OPTIMIZING CYBERDETERRENCE

OPTIMIZING CYBERDETERRENCE

A COMPREHENSIVE STRATEGY FOR
PREVENTING FOREIGN CYBERATTACKS

ROBERT MANDEL

GEORGETOWN UNIVERSITY PRESS
WASHINGTON, DC

© 2017 Georgetown University Press. All rights reserved. No part of this book may be reproduced or utilized in any form or by any means, electronic or mechanical, including photocopying and recording, or by any information storage and retrieval system, without permission in writing from the publisher.

The publisher is not responsible for third-party websites or their content. URL links were active at time of publication.

Library of Congress Cataloging-in-Publication Data

Names: Mandel, Robert, 1949– author.
Title: Optimizing Cyberdeterrence : A Comprehensive Strategy for Preventing Foreign Cyberattacks / Robert Mandel.
Description: Washington, DC : Georgetown University Press, 2017. | Includes bibliographical references and index.
Identifiers: LCCN 2016024168 (print) | LCCN 2016040085 (ebook) | ISBN 9781626164123 (hc : alk. paper) | ISBN 9781626164130 (pb : alk. paper) | ISBN 9781626164147 (eb)
Subjects: LCSH: Cyberterrorism—Prevention.
Classification: LCC HV6773 .M355 2017 (print) | LCC HV6773 (ebook) | DDC
   363.325—dc23
LC record available at https://lccn.loc.gov/2016024168

♾ This book is printed on acid-free paper meeting the requirements of the American National Standard for Permanence in Paper for Printed Library Materials.

18 17   9 8 7 6 5 4 3 2 First printing

Printed in the United States of America

Cover design by Connie Gabbert

The only truly secure system is one that is powered off, cast in a block of concrete, and sealed in a lead-lined room with armed guards.
—Gene Spafford, Purdue University computer science professor and leading cybersecurity expert

Contrary to what the security industry now messages, prevention is *not* a failed strategy.
—Anup Ghosh, chief executive officer and founder of cybersecurity firm Invincea

Contents

	List of Illustrations	ix
	Acknowledgments	xi
	Introduction	1
1	Foreign Cyberthreat Dangers	12
2	Cyberdeterrence Paradoxes	32
3	Obstacles to Forward Progress	43
4	Cyberattack Case Studies	65
5	Case Study Patterns	148
6	Improving Cyberdeterrence Planning	172
7	Improving Cyberdeterrence Execution	190
8	When Cyberdeterrence Works Best	211
	Conclusion	230
	Bibliography	251
	Index	279
	About the Author	289

Illustrations

Figures

I.1.	Distinctiveness of Cyberdeterrence	8
1.1.	Changing Nature of Foreign Cyberthreat	15
1.2.	Cyberattacker and Cyberdefender Preferences	19
1.3.	Underpinnings of Cyberattacker Defiance	27
2.1.	Ideal Cyberdeterrence Dynamics	35
2.2.	Cyberdeterrence Paradoxes	36
3.1.	Obstacles to Forward Progress	60
5.1.	Circumstances Promoting Cyberattack Success	154
5.2.	Cyberdeterrence Case Lessons	163
6.1.	Improving Cyberdeterrence Planning	173
7.1.	Improving Cyberdeterrence Execution	191
8.1.	When Broad Inclusive Cyberdeterrence Is Most Vital	212
8.2.	When Cost and Benefit Optimizations Are Most Vital	216
8.3.	When Public and Private Initiatives Are Most Vital	219
8.4.	When Orthodox and Unorthodox Restraints Are Most Vital	221
8.5.	When Cyberspace and Real-World Responses Are Most Vital	223
8.6.	When Fearful Prevention and Hopeful Persuasion Are Most Vital	225
8.7.	When Cyberdeterrence Neglect Leads to Worst-Case Scenarios	227
C.1.	Broad Inclusive Cyberdeterrence Elements	231
C.2.	How to Integrate and Stabilize Cyberdeterrence Elements	232
C.3.	Cyberdeterrence Legitimacy and Ethics Dilemmas	240
C.4.	Future Cyberdeterrence Prospects	244

Tables

5.1.	Cyberattack Case Background Attributes	149
5.2.	Cyberattack Case Initiator Stimuli	151
5.3.	Cyberattack Case Target Responses	152
5.4.	Cyberattack Case Strategic Outcomes	153

Acknowledgments

Optimizing Cyberdeterrence: A Comprehensive Strategy for Preventing Foreign Cyberattacks—my thirteenth book—has utterly captured my imagination, for it deals with a human-constructed global security threat that in theory should be susceptible to man-made solutions yet in practice appears at least on the surface to defy every remedy. Ever since high school, I have been deeply fascinated with computer hardware and software and the opportunities and dangers embedded in the digital age. Because figuring out how to make cyberdeterrence work better requires a deep and wide integrated understanding of both technical and strategic issues, this investigation was extremely intellectually challenging. I am deeply indebted to my student research assistant Katherine Keller for her hard work and incredibly probing insights and to Don Jacobs of Georgetown University Press for his adept expert shepherding of this project to its completion. I also appreciate the ideas I received from academic colleagues in international relations and computer science and from government defense and intelligence officials. However, I alone take responsibility for any errors found here.

This book is dedicated to the British trio of Charles Babbage, George Boole, and Alan Turing for their role as the earliest computer science pioneers, as well as to those today in the public and private sectors who are tasked with the safety of sensitive data and systems and are struggling with ever-changing threats and technological challenges. This book's aspiration is not only to give the public a glimmer of optimism about the protection of their digital assets but also to assist security officials in their quest to thwart efforts of adversaries who wish to steal, corrupt, or make inaccessible critical data. The best people currently working on cyber protection have to be amazingly creative and nimble in their thinking, and they deserve unbridled admiration and support from the rest of us.

Introduction

Optimizing Cyberdeterrence: A Comprehensive Strategy for Preventing Foreign Cyberattacks presents a distinctive strategic vision for cyberdeterrence to restrain foreign-based cyberattacks. This challenge is particularly daunting because traditional, narrow, direct deterrence (such as Cold War nuclear deterrence) is a poor match for the cyber realm. This book promotes a broader, more inclusive cyberdeterrence designed to alter the cyberattacker's decision calculus. To accomplish this end through this means, *Optimizing Cyberdeterrence* contends that the potential targets of cyberattack need a fluid, integrated mix of strategies that is sensitive to differing circumstances. These strategies encompass (1) moving from just increasing cyberattackers' losses to decreasing any prospects of cyberattackers' gains, both maximizing certainty about high costs and minimizing certainty about high benefits (accounting for culturally different "irrational" adversaries); (2) moving from just national governments making decisions about restraining cyberattackers to including expanded private sector contributions, combining state officials' input with that of private businesses and citizens; (3) moving from just perfecting past and ongoing standard, straightforward cyberattacker countermeasures to developing alternative cyberattacker countermeasures, combining direct, tangible orthodox restraints and indirect, intangible unorthodox restraints; (4) moving from just responding to cyberattackers in kind on the same playing field to adding cross-domain methods on other playing fields—that is, combining cyberspace and real-world responses—and (5) moving from just engaging in draconian intimidation of cyberattackers to finding sensible ways to convince cyberattackers to restrain themselves by combining fear-based physical prevention and hope-based perceptual persuasion.

This book's uniqueness lies in its focus on (1) cyberthreat in the context of other security dangers, considering the relationship of cyberdeterrence with other security policies; (2) comprehensive coverage of twenty-first-century global cyberattack case studies with major security implications; (3) state and non-state threats and responses; (4) improvements in cyberdeterrence planning and execution strategies that combine maximizing high-cost certainty with minimizing high-benefit certainty countermeasures; public and private initiators; direct, tangible orthodox and indirect, intangible unorthodox restraints; cyberspace and real-world responses; and fear-based prevention and hope-based persuasion; (5) identification of conditions where preferred strategies work best; and (6) cyberdeterrence legitimacy and ethics dilemmas. The underlying aspiration is to provide a conceptually probing, empirically rich, and policy-relevant analysis that serves as a springboard from which to spur dramatic improvement in cyberdeterrence.

Exploring cyberdeterrence raises major thorny questions linked to the broader security and strategic studies literature. These issues include (1) the security impacts of technological diffusion, (2) the leveling of the global power hierarchy; (3) the challenges to dominant global values and security norms; (4) the increasingly non-transparent security transactions and indirect means of transnational influence (including social media); (5) the elusive threat initiation and outcome identification; (6) the growing state use of plausible deniability; (7) the increasingly hollow government promises or threats, erosion of state authority, and rising private sector responsibility; (8) the offensive-defensive strategic interrelationships; (9) the long-term stability problems through boomerang effects, action-reaction cycles, and conflict contagion; and (10) the societally divisive trade-offs between openness and secrecy, freedom and stability, safety and justice, fear and hope, and dependence and vulnerability. The common tendency to isolate cyberdeterrence policy from other defense issues thus needs to be overcome.

Distinctiveness of Cyberdeterrence

The concept of deterrence is a key cornerstone of security policy and is based on an assumption that if applied appropriately, targets will avoid undesired behavior because potential aggressors will find it "too risky or too expensive."[1] Although deterrence dynamics and limitations are both well explored and well understood, there are crucial under-examined distinctions between cyberdeterrence and other types of deterrence.

Contrasting Classic Narrow Deterrence to Broad Inclusive Deterrence

Classic narrow deterrence relies on threats of punishment to prevent adversaries, through fear of negative outcomes, from undertaking undesired behavior. Traditionally simple two-party deterrence is "a parsimonious and very attractive proposition" reflected in a relatively strict set of six basic premises "indelibly linked to military force" that during the Cold War were "sufficient to offer insight into strategic deterrence of physical invasion, land capture, or direct attack on US or allied territories by the former Soviet Union and Peoples' Republic of China": a known adversary, a rational target maximizing self-interest, a set of consistent and well-ordered identified preferences, an accurate outcome probability estimation by both sides, a perfect communication between the two sides, and a singular focus on security by both sides.[2] Analysts accepting this definition of narrow deterrence usually question its ability to restrain cyberattacks. They maintain its "credibility is lacking," with such narrow cyberdeterrence being "inherently flawed in that it takes a system developed in one domain (nuclear weapons) and applies it to a non-equivalent domain (cyber)."[3] Moreover, "too many factors—including attribution challenges and sustainability against this vast threat actor landscape—inhibit cyberdeterrence options from achieving their desired outcome in the near term," with cyberspace lacking "the transparency and actor visibility required" for deterrence.[4] Cyberthreat does violate classic deterrence prerequisites, as Western-style rationality, retaliatory threat, unacceptable damage, credibility, and stability are all absent or at least uncertain.[5]

In contrast, the kind of deterrence advocated in this book markedly differs from classic deterrence, notably Cold War nuclear deterrence. "Deterrence in cyberspace is eminently more complicated than deterrence in the Cold War. . . . Even the most sophisticated theories behind nuclear deterrence will prove inadequate for dealing with the complexities of a man-made domain with a virtually infinite number of constantly changing actors, motivations, and capabilities."[6] Broad inclusive deterrence uses a fluid, integrated mix of strategies that are far more multipronged than those in classic deterrence and do "not depend on notions of credible threats, rational actors, or perfect information to work, only that the initiating side understands the drawbacks to its proposed action, and therefore will choose a more restrained approach to the situation."[7] Broad inclusive deterrence does not discard classic deterrence strategies; rather, it augments them with other options that provide more flexible and versatile ways to confront diverse threats. An underlying premise is that differing kinds of threat may require differing combinations of deterrence measures to restrain aggression. In the end, classic deterrence is "merely one part of the picture" for cyberdeterrence.[8] Although some strict constructionists might well reject this broad inclusive approach as encompassing means that go well beyond what they classify as deterrence, this book disagrees, for this distinctive approach still attempts to preemptively compel restraint of outside aggression—the dynamic at the core of all deterrence.

Contrasting Land, Air, and Sea Deterrence to Cyberdeterrence

Regardless of the domain from which a threat originates, the common requirements for all countermeasures are capability, will, and credibility.[9] However, when comparing cyberdeterrence to deterring traditional kinetic attacks, cyberdeterrence seems distinctly disadvantaged. In land, air, and sea deterrence, it seems easier to build up capabilities superior to any adversary's, to blatantly demonstrate abilities to obliterate any attacker, to identify any threat source, and to effectively harden attractive assets. For kinetic warfare "in the physical world, governments have a near monopoly on large scale use of force, the defender has an intimate knowledge of the terrain, and attacks end because of attrition or exhaustion. Both resources and mobility are costly." But for cyberconfrontations "in the virtual world, actors are diverse, sometimes anonymous, [and] physical distance is immaterial."[10]

The contrast with Cold War nuclear deterrence is particularly striking. Cyberdeterrence faces more ambiguity than nuclear deterrence. In the nuclear realm, the "attribution of attack was not a problem; the prospect of battle damage was clear; the 1,000th bomb could be as powerful as the first; counterforce was possible; there were no third parties to worry about; private firms were not expected to defend themselves; any hostile nuclear use crossed an acknowledged threshold; no higher levels of war existed; and both sides always had a lot to lose."[11] Similarly, the prospects for target retaliation for cyberdeterrence differ markedly from those set during the Cold War:

> Cold War deterrence models of assured retaliation do not apply to cyberspace, where it is difficult and time consuming to identify an attack's perpetrator. Whereas a missile comes with a return address, a computer virus generally does not. The forensic work necessary to identify an attacker may take months, if identification is possible at all. And even when the attacker is identified, if it is a nonstate actor, such as a terrorist group, it may have no assets against which ... [one] can retaliate.[12]

Thus cyberdeterrence requires fresh thinking in new directions.

Key categories of difference evident between cyberdeterrence and land, air, and sea deterrence are discovering the emerging threat, identifying it, responding to it, and eliminating it. The highlighted distinctive patterns have great significance in enhancing an understanding of the special challenges surrounding deterrence in cyberspace. Ultimately this improved understanding will help in developing appropriate measures to restrain cyber aggression that deviate sharply from conventional responses to threats from land, air, and sea domains.

Regarding an emerging threat, cyberdeterrence is especially challenging due to ubiquitous, rapidly changing, covert disruptor, cyberattack tools; low disruptor attack expenses and barriers to entry; instantaneous and far-reaching security impacts (where "action at a distance makes systems harder to secure"); huge target vulnerabilities; and heavy external target dependence.[13] The abilities of cyberattackers to create quick, massive, and inexpensive (for the attackers) security breaches constitute a major headache for targets. In contrast, conventional land, air, and sea deterrence seems easier to carry out because the attack tools are overt, attacks are expensive, attacks have a comparatively high barrier to entry and more delayed and contained security impacts, and their targets have lower vulnerabilities, with less externally dependent defenses.

For identifying the threat, cyberdeterrence is challenging due to the ambiguous cyberattacker attribution, the high likelihood of cyberattacker plausible deniability, the irrelevance of geographical proximity, the great difficulty in determining attacker-defender power ratios, and the murkiness in establishing tipping points of critical danger for cybertargets. Not knowing the origins of a cyberattack can be truly debilitating to attempts to prevent future breaches. In contrast, in conventional land, air, and sea deterrence, it is usually easier to identify attackers, geographical distance does provide some security, attacker-defender power ratios are often more clear-cut, and critical damage tipping points can be more readily determined.

In responding to the threat, cyberdeterrence is challenging because targets have trouble demonstrating attack dangers (due to the lower visibility of incursions and consequences) and credible defenses, cyberattackers have few assets that can be held at risk, many target deterrence strategies are not repeatable, determining the proportionality of the targets' responses is confusing, and the targets' use of overwhelming brute force is generally ineffective.[14] A special cyberdeterrence problem involves "holding hostage" the cyberattackers' virtual and physical assets through proportional responses without lowering the target's credibility and the cyberattackers' costs of hostile action.[15] In contrast, conventional land, air, and sea deterrence seems easier given the more ready ability of targets to demonstrate credible defense, the multitude of disruptor assets that can be held at risk, the ability of targets to reuse successful deterrence strategies, the greater clarity in proportionality of target responses, and the higher effectiveness of the targets' use of overwhelming force.

Finally, regarding eliminating the threat, cyberdeterrence is challenging because the cyberattackers' costs and benefits are often intangible, cyberthreats are extremely resilient in the short term, targets often exhibit uncertainty about whether a cyberthreat has vanished, the targets' ability to disarm cyberattackers is low, and the chances of deflecting a cyberthreat to one's allies is high. In contrast, conventional air, land, and sea deterrence seems easier given the more tangible changes in disruptor costs and benefits, the lower resiliency of disruptor threats in the short term, the target's greater certainty that a threat has disappeared, the target's higher ability to disarm disruptors, and the lower probability that deflected disruptor threats will shift to a target's allies. With land, air, and sea deterrence, it is much easier to determine when a threat has been eliminated than it is with cyberdeterrence.

Implications of Cyberdeterrence Distinctiveness

Figure I.1 summarizes the identified differences between (1) classic deterrence and broad inclusive deterrence and between (2) cyberdeterrence and land, air, and sea deterrence. Deterrence in outer space, an underdeveloped combat domain that shares some qualities with cyberdeterrence, is not analyzed here. In the end, the "fifth domain" of combat—cyberspace—appears to be the hardest domain for security policymakers to manage in terms of deterrence.[16]

However, providing a ray of hope for cyberdeterrence is the cyberthreat's unique quality of being man made. Because all cyberspace parameters are human designed and human controlled, "if we are lethally vulnerable to harm in our use of cyberspace, it will largely, if not wholly, be our own fault."[17] A completely human-designed system "is more mutable than other domains" and thus should be susceptible to optimization over time.[18] The most radical last-resort response to such a man-made challenge—although certainly not the most practically applicable one—would be to change completely the parameters of cyberspace itself, and this shift would be inconceivable in any other conflict domain. Nonetheless, even working completely within the existing system, reasonable cyberdeterrence approaches can be developed to manage cyberthreats.

Plan of the Book

This investigation of cyberdeterrence of foreign-based attacks begins by analyzing the rising importance and changing nature of foreign cyberthreat dangers and by evaluating the largely ineffective target responses thus far and the resulting global sea changes. Then the focus moves to the cyberdeterrence paradoxes surrounding efforts to achieve ideal cyberdeterrence dynamics, and a list is presented of obstacles to forward progress, including both the roots of cyberdeterrence failure and the roadblocks to significant cyberdeterrence improvement. Afterward the book emphasizes detailing and drawing wider patterns and implications from case studies of twelve major global twenty-first-century cyberattacks. Based on this assessment, this work suggests specific, feasible ways to improve cyberdeterrence planning and execution and identifies the conditions under which recommended approaches are most needed and work best (along with worst-case scenarios if cyberdeterrence is neglected). The investigation concludes with an overarching analysis of how to integrate and stabilize cyberdeterrence, consider cyberdeterrence legitimacy and ethics dilemmas, address cyberdeterrence paradoxes, and forecast future cyberdeterrence prospects.

Focus of Coverage

This book concentrates on deterring international cyberattacks rather than internal ones (and does not exclusively emphasize those involving the United States). Despite the notoriety surrounding domestic cyberattacks such as Edward Snowden's June 2013 cyberintrusion into National Security Agency data, the cyberattacks most damaging to stability and security tend to be international or transnational rather than local in nature. Indeed, "the most serious and far-reaching consequences will occur from information infrastructure disruptions at the global and regional level."[19] Owing to national sovereignty concerns, internal and external resentment and frustration—along with worries about sinister motivations—seem highest when cyberthreats emerge from foreign rather than domestic sources. Compared to localized cyberthreats, cross-boundary cyberattacks seem more complicated and more dependent "on the skill level and resources of the attacker," and compared to domestic cyberdeterrence, foreign cyberdeterrence seems more challenging because it cannot simply deflect cyberthreats away from one country to land on another.[20] Because cyberattacks are not initiated exclusively by states or on states, this global focus includes transnational non-state groups, multinational corporations, and international organizations as well as national governments (with less emphasis on individual initiators or targets). The spotlight is on twenty-first-century cyberattacks because fears of damage emanating from cyberspace activity have dramatically escalated in this period.

The emphasis is on deterring major cyberattacks that fundamentally threaten state and human security rather than those cyberattacks whose primary impacts are minor, not security oriented, or just profit related, because

FIGURE I.1.
Distinctiveness of Cyberdeterrence

Traditional

CLASSIC DETERRENCE

Threats of Punitive Action Restrain Adversaries
Target Threat Can Easily Be Made Credible
Target Threat Needs to Aim Directly at Adversary
Tangible Damage Threats Are Essential
Adversaries Are Known
Adversaries Are Rational
Adversaries Have Clear, Well-Ordered Preferences
All Parties Accurately Estimate Outcome Probabilities
Contending Parties Have Perfect Communication
All Parties Are Security Focused

Nontraditional

BROAD INCLUSIVE DETERRENCE

Punitive Threats Are Insufficient to Restrain Adversaries
Target Threat Is Harder to Make Credible
Target Response Can Aim Indirectly at Supporters
Intangible Responses Can Help Restrain Adversaries
Attribution of Adversaries Is Harder
Adversaries May Be Irrational or Culturally Different
Adversaries' Preferences May Be Fluid and Murky
Outcome Estimates May Be Inaccurate
Contending Parties Have Poor, Distorted Communication
Adversaries May Have Key Non-security Concerns

FIGURE I.1. *continued*

	Traditional	Nontraditional
	LAND, AIR, AND SEA DETERRENCE	**CYBERDETERRENCE**
Discovering Emerging Threat	Less Common, More Stable, Overt Disruptor Attack Tools Higher Attack Expenses and Barriers to Entry More Delayed and Contained Security Impacts Lower Target Vulnerabilities Lower External Dependence of Target Defenses	Ubiquitous, Fluid, Covert Disruptor Attack Tools Low Attack Expenses and Barriers to Entry Instantaneous and Far-reaching Security Impacts High Target Vulnerabilities High External Dependence of Target Defenses
Identifying Threat	Lower Ambiguity in Disruptor Attribution Lower Chance of Disruptor Plausible Deniability Higher Relevance of Geographical Proximity Easier to Judge Attacker-Defender Power Ratio More Evident Target Tipping Points for Critical Danger	High Ambiguity in Disruptor Attribution High Chance of Disruptor Plausible Deniability Low Relevance of Geographical Proximity Hard to Judge Attacker-Defender Power Ratio Uncertain Target Tipping Points for Critical Danger
Responding to Threat	Easier to Show Attack Dangers and Credible Defense Many Disruptor Assets to Hold at Risk More Reusable Target Deterrence Strategies Clearer Target Proportionality of Response More Effective Overwhelming Brute Force by Target	Hard to Show Attack Dangers and Credible Defense Few Disruptor Assets to Hold at Risk Few Repeatable Target Deterrence Strategies Unclear Target Proportionality of Response Ineffective Overwhelming Brute Force by Target
Eliminating Threat	More Tangible Change in Disruptor Costs/Benefits Lower Short-Run Resiliency of Disruptor Threats Higher Target Certainty that Threat Has Vanished Higher Target Ability to Disarm Disruptor Lower Chance of Threat Moving to Target Allies	Intangible Change in Disruptor Costs/Benefits High Short-Run Resiliency of Disruptor Threats Low Target Certainty that Threat Has Vanished Low Target Ability to Disarm Disruptor High Chance of Threat Moving to Target Allies

"what really matters to political leaders is the political [security] consequence of a cyber attack, not the mere fact of a cyber attack."[21] Although cyberattacks causing financial losses may be highly disruptive, such as the 2009 Chinese cyberattacks on Google or the 2014–15 cyberattacks on retail giant Target, hardware chain Home Depot, and insurance provider Anthem, those cyberattacks with major security implications usually directly or indirectly affect the survival of national governments, critical infrastructures, and mass populations. As a result, political-military cyberespionage receives more attention than economic cybercrime areas such as digitally distributing child pornography, sharing commercial trade secrets to disrupt competitors or to gain market advantage, committing financial fraud, or stealing intellectual property.

This investigation concentrates on deterring intentional rather than accidental cyber disruptions. Unintended breaches are quite common. "While the public tends to see hackers behind every breach, actually slightly less than half of breaches, 47%, are caused by malicious or criminal attacks. Twenty-nine percent involved system glitches while 25% were the result of human error or negligence."[22] Although unintended jolts can be damaging, the technological means of minimizing their damage are better known and more predictably developed (even if not always properly implemented). In contrast, because intentional cyberattacks are constantly evolving and incorporate discontinuous innovative leaps, preventing them or overcoming relevant vulnerabilities is much harder. However, without accurate intelligence, "differentiating a network attack from accidental factors (such as a surge in demand for certain information on the network) or implementation mistakes (such as errors in the portion of a server's operating system that processes network traffic) is neither quick nor easy."[23]

Intended Audience

This book's intended audience is both experts and novices interested in understanding the security opportunities, limitations, and trade-offs surrounding foreign cyberdeterrence. With the needs of practitioners specifically in mind, the analysis goes well beyond identifying broad, intractable problems to suggesting specific, feasible solutions and to identifying when such solutions are most needed. The diversity and rapid pace of cyberspace challenges ought to elicit considerable humility and caution on the part of both participants and observers, thwarting any air of definitive certainty in anyone's recommended policy improvements. However, this analysis does not allow this tentativeness to interfere with its quest to improve concerted, coherent, well-integrated cyberdeterrence.

Although normally cybersecurity discussions are full of arcane technical jargon and obscure acronyms—many of which are unintelligible to the general public—this book consciously avoids off-putting terminology and makes key concepts accessible to readers without a computer science or international relations background. Key insights are summarized in figures and tables to maximize intelligibility. The book's mission is to spread both awareness and impetus to act and improve cyberdeterrence in a world where virtually everyone has sensitive data and systems needing protection but where few feel that they have the expertise to address existing vulnerabilities successfully. The underlying hope here is to allay growing global fears and ensuing panic that could prevent the emergence of effective and legitimate cyberattack responses.

Notes

1. Lewis, *Cross-Domain Deterrence*, 1.
2. Hunt and Chesser, *Deterrence 2.0*, 47–48, 50.
3. Valeriano and Maness, *Cyber War*, 13, 47.
4. Iasiello, "Is Cyber Deterrence," 54.
5. Stevens, "Cyberwar of Ideas?," 152; and Morgan, *Deterrence Now*, 8.
6. Sterner, "Deterrence in Cyberspace," in Butterworth et al., *Returning to Fundamentals*, 27.
7. Valeriano and Maness, *Cyber War*, 56.
8. Davis, "Deterrence, Influence," 3.
9. Cooper, "New Framework for Cyber Deterrence," in Reveron, *Cyberspace and National Security*, 109.
10. Nye, *Cyber Power*, 5.
11. Libicki, *Cyberdeterrence and Cyberwar*, xvi.
12. Lynn, "Defending a New Domain," 99.
13. Schneier, *Beyond Fear*, 97.
14. For a more general context of when brute force is most effective, see Mardel, *Coercing Compliance*.
15. See, for example, Weiner, "Searching for Cyber-Deterrence."
16. Lord and Sharp, *America's Cyber Future*, 1:32.
17. Gray, *Making Strategic Sense*, 39.
18. Russell, *Cyber Blockades*, 3.
19. Tiirmaa-Klaar, "Cyber Security Threats," 2.
20. Hodges and Creese, "Understanding Cyber-Attacks," in Green, *Cyber Warfare*, 59.
21. Lindsay, "Stuxnet and the Limits," 398.
22. Weise, "Average Cost."
23. Shimeall, Williams, and Dunlevy, "Countering Cyber War," 18.

CHAPTER 1

Foreign Cyberthreat Dangers

In the United States at least, there is no security threat today that government policymakers, private businesses, and the public fear more than major cyberattacks. For example, since 2013 the American director of national intelligence has named cyberthreat as "the number one strategic threat to the United States, placing it ahead of terrorism for the first time since the attacks of September 11, 2001."[1] The relative invisibility, tracking difficulty, inexpensive initiation, technical obtuseness, fluid content, speedy impact, and broad scope of cyberthreat make it seem unintelligible, unpredictable, unmanageable, and ultimately catastrophic. On a global level, potential victims find themselves both frustrated and baffled about how to cope with cyberthreat more successfully. In light of this threat, this chapter analyzes the rising perceived importance of foreign cyberthreat, its changing nature, the legacy of ineffective target responses, and the ramifications of resulting global sea changes.

Rising Perceived Importance of Foreign Cyberthreat

Since the 1990s cyberattacks on global computer networks have risen in number (as well as in sophistication), reaching 1.7 billion in 2013, up from 1.6 billion in 2012.[2] For the United States, over time "the frequency and sophistication of intrusions into U.S. military networks have increased exponentially."[3] In 2011 the Government Accountability Office estimated that "the number of unauthorized access or installations of malicious software on U.S. government computers has increased by 650 percent since 2006."[4] From October 2011 through February 2012, the Department of Homeland Security reported over 50,000 cyberattacks on private and government networks, with 86 on critical infrastructure networks.[5] In 2014 a report to Congress revealed that "hackers have penetrated, taken control of, caused damage to and/or stolen sensitive personal and official information from computer systems at the Departments of Homeland Security, Justice, Defense, State, Labor, Energy, and Commerce; NASA [National Aeronautics and Space Administration]; the Environmental Protection Agency; the Office of Personnel Management; the Federal Reserve;

the Commodity Futures Trading Commission; the Food and Drug Administration; the US Copyright Office; and the National Weather Service."[6] Aside from governments, cyberattacks also have targeted private businesses. For example, in 2010 "proprietary corporate data, e-mails, credit-card transaction data and login credentials at companies in the health and technology industries," involving over 75,000 computers at more than 2,500 businesses in 196 countries, were hacked.[7] Today nobody seems immune—regardless of the protection system—to cyber penetration.

The monetary scope of the damage wrought in cyberattacks has also grown. Regarding government targets, in 2009 the Pentagon reported that costs of repairing cyberattack damage—in terms of "manpower, computer technology, and contractors hired to clean up after both external probes and internal mistakes"—was more than $100 million a year.[8] Outside of government targets, in 2008 cybercriminal groups reportedly stole more than $1 trillion in global data and intellectual property.[9] Critical infrastructure operators across the globe report that their networks and control systems are "under repeated cyberattack, often from high-level adversaries like foreign nation-states," and that in 2010 their downtime costs from such breaches exceeded $6 million per day.[10] In May 2013 the Commission on the Theft of American Intellectual Property reported that hackers cost the United States $300 billion a year.[11] The cost of cyberattacks on private business is dramatically rising as well. Including abnormal turnover of customers, reputation loss, diminished goodwill, and paying for credit reports and aid to affected customers, the average cost of a computer breach in 2015 was $3.79 million for large private companies globally, up 23 percent from 2013; and it ran $6.5 million for American companies, up 11 percent from 2013.[12] Although such estimates are inherently imprecise, they do provide a glimmer of the massive, global financial impact of cyberintrusions.

Even more than most global threats, cyberspace dangers can certainly be socially constructed to a great extent. Given that cyberspace is man made, objectively determining to what extent cyberthreat is actually rising or actually poses greater dangers than other security threats would be extremely difficult. However, to call cyberthreat completely artificial and illusory goes too far, for tangible cyberattacks have generated concrete damage to data, information systems, and (indirectly) physical structures. Moreover, regardless of the level of existing threat, there is little doubt that government officials, corporate executives, and the public are now more scared of cyberattacks than ever before in the digital age.

Changing Nature of Foreign Cyberthreat

Possessing a unique set of characteristics, the virtual domain of cyberspace is now as important a source of threat as the physical domains of land, sea, air, and space.[13] However, considerable confusion surrounds the rapidly changing cyberthreat. Continuing transformations in cyberattackers, their goals and motivations, their targets, and their attack styles have complicated understanding ongoing trends. Figure 1.1 summarizes the changing nature of foreign cyberthreat.

Cyberattackers

Not surprising, the most dangerous cyberattackers come from "groups with the resources and commitment to relentlessly target a company or government agency until they succeed in breaking in and then take value out."[14] Thus, today "the main threats no longer come from teenage hackers or petty criminals, although such actors are still around; instead, sophisticated criminals and state-sponsored spies pose the most danger for businesses and governments."[15] The Government Accountability Office lists the primary cyberattack sources as intelligence services, criminal groups, hackers and hacktivists, disgruntled insiders, and terrorists.[16]

Cyber disruption has wide appeal, requiring no more than "a powerful computer, a keen mind, and an underlying grudge."[17] The initiators range from "script kiddies" to "elite hackers" and from rich states and poor states. Cyberattacks' attraction to both the powerful and the weak lies in their "low relative cost, high potential impact and general lack of transparency. Powerful actors such as the United States can combine cyber power with existing military capabilities, economic assets and soft power networks. Less powerful actors—states, organizations, individuals or any combination thereof—can gain asymmetrically in cyberspace by inflicting extensive damage on vulnerable targets."[18] Major powers seeking to protect the status quo often may find themselves thwarted by cyberinitiatives from smaller, weaker players.

Unlike many other forms of aggression, most states with relevant capabilities have not been reluctant to engage in foreign cyberintrusion, leading to intensified international cross penetration. Following security dilemma logic, other states can see a given state's offensive cyberdefense strategy as violating their sovereignty. For example, former US deputy secretary of defense William Lynn suggests that over a hundred foreign intelligence organizations have been illegitimately trying to break into American defense networks.[19] Today's tightly

FIGURE 1.1
Changing Nature of Foreign Cyberthreat

Cyberattackers and Their Goals/Motivations

Cyberattacker Type	*Goal/Motivation*
Criminal Groups	Financial Gain through Theft
Disgruntled Insiders	Getting Back at Employers
Government Intelligence Services	Political Espionage, Economic Advantage, or Warfare Tool
Hackers	Satisfying Personal Agendas or Virility Tests
Hacktivists	Disrupting the Functioning of Institutions
Multinational Corporations	Industrial Espionage or Competitor Disruption
Terrorists	Advancing Political Causes

Direction of Cyberattacker Change
Greatest Danger Moving from Teenage Hackers and Petty Criminals to Sophisticated Criminals and State-Sponsored Spies with Substantial Resources and Commitment

Cyberattacker Threat Styles

Range of Threat Styles
Blocking Internet Access
Causing Catastrophic Failures of Physical Systems
Corrupting Sensitive Data
Defacing Websites
Deleting, Stealing, or Falsifying Information
Interfering with Command-and-Control Structures
Overloading Networks
Penetrating Networks to Exfiltrate Political or Economic Secrets

Direction of Threat Style Change
Greatest Danger Moving from Large-Scale Theft and Disruption of Computer Operations to More Lethal Attacks that Destroy Systems and Physical Equipment

networked information systems can serve equally as weapons to penetrate foreign databases and as targets needing protection.[20]

At the same time, cyberthreats are growing from non-state sources, which exhibit subtle and varied modes of "informal penetration."[21] With the flood of digital information, "power is migrating to small, non-state actors who can organize into sprawling networks more readily than can traditional hierarchical nation-state actors."[22] Cyberattackers "represent simply the latest stage in the development of a long line of technologically-enabled combatants with interests opposed to the system of states."[23] Much cyber sabotage, espionage, and subversion emanate from politically motivated hacktivists and cyberspies (not necessarily sponsored by state governments), as "nonstate actors, intelligence services, and militaries increasingly penetrate information technology networks for espionage and influence."[24] Indeed, a key current cybersecurity deficiency is its state-centric focus, ignoring the recent erosion of state sovereignty and downplaying the pivotal role not only of non-state cyberattackers but also of non-state cyberdefenders such as private companies and private citizens.[25]

Complicating cyberdeterrence efforts are the subtle and fluid relationships cyberattackers have with each other. Three types of covert, nefarious collusion have recently flourished between (1) states and non-state groups, (2) differing types of non-state groups, and (3) cyberattackers and disgruntled insiders within targets. Regarding the first set of linkages between states and non-state groups, such collusion often supports national government plausible deniability, with the collaboration initiated in both directions:

> States are often mistakenly identified as non-state actors, and vice versa. To make matters worse, ties between the two are increasing. First, a growing number of "patriotic cybercriminals" ostensibly wage cyber war on behalf of governments (examples include Chechnya and Kosovo in the 1990s, China in 2001, Estonia in 2007, Georgia in 2008, and every year in the Middle East). Second, cybercrime organizations offer anyone, including governments, cyber attack services to include denial-of-service attacks and access to previously compromised networks.[26]

Because of the "arms bazaar of cyber weapons," "states that lack indigenous capabilities but wish to do harm to the United States or its allies may co-opt or simply buy/rent the services and skills of criminals and hackers to help design and execute cyber attacks."[27]

Regarding the second set of linkages among non-state groups, "alliances of convenience are possible among non-state actors (terrorists and criminal groups, and even individuals) to fill capability gaps" and to "generate force multiplier effects."[28] Extremist, politically motivated hacktivists and economically motivated hackers can easily find kindred spirits in cyberspace, and forming "unholy alliances" increases the chances that "the most malicious actors will collaborate with those who possess the most advanced capabilities" or intelligence.[29] "When terrorist groups do not have the internal technical capability, they may hire organized crime syndicates and cybercriminals through underground digital chat rooms" to move money and smuggle arms and drugs across national boundaries, acquiring in the process access to those with considerable cyber expertise.³⁰ Illustrating this non-state collusion pattern, digital linkages exist among the Palestinian Islamic Jihad, Hezbollah, and Izzedine-Al-Qassam, the military wing of Hamas.³¹

Regarding the third set of linkages between cyberattackers and disgruntled insiders, "disgruntled insiders keen to extract revenge" often assist in cyberattacks.³² This insider cyberthreat is "largely misunderstood and underestimated. Although some security experts estimate that as much as 85 percent of all computer crimes are committed by insiders, media reports have focused primarily on external computer hackers and traditional threat actors."³³ Exemplifying this pattern is "the reported collusion between Iran and company insiders at Saudi Aramco to incapacitate tens of thousands of the firm's machines in 2012."³⁴ As linkages among cyberattackers become tighter and more multifaceted, targets or outside observers find it increasingly difficult to detect accurately the network hierarchy or to determine exactly who is doing what in order to focus cyberdeterrence efforts.

State and non-state cyberattackers exhibit differing "risk propensities," with the strategic advantage pursued sometimes being offensive—that is, "to change the status quo"—and sometimes being defensive, or "to prevent others from changing the status quo."³⁵ On the one hand, for great powers, cyberattacks can allow a non-boots-on-the-ground thwarting of foreign threats. Although such actions are framed as retaliatory or defensive, outside observers may view them as illegitimate and norm violating, especially when they are done preemptively. On the other hand, for unruly rogue states and terrorist groups, cyberattacks can increase global anarchy, which can overturn the power hierarchy and undermine global security. During a global confrontation, those wanting "to challenge the current *status quo*" often conclude that offensive cyberattacks are "best used against civilian targets (for example, the most visited websites on the Internet) . . . in conjunction with other forms of warfare."³⁶ Damaging civilian targets such as communication lines can undercut military command and control, and the threshold of significant damage to them may be harder to detect.³⁷

Cyberattacker Goals and Motivations

Many analysts assume perpetrator goals and motivations in cyberspace are unintelligible. "Hacking appears to be, like most crime, something that malicious people do for reasons that don't always seem to make sense. Why would a talented computer programmer choose to write a virus rather than write a program that might be more useful and, potentially, economically more rewarding?"[38] However, because not all cyberattackers are equally dangerous, "to effectively deter an individual or entity and thereby prevent it from accomplishing its goal—or ideally, prevent it from acting in the first place—it is imperative to understand fully just what the initiating party hopes to achieve."[39]

Cyberattacker preferences differ sharply from those of cyberdefenders, with key differences in cyberintrusion aspirations (attack costs and attack benefits), cyberintrusion repercussions (value challenges and image changes), cyberintrusion confusions (outcome clarity and perpetrator identity), and cyberintrusion reactions (response types, resulting interactions, ensuing involvements, and real-world leakages). The US Army identifies four types of cyberattack goals: (1) loss of integrity, where data is modified improperly; (2) loss of availability, where mission-critical information systems are rendered unavailable to authorized users; (3) loss of confidentiality, where critical information is disclosed to unauthorized users; and (4) physical destruction, where information systems create physical harm through commands that cause deliberate malfunctions.[40] Figure 1.2 summarizes the sharply contrasting differences in cyberattacker and cyberdefender preferences.

Objectives vary according to the type of cyberattacker: "hackers, zealots or disgruntled insiders, to satisfy personal agendas; criminals, for personal financial gain, etc.; terrorists or other malevolent groups, to advance their cause; commercial organizations, for industrial espionage or to disrupt competitors; nations, for espionage or economic advantage or as a tool of warfare."[41] Some geeky young computer hackers desire just to test their virility and gain social status by breaching secure data systems. In economically motivated cyberattacks, cybercriminals are motivated by greed for profits—a 2007 study revealed that 67 percent of Web attacks were profit motivated—and use financial fraud or theft of critical data to gain inside information or to alter databases for economic benefits.[42] As opposed to casual hackers and petty thieves, organized cybercriminals are distinguished by their willingness to spend more time and effort for a larger payoff, with their cyberattacks "characterized by a greater amount of planning, a longer period of time to conduct the activity, more financial backing to accomplish it, and possibly corruption of, or collusion with, insiders."[43] In politically motivated cyberattacks, subversive hacktivists seek to disrupt the functioning of government institutions, to alter a government's policies or its citizen support, or to impede the military's command-and-control capabilities to organize, assess, and disseminate data while fostering fear and dissension among soldiers and civilians. Contrasting economically motivated and political-military-motivated cyberattacks, state security is more directly harmed by cyberespionage of political and military secrets, while

FIGURE 1.2.
Cyberattacker and Cyberdefender Preferences

	CYBERATTACKER PREFERENCES	**CYBERDEFENDER PREFERENCES**
CYBERINTRUSION ASPIRATIONS		
Attack Cost	Low-Risk Inexpensive Operation	High-Risk Expensive Operation
Attack Benefit	Target Severely Damaged and Incapacitated	Attacks Prevented/Target Missed, Critical Data/Infrastructure Preserved
CYBERINTRUSION REPERCUSSIONS		
Value Challenge	Target Defense Efforts Undermine Freedoms/Lifestyle	Target Defense Efforts Leave Existing Freedoms/Lifestyle Intact
Image Change	Recognition of Unanticipated Offensive Capability/Style	Recognition of Defensive Target Prowess
CYBERINTRUSION CONFUSIONS		
Outcome Clarity	Attack Impact Unambiguously Successful	Initiators Have No Idea if Attack Successful
Perpetrator Identity	Attribution Troubles Impede Detection/Accountability	Ready Ability to Identify Attack Perpetrators
CYBERINTRUSION REACTIONS		
Response Type	Target Division and Confusion about What to Do	Unified and Coordinated Target Response
Resulting Interaction	Distracting Resource-Draining Action-Reaction Cycles	No Persistent Repercussions or Negative Entanglements
Ensuing Involvement	Inspiration to Imitators and Third-Party Contagion	Containment and Isolation of Attacks
Real-World Leakage	Battle Remains In Cyberspace	Battle Enlarges to Include Real-World Sanctions

human security is more directly harmed by cybertheft of intellectual property or personal data.

Cybertargets

Cybertargets strictly defined are computers or computer networks, but they commonly refer more broadly to cyberattack victims.[44] Targets span states, non-state groups, private companies, individuals, or international organizations, and they include "individual personal computers; private business internal networks; major intercorporate networks, such as those used for money transfers between banks; or national security command, control, communications, and intelligence (C^3I) networks."[45] Cyberthreats may often "not target states, but societies and individuals," with innocent civilians frequently suffering the direst consequences.[46]

The most damaging cyberattacks can incapacitate entire societies by targeting critical infrastructure—that is, the systems and assets whose incapacitation or destruction would have "a debilitating impact" on the political or economic security of a country or the health and safety of its citizenry, encompassing telecommunications, electrical power systems, gas and oil storage and movement, banking and finance, transportation, water supply, and emergency services.[47] Adversaries who politically target the United States—which "as the most wired nation on earth" offers "the most targets of significance"—seek "to disrupt the nation's critical civilian and military infrastructures."[48] These "potential state and non-state adversaries conduct malicious cyber activities against US interests globally and in a manner intended to test the limits of what the United States and the international community will tolerate," as the "vulnerable data systems present state and non-state actors with an enticing opportunity to strike" since they believe they can avoid negative consequences.[49] Because usually critical infrastructure is so extensive and vulnerable, most targets apply selective protection only to their most important assets.

Cyberattack Styles

Over time the US Cyber Command asserts that cyberattacks "are escalating from large-scale theft and disruption of computer operations to more lethal attacks that destroy systems and physical equipment."[50] Microsoft's senior cybersecurity expert notes that "the most common malicious cyber activities have ... shifted from the criminal or mischief to the downright destructive."[51] In early 2015 widespread concern emerged about BlackEnergy, malware allegedly developed by a Russian hacking group known as Sandworm and identified by the US Department of Homeland Security as located "deep within the industrial control systems that operate critical infrastructure."[52] Although BlackEnergy was initially designed to steal information, Kyle Wilhoit, a senior threat researcher at cybersecurity firm Trend Micro, "fears this tool of espionage could be turned to sabotage."[53]

Cyberattack styles are diverse and "can run the gamut from website defacement to packet-flooding a host to cut it off from the Internet; from covertly penetrating a network to manipulate or exfiltrate information to deliberately causing catastrophic failures of physical systems."[54] Such attacks disrupt confidentiality (cyberespionage), integrity (sabotage of the operation of critical civilian or military information systems), and availability (attempts to take information systems offline).[55] Cyberattacks can entail information overload, sensitive data corruption, information deletion or falsification, and insertion of unauthorized outside control that interferes with existing command-and-control structures. Cyberattackers typically engage in four activities: (1) reconnaissance, when learning about target vulnerabilities; (2) exploit delivery, when a target's defenses are penetrated; (3) payload injection, when tasks achieving an attacker's mission are performed; and (4) exfiltration and cleanup, when data is stolen and breaches are concealed.[56] Popular cyberintrusion modes include "botnets," or networks of unsuspecting private computers that are infected with insidious malware and turned into "zombies," and "spear phishing," or tricking people to click on malicious links that download malware onto their systems. Although it has been commonly assumed that "cyber war and economic espionage are largely associated with states, and cyber crime and cyber terrorism are mostly associated with non-state actors," recently these associations have become a lot murkier.[57]

While cyberattackers usually operate in secret, occasionally they actively seek publicity. If a terrorist cyberattack became widely known, then "concern by many citizens and cascading effects might lead to widespread disruption of critical infrastructures"; for example, "an attack on the international financial system's networks could create a fiscal panic in the public that could lead to economic damage."[58] In addition, social media provides a ready vehicle to promote a distorted portrayal of target vulnerability and initiator supremacy.

The styles of cyberattack on military and business targets differ but can be equally paralyzing. Cyber assaults on military targets can include denial of service and data and supply chain corruption via a combination of kinetic and non-kinetic attacks, and the results can be devastating: "U.S. guns, missiles, and bombs may not fire, or may be directed against our own troops," and "resupply, including food, water, ammunition, and fuel may not arrive when or where needed."[59] The virtual disabling of military command and control can be as crippling to war-fighting capabilities as physically destroying military equipment. Similarly, cyberattacks could devastate global business and result in different types of network damage: it can be localized, costing potential sales and hardware damage repair; it can be broader, crippling an entire economy given its Internet dependence; or it can be kinetic, damaging critical infrastructure such as power plants.[60] Escalating globalization makes it hard to contain financially devastating cyberattacks.

Cyberattacks may be random or targeted, may have origins from inside or outside a networked system, and may be designed for data integrity loss or data leakage. Cyberthreat victims are usually most prepared for targeted external attacks, although random or internally initiated attacks can be equally dangerous. In comparing attacks in which critical data is corrupted (including distributed denial-of-service attacks) or leaked out, both attack styles could be harmful and hard to detect or prevent in terms of damage done to important networked computer systems. Corrupted data can interfere with the basic ability of a government or business organization to function, while leaked data can interfere with carefully formulated strategies that are ready to go, rendering them useless. For cybertargets, it is ironic that having a massive amount of sensitive, protected information uncontrollably flow across national boundaries can be just as debilitating as having that flow interrupted or corrupted. Keeping in mind that cyberattack goals and outcomes are frequently not contained within cyberspace, it is difficult to prioritize cyberattack styles in terms of their overall devastating security impact or overall cyberdeterrence value, for regardless of which style is implemented, the net result could seriously directly or indirectly compromise individual, national, regional, or global security.[61]

Even though there is no inherent reason cyberoffense should have an advantage over cyberdefense, and despite substantial public and private security investment in cybersecurity, so far innovative changes in offensive cyberattack techniques have generally outpaced defensive cyber protection. Within rapidly changing cyberspace, "malicious actors have sophisticated tools and techniques that can defeat current defenses," and these unruly parties initiate "ever more sophisticated cyberattacks" in which "smart attackers react to the countermeasures and modify their attacks accordingly."[62] Dmitri Alperovitch, cofounder and chief technology officer at CrowdSource, concludes dismally,

> What we have witnessed over the past five to six years has been nothing short of a historically unprecedented transfer of wealth—closely guarded national

secrets (including those from classified government networks), source code, bug databases, email archives, negotiation plans and exploration details for new oil and gas field auctions, document stores, legal contracts, supervisory control and data acquisition (SCADA) configurations, design schematics, and much more has "fallen off the truck" of numerous, mostly Western companies and disappeared in the ever-growing electronic archives of dogged adversaries.[63]

It is both highly remarkable and highly disconcerting to realize "how steeply new technology has tipped the balance in favor of those—from free-lance hackers to Russian mobsters to terrorists to states like China and Iran—who want to learn the secrets we keep, whether for national, corporate, or personal security."[64]

Ineffective Target Responses to Foreign Cyberthreat

In response to growing cyberthreat fears, global leaders within potential targets have elevated its security priority. Although much of the public sees cybersecurity as a new concern, national government officials have long viewed this issue "as a major challenge for public policy," but recently their alarm has escalated.[65] Echoing a 1995 *Washington Post* warning, in October 2012 US secretary of defense Leon Panetta claimed that cyberthreat could produce a "cyber Pearl Harbor," destroying property and human life.[66] Public concern has also grown, with about 70 percent of Americans viewing foreign cyberincidents as a major security threat to the United States.[67] Even if these perceived cyberthreat risks are overblown, they still are important because they reflect genuine deep-seated insecurity fears on the part of leaders and citizens alike.

As a result, countries have begun to take concrete steps to address cyberthreat, with each countermeasure involving significant trade-offs. Indeed, "every state in the world now has at least some form of cyber-defence programme, and over 120 states are working on cyber-attack programmes."[68] In the United States, the Department of Defense has been actively "training thousands of troops to wage war on digital battlefields."[69] It "now operates 15,000 networks and seven million computing devices across 4,000 installations in 88 countries" that are designed to help the United States "anticipate, detect and respond to national security threats with remarkable precision and effectiveness."[70] Despite budget cutting, in January 2014 the House of Representatives approved a budget allocating $447 million to the Defense Department's Cyber Command, more than doubling what it had received for 2013.[71] In March 2014 Secretary of

Defense Chuck Hagel announced that the Cyber Command fighting force will number 6,000 by 2016, making it one of the world's largest units and facilitating "full-spectrum cyber capabilities" in crises.[72] To fulfill the growing global demand for cyber protection, cybersecurity firms have been sprouting up like weeds all over the world, with profits soaring.[73] As of 2015 global spending on cybersecurity approached $70 billion per year and was growing by about 10–15 percent annually, "with no deceleration in sight."[74]

Despite these steps and growing cyberattack experience, cyberthreat countermeasures have often failed, with standard operating procedures especially deficient in forestalling cyberattacks. The keynote speaker at the world's largest computer security conference in April 2015, Chief Executive Officer Amit Yoran of computer security firm RSA Security, stated that "we are losing this contest. The adversaries are out-maneuvering the industry, out-gunning the industry, and winning by every measure. . . . What we've been doing for decades isn't getting the job done."[75] Each government struggles "to stop leaks of its most legitimately held secrets," and "personal information continues to be for sale on the criminal market by the boatload."[76] Countermeasures have often backfired, with target systems becoming unavailable or system integrity and confidentiality being compromised.[77] Worst of all, many affected users "may not realize when data has been maliciously, surreptitiously modified, and make decisions based on the altered data," and when this blissful ignorance applies to advanced military control systems, "effects could be catastrophic."[78]

Simply increasing expenditures on cybersecurity resources alone can be futile. Despite huge government and business cybersecurity expenditures, "they're continually under attack," and "even as the world is becoming completely reliant on computers in every part of our lives, we're still in the Dark Ages when it comes to security."[79] Many officials "still mistakenly equate increased network security budgets with a direct and corresponding reduced vulnerability to cyber threats."[80]

In the past, cyberthreat has often paralyzed or debilitated cyber victims, preventing them from undertaking even simple preemptive measures and leaving them highly vulnerable. A 2014 US government report argued that "federal agencies are ill-prepared to defend networks against even modestly skilled hackers," and it goes on "to paint a broader picture of chronic dysfunction, citing repeated failures by federal officials to perform the unglamorous work of information security."[81] Indeed, "for years adversaries have infiltrated U.S. systems, sometimes detected, sometimes deflected, but almost never deterred."[82] James Cartwright, a retired Marine general and the former vice chair of the Joint Chiefs of Staff, has urged the US government "to hold China and other countries that sponsor hackers accountable" and to "implement a clear policy on how it responds to cyberattacks." He observed, "Right now we have the worst of worlds," for "if you want to attack me you can do it all you want, because I can't do anything about it. It's risk free, and you're willing to take almost any risk to come after me." He insists that targets need "to say, if you come after me, I'm going to find you, I'm going to do something about it."[83] Although this predicament is changing, targets still have a long way to go to attain dependable protection. In April 2015 US government officials admitted that their global "reliance on the confidentiality, availability, and integrity of data stands in stark contrast to the inadequacy of our cybersecurity."[84]

Given the dismal effectiveness record, one might expect that most countries would be rapidly developing new and different cyberthreat countermeasures, but in many cases warnings about cyberthreat response inadequacy have fallen on deaf ears. Rhetoric has been a great deal more impressive than reality. Heads-of-state have largely rattled sabers, promising significant hardening of attractive assets, promoting greater resiliency and redundancy, and threatening severe retaliation if cyberattacks persist. US president Barack Obama's 2009 comments illustrate this strong rhetoric: "From now on, our digital infrastructure—the networks and computers we depend on every day—will be treated as they should be: as a strategic national asset. Protecting this infrastructure will be a national security priority. We will ensure that these networks are secure, trustworthy and resilient. We will deter, prevent, detect, and defend against attacks and recover quickly from any disruptions or damage."[85] Yet the ensuing reality of cyberattacker restraint has been largely disappointing. "In place of grave warnings of the harm attackers will suffer are assertions we are getting serious about this and instituting new bureaucratic arrangements for doing so," but little evidence is cited of attackers actually being punished.[86]

Resulting Global Sea Changes

Due to ineffective target responses, globally most cyberattackers seem decidedly unfazed by Western response threats. These aggressors (1) doubt that threatened cybertarget countermeasures will actually be carried out, (2) recognize the underlying hypocrisy in attempts to restrain cyberattacks by those cybertargets who also initiate cyberintrusions, (3) discover ways to circumvent or undermine hardships that cybertargets try to impose when they actually apply countermeasures, (4) develop in a creative and fluid manner innovative cyberattack methods that directly overcome the barriers imposed by cybertarget countermeasures, (5) make ongoing cyberattack efforts harder to detect by increasing their secrecy and non-transparency, and (6) claim publicly not to care about the punitive consequences of ensuing cybertarget sanctions. Because of these defiant reactions, "despite over a decade of US government and private sector investment in network defenses designed to reduce our vulnerability to cyber intrusion, the two key national security threats from cyber adversaries—cyber espionage and cyberattack against critical infrastructure—are increasingly severe."[87] Furthermore, "despite productive efforts by the U.S. government and the private sector to strengthen cyber security, the increasing sophistication of cyber threats continues to outpace progress."[88] Figure 1.3 summarizes the underpinnings of this cyberattacker defiance.

Twenty-first-century cyberspace contributes to a world "fraught with a range of perils" previously unseen.[89] Because modern technology allows individuals to wield incredible disruptive power and to attack or be attacked from any part of the globe, national government leaders now recognize that the global system's parameters may be changing and routinely discuss "weapons of mass disruption" in cyberspace along with traditional weapons of mass destruction.[90]

Global chaos could result from unchecked cyberattacks, and "the cyber domain is the perfect breeding ground for political disorder and strategic instability."[91] "The main effect of cyberspace on the present international order is subversive," as it alters the relative power not only among states but also between states and non-state groups by allowing such groups "to perform acts of 'resistance' in places and on a scale which never before could they have done."[92] Cyberattacks could generate system-wide shocks "as devastating as any conventional means of conducting armed conflict."[93]

Overall, the world is now in the midst of a technological sea change. "Humanity is undergoing a transformation from the Industrial Age characterized by machinery, factories, urbanization and measured change where resources, production and optimization were the source of wealth and power, to an Information Age, defined by knowledge and networks, interconnectedness, globalization, adaptability, agility, innovation and rapid change. New rules sets are emerging that cannot be predicted and with them come opportunities, creativity and societal dislocations that often breed violence and instability."[94]

The microchip, along with other strategic breakthroughs, is "transforming warfare in the same way the musket did in the 1600s and the atom bomb did in 1945." The new "digital battlefield" now "weds precision-guided long-range weapons to high-tech information and surveillance systems that enable commanders to direct the action from thousands of miles away, and so on down to the smallest computerized gizmo that springs from the mind of a military

FIGURE 1.3.
Underpinnings of Cyberattacker Defiance

LOW PERCEIVED CYBERDEFENDER CREDIBILITY
Cyberattackers doubt that threatened target countermeasures will actually be carried out

HIGH PERCEIVED CYBERDEFENDER HYPOCRISY
Cyberattackers recognize the inconsistency when those targets who initiate cyberintrusions attempt to restrain cyberattacks

HIGH CYBERATTACKER PUNISHMENT RESILIENCY
Cyberattackers discover ways to circumvent or undermine hardships imposed when targets actually apply countermeasures

HIGH CYBERATTACKER OBSTACLE ADAPTABILITY
Cyberattackers develop creatively and fluidly innovative ways to overcome the barriers imposed by target countermeasures

HIGH CYBERATTACKER OPERATIONAL SECRECY
Cyberattackers increase their secrecy and non-transparency, making their ongoing disruptive efforts harder to detect

LOW PROFESSED CYBERATTACKER
Cyberattackers claim publicly not to care about the punitive consequences of ensuing target sanctions

planner."[95] The outcome can undermine global authority structures and erode national sovereignty.[96] Because no networked, electronically stored data is secure, the power of any legitimate body seeking to protect sensitive information diminishes.[97] Although in theory this transformation could be as much a force for stability and peace as for instability and disruption, in practice its tendency to render irrelevant traditional power elements and rules of the game while leveling the international playing field tilts its impact decidedly in the second rather than in the first direction.

Given the increasing centrality of digital information and communications systems in most countries, these sweeping global changes fundamentally challenge the public's trust and confidence in the capacity of national governments to provide ironclad protection, of critical infrastructures to provide functional continuity in public services, of private companies to provide uninterrupted goods and services, and of private citizens to experience security, privacy, and freedom in their digital assets. Among government defense personnel, this loss of trust can be devastating: "Military commanders may rapidly lose trust in the information and ability to control U.S. systems and forces; once lost, that trust is very difficult to regain."[98] Among private parties, "even localized damage to some critical part of infrastructure (or even symbols of the nation, such as national monuments) could have a massive effect on public confidence."[99] Little global confidence exists today about future data and system security, with scant hope among governments, businesses, or the public that information, transportation, and communications systems can reliably be fully protected from disruptive domestic and foreign cyberattacks. Major cyber breaches that exposed gaping vulnerabilities in government and multinational corporation systems have both decreased public confidence in public and private authorities' abilities to provide future protection and increased cyberattackers' confidence in their abilities to undertake future data breaches. Indeed, "one major effect of cyberspace is that it makes it easier to subvert and harder to govern."[100]

As evidenced by recent major cyberattacks, especially Edward Snowden's June 2013 National Security Agency breach, empowered non-transparent hackers can use sovereignty-reducing subversion to expose state security secrets and force unwanted national government transparency about both hidden agendas and closet vulnerabilities. Such transparency is decidedly "awkward for democracies" and an "anathema to autocracies."[101] Malevolent foreign extremist agents of digital subversion are usually fully aware that "the main benefit of attacks on critical infrastructure is not the immediate damage they inflict, but the collateral consequences of eroding the public's trust in services on which it depends."[102] System administrators may fail to realize fully that invoking this fear rather than gaining data access is often the ultimate hacking goal.

Successful cyberattackers are very astute in assessing the twenty-first-century global security environment and harbor no illusions that they are in an orderly international setting with common, accepted constraining rules of acceptable behavior. They reasonably assume that many other parties—including respected, advanced industrial societies—have chosen and will continue to choose to participate in cyberspace behavior that is just as easily classified as disruptive. Cyberattackers have been much quicker than cyberdefenders to adjust to the new tools at their disposal and understand that cyberspace success associates with operational secrecy; persistent use of low-risk, unanticipated methods; exploitation of cross-national ethnic and ideological subversive ties; clever image manipulation; and tactical and locational fluidity. Regardless of the actual risks posed by foreign cyberthreats, the perceived distrust engendered by foreign cyberattacks—if left unmanaged—could ultimately unravel the stabilizing fabric of the entire international system.

Overall Comments

As global concern about cross-border cyberthreat has grown in recent decades, there has been increased diversity in cyberattackers and their goals, motivations, targets, and attack styles. Given the ineffectiveness of cyberdefenders, the frequency and severity of cyberattacks have not diminished, and many hacking groups now seem emboldened. So far the danger posed by the latest cyberattackers and breach modes has been rising much faster than the sophistication of the victims' responses. Parallel to the broader strategic challenge of attempting to deter covert, dispersed, and decentralized real-world attacks from violent, armed non-state groups (theories about such groups "have direct relevance" to cyberspace), the net result may be a sea change that produces global disorder and instability.[103]

Notes

1. US Department of Defense, *DoD Cyber Strategy*, 1, 9.
2. Umbach, "Cyber Threats"; and "Innovative U.S. Cybersecurity," *Homeland Security News Wire*.
3. Lynn, "Defending a New Domain," 97.
4. Grow and Hosenball, "Special Report."
5. Schmidt, "New Interest."
6. Minority Staff, *Federal Government's Track Record*, 3.
7. Nakashima, "Large Worldwide Cyber Attack," A3.
8. "Fighting Cyber Attacks," *Homeland Security News Wire*.
9. Weber, "Cybercrime Threat Rising Sharply."
10. Baker, Waterman, and Ivanov, *In the Crossfire*, 3.
11. Davidson, "China Accuses U.S."
12. Weise, "Average Cost"
13. Reveron, "Introduction," in Reveron, *Cyberspace and National Security*, 4.
14. Lewis, *Cyber Threat and Response*, 2.
15. Lachow, *Active Cyber Defense*, 1–2.
16. US Government Accountability Office, *Cybersecurity*.
17. Kerry, *New War*, 123.
18. Lord and Sharp, *America's Cyber Future*, 1:20.
19. Lynn, "Defending a New Domain," 98–99.
20. Rattray, *Strategic Warfare in Cyberspace*, 99–100.
21. For the global rise of armed non-state groups as a context for this growth in non-state cyberattackers, see Mandel, *Global Security Upheaval*. See also Mandel, *Changing Face*, 30. An astute early formulation of this trend is found in Scott, *Revolution in Statecraft*.
22. Arquilla and Ronfeldt, "New Epoch," in Arquilla and Ronfeldt, *In Athena's Camp*, 5.
23. Hunt and Chesser, *Deterrence 2.0*, 33.
24. Reveron, "Introduction," 3.
25. Hunt and Chesser, *Deterrence 2.0*, 50.

26. Geers et al., *World War C*, 5.
27. Cilluffo, Cardash, and Salmoiroghi, "Blueprint for Cyber Deterrence," 8.
28. Ibid., 5.
29. Lord and Sharp, *America's Cyber Future*, 1:26.
30. Theohary and Rollins, *Terrorist Use*, 4.
31. Hunt and Chesser, *Deterrence 2.0*, 71.
32. Giacomello, "Information Society," in Anttiroiko and Malkia, *Encyclopedia of Digital Government*, 1529, 1533.
33. Brenner and Goodman, "In Defense of Cyberterrorism," 55; and Krepinevich, *Cyber Warfare*, 46.
34. Kello, "Meaning of the Cyber Revolution," 37.
35. Hunt and Chesser, *Deterrence 2.0*, 3; and Libicki, "Pulling Punches in Cyberspace," in National Research Council, *Proceedings*, 123.
36. Giacomello, "Bangs for the Buck," 401.
37. Libicki, *Cyberdeterrence and Cyberwar*, 153.
38. Thomas, *Hacker Culture*, 7.
39. Cilluffo, Cardash, and Salmoiroghi, "Blueprint for Cyber Deterrence," 12.
40. US Army Training and Doctrine Command, *Critical Infrastructure Threats*, VII-3–VII-4.
41. Hundley and Anderson, "Emerging Challenge," in Arquilla and Ronfeldt, *In Athena's Camp*, 232.
42. SPAMfighter News, "Most Web Hacks."
43. Conklin et al., *Principles of Computer Security*, 9. For a broader perspective on criminal motivations, see Mandel, *Dark Logic*.
44. Lin, "Operational Considerations," in Reveron, *Cyberspace and National Security*, 38.
45. Solomon, "Cyberdeterrence between Nation-States," 11.
46. Krahmann, "From State to Non-State Actors," in *New Threats*, 7.
47. Jensen, "Cyber Deterrence," 777; and US Army Training and Doctrine Command, *Critical Infrastructure Threats*, 1, 5.
48. McConnell, "To Win the Cyber-War," B1; and McConnell, "Cyber Insecurities," in Lord and Sharp, *America's Cyber Future*, 2:28.
49. US Department of Defense, *DoD Cyber Strategy*, 9, 2.
50. "Cyber Attacks on U.S.," *Homeland Security News Wire*.
51. Burke, "Why Microsoft's Craig Mundie."
52. Ernst, "Is This the Future?"
53. Ibid.
54. Guinchard, "Between Hype and Understatement," 88; and Solomon, "Cyberdeterrence between Nation-States," 11. See also Valeriano and Maness, "Persistent Enemies and Cyberwar," in Reveron, *Cyberspace and National Security*, 141.
55. Alperovitch, "Towards Establishment," in Czosseck, Tyugu, and Wingfield, *Proceedings*, 89–90.
56. Hodges and Creese, "Understanding Cyber-Attacks," 39.
57. Nye, "Power and National Security," in Lord and Sharp, *America's Cyber Future*, 2:16.
58. Theohary and Rollins, *Terrorist Use*, 5–6.
59. Defense Science Board, *Resilient Military Systems*, 5.
60. Kesan and Hayes, "Thinking through Active Defense," in National Research Council, *Proceedings*, 327.
61. Kello, "Meaning of the Cyber Revolution," 19.
62. Lewis, *Cyber Threat and Response*, 1; and Schneier, *Beyond Fear*, 80.

63. Alperovitch, *Revealed: Operation Shady RAT*, 2.
64. Brenner, *Glass Houses*, 2.
65. Clark, Berson, and Lin, *At the Nexus*, vii–viii.
66. Munro, "Pentagon's New Nightmare," C3; and "Leon Panetta," *Washington Post*.
67. Stokes, "'Extremists, Cyber Attacks.'"
68. Green, *Cyber Warfare*, 3.
69. "Twelve Chinese Hacker Groups," *Homeland Security News Wire*.
70. Lord and Sharp, *America's Cyber Future*, 1:12.
71. "House Approves," *Homeland Security News Wire*.
72. Nakashima, "U.S. Cyberwarfare Force."
73. Weinschenk, "Cyber Security's New."
74. Libicki, Ablon, and Webb, *Defender's Dilemma*, xi–xii.
75. Weise, "Computer Security."
76. Brenner, *Glass Houses*, xi.
77. Bronk, "Treasure Trove," 27.
78. AGT Intelligence, "Objectives of Cyber Attacks."
79. Weise, "Computer Security."
80. Raymond, "Paradoxes of (Cyber) Counterinsurgency."
81. Timberg and Rein, "Senate Cybersecurity Report."
82. Defense Science Board, *Resilient Military Systems*, 4.
83. "Twelve Chinese Hacker Groups," *Homeland Security News Wire*.
84. US Department of Defense, *DoD Cyber Strategy*, 1, 9.
85. Obama, "Remarks."
86. Morgan, "Applicability of Traditional Deterrence," in National Research Council, *Proceedings*, 58.
87. Kramer and Teplinsky, "Cybersecurity and Tailored Deterrence," 1.
88. Lord and Sharp, *America's Cyber Future*, 1:7.
89. Cilluffo, Cardash, and Salmoiroghi, "Blueprint for Cyber Deterrence," 10.
90. Wittes and Blum, *Future of Violence*, 5.
91. Kello, "Meaning of the Cyber Revolution," 32.
92. Betz and Stevens, *Cyberspace and the State*, 104.
93. Green, *Cyber Warfare*, 2.
94. Hunt and Chesser, *Deterrence 2.0*, 3.
95. Silverstein, "Buck Rogers," 23.
96. Nichiporuk and Builder, "Societal Implications," in Arquilla and Ronfeldt, *In Athena's Camp*, 296–97.
97. Wittes and Blum, *Future of Violence*, 93–94.
98. Defense Science Board, *Resilient Military Systems*, 5.
99. Clark, Berson, and Lin, *At the Nexus*, 15.
100. Betz and Stevens, *Cyberspace and the State*, 135.
101. Ibid., 135, 138.
102. Flynn, "Brittle Superpower," in Auerswald et al., *Seeds of Disaster*, 32.
103. Russell, *Cyber Blockades*, 23.

CHAPTER 2

Cyberdeterrence Paradoxes

To restrain cyberthreat, it is essential to develop a better cyberdeterrence framework than that commonly used today.

> We have reached a tipping point. The costs to our national and economic security are high and continue to grow higher. Whether from nation states intent on stealing military, political or economic secrets, attacking our critical infrastructures, pilfering corporate intellectual property and R&D [research and development] or from criminals engaging in theft, fraud and other cybercrimes, the initiative continues to remain with the attacker. It's time to engage in cyber deterrence through a strategy to dissuade, deter, and compel would-be attackers.[1]

Thus, after presenting the ideal cyberdeterrence dynamics in this chapter, the key surrounding cyberdeterrence paradoxes complicating the pursuit of this ideal are explained and analyzed.

Cyberdeterrence embodies both benefits and drawbacks. The advantages of cyberdeterrence are that it (1) is proactive and preemptive, focused on attempting to prevent cyberattacks before they occur rather than engaging in more common reactive, after-the-fact responses; (2) lowers security risks because immature threats are unlikely to be as harmful; (3) decreases long-run cyberattack frequency and severity; (4) forestalls the extensive societal damage that after-the-fact responses allow in the interim; and (5) compared to continuous conflict, reduces defense resource expenditures.[2] The disadvantages are that the earlier one takes action, the more fragmentary and ambiguous is one's intelligence and the greater are the political risks of a false alarm, sizable collateral damage, or global illegitimacy.

Ideal Cyberdeterrence Dynamics

The ideal dynamics of broad inclusive cyberdeterrence involve targets integrating a fluid mix of strategies to restrain significant cyberattacks by altering their adversaries' decision calculus. Although clearly not always attainable within today's anarchic global security setting, these ideal dynamics highlight the process that targets should strive to reach by taking early preemptive steps that nip the cyberthreat in the bud before it can cause tangible harm.

First, an emerging cyberthreat is evident when adversaries seek to disrupt the governmental and societal functioning of their targets by means of cyberattack. Second, identifying a cyberthreat requires targets to recognize critical assets that need protection, to become aware through early warning systems that they are impending cyberattack victims, to achieve attribution via focused intelligence on aggressors, and to determine through threat analysis their associated risks and vulnerabilities.

Next, responding to a cyberthreat occurs in two ways. In one part of this response, targets initiate defensive and offensive countermeasures against threat sources and their supporters, sponsors, or patrons. A second component involves communicating clearly the general thrust but not the specific content of these measures to adversaries. Targets must also demonstrate their capability and will to respond, foster public-private cooperation, and enhance their response legitimacy by spreading norms of restraint and by garnering internal and external support for these countermeasures. Choosing cyberthreat responses requires targets to specify tailored deterrence objectives; to evaluate and alter the adversary's strategic calculus; to identify desired changes in adversary conduct, including restraining conflict escalation and contagion; to assess alternative responses to trigger desired changes; to execute deterrence responses and monitor and assess adversary reactions to them; and to adjust responses as the deterrence situation evolves.[3]

Fourth, eliminating a cyberthreat occurs when adversaries decide to cease and desist cyberattacks given their certainty about higher-than-expected cyberattack costs (through cyber, military, political, and economic sanctions and negative global blowback) and lower-than-expected cyberattack benefits (through targets' hardening of vital assets, avoiding single-system reliance, using diversionary mechanisms, and fostering outcome assessment errors). These ideal cyberdeterrence dynamics are summarized in figure 2.1.

Retired US Marine general and former vice chair of the Joint Chiefs of Staff James Cartwright sums up ideal cyberdeterrence as involving a target convincing its adversaries that they will pay a steep price for any breach undertaken, that the target can alter any costs of such a confrontation to its advantage, and that the target possesses credible means to carry out these policies.[4] Overall, targets first attempt to prevent cyberattacks from occurring, but if attacked, then targets attempt to thwart the attacker from achieving its goals;

and if damaged, then targets try to limit its amount and to reconstitute affected systems expeditiously. Finally, targets must learn from the attack and improve their protection.⁵

Major Cyberdeterrence Paradoxes

Many analysts agree that cyberdeterrence involves "a process laden with paradoxes and contradictions," with the principal contentious issues not only being difficult for societies to grapple with and resolve but also being conducive to internal and external tensions.⁶ The four key paradoxes, summarized in figure 2.2, are (1) a cyber-sophistication vulnerability paradox linking connectivity level, digital awareness, and cyberthreat; (2) a cyber-restraint hypocrisy paradox encompassing difficulties in limiting global aggression when involved in both cyberdefense and cyberoffense; (3) a cyber-publicity muddle paradox emphasizing openness-secrecy trade-offs in inducing adversary compliance; and (4) a cyber-liberty tension paradox revealing a contradiction between promoting Internet freedom and promoting Internet security. Together these paradoxes reflect ambiguity and disagreement about inherent trade-offs embedded in cyberdeterrence.

Cyber-Sophistication Vulnerability

Cyberdeterrence involves a fundamental paradox regarding connectivity level, digital awareness, and threat. On the one hand, "the less sophisticated and widespread a country's connection to the internet, the lesser the cyber-threat. The more services are on line, the higher the risk of cyber-attack. On the other hand, the countries best prepared to react to a cyber-attack are those that are cyber and internet literate."⁷

Regarding cyberattack vulnerability, the digital world exhibits mixed impacts:

> Global interconnectivity both strengthens us and moderates us at the same time. We are strengthened because we are better connected to others than ever before and thus capable of spreading the seeds of liberty and opportunity to populations that yearn for it and where the lack of it is still being justified. We are moderated by this interconnectivity because others can more easily exploit the seams and turn our freedoms against us to infect with vitriolic propaganda that violently radicalizes populations across this interconnected Web.⁸

FIGURE 2.1.
Ideal Cyberdeterrence Dynamics

EMERGING CYBERTHREAT

1. Appearance of Adversaries Who Seek to Disrupt Designated Targets' Governmental and/or Societal Functioning

2. Selection by These Adversaries of Cyberattack as Their Preferred Mode of Intrusion into Designated Targets

↓

IDENTIFYING CYBERTHREAT

3. Awareness through Early Warning Systems Protecting Key Assets of the Likelihood of Becoming Victims of Cyberattacks

4. Attribution of Cyberattackers by Targets through Intelligence and Determination of Risks/Vulnerabilities through Threat Analysis

↓

RESPONDING TO CYBERTHREAT

5. Initiation by Targets of Defensive and Offensive Countermeasures
6. Clear Communication to Adversaries of These Measures' General Thrust

7. Effectiveness Promotion—Capability/Will and Public-Private Cooperation
8. Legitimacy Enhancement—Internal-External Support and Restraint Norms

↓

ELIMINATING CYBERTHREAT

9. Development by Adversaries of Certainty about Higher Costs and Lower Benefits of Cyberattacks

10. Decision by Adversaries to Cease and Desist from Initiating Significant Cyberattacks on Designated Targets

Sophisticated information and communications systems have improved the way major powers can fight wars but also have made military command and control more vulnerable to attacks.[9] Thus, cyberspace is both a blessing and a curse for security, creating opportunities and vulnerabilities for liberal, democratic advanced industrial societies.

President Barack Obama has stated, "It's the great irony of our Information Age—the very technologies that empower us to create and to build also empower those who would disrupt and destroy."[10] Put differently, "the network connectivity that the United States has used to tremendous advantage, economically and militarily, over the past 20 years has made the country more vulnerable than ever to cyber attacks."[11] Cyber capabilities can serve purposes perceived as legitimate or illegitimate, so it seems impossible to ban destructive

FIGURE 2.2.
Cyberdeterrence Paradoxes

CYBER-SOPHISTICATION VULNERABILITY
Paradoxical Link among Connectivity Level, Digital Awareness, and Threat
More sophisticated and widespread Internet connections and online services tend to increase perceived and actual cyberthreat

CYBER-RESTRAINT HYPOCRISY
Paradoxical Limitation of Aggression by Parties Pursuing Both Cyberdefense and Cyberoffense
More disruption of adversaries' defense information systems tends to jeopardize protection of one's own defense systems

CYBER-PUBLICITY MUDDLE
Paradoxical Choice between Openness and Secrecy in Inducing Cyberattacker Compliance
More covert cyberattack responses tend to lower outside friend support and foe restraint, while more overt responses tend to allow adversaries to circumvent or overcome them

CYBER-LIBERTY TENSION
Paradoxical Contradiction between Internet Freedom and Internet Security
More secure cyber protection tends to clash with widespread democratic expectations of freedom, privacy, and transparency

or vulnerability-increasing ones and promote constructive or vulnerability-decreasing ones. Moreover, negative impacts are not restricted to those from outside initiatives, for one's own use of cybertechnology can inadvertently harm one's own society.

Cyber-Restraint Hypocrisy

Many states face an offensive-defensive cyberdeterrence paradox. The incentives to disrupt the defense information systems of one's enemies seem identical to those for protecting one's own systems. Indeed, "as everyone becomes increasingly dependent on automated information systems, the value of maintaining and securing them rises; conversely, the value to an adversary of gaining access to the system, denying service and corrupting its contents, also rises."[12] In a perverse variation of the golden rule, cyberdeterrence can entail "a capability in cyberspace to do unto others what others may want to do unto us."[13] Moreover, given a shared global infrastructure, "the systems we want to undermine are often the very same systems we want to protect."[14]

The United States faces particular challenges in this regard. Although "the nation [is] most often cited as a model in dealing with cybersecurity, . . . executives from many nations, including many U.S. allies, rank the United States as the country 'of greatest concern' in the context of foreign cyberattacks."[15] The US defense community's interest in cybertools stems both from its own vulnerability—"the United States, in civilian as well as military matters, is more dependent on electronic information systems than is anyone else in the world"—and from its enemies' vulnerability. A cyberconfrontation "may be as much an opportunity as it is a threat."[16]

It is difficult to push global norms of cyber restraint and cyber protection if one simultaneously is a major cyberthreat source. In cyberspace, while the US government does not see pursuing both offensive and defensive initiatives as contradictory, "Chinese writers hasten to compare the United States to 'a thief crying stop thief.'"[17] Because "the United States wants a secure cyberspace but its intelligence agencies have found enormous utility in using their own computer hacking capabilities to collect confidential information from foreign adversaries," the question arises about "how the U.S. government can push for global cybersecurity while at the same time using cyber means to collect intelligence on potentially threatening regimes such as Iran."[18] The international community is skeptical about lofty universal principles that endorse the legitimacy of offensive cyber action as well as the need for coordinated international defensive measures. This paradox separates cyberdeterrence from other forms of deterrence, where major powers push the status quo and rarely engage in exactly the same kind of global aggressive behavior from which they are trying to protect themselves.

This offensive-defensive cyberspace mix can create a real cyberdeterrence bind as illustrated by three US National Security Agency (NSA) dilemmas. First, the NSA apparently regularly engineers, discovers, or purchases "zero-day" vulnerabilities, which are software defects unknown to vendors, and then stores them for use in its own offensive cyberattacks. This behavior, however, creates a difficult choice for the agency: "It can hoard a zero-day for offensive purposes but leave all computer systems affected by the zero-day vulnerable to exploitation or attack [by adversaries of the United States]; or it can disclose the vulnerability and allow it to be patched, enhancing defense at the cost of a potential offensive tool."[19]

Second, the 2013 NSA leaks about US offensive cyberespionage efforts specifically undercut its cyberdeterrence of the People's Republic of China. "Edward Snowden's revelations about the U.S. government's extensive online-surveillance programs have been a propaganda boon in China, and Beijing has raced to paint the Obama Administration as hypocritical for admonishing the Chinese government for cyberattacks while apparently committing plenty of its own."[20] While the United States accepts the legitimacy of mutual government military cyberespionage for political security purposes—covertly discovering adversaries' offensive capabilities and defensive vulnerabilities—it vehemently opposes state-sponsored intellectual property theft for economic gain.

Third, in April 2014, when the Heartbleed computer bug proliferated, rumors (later disconfirmed) spread that the NSA knew about it in advance because "the agency regularly seeks out similar security flaws, and turns some of them into cyberweapons."[21] These three NSA dilemmas serve to highlight the complexities of undertaking coherent and mutually reinforcing offensive and defensive action simultaneously in cyberspace.

Cyber-Publicity Muddle

A paradox exists about how public, explicit, and transparent targets should choose to make their response to cyberthreats. On the one hand, regardless of whether resulting damage is widely known, if a government keeps its offensive and defensive countermeasures in response to a cyberattack secret, then the advantage is that adversaries cannot easily adjust to whatever changes were made. The disadvantages to such secrecy are that outside support for targets from their allies would decline, and deterrence effects on other enemies would lessen because they would neither be intimidated nor discouraged by the unknown response. On the other hand, if a government makes its response to a cyberattack public, explicit, and transparent, then the advantage is that with proper signaling it can have some deterrent effect by intimidating or discouraging adversaries. Advertising cyberwar capabilities can "back up a deterrence strategy," "dissuade other states from conventional mischief or even from investing in mischief-making capabilities," and "reduce the other side's confidence in the reliability of its information, command and control, or weapon systems."[22]

However, the disadvantage of this advertising is that adversaries could easily make adjustments to circumvent or overcome policy. Indeed, "companies and public institutions are often hesitant to describe publicly the nature or success of attacks on their computer systems, partly for fear of providing information that would be useful to the individuals or countries mounting the efforts."[23] For the United States in particular, great uncertainty surrounds "the appropriate balance between publicizing U.S. efforts to develop cyber capabilities in order to discourage/deter attackers and keeping them secret in order to make it harder for others to foil them."[24] In today's globalized world, international expectations may be for a higher level of transparency about cyberattacks and cyber responses than cybertargets are comfortable with in terms of their own cybersecurity.

If "overheated rhetoric" accompanies publicity about cyberthreat responses, then outside outcome expectations can become unrealistically high. "After years of framing cyber attack in terms of war and large-scale natural disaster, policy makers might find it difficult to authorize such an attack [in response to threat] and then be disappointed when the results do not live up to the hype."[25] Both the citizens within states trumpeting sophisticated cyber responses and the allies of such countries can end up expecting way too much in terms of preventing future cyberattacks. Consequently, better balance is needed between causing domestic citizens or foreign observers to presume too little or too much from cyberattack responses. Given the effort and expense to launch a comprehensive cyberdeterrence program, the "bang-for-the-buck" question is also quite central for cybertargets.

Ironically, publicizing strong target cyber protection measures may sometimes make cyberattacks more frequent and severe. Adversaries may view escalating safeguards as an invitation to instigate cyberattacks, if only to demonstrate the imperviousness to any such restraint. Similar to waving a red flag in front of a bull, bragging about protective measures instead of improving cybersecurity could make intrusion more enticing because of the external prestige derived from penetrating such secure systems. Many "individual hackers seeking to prove their technical prowess," and even some states, believe that successful cyberattacks can signal "a manifestation of modernity and prowess: the counterpart of the gatling guns, dreadnoughts and B52s that signalled 'top nation.'"[26] Hackers may derive pleasure in writing code that can overcome even the toughest protection. The United States is in their bull's-eye, for "its iconic status as the most powerful organization in the world has recently made it the crown jewel of hackers worldwide."[27]

For most cyberattacks, neither initiators nor targets choose to publicize details, with victims being especially reluctant to discuss openly a cyberattack's full effect even though such revelations could help others protect themselves.[28] Indeed, "states or private entities are likely to have strong incentives not to discuss the technical details of informational security breaches or reveal their own capabilities to adversaries or third parties." For example, the US government "waited two years before disclosing that in 2008 it suffered 'the most significant breach of U.S. military computers ever' when a flash drive inserted into a U.S. military laptop surreptitiously introduced malware into the Pentagon's classified and unclassified computer systems." It only "disclosed few details about the extent of harm and said nothing about its knowledge of the likely perpetrators."[29]

For most targets, such incentives to hide cyberattack details and the scope of resulting devastation apply to both domestic citizens and international observers. Non-transparency appears to be the norm among states about not only their cyber responses and cyber impacts but also their cyber capabilities. Only four countries publicly admitted they had offensive military cyber programs in 2011, twelve countries did so in 2012, and forty-six countries in 2013.[30] Aside from national governments, private companies let "most such cases go unpublicized if not altogether unreported" due to "reputational and other concerns by the victim."[31] Such policies lead to low global visibility of cyberintrusions.

Cyber-Liberty Tension

Cyberspace engenders growing freedom-security tensions, which are exemplified by two "simultaneous and potentially contradictory efforts" by US government security officials: "On the one hand, they seek to secure the United States against cyber attacks, pushing for greater online transparency and attribution. On the other, they promote Internet freedom, advocating privacy and providing tools through which individuals can act anonymously online."[32] Although some analysts argue that cyberspace "freedoms and liberties actually provide security," cyberspace can alter the "liberty-privacy-security symbiosis" and trigger difficult policy choices.[33] They also maintain that "we in the West are going to face a tough choice because the governments that don't like free speech on the internet are going to put us in the position of choosing between free speech and cyber-security."[34] Democracy creates openness, freedom, privacy, and transparency expectations that can clash with cybersecurity. Indeed, "as important as it is to protect the key welfare benefits derived from cyber connectivity, some values such as life and liberty may be ranked as more important in national security, and connectivity that creates vulnerabilities that endanger those values may be sacrificed."[35]

Public insistence on privacy and resistance to surveillance—despite its role in deterrence—and to Internet restriction, meanwhile, is consistently high. In a 2008 poll of 22,512 respondents in twenty-two countries, the vast majority believed that "the government should not have the right to limit access to the Internet."[36] If a foreign rather than domestic government moves to restrict this access, then public resistance is even higher.

The roots of this tension are in differing cybersecurity expectations both between private citizens and national governments and between cyberattackers and cyberdefenders. Indeed, the "concept of information warfare is very dangerous from a civil liberties point of view." Some demand that "in order to ensure our survivability in an information war, the military should make use of all 'national assets and use all sectors of society,'" including "all privately owned computers, fax machines, computer bulletin boards and . . even the assets of international corporations."[37] Much of the public resists intrusive cybersecurity measures given the invisibility of their benefits and the concreteness of their liberty-constraining costs. If targets chose to define freedom strictly as freedom from cyberattacks, and the attack rate actually fell, then the public might be more accepting of these restrictive measures. This limited notion of freedom, however, is decidedly not globally endorsed.

Western analysts differ markedly about the freedom-security balance in cyberspace. Some argue that Internet freedom and privacy are basic rights for every individual and are not to be tampered with under any conditions, while others contend that protecting the security of critical infrastructure should always take precedence. The US government typically handles such issues "by sacrificing the security of the global communications infrastructure to maximize the capacity of intelligence and national-security agencies to track and undermine adversaries," but many find this objectionable.[38]

This intense cybersecurity debate relates more broadly to protecting individual human rights versus promoting collective security. Vast value differences impede a globally acceptable balance. "Constructing acceptable international norms that balance America's cyber security interests with the desire to maintain an open and free Internet can be difficult, given both the opposition of authoritarian regimes" and "the disjunction between the U.S. position on free expression and those of even America's closest democratic partners."[39] So far it has been exceedingly difficult for opposing parties to achieve understanding and a middle-ground, mutually acceptable compromise regarding these areas of deep value divides.

Overall Comments

Although most of the strategic tensions highlighted by the four cyberdeterrence paradoxes are not unique to cyberdeterrence and appear in other kinds of security initiatives—such as in counterinsurgency—they seem particularly acute in the cyber domain. They substantially interfere with the direct pursuit of the ideal cyberdeterrence dynamics. From a policy standpoint, each tension elicits a sensitive balancing act of managing competing interests by those pursuing cybersecurity.

Notes

1. Cilluffo and Siers, "Cyber Deterrence."
2. Goodman, "Cyber Deterrence," 103; and Libicki, *Cyberdeterrence and Cyberwar*, 103.
3. Kugler, "Deterrence of Cyber Attacks," in Kramer, Starr, and Wentz, *Cyberpower and National Security*, 330.
4. Center for Strategic and International Studies, *Global Security Forum*, 3.
5. Lukasik, "Framework for Thinking," in National Research Council, *Proceedings*, 99.
6. Valeriano and Maness, *Cyber War*, 61.
7. Security and Defence Agenda, *Cyber-Security*, 48.
8. Hunt and Chesser, *Deterrence 2.0*, 3.
9. Rattray, *Strategic Warfare in Cyberspace*, 2.
10. Obama, "Remarks."
11. Defense Science Board, *Resilient Military Systems*, 15.
12. Libicki, "Information War," 416–17.
13. Libicki, *Cyberdeterrence and Cyberwar*, 27.
14. Kroll, "Cyber Conundrum," 9.
15. Baker, Waterman, and Ivanov, *In the Crossfire*, 25.
16. Berkowitz, "Warfare in the Information Age," 59–66.
17. Lindsay, "Impact of China," 8.
18. "Contradictions in U.S. Cybersecurity Policy," *Homeland Security News Wire*.
19. Goldsmith, "Cyber Paradox."
20. Davidson, "China Accuses U.S."
21. Sanger and Perlroth, "U.S. Denies It Knew."
22. Libicki, *Brandishing Cyberattack Capabilities*, xi.
23. Sanger and Markoff, "I.M.F. Reports Cyberattack."
24. National Research Council, *Proceedings*, 364.
25. Lawson, "Overheated Rhetoric."
26. McConnell, "Cyber Insecurities," 28; and Arnold, "Cyber War in Ukraine."
27. Haley, "Theory of Cyber Deterrence."
28. Hodges and Creese, "Understanding Cyber-Attacks," 48.
29. Waxman, "Cyber-Attacks," 444.
30. Lewis, "Truly Damaging Cyberattacks."
31. Baker, Waterman, and Ivanov, *In the Crossfire*, 8.
32. Fontaine and Rogers, "Internet Freedom," in Lord and Sharp, *America's Cyber Future*, 2:145.
33. Schneier, *Beyond Fear*, 246; and Wittes and Blum, *The Future of Violence*, 141.
34. Security and Defence Agenda, *Cyber-Security*, 48.
35. Nye, "Power and National Security," 15.
36. "International Public Opinion," WorldPublicOpinion.org.
37. DiNardo and Hughes, "Some Cautionary Thoughts."
38. Kroll, "Cyber Conundrum," 9–10.
39. Fontaine and Rogers, "Internet Freedom," 153.

CHAPTER 3

Obstacles to Forward Progress

Numerous obstacles impede restraining foreign cyberattacks, including systemic roots of failed cyberdeterrence and cyberdeterrence improvement roadblocks. Some blockages are immovable, others can be circumvented, and still others can actually be reduced. Identifying and analyzing these obstacles can provide critical clues about what to avoid in pursuing broad inclusive cyberdeterrence.

Today many pessimistic analysts conclude that cyberdeterrence is impossible or at least highly unlikely. Sentiments persist that "there is no identifiable protection model that will keep pace with the evolution and sophistication of cyber threats."[1] The most cynical critics claim that "the anonymity, the global reach, the scattered nature, and the interconnectedness of information networks greatly reduce the efficacy of cyber deterrence and can even render it completely useless."[2] This view often rests on fatalistic assumptions that obstacles will always thwart cyberdeterrence and that cyberattackers will always maintain the upper hand over cyberdefenders, reinforcing an acceptance of cyber penetration without significant recourse.

Other more optimistic observers minimize cyberattack threat because such disruptions have not yet directly led to a massive loss of human life or to property damage; thus, they classify fear of cyberattacks as dysfunctional threat-inflating "cyber hype."[3] Because cyberconfrontations directly target the communication and database infrastructure rather than human enemies, cyber disruption "seems to possess the redeeming quality of being 'much more humane' than real-world warfare since the only intended casualties would be the crippling of information flow, convenience, and comfort."[4] Further, new nonlethal methods of electronic warfare seem in several instances to have "greatly limited" human casualties.[5] One strategist surmises that "while much about cyber is cloaked either in official secrecy or is shrouded in a fog of uncertainty because of the subject's immaturity, nonetheless it is safe enough to say now that cyber peril should not be regarded as a nuclear-like danger or set of dangers."[6]

Still other hopeful observers go a step further and contend that cyberattacks may even beneficially lower security risks.

> Cyber attacks diminish rather than accentuate political violence by making it easier for states, groups, and individuals to engage in two kinds of aggressions that do not rise to the level of war: sabotage and espionage. Weaponized computer code and computer-based sabotage operations make it possible to carry out highly targeted attacks on an adversary's technical systems without directly and physically harming human operators and managers. Computer-assisted attacks make it possible to steal data without placing operatives in dangerous environments, thus reducing the level of personal and political risk.[7]

Cyberattacks certainly have directly generated less significant real-world damage than conventional kinetic military attacks have. However, this argument and related claims may overly downplay the rapid pace at which cyberconfrontations are changing, with new offensive and defensive tools and new responses to countermeasures potentially altering the past pattern of expected security consequences.

Failed Cyberdeterrence Systemic Roots

The systemic roots of failed cyberdeterrence are (1) porous digital infrastructure design; (2) initiator-target cyber expertise imbalance; (3) proliferating cyberattack tools; (4) overly static, rigid, predictable, and narrow cyberdeterrence strategies; and (5) growing target cyberspace dependence and addiction. These roots shed deeper light on the earlier discussion of why target responses to foreign cyberthreat have been so ineffective. The majority of these systemic roots are extremely difficult to change in today's world.

Porous Digital Infrastructure Design

Cyberdeterrence failure stems most fundamentally from the purposely open architecture of the Internet, which was originally constructed for ease of use rather than for security.[8] Cybersecurity firm Darktrace's chief executive officer Andrew France argues that "the Internet was never designed to be secure, and if you attach your critical national infrastructure to it, then you're asking for trouble."[9] Given this architecture, and the continuing role of externally accessible computer networks in military and economic power, "they are at risk."[10]

The Center for Strategic and International Studies confirms that "porous information systems have allowed our cyberspace opponents to remotely access and download critical military technologies and valuable intellectual property—designs, blueprints, and business processes—that cost billions of dollars to create."[11] Furthermore, having databases within this open architecture be dependent on nonnative hardware and software components can magnify these dangers. For example, in the United States, the extensive reliance on "inherently insecure architectures with increasing use of foreign-built components" accentuates supply chain vulnerabilities.[12]

Initiator-Target Cyber Expertise Imbalance

Cyberdeterrence failure is also due to both the rise of tech-savvy non-state groups that are more immune than states are to countermeasures, and the prevailing ignorance of many security policymakers about cyberspace. In the minds of many practitioners, recent rapid technological advances have appeared to favor cyberattackers, "leaving defenders to play catch-up."[13] This perceived imbalance can cause cyberattack victims to feel vulnerable and hamstrung in their sense of helplessness to curtail cyberthreats. State targets often misjudge cyberthreats and responses to them. The immediate impulse is to strike out and retaliate against cyberattackers, but they are often difficult to identify and constantly morphing and on the move.

Even today many political leaders seem befuddled by cyberspace, and their ignorance about their own governments' cybersecurity is "alarming."[14] Most have very "limited understanding of technology, often due to their age."[15] Even at lower levels, "middle-aged analysts and operators are unlikely to possess the cutting edge expertise on what is happening in the cyber domain or more important, what approaches may be useful for deterrence in this emerging world."[16] Network administrators complain about insufficient "top-notch computer gumshoes to track down the foreign rings," and "their hands are often tied by the strict rules of engagement."[17] Moreover, a cyberdeterrence-inhibiting chasm exists between those who are tech-savvy and those who are strategy-savvy: "Senior people in the ranks of strategic studies have by and large ignored the growing cyber challenge, while those who are technically highly cyber knowledgeable typically have scant background in strategy."[18] The split can result in a void of valuable integrated analysis conducive to cyberattack restraint.

Today disruptive individuals and groups are acquiring cyberattack know-how at an amazing pace. An official with the National Infrastructure Protection

Center (formerly part of the Federal Bureau of Investigation and now part of the Department of Homeland Security) warned that "the threat of cyberterrorism will grow in the new millennium, as the leadership positions in extremist organizations are increasingly filled with younger, Internet-savvy individuals" who are now able to "threaten the sovereignty and wellbeing of nation-states, oftentimes from the comfort of their own homes."[19] Although powerful states often dismiss the technological capabilities of non-state disruptors, in cyberspace such groups are often light years ahead of the game.

Proliferating Cyberattack Tools

A related pervasive root of cyberdeterrence failure is found in rapid digital innovation and proliferating cyberattack technologies, with the best cyberweapons being covert—that is, "intended to achieve effects without adversaries even realizing that they have been targeted."[20] Swift technological diffusion facilitates amazing networking and communication, and the inexpensiveness, availability, and unregulated nature of the facilitating tools makes them "highly accessible."[21] Many cyberattack tools are so low cost and easy to use that anyone could readily download, copy, or apply them within a supply chain where key components are developed and sold globally.[22] For example, today hackers can buy BlackEnergy or NetBot Attacker—cyberattack tools made by Russian and Chinese hackers, respectively—"for less than $100 apiece."[23] If tools are unavailable through open commercial channels, hackers can easily find criminal providers. As technological complexity rises, vulnerabilities become subtler.[24] Despite the reliance of sophisticated breaches on technical expertise, target intelligence, and complex compromise-minimization strategies, the low cost of cyberattacks and the ubiquitous availability of cyberattack tools make breaches highly appealing to aggressors because such assaults seem a whole lot easier than "developing, maintaining, and using advanced military capabilities."[25]

Malicious disruptive forces benefit from these diverse, readily available hacking tools and from reduced barriers to entry.[26] In the eyes of many analysts, "for the moment the 'bad guys' have the upper hand—whether they are attacking systems for industrial or political espionage reasons, or simply to steal money—because the lack of international agreements allows them to operate swiftly and mostly with impunity."[27] Cyberattackers can easily develop weaponized code with the potential to disrupt state and human security and to wreak global havoc.[28]

Overly Static, Rigid, Predictable, and Narrow Cyberdeterrence

Existing cyberdeterrence measures have not been nimble. "Many current defensive security architectures have a lot in common with the Maginot Line [the expensive French fortifications that the German army simply bypassed in World War II] in that they are stiff, inflexible, and overly complex. Having more layers of similar static defenses does not equate to greater security. A defensive architecture that depends on a static approach using signatures and compliance-based standards is something that hackers will beat every time."[29]

In today's world, "cyber attack methods evolve so quickly that static, predictable defenses are doomed to fail."[30] Heavy reliance on standard defense measures—such as simple password protection, primitive antivirus software, and skimpy firewalls—reflects the unfounded assumption that these rudimentary policies are sufficient to prevent cyberattacks. Even with these elementary steps, monitoring and enforcement have been lax. Maintaining system integrity necessitates not only safeguards against unwanted external intrusions into data and communications systems but also immediate detection and speedy adjustment and restoration when such breaches occur. The performance of government and business targets in these last two areas, however, has been woeful.

Growing Target Cyberspace Dependence/Addiction

Cyber dependence has been growing rapidly in recent years, with cyberspace now integrated into every aspect of modern life.[31] Globally over the last decade, the number of people with Internet access has increased by over two billion people; and for the US economy in 2015, from 3 percent to 13 percent of business value is generated by Internet-related businesses.[32] Military cyber dependence is especially massive, with digital technology in the US military—consisting of fifteen thousand networks and seven million computing devices across hundreds of installations in dozens of countries and employing over 900,000 people—facilitating logistical support, command-and-control systems, real-time provision of intelligence, and remote operations.[33] Fueling this cyber dependence is an ever-increasing technological efficiency, as "computing power doubled every 18 months for 30 years, and by the beginning of the twenty-first century it cost one-thousandth of what it did in the early 1970s."[34]

Even during wartime, digital network dependence is pivotal. Warfare is "no longer primarily a function of who puts the most capital, labor and technology on the battlefield, but of who has the best information about the battlefield."[35] Modern warfare now requires speedy and reliable data on remote targets and coordinated multifaceted strategy and tactics in the field, and operating blind—even with overwhelming force advantages—is a sure path to defeat. So cybersecurity has become as critical as military preparedness, troop strength, and advanced weapons systems to succeed in modern warfare. If a computerized system "becomes the center of gravity for modern militaries, it becomes the logical target of others"; thus, "information warfare is often cited as the *leitmotif* of early 21st century conflict."[36] One analyst quips, "If you want to shut down the free world, . . . the way you would do it is not to send missiles over the Atlantic Ocean—you shut down their information systems and the free world will come to a screeching halt."[37]

As noted in chapter 2's discussion of cyberdeterrence paradoxes, cyber dependence creates security vulnerability. Given the "ever-expanding dependency on cyberspace, [the] isolation, corruption, or elimination of cyberspace" could end "life as we know it."[38] Moreover, the "openness and dynamism that led to the Internet's rapid expansion now provide dangerous state and nonstate actors with a means to undermine U.S. [and global] interests."[39]

The psychological impact of cyberspace dependence and addiction is extremely dangerous. Government officials, business executives, and private citizens no longer see digital access and reliability as a luxury but as a basic need and, within some societies, as a basic human right. There is little tolerance of any form of downtime or delayed or interrupted access, with people incessantly demanding that disruptions be fixed immediately and growing highly anxious and angry if they are not. The widespread underlying expectations involve unrestricted, ready, fast, and reliable access to all digital assets deemed vital, simultaneously accompanied by security and confidentiality for all sensitive digital assets. Because in today's interpenetrated world this combination is next to impossible to achieve, and because the reliance of governments, businesses, and citizens on digital assets is growing by leaps and bounds, those people who are most dependent on cyberspace are the ones who experience almost constant frustration in dealing with a lifestyle predicament that they believe can and should be quickly remedied. Rather than seek ways to reduce this vexing cyber dependence, instead the most common response has been to escalate insistence that relevant authorities work harder to find a satisfactory solution. In the process, there appears to be little understanding among consumers—including those in government and business—of the frailty of much network connectivity and cybersecurity.

Roadblocks at Differing Societal Levels

Cyberdeterrence roadblocks at differing societal levels include political regime constraints, citizen attitude difficulties, and intractable global tensions. Existing blockages are neither primarily top down nor bottom up; instead, they pervade all parts of society. State constraints seem easiest to address, while global system tensions seem hardest to manage.

State Government Level: Political Regime Constraints
Impediments Posed by Government Bureaucratic Inertia

A key obstacle to forward progress, particularly within large bureaucracies in democratic states, is the difficulty in updating outmoded unwieldy government structures and entrenched attitudes.[40] The peripheral status of information technology workers is a hindrance here. A general failure exists among government agencies "to hire top-notch information technology workers, pay them enough, and give them enough clout to enforce routine security practices. . . . Higher up the chain of command, agency directors are rarely held accountable for security failures . . . because it is often unclear who is responsible."[41] Traditional state bureaucracies have been unused to giving those safeguarding cybersecurity the authority they need to promote effective cyber protection of vital data and networked systems.

The sluggishness promoted by bureaucratic inertia and outmoded standard operating procedures poses a critical roadblock for cyberdeterrence because "governments tend to move slowly, but with cyber-security we need to move fast."[42] For cyber protection, milliseconds can make a difference, with the ideal being to "respond to attacks before they happen or even before they arrive."[43] Government officials are often reluctant to experiment with new modes of data protection that are perceived as too risky. In the defense sector, too frequently shortsightedness, narrow-mindedness, predispositions against outside-the-box thinking, and intellectual complacency have prevailed. Low accountability, ignorance about technology, and lack of authority for the few tech-savvy officials—all combine to impede cyberdeterrence success. Particularly within huge government organizations, this sluggishness is hard to overcome.

Perhaps the most far-reaching danger from this inertia regarding cyberspace is how it can undermine a state's political authority. Modern systems of authority rely on complex command-and-control systems to function, depending on database management and effective communication among components to keep track of what is going on, to make decisions, and to provide necessary services. National defense systems, in particular, heavily rely on this kind of elaborate network to give an early warning of any impending danger and to formulate quick and effective responses. Legitimate political authority now rests heavily on data and communication credibility due to digital command and control; thus, if bureaucratic inertia leads national governments to seem visibly unable to protect their sensitive military and critical civilian infrastructure data, their political authority is directly undermined.

Impediments Posed by Mutual Government-Business Friction

Often those recognizing the paramount importance of cyberthreats inappropriately place all of the responsibility for protection—and all the blame for failure—on national governments. When private firms suffer cyberattacks, they often blame inadequate state protection for the resulting problems. Some observers inside and outside of government believe strongly that the cyberthreat challenge is so sophisticated that only national governments possess the appropriate resources and tools to address it effectively. These analysts stress the need for the type of completely standardized response that only a central state regime could provide. For example, a 2012 US government report emphasized the call for "increased federal involvement in protecting the nation's privately-owned critical infrastructure" because recent cyber protection failures "aren't due to poor practices by the private sector" but rather to "real lapses by the federal government."[44] However, this concerted focus on top-down state cyber protection ignores the critical role played by bottom-up protection initiatives from private citizens and private companies and the need to find ways to overcome existing public-private cybersecurity distrust.

Numerous government roadblocks exist to information sharing with private business. Sometimes key government officials inadvertently retard bottom-up cyber protection responsibility by making ill-advised statements. For example, "when U. S. military officials hype cyberwar, it leads the public to believe that the Pentagon is in charge of dealing with the threat," whereas "companies and individuals need to take responsibility for their own security."[45] At other times, government officials are reluctant to share information because they fear that sharing secret data with companies would lead to security leaks. The resulting security classification requirements can be decidedly off-putting to business leaders, many of whom lack security clearance and are unwilling to submit to the process necessary to obtain it. In still other circumstances, such public-private collaboration faces "legal, commercial, and transactional impediments."[46] Public-private information sharing often tends to be skewed, with widespread business concerns feeling that it is "a one-way street" (private to public only). As one chief security officer put it, "When it comes to getting truly useful information back from the government—warnings or advice about the use of resources—[we get] nothing at all."[47] Although in the United States the government has attempted to address this issue by giving security clearances to key industry executives, progress in this regard "has been uneven."[48] Governments face a delicate balance in signaling that they are playing a vital role in providing cyber protection while at the same time encouraging private parties to provide their own protection.

Turning to business roadblocks in sharing with governments, private companies often need special prodding to share cyberdeterrence information. Even though almost two-thirds of business security experts polled believed that sharing cyberthreat intelligence could have prevented cyberattacks on their companies, businesses are often reluctant to provide their own cyber protection; instead, they rely on the government and try to avoid the high costs of cybersecurity, which they see mainly "as inherently military or law-enforcement responsibilities."[49] Furthermore, private companies are often reluctant to talk to governments about cyberattacks because "they aren't keen to reveal vulnerabilities to competition or to consumers."[50] Companies are afraid that if word gets out that they have been cyberattack targets, then their image among their customers and within the business community will suffer. Indeed, a cyberattack's effect on the company's reputation is the biggest concern for company security officers, as all it takes is a whisper of a possible problem to make a company's stock take a dive.[51] Larry Clinton, president of the Internet Security Alliance, said that requiring businesses to publicly disclose their security statuses might cause corporations to feel that they may be "named and shamed" for finding security breaches.[52] Furthermore, private companies worry that data provided could be "misused by government" and that transparency with governments could lead to more onerous regulations.[53] As a result, private sector cyber protection initiatives have been woefully inadequate. A 2011 survey revealed that although 73 percent of responding companies had been hacked, "88 percent of them spent more money on coffee than on securing their Web applications."[54]

These contrasting government and business perceptions of cyber cooperation are linked to pervasive attitudes of public-private distrust. Government and business are "dominated by two different cultures."[55] For private multinational corporations, which control most critical infrastructure, governments are viewed as "partners," "regulators and policemen," and "owners, contractors and customers; but they are also seen as aggressors, infiltrators and adversaries"; consequently, many corporate information technology officers are "skeptical" about governments' "ability to deter or protect against cyberattacks."[56] Moreover, both sides have few incentives to change and adapt. "Private enterprises have little incentive to publicly identify their own vulnerabilities," particularly "in the cyber domain, where the private sector actors are notoriously distrustful of government interference and regulation. And ... government institutions like the NSA with (perhaps) superior knowledge of threat signatures and new developments in the arsenal of cyber attackers are deeply reluctant to share their hard won knowledge with the private sector at the risk of compromising their own sources and methods."[57] Such mutual fears can stymie meaningful government-business cyberdeterrence cooperation, and any following cyberattacks can cause dysfunctional mutual finger-pointing.

This pervasive public-private distrust is illustrated by problems surrounding US president Barack Obama's 2012 Enhanced Cybersecurity Services program, which security experts widely praised in its conception. Launched to promote cybersecurity by giving approved businesses access to classified cyberthreat information and the ability to sell cybersecurity services to critical infrastructure targets, the program quickly bogged down. Two years later, government officials stated that "Congress' failure to pass new legislation allowing companies to share information on cyberattacks without the risk of antitrust action or shareholder liability suits has diminished efforts to improve private sector cyber defenses."[58] Thus, overcoming the public-private information-sharing logjam would appear to require some basic attitude changes on both sides.

Public Level: Citizen Attitude Difficulties
Impediments Posed by Fatalistic Fears

The public's fears about cyberspace abound, fueling "worst-case" apprehensions. They include escalating problems in three areas: knowledge, manipulation, and falsification of personal data; elimination of credible information sources, confusing the public voice needed for democratic functioning; and personal and national vulnerability, where even with sizable military forces no way exists to protect oneself and one's society from cyber penetration. Such subjective fears can yield receptivity to protection initiatives but not overcome cynicism about their value.

However, often the public is unaware of the indirect human costs of cyberattacks. "While an information attack may avoid direct human casualties, there may be considerable indirect death and damages. Disrupting the information infrastructure of another nation will shut down hospitals, cause planes and trains to crash, cause starvation in isolated regions, etc. Though there are no direct casualties when logic bombs destroy the information infrastructure of another nation, they may cause significant collateral death, most likely civilian."[59]

Acting in cyberspace may mask the extent of mass public harm. For example, disrupting power infrastructure, which serves consumer and corporate energy needs, may cause some citizens to freeze to death; or a cyberattack on a computer server may prevent a hospital from performing life-saving surgeries on patients. Indeed, "the public (and often the industry) understanding of this significant national security threat is largely minimal due to the very limited number of voluntary disclosures by victims of intrusion activity compared to the actual number of compromises that take place."[60]

Impediments Posed by Threatened Dominant Values

Cyberattack dangers are not restricted to disrupting vital databases and crippling critical infrastructure. In addition, they can challenge deep-seated national beliefs. "What can be held at risk as we seek to deter the violent metastasis of ideas propagated over the Internet? How can we prevail in a global marketplace of ideas without compromising our own sacred values?"[61] For example, jeopardizing the notion of American exceptionalism is the country's recognition of its cyber vulnerability and the urgent need for improved cyber protection.

As suggested in the cyberdeterrence paradoxes discussion in chapter 2, cyberdeterrence can challenge moral values. In the United States, for example, any discussion of cybersecurity "at the strategic level must occur in the context of the moral nature of communication in a pluralistic, secular, democratic society.... The question must be raised whether using the techniques of information warfare at the strategic level is compatible with American purposes and principles."[62] Culturally dissimilar societies may address different areas of value incompatibility.

In many countries, the push for freedom is at the root of this challenge. Indeed, "as long as major governments desire unimpeded operational freedom in cyberspace, it will continue to be the Wild West."[63] The global spread of democracy and liberal enlightened values may clash with cyberdeterrence's need for effective monitoring of morphing digital dangers. Many subtle cyberthreats are quite elusive, so a new balance may be necessary between these pervasive security needs and the demands from civil liberties and right-to-privacy advocates.

International System Level: Intractable Global Tensions
Impediments Posed by Global Agreement Troubles

Reaching agreement on meaningful global cyberattack regulation is daunting because "coordinating such diverse stakeholders with such varied values will not happen quickly or easily."[64] Trying to assemble a broad, anti-cyberthreat multilateral coalition can often critically delay needed action. Given differing cyberattack priorities, definitions, verification obstacles, and cyber rights and values, "it will be difficult to achieve international agreement on legal interpretation and to enforce it with respect to cyber-attacks."[65]

Even when cyberspace agreements are reached, they can be undercut easily. First, there are multiple unsavory roundabouts: embargo-bypassing transshipment of cyberattack hardware or software components (with the least restrictive routes chosen to maximize illicit success), firewall-bypassing cyberattack viruses and malware, and identity-bypassing morphing cyberattackers. Because many cybercrime groups are transnational, they can corrupt state officials of various nationalities in different countries to move cyber components internationally.[66] Second, formal international accords may simply make nefarious cyber disruption more covert (pushing cyber transactions into a seamy underground black market) and more difficult to track and interdict. Global laws may "simply prompt more sophisticated and geographically dispersed law evasion techniques," complicating cyberattack restraint.[67] Third, agreements and laws can end up one step behind rapidly changing cyberattack innovations, rendering such pacts irrelevant.

Impediments Posed by Global Power Shifts

Cyberthreat can upset existing global power hierarchies. Specifically, "the characteristics of cyberspace reduce some of the power differentials among actors," and "the largest powers are unlikely to be able to dominate this domain as much as they have others like sea or air."[68] In cyberspace, status quo–seeking major powers may see their vast military superiority undercut, while subversive parties at the bottom of the global pecking order may gain ground.

US global political-military hegemony is now in danger. According to the Defense Security Service, "every time our adversaries gain access to sensitive or classified information and technology, it jeopardizes the lives of our warfighters, since these adversaries can exploit the information and technology to develop more lethal weapons or countermeasures to our systems."[69] Cyberattacks provide adversaries a means to overcome overwhelming US conventional military power "in ways that are instantaneous and exceedingly hard to trace."[70] In the end, global technological diffusion has "placed the United States in a permanently more vulnerable and even fearful mode."[71]

Moreover, US global industrial competitiveness is threatened as well. "The immediate benefits gained by our opponents are less damaging, however, than is the long-term loss of U.S. economic competitiveness. We are not arming our competitors in cyberspace; we are providing them with the ideas and designs to arm themselves and achieve parity. America's power, status, and security in the world depend in good measure upon its economic strength; our lack of cybersecurity is steadily eroding this advantage."[72] An intelligence official has said $1 billion and twenty capable hackers could "shut down America."[73]

Roadblocks with Differing Time Frames

Cyberdeterrence roadblocks with differing time frames include immediate short-term defective cyberthreat detection; medium-term problem-solution mismatches; and distant, long-term, unintended pernicious implications. All of these obstacles are highly interrelated. Most cybertargets prioritize the immediate roadblocks, however, leaving the distant ones to be dealt with later.

Short-Term Defective Cyberthreat Detection
Impediments Posed by Perpetrator Attribution Difficulties

Attribution, or identifying cyberattack initiators, is often cited as the key impediment to cyberdeterrence.[74] The elusive far-flung origins of cyberattacks—"including cybercafés, open Wi-Fi nodes, and suborned third-party computers"—compound attribution problems, as these attacks "do not require expensive or rare machinery" and "leave next to no unique physical trace."[75] Indeed, "the nature of the digital domain lends itself to anonymity," where "attackers can easily conceal, erase, or even spoof [deceiving targets about the true perpetrator] the original source of an attack, leaving behind no identifiable physical tracks."[76] In 2009 US director of national intelligence Dennis Blair reported to Congress that identifying a cyberattacker "often takes weeks and sometimes months of subsequent investigation" and admitted that "even at the end of very long investigations you're not quite sure who carried out the offensive," for in cyberspace "ambiguity is ubiquitous and reinforces the normal fog of war."[77] In a 2011 survey, only 6 percent of cybertargets detected cyberattackers via internal methods. The remaining 94 percent only learned that they were victims from external sources such as law enforcement because typically a cyberattack remains undetected longer than a year.[78]

Attribution is especially complicated when non-state groups launch cyberattacks with ambiguous state support. Emerging threats have been typically covert, dispersed, decentralized, adaptable, and fluid, with threat sources relatively difficult to identify, monitor, target, contain, and destroy. Further, these groups' past actions are not necessarily a sound guide to their future behavior.

Cyberdeterrence usually involves decision making with reservations and "high degrees of uncertainty about the source of the attack, and the motivations of the perpetrator."[79] Given the combination of unknown information about a cyberattack and technical unfamiliarity with the challenge, policymakers often feel immobilized. Equally problematic, "sometimes leaders may feel more confident of their attributions of villainy than the objective evidence might support."[80] Michael Chertoff, former head of the US Department of Homeland Security, notes a classic government security problem: "There are often times we know [who has attacked us], but we can't publicly prove it without revealing intelligence sources and methods; you have to decide whether to act on the basis of evidence you cannot reveal."[81]

These attribution difficulties generate key security problems. First, following cyberattacks, counterproductive finger-pointing often ensues. Sometimes the wrong initiator is accused, and sometimes the wrong motivation—such as obtaining information versus inflicting damage—is assumed.[82] Such misguided accusations can be incredibly dangerous. A sustained 1998 breach of the Pentagon's computer networks caused officials to be on the verge of launching a cyber counterstrike against China "when a little more investigation showed that the attacker was not the Peoples Liberation Army but bored teenagers in Cupertino, California."[83] In extreme cases, attribution errors can generate external hostility; thus, accurate attribution may be absolutely essential to convince neutral international observers that "retaliation is not aggression."[84] Second, even if a target does attribute the cyberattack correctly, the net long-term result could backfire, causing cyberattackers "to cover their tracks more carefully and continue attacking" in the future or to increase their investment in their disruptive planning.[85]

Impediments Posed by Cyberattack Plausible Deniability

Closely related to attribution difficulties, plausible deniability—that is, the ability to deny any involvement in cyber-disruptive activity when evidence is lacking—is quite common among cyberattackers, especially the Russians and the Chinese. This type of behavior is not new, as plausible deniability regarding a state's use of mercenaries was first mentioned explicitly in the seventeenth century.[86] Presenting proof of culpability to today's cyberoffenders often would reveal too much about target intelligence capabilities, and in any case offenders would claim it was fabricated. Punishment sanctions rely heavily on knowing the identity of cyberattackers, but "it is hard to find a smoking keyboard in cyberspace since the domain is made for plausible deniability."[87] It is highly advantageous and relatively easy for a state to employ "non-state proxy 'cyber patriots' or terrorist organizations to both conduct the attacks and claim responsibility for them as a way of creating plausible deniability for itself and presenting its adversary with no real targets against which to retaliate."[88] States often brazenly deny having done anything wrong regardless of evidence of complicity, which may involve sponsorship, tacit control, or simply tolerance of a cyberattack.[89] Precisely because attribution is so difficult in cyberspace, plausible deniability by states is often globally credible and not usually definitively challenged even after considerable investigation.

Special circumstances increase the frequency and effectiveness of today's use of plausible deniability. First, Arbor Networks cybersecurity expert Jose Nazario explains how the diffusion of cyberattack tools facilitates the availability of the plausible deniability option: "The cheap and easy availability of the tools and weapons—botnet armies, hacker groups, and the like—have caused governments around the world to eye this approach as a means of silencing enemies." He points out that these "tactics and tools ... make an excellent attack tool with plausible deniability for the attack director."[90] Second, plausible deniability possibilities increase in cyberspace if cyberattackers have liaisons with other third-party state or non-state parties that are supportive of cyberattacks. Indeed, "such arrangements further compound the attribution challenge (who is responsible) and provide for additional plausible deniability."[91] Because today aggressors can frequently benefit from cyberattacks while avoiding accountability through plausible deniability, it seems reasonable to anticipate that the use and sophistication of this technique will grow in the future.[92]

Medium-Term Problem-Solution Mismatches
Impediments Posed by Inappropriate Deterrence Models

As discussed earlier, because much cyberdeterrence policy still derives from Cold War nuclear deterrence, such approaches seem decidedly archaic and "have little relevance today."[93] Yet cybersecurity policymakers have often seemed reluctant to abandon outmoded and inappropriate deterrence models, reducing their openness to alternative, unorthodox options. In trying to prevent cyberattacks, "applying possibly anachronistic notions of deterrence to such a threat may lead decision makers away from the most creative approaches, and constructive responses, to these challenges."[94]

As a result of this common reliance on obsolete models, policymakers have not responded well, particularly to new cyberchallenges. Inadequacies seem especially on display when encountering in cyberspace "asymmetric vulnerability to attack, new classes of opponents with very different tolerance of risk, and the difficulty of crafting a proportional and credible threat" to deter future cyberattacks.[95] Signaling credible target cyberdefenses to adversaries in a manner that persists over time has been incredibly hard given that frequently "the demonstration of a cyber-capability quickly renders that capability useless" for deterrence purposes.[96] As a result, the quest for durable cyberdeterrence continues.

Impediments Posed by Endless Protection Needs

Cyber vulnerability is so deep and wide that it is hard to know where to begin, as the potential asset list requiring protection "seems endless—air traffic, financial sector, national elections, water, even electricity."[97] In addition, the list of possible state and non-state cyber aggressors wishing to penetrate these targets appears to be unlimited, while the means to do so keep spreading, the visible probabilities of costly apprehension and punishment remain low, and the perceived benefits of such penetration continue to be high and seem to be immediate and sizable. In cyberspace, the opportunity to exploit human vulnerability "appears endless."[98] For many cybersecurity analysts, even the specter of cyberterrorism "conjures up an endless list of doomsday scenarios."[99]

Logically, potential cyberattack targets would wish to prioritize the most vital assets, especially critical infrastructure, needing protection. However, doing such security prioritization in an appropriate manner—taking into account both asset importance and asset vulnerability—is extremely challenging due to the scarcity of both sophisticated theoretical models and reliable comprehensive empirical evidence to support such calculations. Moreover, predicting where cyberattacks are likely to occur has been exceedingly difficult given the involvement of multiple types of initiators with various goals and methods. Further, rapidly evolving cybertechnology has left policymakers "with little historical precedent to inform their expectations."[100] Thus, highly vulnerable societies often feel stymied in trying to find effective and legitimate ways to reduce their huge susceptibility to cyberattack.

Long-Term Unintended Pernicious Implications
Impediments Posed by Possible Boomerang Effects

Perhaps the greatest danger from engaging in offensive cyberdeterrence is becoming a target of the same kind of penetration. In the words of one analyst, there is "the genie-in-the-bottle syndrome to think about," as "once a cyber-attack has been unleashed, who's to say that in the interconnected world your carefully constructed virus won't spread to the networks of friendly or neutral nations?"[101] Cybersecurity expert Eugene Kaspersky asserts that "in cyberspace, everything you do—it's a boomerang—it will get back to you."[102] So the potential is high for unpredictable results, out-of-control tit-for-tat escalation spirals, and undesired threat contagion within cyberspace, all of which jeopardize prospects for long-term stability.

Cyberdeterrence backfire effects can foster a loss of credibility and an image of flailing futility. Citizens, especially in democracies, get angry when they see large, unproductive cybersecurity expenditures that appear to do little other than provoke further retaliation. Because successful cyberdeterrence efforts are largely unseen by the public, most people hear about only the cyberdeterrence failures and the growing frequency and severity of cyberattacks, leaving them frustrated due to their perceived escalating vulnerability. Besides this negative public reaction to cyberdeterrence boomerang effects, resentment may emerge from outsiders about both defensive cyberdeterrence failures and offensive cyberdeterrence successes because they may question the legitimacy of cyberintrusion into other states' affairs.

Impediments Posed by Dual-Use Technologies

Because cyberattack tools most commonly rely on dual-use technologies, law enforcement authorities find it difficult to regulate cyberweapons effectively.[103] Malware is much easier to conceal than kinetic weapons, and an agreement to limit cyberattacks "would likely conflict with the privacy rights of individuals and the intellectual property rights of both individuals and corporations."[104] From a software standpoint, computer code involved in cyberattacks can be mixed with legitimate code for surveillance or for system maintenance, complicating its identification and isolation. From a hardware standpoint, key components of computer systems and networks—such as routers and sensors—could serve either functional or dysfunctional purposes, depending on who controls them. The same technologies that benevolent governments use "legitimately and legally for national security and law enforcement" can be adopted by malevolent governments to "track opposition and facilitate human rights abuses."[105]

So banning cyberattack software or hardware could easily handicap legitimate or even essential uses of such technologies. Although US export controls attempt to prevent the purchase of "sensitive dual-use components and systems," cyberattackers often can easily sidestep such regulations by taking advantage of transshipment through more lax third-party countries.[106] If international

FIGURE 3.1.
Obstacles to Forward Progress

Roots of Cyberdeterrence Failure

POROUS DIGITAL INFRASTRUCTURE DESIGN
Purposely Open Architecture of the Internet
Insecure Database Design Reliant on Foreign Components

INITIATOR-TARGET CYBER EXPERTISE IMBALANCE
Tech-Savvy Non-state Groups Relatively Immune to Sanctions
Cyber Ignorance among Target State Leaders and Citizens

PROLIFERATING CYBERATTACK TOOLS
Rapid Development and Impact of Digital Innovation
Globalized Spread of Easy-to-Use Cyberattack Technologies

OVERLY STATIC, RIGID, PREDICTABLE, AND NARROW CYBERDETERRENCE
Static Predictable Defenses Always Penetrated by Cyberhackers
Avoidance of Creative Options Due to Outmoded Deterrence Notions

GROWING TARGET CYBERSPACE DEPENDENCE/ADDICTION
Integration of Cyberspace into Every Aspect of Modern Life
Greed, Power Hunger, and Frustration Abound in Cyberspace

Cyberdeterrence Improvement Roadblocks

ROADBLOCKS AT DIFFERING SOCIETAL LEVELS

State Government Level
POLITICAL REGIME CONSTRAINTS
Impediments Posed by Government Bureaucratic Inertia
Impediments Posed by Mutual Government-Business Friction

Mass Public Level
CITIZEN ATTITUDE DIFFICULTIES
Impediments Posed by Fatalistic Fears
Impediments Posed by Threatened Dominant Values

International System Level
INTRACTABLE GLOBAL TENSIONS
Impediments Posed by Global Agreement Troubles
Impediments Posed by Global Power Shifts

ROADBLOCKS WITH DIFFERING TIME FRAMES

Short Term
DEFECTIVE CYBERTHREAT DETECTION
Impediments Posed by Initiator Attribution Difficulties
Impediments Posed by Cyberattack Plausible Deniability

Medium Term
PROBLEM-SOLUTION MISMATCHES
Impediments Posed by Inappropriate Deterrence Models
Impediments Posed by Endless Protection Needs

Long Term
UNINTENDED PERNICIOUS IMPLICATIONS
Impediments Posed by Possible Boomerang Effects
Impediments Posed by Dual-Use Technologies

---

regulation is imposed and enforced, the net result could be increased black market acquisition of dual-use cyberweapons, with some countries "that encounter what they perceive as delays in acquiring desired technology, including dual-use systems, through legitimate avenues" instead turning "to illicit methods."[107] The public would be extremely upset if communication, privacy, or freedom of expression was restricted simply because some of the technologies facilitating these activities could potentially be manipulated by nefarious outsiders in ways that cybersecurity officials think could promote cyberattacks.

Overall Comments

Figure 3.1 comprehensively summarizes the obstacles to be overcome in order to restrain global cyberattacks, encompassing systemic roots of failed cyberdeterrence and cyberdeterrence improvement roadblocks. The systemic roots of failed cyberdeterrence include porous digital infrastructure design; initiator-target cyber expertise imbalance; proliferating cyberattack tools; overly static, rigid, predictable, and narrow cyberdeterrence; and growing target cyber dependence and cyber addiction. Although porous protection, expertise imbalance, proliferating attack tools, and rigid responses characterize many of today's global security challenges, policymakers have more experience in dealing with them in the real world than in cyberspace. The cyberdeterrence improvement roadblocks include those at different societal levels and with different time frames. While the plethora of seemingly insuperable impediments to achieve cybersecurity may appear at first glance vast enough to discourage any cyberdeterrence initiative, this book contends that with resolve and creativity each obstacle can be surmounted, circumvented, or bypassed.

Notes

1. Baker, Waterman, and Ivanov, *In the Crossfire*, 33.
2. Lan and Xin, "Can Cyber Deterrence Work?," in Nagorski, *Global Cyber Deterrence*, 1.
3. Valeriano and Maness, *Cyber War*, 1.
4. Molander and Siang, "Strategic Information Warfare."
5. Kuschner, "Legal and Practical Constraints."
6. Gray, *Making Strategic Sense*, 35.
7. Rid, "Cyberwar and Peace," 77–78.
8. Lord and Sharp, *America's Cyber Future*, 1:20–24.
9. "Russian Cyber Attacks," Channel 4 News.
10. Libicki, *Cyberdeterrence and Cyberwar*, xiii.
11. Lewis, *Securing Cyberspace*, 13.
12. Defense Science Board, *Resilient Military Systems*, 1.
13. Schneier, *Beyond Fear*, 101.
14. Geers, *Strategic Cyber Security*, 50.
15. Security and Defence Agenda, *Cyber-Security*, 13.
16. Hunt and Chesser, *Deterrence 2.0*, 18.
17. Thornburgh, "Invasion of the Chinese Cyberspies," 35.
18. Gray, *Making Strategic Sense*, vii.
19. "U.S. Official Warns," *Nando Times*; and Herzog, "Estonian Cyber Attacks," 54.
20. Raymond, "Paradoxes of (Cyber) Counterinsurgency."
21. Hunt and Chesser, *Deterrence 2.0*, 12; and Rattray, *Strategic Warfare in Cyberspace*, 141.
22. Clark, Berson, and Lin, *At the Nexus*, 17.
23. "Political Denial-of-Service Attacks," *Homeland Security News Wire*.
24. Schneier, *Beyond Fear*, 90.
25. Lindsay, "Impact of China," 44; and Office of the Under Secretary of Defense, "Report of the Defense Science Board."
26. Lord and Sharp, *America's Cyber Future*, 1:20–24; and Lynn, "Defending a New Domain," 100.
27. Security and Defence Agenda, *Cyber-Security*, 3.
28. Kello, "Meaning of the Cyber Revolution," 23; and Defense Science Board, *Resilient Military Systems*, 1.
29. Lewis, *Cyber Threat and Response*, 4.
30. Geers, *Strategic Cyber Security*, 100.
31. Lord and Sharp, *America's Cyber Future*, 1:20–24.
32. US Department of Defense, *DoD Cyber Strategy*, 1.
33. Lynn, "Defending a New Domain," 98.
34. Nye, *Cyber Power*, 1–2.
35. Arquilla and Ronfeldt, "Cyberwar Is Coming!," in Arquilla and Ronfeldt, *In Athena's Camp*, 23. See also "Fierce Cyber War Predicted," CNN.
36. Libicki, "Information War," 411–12.
37. Havely, "Why States Go to Cyber-War."

38. Russell, *Cyber Blockades*, 3.
39. US Department of Defense, *DoD Cyber Strategy*, 1.
40. Baker, Waterman, and Ivanov, *In the Crossfire*, 33.
41. Timberg and Rein, "Senate Cybersecurity Report."
42. Security and Defence Agenda, *Cyber-Security*, 32.
43. Lynn, "Defending a New Domain," 103.
44. Minority Staff, *Federal Government's Track Record*, 2.
45. Rid, "Cyberwar and Peace," 87. See also "Private Sector Responsible," *Homeland Security News Wire*.
46. Lewis, *Cyber Threat and Response*, 7.
47. Baker, Waterman, and Ivanov, *In the Crossfire*, 27, 38. Brackets in original.
48. Ibid., 38.
49. "Innovative U.S. Cybersecurity Initiative," *Homeland Security News Wire*; and Solomon, "Cyberdeterrence between Nation-States," 7.
50. Security and Defence Agenda, *Cyber-Security*, 35.
51. Libicki, Ablon, and Webb, *Defender's Dilemma*, xv.
52. Etzioni, "Cybersecurity in the Private Sector," 62.
53. Security and Defence Agenda, *Cyber-Security*, 33.
54. HelpNet Security, "73% of Organizations Hacked."
55. Kesan and Hayes, "Thinking through Active Defense in Cyberspace," 338.
56. Baker, Waterman, and Ivanov, *In the Crossfire*, 25.
57. Rosenzweig, "Achieving Cyber Deterrence," in National Research Council, *Proceedings*, 254.
58. "Russia May Launch,' *Homeland Security News Wire*.
59. Lewis, "Information Warfare."
60. Alperovitch, *Revealed: Operation Shady RAT*, 23.
61. Hunt and Chesser, *Deterrence 2.0*, 3.
62. Stein, "Information War—Cyberwar—Netwar," in Schneider and Grinter, *Battlefield of the Future*, 159.
63. Baker, Waterman, and Ivanov, *In the Crossfire*, 31.
64. Finnemore, "Cultivating International Cyber Norms," in Lord and Sharp, *America's Cyber Future*, 2:90.
65. Security and Defence Agenda, *Cyber-Security*, 3, 27; Nye, "Power and National Security," 19; and Waxman, "Cyber-Attacks," 425.
66. Williams, "Combating Transnational Organized Crime," in Pumpfrey, *Transnational Threats*, 191.
67. Andreas and Nadelmann, *Policing the Globe*, 245–46.
68. Nye, *Cyber Power*, 1.
69. Defense Security Service, *Targeting U.S. Technologies*, 5.
70. Lynn, "Defending a New Domain," 108.
71. Hunt and Chesser, *Deterrence 2.0*, 2.
72. Lewis, *Securing Cyberspace*, 13.
73. Laqueur, "Postmodern Terrorism," 35.
74. Geers et al., *World War C*, 5.
75. Libicki, *Cyberdeterrence and Cyberwar*, xvi.
76. Haley, "Theory of Cyber Deterrence"; and Lan and Xin, "Can Cyber Deterrence Work?," 1.

77. "U.S. Slow to Pinpoint," *Homeland Security News Wire*; and Nye, *Cyber Power*, 5.
78. Lachow, *Active Cyber Defense*, 2.
79. McDermott, "Decision Making," 227.
80. Ibid., 232.
81. Waterman, "Obama Hits Pause." Brackets in original.
82. Krepinevich, *Cyber Warfare*, 49.
83. Lewis, *Computer Espionage*, 1.
84. Libicki, *Cyberdeterrence and Cyberwar*, xvi.
85. Ibid., 49, 87.
86. Thomson, *Mercenaries, Pirates*, 21.
87. Cilluffo, Cardash, and Salmoiroghi, "Blueprint for Cyber Deterrence," 15.
88. Krepinevich, *Cyber Warfare*, 49–50.
89. Nazario, "Politically Motivated," 15.
90. Ibid., 12.
91. Cilluffo, Cardash, and Salmoiroghi, "Blueprint for Cyber Deterrence," 5.
92. Nazario, "Politically Motivated," 18.
93. Morgan, "Applicability of Traditional Deterrence," 75.
94. McDermott, "Decision Making," 229.
95. Lewis, "Cyber Deterrence." See also Wittes and Blum, *Future of Violence*, 66.
96. Weiner, "Searching for Cyber-Deterrence."
97. Geers, *Strategic Cyber Security*, 28.
98. Libicki, *Cyberdeterrence and Cyberwar*, 123.
99. Giacomello, "Bangs for the Buck," 387.
100. Lynn, "Defending a New Domain," 101.
101. Havely, "Why States Go to Cyber-War."
102. Vincent, "Russian Nuclear Power Plant."
103. US Department of Defense, *Cyberspace Policy Report*, 8.
104. Caldwell and Williams, *Seeking Security*, 173.
105. Negroponte, Palmisano, and Segal, *Defending an Open*, 63.
106. Defense Security Service, *Targeting U.S. Technologies*, 28.
107. Ibid., 60.

CHAPTER 4

Cyberattack Case Studies

The selected transnational cyberattacks in this chapter empirically highlight both cyberthreat dangers and cyberdeterrence challenges. In chronological order, the twelve considered cases are (1) Chinese cyberattacks on the United States (called Titan Rain) from 2003 to 2007, (2) Chinese cyberattacks on international organizations (called Operation Shady RAT) starting in mid-2006, (3) cyberattacks from pro-Russia hackers on Estonia in April and May 2007, (4) cyberattacks by pro-Russia criminal hackers on Georgia during the Russian invasion of Georgia in August 2008, (5) cyberattacks from a criminal organization (supported by Hamas and Hezbollah) on Israel during the Gaza Strip offensive in January 2009, (6) US and Israeli cyberattacks on Iranian computers (called Stuxnet) in July 2010, (7) cyberattacks by the hacktivist group Anonymous on the International Monetary Fund (IMF) in June 2011, (8) Iranian cyberattacks on the Saudi Arabian oil company Aramco in August 2012, (9) cyberattacks by the pro-Assad Syrian Electronic Army (SEA) on western Europe and the United States from April 2013 until the present, (10) cyberattacks by pro-Russia hackers on the Ukraine in March 2014, (11) North Korean cyberattacks on Sony Pictures Entertainment in November 2014, and (12) the Islamic State of Iraq and Syria (ISIS) cyberattacks on US Central Command (CENTCOM) in January 2015.

Each case is presented in parallel fashion. The analysis covers the description, attribution, and security impact of the cyberattacks; the response to the cyberattacks; and the lessons for improving cyberdeterrence. The overarching goal is to facilitate comparative cross-case analysis and discover overarching patterns that suggest what might succeed and what might fail in restraining future cyberattacks.

Because the cases focus on cyberattacks, their utility for deriving cyberdeterrence lessons is a bit indirect and nonlinear. What contributes to cyberattack success tends to increase cyberdeterrence failure. Because cyberdeterrence successes are often secret, without making cyberspace incidents public, the cases in this chapter highlight cyberdeterrence failures and study how critical systems failures produce critical lessons about needed vulnerability-reducing improvements.¹ In other words, limits on publicly available evidence prevent the usual comparison of circumstances surrounding cyberdeterrence failures and successes because the successes are usually classified. However, it is possible to glean more valuable insights about needed cyberdeterrence improvements from failures than from successes.

The case studies of twenty-first-century global cyberattacks with major security implications provide incisive ideas about what needs to be done to advance forward-thinking cyber protection. In each case determining the lessons for improving deterrence focuses on what might have converted failure to success if appropriate steps had been taken. Although by necessity the cases rest on fragmentary evidence, this analysis makes every effort to unearth multiple sources of information about key insights to increase the validity and reliability of findings and balanced and dispassionate conclusions about the nature and implications of what occurred.

Chinese Cyberattacks on the United States: Titan Rain

Cyberattacks' Description

Beginning in 2003 and lasting through 2007, a series of highly successful cyberespionage attacks penetrated the networks of the US Departments of Defense, State, Energy, and Homeland Security; those of the National Aeronautics and Space Administration, the Redstone Arsenal, and the US Army Information Systems Engineering Command; those of defense contractors such as Lockheed Martin and Sandia National Laboratories; and those of certain international organizations, including the World Bank. These cyberattacks were code-named Titan Rain for a Chinese scanner program that probes national defense and high-tech industrial computer networks, looking for vulnerabilities.² The cyberattackers downloaded terabytes of data. "Methodical and voracious, these hackers wanted all the files they could find, and they were getting them by penetrating secure computer networks at the country's most sensitive military bases, defense contractors and aerospace companies."³

During this period, far more attempts to scan Defense Department systems came from the People's Republic of China than from any other country, and hackers heavily used Chinese websites to target US computer networks, "successfully breaching hundreds of unclassified networks," according to several US government officials.⁴ American officials called a June 2007 Chinese military hacking attack into a Pentagon military computer network "the most successful cyber attack on the US Defense Department" up to that time.⁵

Cyberattacks' Attribution

Multiple investigators were able to trace the origin of the attacks to computers in Guangdong, China.[6] These cyberattacks were purportedly orchestrated by Chinese hackers whose aim was to steal as much technology as possible, especially politically sensitive military secrets. "Titan Rain's objective was to exfiltrate sensitive data" by penetrating target computer systems; copying everything on their hard drives; sending it to computers in South Korea, Hong Kong, and Taiwan; and later routing it "to computers in China's Guangdong province."[7] This multifaceted operation had been executed with pinpoint precision for years.

The direct involvement of the Chinese government in Titan Rain was suspected but remained unconfirmed, although a network security analyst at a major US defense contractor who studied Titan Rain since 2003 stated that "this has been going on so long and it's so well organized that the whole thing is state sponsored, I think."[8] SANS Institute research director Allan Paller contended that because the cyberattacks emerge from individuals "'with intense discipline, ... no other organization could do this if they were not a military organization.' The perpetrators 'were in and out with no keystroke errors and left no fingerprints, and created a backdoor in less than 30 minutes. How can this be done by anyone other than a military organization?'"[9] Moreover, a federal law enforcement official said that the US Federal Bureau of Investigation (FBI) was "aggressively" pursuing the possibility that the Chinese government was behind the attacks, even though American analysts were split on whether the breach represented a direct, concerted Chinese government initiative to penetrate US government networks and spy on sensitive data.[10] "Some in the Pentagon are said to be convinced of official Chinese involvement; others see the electronic probing as the work of other hackers simply using Chinese networks to disguise the origins of the attacks."[11] No conclusive evidence of Chinese government culpability ever emerged in this case.

Despite suspicions of the Chinese military establishment's involvement in the cyberattacks, after the breaches Beijing consistently denied responsibility. The Chinese government did not cooperate with US investigations of Titan Rain, and China's State Council Information Office, speaking for the government as a whole, argued that the charges about cyberspying and Titan Rain were "totally groundless, irresponsible and unworthy of refute."[12] Similarly, during a news briefing in May 2013, Chinese assistant foreign minister Zheng Zeguang adamantly insisted that "China opposes all forms of cyberattacks" and "is also a victim of hacking."[13] However, later on the Chinese government finally admitted to the world that it had offensive digital weapons teams "on both the military and civilian-government sides." In March 2015 discarding China's previous "fig leaf of quasi-plausible deniability," an influential publication from the top research institute of the Chinese People's Liberation Army finally formally acknowledged that "the country's military and its intelligence community have specialized units for waging war on computer networks."[14]

Cyberattacks' Security Impact

Even though it is possible that many Americans exaggerated "the threat from China" in cyberspace, a US government official anonymously interviewed about the security impact of Titan Rain said, "The scope of this thing is surprisingly big."[15] Several government analysts who protect military networks asserted that "Titan Rain is thought to rank among the most pervasive cyberespionage threats that U.S. computer networks have ever faced."[16] Indeed, the US-China Economic and Security Review Commission cited this Chinese cyberespionage as having been the "single greatest risk to the security of American technologies."[17]

The potential security damage from Titan Rain was huge, as suggested by early indications of "Titan Rain's ability to cause widespread havoc" in a November 2003 government report: "Hundreds of Defense Department [DOD] computer systems had been penetrated by an insidious program known as a 'trojan,'" which allowed "an unknown adversary not only control over the DOD hosts, but also the capability to use the DOD hosts in malicious activity" or to shut them down.[18] In addition to the United States, "the attacks were also stinging allies, including Britain, Canada, Australia and New Zealand, where an unprecedented string of public alerts issued in June 2005 ... also referred to Titan Rain-related activity."[19] In 2007 Whitehall officials in Great Britain reported that "Chinese hackers, some believed to be from the People's Liberation Army, have been attacking the computer networks of British government departments," including the Foreign Office.[20]

The success of the Titan Rain cyberattacks later spawned a series of cyberattacks on the United States emanating from China. Apparently, "Titan Rain was only the start. According to security experts, state-sponsored individuals in China were hacking into systems belonging to all the biggest factories and companies, seeking industrial data and intellectual property."[21] The focus of Chinese cyberintrusions appears to have changed over time. A 2011 report noted that "in the past, Chinese cyberattacks primarily targeted the U.S. government, but in the last decade, hackers have focused more and more on private businesses, especially defense contractors and businesses in energy, finance, and other critical sectors."[22] The Defense Science Board prepared a May 2013 study for the Pentagon that says, "Chinese government hackers have also been able to penetrate the computer networks of all the major U.S. defense contractors, stealing the designs and specifications of the most advanced weapon system in the U.S. arsenal, and gaining insights into broad technologies on which U.S. military advances are based."[23] In July 2013 China was reportedly behind 70 percent of the efforts to steal intellectual property and trade secrets from the United States.[24]

Two well-known troublesome illustrations of the successor cyberattacks on the United States that emanated from China are Aurora and Night Dragon. Occurring in 2009 (disclosed in January 2010) and probably initiated by a highly sophisticated Chinese hacking group called Hidden Lynx, the Aurora cyberespionage attacks targeted Google and two dozen other information technology companies—including Adobe, Juniper, and Cisco—in an effort to access and change these companies' source code.[25] The Night Dragon cyberattacks occurred in November 2009 and harvested sensitive intellectual property from global oil, gas, and petrochemical companies using progressive intrusions into targeted infrastructure.[26]

Chinese cyberattacks on the United States persisted over time. In April 2009 China allegedly was behind cyberspies' breaking into the Pentagon's $300 billion Joint Strike Fighter project, which at the time was the Defense Department's most expensive weapons program.[27] In November 2011 the security company Symantec accused Chinese hackers of having targeted in 2010 fifty chemical and military companies, including multiple Fortune 500 firms.[28] On February 19, 2013, cybersecurity firm Mandiant showed a link between "the most sophisticated Chinese hacker groups, groups [near Shanghai] conducting the most threatening attacks on the United States," and "the headquarters of China's military intelligence lead unit."[29] Later that same month, the Department of Homeland Security reported that China hacked into twenty-three gas pipeline companies, possibly for sabotage purposes.[30] In March 2013 US president Barack Obama publicly acknowledged that "some, but not all, hacking originating from China was state sponsored."[31] In May of that year, a Pentagon report to Congress claimed that "numerous computer systems around the world, including those owned by the U.S. government, continued to be targeted for intrusions, some of which appear to be attributable directly to the Chinese government and military."[32] On June 4, 2013, Kaspersky Lab revealed details on NetTraveler—a data exfiltration tool infecting the data systems of more than three hundred fifty high-profile diplomats, military contractors, and government agencies in forty countries, including the United States—with direct ties to China and "loosely connected with Titan Rain."[33] In February 2014 the security company McAfee claimed that Chinese hackers had stolen data from oil companies in the United States, Greece, Taiwan, and Kazakhstan about oil field bidding, financing, and operations.[34]

Response to the Cyberattacks

The Titan Rain computer attacks gave "added impetus to Pentagon moves to adopt new detection software programs and improve training of computer security specialists.... 'It's a constant game of staying one step ahead.'"[35] This concern about cybersecurity was particularly acute for the Pentagon because with "more computers than any other agency—about five million worldwide—it is the most exposed to foreign as well as domestic hackers." Over the past several years, in response to the Chinese cyberthreat, "the Defense Department has taken steps to better organize what had been a rather disjointed approach to cyber security by individual branches of the armed forces."[36] Sandra Bell, head of the Royal United Services Institute's Homeland Security and Resilience Department, said that the attacks from China on the Pentagon's computer system were "very much a wake-up call."[37]

The Titan Rain cyberattacks specifically heightened the Americans' vigilance and concern about the increasing scope and impact of Chinese military activities and their extension of military power overseas. US defense secretary Donald Rumsfeld warned in June 2005 that China's military spending threatened the security balance in Asia, and the July 2005 Pentagon annual report on Chinese military power said that the People's Liberation Army saw computer network operations as "critical" in seizing "the initiative" and establishing "electromagnetic dominance" early in a conflict to increase effectiveness in battle.[38] Richard Clarke, a former terrorism adviser to presidents Bill Clinton and George W. Bush, cautioned that "Beijing is successfully stealing research and development, software source code, manufacturing know-how and government plans. In a global competition among knowledge-based economies, Chinese cyberoperations are eroding America's advantage.... The attacks ... are aimed at providing China with a strategic parity with the United States."[39] On May 19, 2014, the US Justice Department indicted five Chinese military officers on the charge of industrial espionage, involving stealing data from six US companies, and in the process for the first time for another national government, it formally accused China of such cyberspace treachery and of "inaugurating a major escalation of tensions with China over economic spycraft."⁴⁰ There is disagreement about the impact of these indictments. In late 2015 an American official observed that "for a period of time following the indictments, there was a very significant decrease" in cyberattacks by the People's Liberation Army, but in early 2016 the director of the National Counterintelligence and Security Center concluded that "there is no evidence China has curtailed its economic espionage."⁴¹

One key constraint on a strong US response to Chinese cyberattacks has been the economic interdependence between the two countries. Given sensitivities in American-Chinese relations, at the time of Titan Rain and for many years afterward, "the U.S. government, for its part, has been fecklessly circumspect in calling out the Chinese.... Like so many Rip Van Winkles, most of Washington has been asleep while [Chinese] cyber-attacks proliferated."⁴² In late 2013 the US-China Economic and Security Review Commission admitted that the ongoing public shaming of China "only served to quell the attacks for a short amount of time." Indeed, the unit of the People's Liberation Army responsible for these attacks "chilled out for about a month after the bad press," after which it "ramped its attacks back up to previous levels."⁴³ Stopping the attacks "without soiling Sino-American relations" proved difficult.⁴⁴ In the end, both China and the United States "still have incentives to moderate the intensity of their exploitation in order to preserve the benefits that make exploitation worthwhile in the first place," leading to "a relentlessly irritating but indefinitely tolerable stability in the cyber domain" where "one can expect the risk of unwanted escalation from cyber to other military domains to deter both sides from resorting to more destructive forms of computer network attack in most situations."⁴⁵

Lessons for Improving Cyberdeterrence

A key lesson from the Titan Rain cyberattacks is the need for clearer network administrator communication with policymaking superiors about cyberintrusions. Indeed, "if the Titan Rain attacks taught the information security community anything, it is that IT [information technology] administrators need to know how to articulate the dangers of cyberspace to upper management."⁴⁶ Regarding the existence of a cyberattack, in 2005 SANS Institute research director Paller contended that "the American strategy in the last couple of years has been to keep it secret.... That may make people feel good but it doesn't help you defend things. [Secrecy] benefits the attackers, not the victims."⁴⁷ Although such open communication, including security-reducing leaks and embarrassing admissions of failure, can be risky, it generally seems worthwhile.

A second cyberdeterrence lesson from the Titan Rain cyberattacks is that with clever state or non-state cyberespionage, definitive attribution may be impossible. In particular, "the last thing that an intelligence service that had successfully penetrated an opponent's networks would want is to be noticed. . . . If someone stumbles across the effort, you will want to have covered your tracks well enough that blame cannot be ascribed."[48] In many such cases, having the primary thrust of one's cyberdeterrence policy be heavily focused on the commitment of tons of time, money, and resources to identify cyberattackers definitively may prove to be misguided.

A third and final lesson is that given these attribution difficulties in cases such as Titan Rain and the focus on covert cyberespionage, cyberdeterrence may be better served putting a greater emphasis on defensive protection rather than on offensive retaliation. In preventing computer espionage, "the U.S. should worry less about who is attacking—assume everyone is attacking—and pay more attention to basic [defensive] security measures—authenticating users, encrypting data, regular patching, and monitoring systems for intrusions."[49] This protection-oriented approach can deal with a much wider range of cyberespionage threats than can responses focused on particular threats emanating from particular initiators.

Chinese Cyberattacks on Organizations: Shady RAT

Cyberattacks' Description

As a five-year series of cyberattacks that started in mid-2006, Operation Shady RAT hit at least seventy-two organizations worldwide, encompassing twenty government agencies, seven international organizations, twenty-six private commercial companies, thirteen defense contractors, two think tanks, and two nonprofit organizations.[50] The specific targets included the International Olympic Committee (affecting the 2008 Summer Olympics), the United Nations, the Association of Southeast Asian Nations, and the World Anti-Doping Agency. Although the majority of targets—forty-nine—were located in the United States, isolated cyberattacks also hit targets in Canada, South Korea, Taiwan, Japan, Switzerland, the United Kingdom, Indonesia, Vietnam, Denmark, Singapore, Hong Kong, Germany, and India.[51] The operation's name was derived from the common security industry acronym for the term "remote access tool," RAT. Released in 2011, the formal report from cybersecurity firm McAfee that revealed Operation Shady RAT named only seventy-two affected companies, but Dmitri Alperovitch, at the time McAfee's vice president of threat research, said that "it is fair to assume that the number of victim organizations goes well into the thousands."[52]

Cyberattacks' Attribution

Most analysts believed that the People's Republic of China was directly behind these cyberattacks. Circumstantial evidence certainly supports this conclusion: "The operation targeted a broad range of public- and private-sector organizations in almost every country in Southeast Asia—but none in China; and most of Shady RAT's targets are known to be of interest to the People's Republic."[53] James Lewis, a leading cybersecurity expert and director and senior fellow of the Strategic Technologies Program at the Center for Strategic and International Studies, concluded that "all the signs point to China."[54] Indeed, "the interest in the information held at the Asian and Western national Olympic Committees, as well as the International Olympic Committee (IOC) and the World Anti-Doping Agency in the lead-up and immediate follow-up to the 2008 Olympics was particularly intriguing and potentially pointed a finger at a state actor behind the intrusions, because there is likely no commercial benefit to be earned from such hacks." Moreover, "hacking the United Nations or the Association of Southeast Asian Nations (ASEAN) Secretariat is also not likely a motivation of a group interested only in economic gains."[55]

Bruce Sterling, a cybersecurity expert writing in *Wired* magazine, provided compelling logic for China's being the initiator of the Operation Shady RAT cyberattacks:

> I see little reason to doubt that it's really happening. Because it makes sense. If you've got enough manpower, it's pretty simple to do. The Chinese have means, motive and opportunity to do it. Nobody's going to punish them for doing it. Everybody knows they've been at it for years. I've been posting it on this blog for years. Why would they not just keep doing it? The upside is huge and the downside is minimal.
>
> They've got enough of a centrally-directed state apparatus left that they can derive some real benefit from cyberespionage. Others don't. . . .
>
> Cyberespionage is an aspect of Chinese soft power. It's part of an advantage their covert, disciplined and centralized system possesses, which the globalized, flat-world system of the Washington Consensus simply lacks. It's just a unique Chinese strategic advantage.[56]

Thus, compared to other countries, China appeared to be uniquely suited to undertake this kind of successful foreign cyberespionage.

However, there was not complete consensus on the attribution of Operation Shady RAT. For example, Amichai Shulman, chief technical officer and cofounder of the cybersecurity company Imperva, said that "rather than a government being to blame ... this appears to be a targeted criminal hacking, a growing scourge where botnet farmers infect computers with automated spear phishing campaigns."[57] Nonetheless, most "other experts agree with McAfee's speculation that the attack originated from a nation-state."[58]

Cyberattacks' Security Impact

The scope of the security impact of Operation Shady RAT was apparently huge. McAfee vice president Alperovitch concluded, "After painstaking analysis of the logs, even we were surprised by the enormous diversity of the victim organizations and were taken aback by the audacity of the perpetrators.... Virtually everyone is falling prey to these intrusions, regardless of whether they are the United Nations, a multinational Fortune 100 company, a small, non-profit think tank, a national Olympic team, or even an unfortunate computer security firm."[59] Operation Shady RAT involved the most dangerous kind of advanced persistent threat, which when compared to other types of cyberattacks, "are much more insidious and occur largely without public disclosures. They present a far greater threat to companies and governments, as the adversary is tenaciously persistent in achieving their objectives."[60]

However, some controversy surrounds the security impact of Operation Shady RAT. Cybersecurity analysts from McAfee's two primary rival cybersecurity companies—Eugene Kaspersky, the head of Kaspersky Lab, and Hon Lau, a cybersecurity researcher with Symantec—sharply disagreed with McAfee's analysis, calling it "alarmist" and claiming that the cyberattacks involved in Operation Shady RAT were not nearly as sophisticated or dangerous as McAfee contended. Kaspersky asserted that "we conducted detailed analysis of the Shady RAT botnet and its related malware, and can conclude that the reality of the matter (especially the technical specifics) differs greatly from the conclusions made by Mr. Alperovitch." Instead, it exhibited "very low proliferation—as confirmed by our cloud-based cyberthreat monitoring system and by other security vendors. It has never been on the list of the most widespread threats."[61]

In contrast, other cybersecurity experts agreed with McAfee's dire conclusions and believed that the cyberthreat involved was extremely severe and demanded action. Gretchen Hellman, vice president of product management at cybersecurity firm Vormetric, stated that "Operation Shady RAT is a clear example of how prevalent sophisticated, targeted cyberespionage is" and how what is needed is "a sense of urgency and recognition that advanced persistent threats are a reality."[62] Anup Ghosh, chief executive officer and founder of the cybersecurity firm Invincea, concurred and stated, "We do believe that what we are witnessing is wholesale theft of the nation's IP [Internet Protocol] that will affect our competitiveness on a global scale in future years to come."[63]

Response to the Cyberattacks

The responses by the victims of Operation Shady RAT were not impressive. Although "the shortest time that an organization remained compromised was less than a single month," this duration brevity was not "an indication of the rapid reaction of information security teams in those organizations, but perhaps merely evidence that the actor was interested only in a quick smash and grab operation that did not require a persistent compromise of the victim."[64] Ghosh argued that "these attacks illustrate that the security industry as a whole has failed in its mission to protect corporate, government and citizens against these attacks. . . . It is time to stop blaming users for clicking on links and attachments, time to stop blaming the companies and agencies who are victim to these attacks, and time to start innovating in security again so we fight 21st century attacks with 21st century technologies."[65]

In direct response to McAfee's revelation of Operation Shady RAT, calls for action from government officials were impressive. Department of Homeland Security secretary Janet Napolitano stated that "we obviously will evaluate it and look at it and pursue what needs to be pursued."[66] White House spokesman Jay Carney said, "We're aware of the report. Detecting and blocking cyberintrusion is a key cybersecurity goal for this administration." Moreover, Col. Rivers Johnson, the spokesman for US Cyber Command at Fort Meade, said, "the agency was doing best possible to protect the country from cyberattacks."[67] Operation Shady RAT attracted considerable high-level attention from the US government, with Dmitri Alperovitch providing "confidential briefings on Shady RAT to senior White House officials, executive-branch agencies, and congressional-committee staff."[68] Senator Dianne Feinstein (D-CA), chair of the Senate Select Committee on Intelligence, concluded after reviewing the McAfee report on Shady RAT that "this is further evidence that we need a strong cyber-defense system in this country, and that we need to start applying pressure to other countries to make sure they do more to stop cyber hacking emanating from their borders."[69] Furthermore, after a short time following the cyberattacks, most targets removed the malware, and US law enforcement agencies were "on the case to shut down the operation."[70]

Nonetheless, there is no public evidence that these cyberattacks by themselves stimulated necessary dramatic changes in national responses to emerging cyberthreats. Indeed, outside of the United States, many victims of Shady RAT either denied that they had been attacked or ignored McAfee's offer to provide more details of how networks had been compromised and to help victims to prevent future infiltrations.[71] Alperovitch said, "We've seen this before. . . . Victims don't want to know they're victims. I guess that's just victim psychology: if you don't know about it, it's not really happening."[72] However, Hellman of Vormetric argued that because "unstructured data stores in the United States hold trillions of dollars' worth of intellectual property—which Operation Shady RAT has demonstrated is a valuable target . . . [i]nformation defense for valuable unregulated data—such as IP—requires full defense in depth applied directly to data, including intelligent encryption, strong access control and solid system security as preventative measures, and real-time activity monitoring."[73]

Lessons for Improving Cyberdeterrence

A key lesson from Operation Shady RAT is the universal vulnerability to cyberattacks, thus highlighting the worldwide need to be concerned about cyber protection. Alperovitch said, "I am convinced that every company in every conceivable industry with significant size and valuable intellectual property and trade secrets has been compromised (or will be shortly), with the great majority of the victims rarely discovering the intrusion or its impact. . . . This is a problem of massive scale that affects nearly every industry and sector of the economies of numerous countries, and the only organizations that are exempt from this threat are those that don't have anything valuable or interesting worth stealing."[74] Deluding oneself into thinking one's data is safe—whether within a public or private organization—is simply asking for trouble.

A second lesson from Operation Shady RAT is that the sharp disagreement among experts—notably those at McAfee, Kaspersky Lab, and Symantec —on the significance of the cyberattack points to the need to develop more uniform yardsticks to measure the security impact of cyberattacks and, by extension, the success or failure of cyberdeterrence and the need to seek opinions from multiple sources before drawing policy conclusions about cyberthreat significance. Even if unambiguous evidence about a cyberattack and its immediate consequences is discovered—a highly unusual circumstance—it appears the only way consensus about cybersecurity priorities would likely emerge is if greater global standardization existed about how to gauge the repercussions of major breaches systematically. At the very least, it would seem important that vulnerable targets should develop internally coherent, consistent, and accepted measures for assessing the outcome significance of perturbations in cyberspace.

A final lesson from Operation Shady RAT is that even major cybersecurity breaches may be deemed insufficient by target decision makers to trigger a major overhaul in existing cyberdefenses. Even though former US deputy secretary of defense William Lynn revealed in March 2011 that "the Pentagon had recently suffered its largest ever cyberbreach, with 24,000 data files stolen from the network," and despite the stunning revelations contained in the McAfee report on Operation Shady RAT shortly afterward, the US government's response to the report in terms of actual cybersecurity transformation was decidedly underwhelming.[75] On every level, there apparently are widespread disincentives for security officials to recognize and report cyberattacks, let alone to taking the necessary steps to prevent their occurrence in the first place.

Russian Cyberattacks on Estonia

Cyberattacks' Description

The backdrop to the cyberattacks on Estonia was a long history of ethnic tension between Estonia and Russia, dating back to the Soviet annexation of the Baltic states in 1940 and the ensuing relocation of hundreds of thousands of ethnic Russians to Estonia. When the Cold War ended, the Estonian government quickly took steps to minimize Russian influence on Estonian culture.

> Whereas the newly formed governments of Latvia and Lithuania—Estonia's two Baltic state neighbors—extended universal citizenship to all people living within their borders (making great strides to integrate these disparate ethnic groups into one cohesive populace), Estonia refused to do so. Instead, the Estonian government insisted that all non-ethnic Estonians be treated as foreigners, thus forcing any ethnic Russian desiring Estonian citizenship to undergo naturalization. Instead of bringing people of all different ethnicities together under the Estonian banner, this policy served as a barrier to further

solidify the division between ethnic Estonians and Russians living within Estonian borders.[76]

Estonia's Russian population felt simmering resentment about these steps.

In early 2007 as Russia became more combative toward the European Union over gas supplies, a six-foot-tall statue called the *Bronze Soldier*—erected in 1947 in the capital city to commemorate the Soviet Red Army's liberation of Estonia from the Nazis—became a trigger for angry, violent anti-Estonia activists.[77] At dawn on April 27, 2007, the Estonian government moved the statue from Tõnismägi Park in central Tallinn to the more secluded Tallinn Military Cemetery, thus escalating the ongoing friction between the ethnic Estonian majority and the Russian minority (constituting about 26 percent of the population in 2007).[78]

The Russian community perceived the action as highly inflammatory and as representing "further marginalization of their ethnic identity."[79] Indeed, "to the ethnic Russian minority, this statue was a symbol of their legitimacy and rights in Estonia. But for some Estonians, it represented a brutal Soviet takeover of their country, and in 2006 these citizens [had] petitioned the Tallinn City Council to demolish the monument."[80] In response to the Estonians' moving the statue, Russian president Vladimir Putin stated, "I find that this is an absolutely short-sighted policy, extremist-nationalist, which does not take into consideration the history connected with the fight against Nazism or today's reality." Russian foreign minister Sergei Lavrov agreed, saying Estonia had a "blasphemous attitude towards the memory of those who struggled against fascism."[81]

Moving the statue triggered deadly rioting, largely by ethnic Russians. Estonian government authorities responded to rioters—who looted shops, burned cars, and threw Molotov cocktails—by deploying tear gas and water cannons; and in Moscow Russian activists blockaded the Estonian Embassy for days.[82] Overall, thirteen hundred people were arrested, a hundred people were injured, and one person was killed.[83] The cyberattacks on Estonia began at 10:00 p.m. on April 26, 2007, but they "remained relatively unnoticed for the first twenty-four hours" until the Estonian minister of defense discovered that he was unable to log on to the prime minister's website.[84] From April 27 to May 18, distributed denial-of-service (DDoS) cyberattacks targeting the country's infrastructure paralyzed the country by knocking completely offline the websites of all government ministries, major banks, news publications, university centers, and key political parties, thus preventing email communication and business or political transactions.

This cyberattack overwhelmed Estonia. It was implemented "through the use of globally dispersed and virtually unattributable botnets of 'zombie' computers ... in places like Egypt, Russia, and the United States ... in a 'swarming' DDoS strategy. Government and bank websites that normally received 1,000 visits a day crashed after receiving upwards of 2,000 hits a second."[85] On May 9, the heaviest day of the cyberattacks and perhaps not so coincidentally when Russia and its allies commemorated Hitler's defeat in Europe, on average over 4 million incoming packets of information per second targeted hundreds of Estonian websites.[86] Incredibly, "it is estimated that a million computers were hijacked and mobilized globally for this distributed denial of service onslaught on the servers of a country of 1.3 million inhabitants."[87] After the statue was moved, many on Russian websites excitedly advocated "a strategy for destroying the e-systems that have become a vaunted success as the arteries of government and business in Estonia."[88]

This coordinated effort was thwarted only when a team of cyber experts attempted to "screen the waves of incoming traffic in order to pinpoint the attacking rogue computers." When they identified an attacking computer's address, the experts "asked network operators throughout the world to block its IP (Internet Protocol)—the data link to the internet—at the source."[89]

Cyberattacks' Attribution

As the cyberattacks subsided, the Estonian government and the North Atlantic Treaty Organization (NATO) began to investigate the origins of the cyber disruption. The Estonian government immediately accused the Russian government because "the Russian government had publicly denounced Estonia's decision to remove the Bronze Soldier memorial," had called "for the Estonian government's resignation," and was said to have "helped to instigate the street riots that took place in Tallinn upon the monument's removal." Moreover, "the Estonian government successfully traced one of the attacks back to an IP address owned by a member of the Russian government."[90] Senior Estonian officials privately contended that "several of the attacking computers were traced directly to the Kremlin."[91]

In 2009 the pro-Kremlin youth group Nashi—which is "nominally independent" from the Russian government but "does the Kremlin's bidding" and is funded by "pro-business owners looking to ingratiate themselves with the regime"—said that it was responsible for the cyberattacks.[92] The claim has not been verified, but "many Estonian experts believe it's credible."[93] The hacktivists appeared to be "a combination of experienced hackers who would contract out their own botnets or write their own malicious programs, and 'script kids' who were, by and large, individual novice hackers who attacked Estonian target sites by following 'how-to' guides found on various hacker websites."[94] Although Estonia never completely isolated and tracked down most of the principal culprits given their "disparate nature," the government did indict one of the attackers, an ethnic Russian student residing in Estonia named Dmitri Galushkevich, in January 2008.[95]

While European Union and NATO experts could not uncover direct evidence of Russian involvement, "it certainly would have been in Moscow's interests to organize DDoS strikes," and Russian officials egged on the hackers "by accusing Tallinn of altering history, perpetrating human rights violations, and encouraging fascism." Although "Russia categorically denied any involvement in the attacks, one unnamed NATO official did not mince words: 'I won't point fingers. But these were not things done by a few individuals. This clearly bore the hallmarks of something concerted.'"[96]

Cyberattacks' Security Impact

The security disruption wrought by these cyberattacks was significant because of the exceptionally high digital dependence in Estonia, which is often called the "most wired country in Europe."[97] "Estonia relies on the Internet for its critical infrastructure; electronic networks are integral to the functioning of government operations, electric power grids, banking services, and even Tallinn's water supply. In Estonia, 97 percent of bank transactions occur online; and in 2007, 60 percent of the country's population used the Internet on a daily basis."[98] Estonia's culture made its citizens "willing to sacrifice some privacy in exchange for [the] efficiency, convenience, and modernity" that cyberspace transactions provide.[99] Estonia's "e-Government" system, which depends on the Internet to make government goods and services available to citizens and businesses, created maximum vulnerability.[100] According to former White House cybersecurity adviser Howard Schmidt, "Estonia has built their future on having a high-tech government and economy, and they've basically been brought to their knees because of these attacks."[101]

The cyberattacks on Estonia directly affected not only state security but also human security, for the attacks "targeted the entire civil and economic infrastructure with the aim of paralyzing the society."[102] Overall, "the scope, sophistication, and duration of these attacks were unprecedented."[103] Besides the fact that "never before had an entire country been targeted on almost every digital front all at once," Estonian defense minister Jaak Aaviksoo noted that "this was the first time that a botnet threatened the national security of an entire nation."[104] It "took an emergency mobilization of all Estonia's special computer-wise expertise and resources—as well as international assistance—to thwart the e-assault and defend the core of the country's extensive electronic infrastructure."[105]

Response to Cyberattacks

In the short run, the Estonian government vainly sought to manage the crisis through isolating the country. It cordoned off its networks from international servers and effectively blocked all international Web traffic. However, as expected with a wired country in an interdependent world, this action "created additional connectivity problems. For example, although Estonians could access their e-mail and online services within Estonia, those travelling abroad could not access e-mail or banking services."[106]

In the medium run, Estonia—a NATO member since 2004—ultimately managed to recover from the cyberattack. This recovery heavily depended on an extensive and rapid international response through the Estonian government's Computer Emergency Response Team (CERT), which sought help from Finnish, German, Israeli, and Slovenian sources to restore network functioning; aid from NATO CERTs; technical assessments of developments from the European Union's European Network and Information Security Agency; and considerable intelligence sharing among Western countries.[107] Estonia could not have emerged from this crisis without outside aid.

In the long run, in April 2008 NATO adopted a unified Policy on Cyber Defence and created the Cyber Defence Management Authority to "centralise cyber defence operational capabilities across the Alliance."[108] Approved in May 2008 and opened in August 2008, the Estonia-based Cooperative Cyber Defence Centre of Excellence became NATO's cybersecurity headquarters and has served since then as an international research consortium designed "to increase international awareness and understanding of information security best practices" and "to promote international cooperation to solve cyber security problems."[109]

Estonia itself took two giant cyberdefense steps, aided by government consensus about the high priority of addressing the foreign cyberthreat. First, in May 2008 a multiagency council led by the Ministry of Defense released the Cyber Security Strategy, spearheading the development and implementation of improved security measures, competence in information security, a legal framework for cybersecurity, international cooperation, and cybersecurity awareness. Then in 2010 the Estonian government created the Cyber Defense League, composed of small, locally operated units of public and private sector citizens who are information technology specialists—including computer scientists, programmers, and software engineers—and would volunteer to assist the Estonian military under a unified military command during a time of cyber crisis.[110] The Cyber Security Strategy was so well formulated that several European countries—notably Germany, the Netherlands, France, and the United Kingdom—later released similar national cyberpolicies, and "there have not been any significant computer network breaches reported in Estonia since the 2007 Attacks."[111] In March 2015 Estonian officials placed "renewed focus on an innovative plan to protect the country's vast digital identity, through the creation of what they call 'data embassies'"—that is, "online storage and remote servers that would be afforded the same protections as traditional embassies."[112]

Lessons for Improving Cyberdeterrence

One lesson from the cyberattacks on Estonia is the need for advanced international coordination and cooperation for smaller, weaker cybertargets. Indeed, "at the moment when 400 times more data are flooding your servers from all the countries in the world, the mitigation can be carried out only with the help of international contacts and networks."[113] Because this collaboration occurred only after the cyberattacks, however, it did not play a key cyberdeterrence role.

A second key lesson from the cyberattacks on Estonia is the extremely high security priority of cyberdeterrence for targets with exceptionally high cyber dependence. Relying totally on cyberspace for basic functioning requires that advanced, sophisticated cyberdefenses (and compelling means promoting adversary restraint) be in place. Although prior to the 2007 cyberattack "the Estonian government heavily financed research and development (R&D) for telecommunications and other Internet-based services and innovations, it did little to explore defensive protocols against any potential cyberattacks that might occur."[114] Despite prior Estonian government research on cybersecurity as it prepared for online national elections in 2005 (which was a global first) and sought to protect against fraud or intrusion in voting, this advanced preparation was insufficient to prevent the 2007 cyberattacks.[115] With the benefit of hindsight, the only cyber resiliency steps Estonia had available before the DDoS cyberattacks appeared to be expanding Internet bandwidth—but doing so proved meager and grossly inadequate to cope with the traffic increase—and severing the international Internet connection. The Estonians cut off the international traffic but at significant costs, including impeding their ability to tell the rest of the world what was transpiring in their country.[116]

A third lesson from this case concerns the incredible dangers surrounding unconventional cyber tactics targeting the civilian population's economic infrastructure instead of exclusively focusing on government political-military targets. If cyberattacks paralyze an entire country, then public panic is likely to be higher, recovery is likely to be more difficult, management is likely to require more internal coordination, and outside assistance is likely to be more essential than it otherwise would be.

Russian Cyberattacks on Georgia

Cyberattacks' Description

Long-standing tensions going back to the early 1990s have existed in Georgia, with two areas—Abkhazia and South Ossetia—being highly partial to Russian rule. Indeed, most residents of Abkhazia and South Ossetia have been granted Russian citizenship and passports, and they seem to want their states to be part of Russia.[117] When Mikheil Saakashvili was elected president of Georgia in 2004, he pledged to institute democratic reforms and to regain control over the separatist regions. In September and October 2006, Georgia expelled six Russian intelligence agents accused of espionage, and Russia responded with a full economic embargo of Georgia, including severing all transportation and communications links. In July 2008 the Georgians and the South Ossetians exchanged artillery fire, and Russia launched a large-scale military exercise near the Georgian border.[118]

In early August 2008 these tensions escalated between Russia-leaning South Ossetia and more democratically oriented Georgia, with each accusing the other of launching hostile artillery barrages, and "on August 8, as world leaders gathered in Beijing to watch the opening ceremony of the Olympic Games, Russian tanks rolled across the border into Georgia."[119] Georgia claimed that South Ossetian forces responded to a cease-fire appeal by intensifying their shelling, "forcing" Georgia to send in troops, while Russia claimed that its forces entered the area simply as a "peacekeeping" operation. On August 8 Russia launched massive air attacks throughout Georgia, and Russian troops engaged Georgian forces in South Ossetia. Russian warships landed troops in Georgia's Abkhazia region and took up positions off Georgia's Black Sea coast. On August 26 Russia officially recognized the two breakaway regions of Abkhazia and South Ossetia. As a result of the Russian-Georgian conflict, nearly 1,000 people died, and in October 2008 the World Bank reported that the fighting in Georgia, South Ossetia, and Abkhazia had displaced about 127,000 persons.[120]

Russian cyberattacks on Georgian websites and network infrastructure began in the summer of 2008. From July 19 to July 20, 2008, the website of the president of Georgia had come under a persistent distributed denial-of-service attack.[121] By late August 7, just prior to the Russian invasion of Georgia, cyberattacks commenced on many Georgian government websites. It appeared "to be the first case in history of a coordinated cyberspace domain attack synchronized with major combat actions in the other warfighting domains (consisting of Land, Air, Sea, and Space)."[122] Immediately after the Russians invaded Georgia on August 8, "substantial" DDoS attacks, linked to multiple botnets, "began to flood into Georgia."[123]

The methods and goals of the cyberattacks against Georgia were similar to those used against Estonia in 2007 as they defaced public Georgian websites (including juxtaposing pictures of Georgian president Saakashvili with those of Nazi leader Adolf Hitler) and led DDoS attacks against numerous political/governmental and financial websites (including the National Bank and the Ministry of Foreign Affairs). In addition to disrupting Georgian communications and altering Georgian websites, the Georgia cyberattacks were "part of information exfiltration activities that tried to steal and accumulate military and political intelligence from Georgian networks."[124] Notably, "the network employed to launch DDoS [attacks] against Georgian websites and servers was itself constituted across over sixty countries, including states allied to Georgia, such as Germany and the United States."[125] To attain their ends, hackers "began collaborating over well-known social media portals like Twitter and Facebook."[126]

Cyberattacks' Attribution

There seems to be "a rather widespread consensus" that the attacks were coordinated from the beginning, as "several Russian blogs, forums, and websites spread a Microsoft Windows batch script that was designed to attack Georgian websites."[127] The Georgian government "blamed Russia for the attacks, but the Russian government said it was not involved."[128] In all likelihood, "the bad guys weren't working for the Russian government or military but it is safe to say that there had to be some complicity here."[129] Georgian National Security Council chief Eka Tkeshelashvili said, "It is, quite simply, implausible that the parallel attacks by land and by cyberspace were a coincidence—official denials by Moscow notwithstanding."[130] Many of the cyberattacks were so closely timed to the corresponding military operations that "there had to be close cooperation between people in the Russian military and the civilian cyber attackers."[131] There is ample "historical evidence that past and present members of the Russian government endorse cyber warfare and/or cyber attacks initiated by their country's hacker population," especially given that "the coordination of and support to attacks took place mainly in the Russian language and was [sic] conducted on Russian or Russia-friendly forums."[132] However, as with the cyberattacks in Estonia, "there is no conclusive proof of who is behind the DDoS attacks, even though finger pointing at Russia is prevalent by the media."[133] Indeed, "paranoid that the Kremlin's hand is everywhere," the West risked "underestimating the great patriotic rage of many ordinary Russians, who," owing to Russian government propaganda, felt that they needed "to crash Georgian Web sites."[134]

The Russian hackers behind the Georgian cyberattacks appeared to have criminal ties. According to Bulgarian security researcher Dancho Danchev, the cyberattacks originated from "a 'hacker militia' of Russian botnet herders and volunteers"—including cybercriminals—who "mobilize themselves without a need for a central location to do so, distribute the targets, discuss the attack approaches, come up with a plan on the coordination, and you have everyone participating."[135] Several analysts have accused the Saint Petersburg–based Russian Business Network, "a network of criminal hackers with close links to the Russian mafia and government," of the cyberattacks on Georgia.[136] The Swedish Defence University conducted an investigation directly linking the cyberattacks on Georgia to organized crime. The website stopgeorgia.ru, which provided information and tools for independent hackers to attack Georgian websites, was extensively involved in criminal activities such as forged passports and stolen credit cards. Russian authorities normally would regulate these activities, but they "remained remarkably passive" in pursuing and prosecuting anyone in this particular case.[137]

Cyberattacks' Security Impact

"Cyberspace played a significant, if not decisive, role in the [territorial] conflict" between Russia and Georgia.[138] The cyberattacks' impact on the Georgian government was substantial even though, unlike Estonia, Georgia's growing information technology infrastructure had a relatively low number of Internet users.[139] The Russian hackers' attack on Georgia's military and government networks was, tactically at least, "highly successful": "54 web sites in Georgia related to communications, finance, and the government were attacked by rogue elements within Russia," and the "very organized and planned" DDoS attacks ended up crippling 90 percent of all Georgian government domain addresses."[140] In terms of the country's two main Internet access and service providers, United Telecom of Georgia and Caucasus Network, United Telecom was "unavailable and incapable of providing service for several days," and Caucasus Network—whose "network infrastructure runs through the war activity zone"—was "flooded with excessive queries."[141] Because of the attacks, from August 9 to August 18 the National Bank of Georgia ordered all banks to cease offering electronic services.[142] The impact of the cyberattacks, however, was short lived. "While the attacks did not have a permanent or even a long-run devastating effect on the Georgian Internet infrastructure, the damage caused by the attacks was most acutely experienced at the time when Georgia was the most dependent on the availability of their information channels."[143]

The cyberattacks also had a marked human security effect on the Georgians and their ability to communicate and gain accurate information, for "as tanks and troops were crossing the border and bombers were flying sorties, Georgian citizens could not access web sites for information and instructions."[144] The unavailability of key Georgian government websites "severed communication from the Georgian government in the early days of the Georgian-Russian conflict—a period that was doubtless the most critical in the events and when the Georgian government had a vital interest in keeping the information flowing to both the international public and to its own residents."[145] This disruption created discouragement and confusion for Georgians. "The heart of the damage lied [sic] in limiting the nation's options to distribute their point of view about the ongoing military conflict—in 'making its voice heard' to the world"—while "simultaneously, Georgia's own public was deprived of information" at an absolutely critical time.[146]

Public cyberattack fears persisted afterward. In early August 2009, Russian hackers attacked a Tbilisi computer user's social media accounts with "a massive and simultaneous denial-of-service attack apparently aimed to prevent the Georgian from posting critical blog entries" marking the first anniversary of the Russian-Georgia War.[147]

Response to the Cyberattacks

Although the cyberattacks surprised Georgia—Evgeny Morozov, a technology consultant based in Berlin, contends that "Georgia was completely unprepared"¹⁴⁸—its eventual response to these attacks was relatively effective, albeit facilitated by outside aid. While some attacked websites were relocated (primarily to the United States, Estonia, and Poland), others remained online, and CERT Georgia, normally the provider of digital technical support to Georgian higher education institutions, coordinated attack mitigation.¹⁴⁹ Georgia minimized the disruptive impact of DDoS attacks "by rehosting its Web sites on U.S. servers with capacious fiber optic connections and adroit system managers."¹⁵⁰ Georgia globally protested the cyberattacks, but "it had no formal avenue to appeal for help," as "international treaties and defense pacts don't clearly obligate anyone to respond to cyber attacks, even when the victim is an ally."¹⁵¹ Nonetheless, according to cybersecurity expert Jose Nazario at Arbor Networks, outside cybersecurity firms helped "to shut down the servers that the hackers used to command their army of infected machines, those bots, to basically get the server shut offline and blocking access to . . . servers, such that those computers will no longer respond to those commands." They also facilitated the ability of global Internet service providers to "identify the traffic and begin blocking specifically that attack traffic, such that other traffic can pass to Georgia."¹⁵² On August 12 two Estonian computer experts arrived to help keep Georgia's networks running during the war, and Poland lent space on its president's Web page so that Georgia could post updates on its conflict with Russia.¹⁵³

An action-reaction cycle commenced following the cyberattacks, with Georgian websites seeing limited retaliation against Russian sites. For example, Georgian hackers launched DDoS attacks against RIA Novosti, a Moscow-based news service.¹⁵⁴ These retaliatory cyberattacks demonstrated that the original Russian hacker cyberattacks were not totally effective in silencing the voice of the Georgians.¹⁵⁵ Overall, such "hacker wars between (often quite talented) patriotic amateur hackers, cyber militias, and organized criminal gangs have become a widely accepted de facto form of nation-state conflict over the past twenty years."¹⁵⁶

Lessons for Improving Cyberdeterrence

First, heightened vulnerability results when a country depends on foreign Internet connections. The cyberattacks on Georgia ended up "exposing its reliance on Russian Internet pipelines" and the associated dangers.¹⁵⁷ Given that many former Soviet states are poorly connected to the Internet and are increasingly reliant on Russia, "the attack highlights the leverage some countries have gained over adversaries by laying down fiber-optic cables and providing cheap Internet services."¹⁵⁸

Second, international assistance is vital when hackers associated with a much larger power attack a small, non-tech-savvy country. As Nazario points out, "If we are to successfully defend national infrastructure against the sorts of attacks that affected Estonia and Georgia, then we must be open to all forms of assistance" and take advantage of the reality that "in both cases the public were firmly on the side of the victim."[159] Some situations require a certain sobering humility about one's own cyber capabilities, accompanied by a willingness to sacrifice certain traditional elements of national sovereignty.

Third, the internationalization of the conflict between Russia and Georgia increased the volatility of its security consequences. Because both cyberattack and cyberdefense strategies involved multiple states, "such actions call into question the neutrality of third countries," and "in a context where DDoS and malicious hacking are portrayed as acts of war, they can also lead to a dangerous and unpredictable escalation."[160] The potential for ominous tit-for-tat cycles seems quite high in such circumstances.

Fourth, in today's global security setting a virtual war in cyberspace can be just as significant—in terms of achieving both a military wartime victory and strategic postwar goals—as a real kinetic battle being fought on the ground. The tight interconnection between the virtual and real wars is striking: "The Russian-oriented hackers/militia took out news and local government web sites specifically in the areas that the Russian military intended to attack in the ground and air domains."[161] Ronald Deibert, director of the University of Toronto's Citizen Lab, asserts that "battles today are as much about ideas and images as they are territories.... If you're a military and intelligence agency, you're going to take down information that is in opposition and control the message."[162] So cyberdeterrence requires the preemptive preservation of open channels of communication to protect target governments and citizens.

Fifth, more than any other case, the cyberattack on Georgia showed that the absence of global restraint norms can leave a target helpless, with no outside party feeling obligated to respond. As Georgia is stuck within Russia's sphere of influence, nobody wanted to risk aiding Georgia. Even when outside sympathy exists—in this case from Western democracies—the absence of meaningful norms or binding agreements can leave cyber victims high and dry.

Cyberattacks on Israel

Cyberattacks' Description

On December 27, 2008, in response to long-standing friction, violence, and instability, the Israeli government launched Operation Cast Lead, a major military offensive in the Gaza Strip involving the aerial bombardment of Hamas targets in the hopes of stopping Hamas rocket attacks into southern Israel. On January 3, 2009, Israel launched a ground offensive in Gaza, sending in thousands of troops. By January 5 Israeli troops had surrounded Gaza City. Both sides were accused of committing war crimes in the battle. The violent conflict ended on January 18, and on January 21 as Israeli troops completed their withdrawal from Gaza, about thirteen hundred Palestinians and thirteen Israelis were dead. The backdrop to the Israeli military offensive was the legacy of over sixty years of civil war, resulting in having "totally estranged people from another. This ethnic, political, and religious division has given a strong foundation to militants inside Gaza . . . and their radical supporters worldwide to attack their enemies most efficiently . . . by propaganda."[163]

In retaliation for this violent conflict, in January 2009 computer hackers "launched an unprecedented attack on Israel's Internet infrastructure."[164] The cyberattacks focused on Israeli government websites, allegedly using at least half a million computers.[165] A long-term pattern of cyber hostilities existed between the two sides of the conflict. For example, in 2006, as tensions rose between Israel and Gaza, "pro-Palestinian hackers shut down around 700 Israeli Internet domains."[166] In December 2008 in an "online backlash to an incursion by Israel Defense Forces (IDF) into the Gaza Strip . . . [h]ackers from the Muslim world self-mobilized to attack tens of thousands of Israeli websites." They defaced "government, hospital, banking, and media sites" and "the websites of thousands of large and small companies" and other organizations by leaving threatening messages or launching denial-of-service attacks to take the websites offline.[167] The January 2009 cyberattacks on Israel, however, were more massive. "Every time the conflict with the Palestinians flares up, Israeli web sites suffer a barrage of virtual assaults. During the fighting in Gaza, however, the attack was unusually severe, consisting of four waves—each stronger than the last, and peaking at 15 million junk mail deliveries per second."[168] Thus the 2009 cyberattacks deserve special attention.

This Gaza cyberconfrontation was decidedly two sided. During the January 2009 Israeli-Hamas battles, "multiple cyber attacks were launched both from Israeli hackers and Palestinian (and pro-Palestinian) attackers."[169] Although most of the cyberattacks were website defacements, some DDoS attacks also occurred.[170] In the end, in Gaza "cyberspace is becoming a platform Israel and pro-Palestinians shift in their virtual two-front battle," in which "Israel is subject to a new war that is hard to stand in front of despite its [having the] most advanced cyber army in the Middle East."[171] Hamas, which came to power in Gaza after the 2006 elections, was "fighting a two-front war, one on the internet and another by ambushes in Gaza houses. Conscious of the fact that it cannot beat the firepower of the Israeli defense forces, the militant regime relies on the power of perception by using a fast and increasingly effective propaganda machine that spans from Gaza City to US living rooms."[172] Both the Israeli government and Hamas have engaged in digital propaganda campaigns over social media that are "seeking to win the hearts and minds of people in the Middle East and elsewhere in the world" regarding the Gaza conflict.[173]

Cyberattacks' Attribution

The source of the cyberattacks on Israel is still officially unidentified. However, Israeli officials did identify the most credible culprit—"a criminal organization from the former Soviet Union, and paid for by Hamas or Hezbollah," two groups both Israel and the United States explicitly identify as terrorists.[174] The Palestinian Hamas in the Gaza Strip publicly called for "an escalation of Internet hacking against Israel. Hamas spokesman Sami Abu Zuhri said, in a statement e-mailed to reporters in the Gaza strip, 'Penetrating Israeli websites means opening a new field of resistance and the beginning of an electronic war against Israeli occupation.'"[175] Boaz Doley, director of the Israeli government's website management system, Tehila, less credibly speculated that "perhaps it's a genius hacker working alone who activated a program that took over hundreds of thousands of computers as a platform to launch the attack."[176]

Cyberattacks' Security Impact

The security impact of these cyberattacks on the Israeli government was significant but very brief. Indeed, a government official said that Tehila had repaired most sites "within 5 to 20 minutes," although a senior official at IDF Home Front Command's headquarters noted that its site, which guides citizens on how to protect themselves during attacks, was down for three hours.[177] The brevity of the downtime was at least partially due to excellent Israeli cyber readiness.

Nonetheless, the 2009 cyberattack success inspired follow-up cyber aggression. Following the 2009 military confrontation, Israel launched two major follow-up military offensives in Gaza. In November 2012 Israel launched Operation Pillar of Defense, an eight-day military operation in Gaza, and on July 8, 2014, the Israel Defense Forces waged Operation Protective Edge in Gaza to undermine Hamas's offensive capabilities there. The cyber responses to the two offensives differed significantly: "In comparison to Operation Pillar of Defense, where the Israeli government faced over 100 million cyber attacks in eight days and IP addresses traced back to Europe and the United States, during Operation Protective Edge, 70 percent of cyber attacks were traced back to Qatar, Hamas' main benefactor."[178]

Over the years, the transnational hacktivist group Anonymous targeted Israeli assets in "protest of Israeli policy toward the Palestinians" in Gaza, leading some observers to question whether Anonymous is "being infiltrated and deceived by Hamas and other pro-terrorist organization affiliates."[179] After Israel's November 2012 Operation Pillar of Defense in Gaza, "Anonymous hacktivists breached and defaced numerous Israeli websites," leaking information and conducting DDoS attacks against the IDF website. The group wrote that "Anonymous has stood by with the rest of the world and watched in despair the barbaric, brutal and despicable treatment of the Palestinian people in the so called 'Occupied Territories' by the Israel Defense Force." The group maintained that after "the government of Israel publicly threatened to sever internet and other telecommunications into and out of Gaza, they crossed a line in the sand." In response, on behalf of the people of Gaza, Anonymous members threatened to "do everything in our power to hinder the evil forces of the IDF arrayed against you. We will use all our resources to make certain you stay connected to the Internet and remain able to transmit your experiences to the world."[180]

Israel claimed that it was barraged by more than 60 million hacking attempts in the 2012 attacks.[181] On April 7, 2013, Holocaust Memorial Day, Anonymous hacktivists attacked key Israeli websites, including those of the Foreign Ministry, the Bank of Jerusalem, the Israeli Defense Ministry, the IDF's blog, and the Israeli president's official website. The group also released the personal data of 5,000 Israeli officials along with that of 600,000 users of the popular Israeli email service Walla.[182] On April 7, 2015, Anonymous used website defacement to try "to wreak an 'electronic holocaust' on Israel ... to erase the country from cyberspace." Its motive for this threat was to "punish" Israel for its "heinous crimes against humanity," citing as evidence its "continuous aggression, bombing, killing and kidnapping of the Palestinian people, as in the last war against Gaza in 2014."[183]

The impact of these follow-up cyberattacks on Israel, whose "government networks are among the most highly attacked in the world," was mixed.[184] Not surprising, the Gaza government information office praised Anonymous's efforts. Palestinian government spokesman Ihab Al-Ghussian asked Allah to "bless the minds and the efforts of the soldiers of the electronic battle." Computer engineer Sami Rouqa at Gaza's Ministry of Information said it had more support: "Palestinians, Saudis, Indonesians, Moroccans, Algerians and Iraqis worked together in the cyber warfare."[185] While Anonymous boasted about its 2013 operations—claiming it had "caused $3 billion ... worth of damage to Israel and targeted more than 100,000 websites, 40,000 Facebook pages, 5,000 Twitter accounts and 30,000 Israeli bank accounts"—Benjamin Decker, a senior intelligence analyst at the Tel Aviv–based consulting firm the Levantine Group, concluded that Israeli cyber infrastructures had incurred little damage "largely due to Israel's pioneering of most cyber-warfare tactics, both offensive and defensive."[186] Similarly Yitzhak Ben Yisrael of Israel's National Cyber Bureau said these hacking efforts had largely failed to shut down key sites or to achieve "any real damage."[187] Former US House Intelligence Committee chairman Rep. Mike Rogers (R-MI) also stated that he did not believe that "Israel's Iron Dome missile defense system, which is credited with preventing all but a few dozen Israeli casualties despite ongoing rocket fire from Hamas, was at risk of being shut down by a cyber attack."[188]

Anonymous did not constitute the only outside hackers to take on Israel after Israeli military actions toward Palestinians in Gaza. In January 2012 a single hacker penetrated several Israeli credit card companies and obtained credit card information for over 400,000 Israelis. Because he believed that "Israel attacks and kills innocent Palestinian people, they commit genocide, [and] they even break legal international rules," the hacker released the data online, hoping to make "Israeli credit cards untrustable in the world" and "to harm Israel financially and socially."[189]

When Israel's Operation Protective Edge began in Gaza in July 2014, the hacker group Izz ad-Din al-Qassam Cyber Fighters—"almost certainly sponsored by the Iranian government"—showed support for the Palestinians by attempting "to flood a core piece of Israel's internet infrastructure, the Domain Name System" (Israel's Web phone book containing personal data about Israeli citizens) and "to take down websites for the national stock exchange and Mossad" (Israel's intelligence and special operations body), but "the attacks caused little trouble."[190] In 2015 Israel discovered that since 2012 skilled hackers had been undertaking a cyberespionage campaign, apparently orchestrated by Hezbollah, that targeted Israeli "military suppliers, telecom companies, media outlets, and universities with malicious software meant to steal sensitive data and monitor its victims."[191]

Response to the Cyberattacks

The Israeli government responded to the cyberattacks by initiating a concerted policy effort to increase preparedness for the future. A Defense Ministry official stated that "we need a uniform standard for all the country's major governmental and economic organizations to ensure that next time there's a big cyber attack, the economy isn't paralyzed completely."[192] In 2011 the Israeli government established a National Cyber Directorate "to help guard against infiltration of the country's government and business computer systems."[193] In November 2012 the Israel Defense Forces, "realizing the dangers of citizen journalism, implored Israelis not to attach locations to tweets or photos reporting rocket attacks or siren alerts to prevent triangulation by Hamas and its allies; Twitter, it seems, is a weapon that can be used by both sides."[194] On February 15, 2015, Israel's Security Cabinet approved a new cyberdefense authority, to be rolled out gradually over three years with an annual budget of $38 million to $50 million.[195] Then on June 15 of that year, "in a historic move indicative of the dangers and potency of the digital medium as a weapon," the commander of the Israeli army established a new IDF unit responsible for all cyber activity.[196]

Lessons for Improving Cyberdeterrence

A few security lessons emerge from the cyberattacks on Israel. First, even the most advanced cyberdefense systems—and Israel is globally renowned for its world-class cybersecurity systems—are vulnerable to penetration by clever hackers. Second, if an ongoing conflict occurs with both sides being cyber-capable, it seems highly likely to start a dangerous action-reaction cycle. Third, even if a state has established a record of credible deterrence against conventional land, sea, and air attacks, that authority does not carry over to cyberattacks. Note that "Israel has repeatedly proved that it responds to physical attack and provocation. No one has that record in cyberspace. Thus, in the absence of such credibility, some sort of decision on retaliation may have to follow quickly once attribution is announced. The longer the gap between attribution and retaliation, the more time the forewarned attacker has to prepare for a return blow."[197] For the Gaza cyberattacks, then, the longer the perpetrator feels it has escaped any form of truly punishing Israeli retaliation, the more empowered it will feel to engage in future cyber-disruptive activity.

The relationship between real-world and virtual attacks in the Gaza conflict appeared to be inverse. In November 2012 when the physical combat between the two sides in Gaza paused, cybersecurity firm CloudFlare's chief executive officer Matthew Prince noticed that the "cease-fire in the physical world ... actually translated into fighting in the cyber world." Although "cyberattacks were part of the recent deadly bombing campaign between Israel and Gaza from the beginning, as hackers aligned with both sides targeted the opposition's websites and servers, . . . when a cease-fire was declared, the fighting's focus moved from the physical space into the digital arena."[198]

Given the global diffusion of cyberattack tools and skills, a key lesson from this confrontation is that it is unwise for any country to be complacent about perceived technological superiority. Even though Israel has consistently adhered to a policy of retaliating following acts of terrorism to "signal to Palestinians in general, and Hamas in particular, that terrorism is costly," this case vividly demonstrates the leveling of the global cyber playing field and consequent cyber signaling difficulties. "Because cyberspace is noisy, both the easily understood and subtle signals (thought to be) present in the nuclear realm may be nearly indecipherable in the new medium. . . . Without clear signaling, it is difficult to distinguish deterrence from aggression."[199] So as a result cybertargets often find that outside observers judge their retaliation as illegitimate.

US and Israeli Cyberattacks on Iran (Stuxnet)

Cyberattacks' Description

In July and August 2010 notoriety surrounded a cyberworm malware called Stuxnet (named after initials found in its code) that was used on Iranian computers, infecting them with destructive viruses. Stuxnet was originally discovered in June 2010 by a Belarus security firm, which "found samples of the code on computers belonging to an unnamed client in Iran."[200] The target of the worm, which is "a cybermissile designed to penetrate advanced security systems," was Iran's nuclear program. Stuxnet "was equipped with a warhead that targeted and took over the controls of the centrifuge systems at Iran's uranium processing center in Natanz."[201] Stuxnet, which had multiple versions, had actually "been at work silently sabotaging centrifuges at the Natanz plant" since June 2009, and already "in January 2010, inspectors with the International Atomic Energy Agency visiting the Natanz uranium enrichment plant in Iran noticed that centrifuges used to enrich uranium gas were failing at an unprecedented rate."[202]

As a malicious worm infecting computers running on the Microsoft Windows operating system, Stuxnet was one model of a programmable logic controller (made by the German company Siemens) that was used to "drive and regulate the motors, valves, and switches in a wide range of industrial applications." Once it gained control in the nuclear plant, "the virus directed the centrifuges to operate at unsafe speeds" and resulted "in their physical damage, evidently in some cases to the point of destruction, requiring costly and time-consuming repairs, thereby delaying Iran's uranium enrichment efforts."[203] Stuxnet "disguises all of this activity by sending commands to shut off warning and safety controls that would normally alert plant operators."[204] Because the nuclear facility's computers were air gapped from the Internet, the attackers designed a version of the cyberweapon to spread via USB flash drives, first infecting computers belonging to outside companies that were presumably connected to the Iranian nuclear program. Stuxnet "was unlike any other virus or worm that came before. Rather than simply hijacking targeted computers or stealing information from them, it escaped the digital realm to wreak physical destruction on equipment the computers controlled."[205]

Inventing the highly complex Stuxnet worm was not a simple task. Its creation was expensive, taking "8 to 10 people six months to write," and it required extensive pre-release testing and intelligence collection to perfect its targeting. "Whoever wrote Stuxnet was willing to spend a lot of money to ensure that whatever job it was intended to do would be done."[206] Apparently "Stuxnet's creator took several swipes at Iran's nuclear facilities before hitting paydirt, but each tweak also made the worm more likely to break out and cause collateral damage in untargeted networks."[207] This malware was so well designed that "computer security specialists who have examined it were almost certain it had been created by a government and is a prime example of clandestine digital warfare."[208] Ralph Langner, a German cybersecurity expert who was among the first to study and raise alarms about Stuxnet, said, "This is not some hacker sitting in the basement of his parents' house. To me, it seems that the resources needed to stage this attack point to a nation state."[209]

Seán McGurk, the head of the National Cybersecurity and Communications Integration Center at the US Department of Homeland Security, in his 2010 testimony before Congress called Stuxnet a "game changer," representing a large and complex threat with capabilities never seen before. He stated, "This code can automatically enter a system, steal the formula for the product you are manufacturing, alter the ingredients being mixed in your product, and indicate to the operator and your anti-virus software that everything is functioning as expected."[210] Stuxnet was "carefully crafted, not only to evade detection, but to cause damage that would be mistaken for system design flaws or operational errors," and once it found the targeted device, "it would lie dormant for two weeks, recording operational data from the centrifuge cascades that it would play back later to indicate continued normal conditions to system operators."[211] In the end, Stuxnet was "the world's first known cyber super weapon designed specifically to destroy a real-world target" and was hailed as "the most sophisticated cyberweapon ever created."[212]

Cyberattacks' Attribution

Given that Stuxnet's developers "were uncommonly thorough about not leaving clues in their code," their identity may never be definitively confirmed.[213] However, after considerable investigation, the Stuxnet worm appears to have been created in the United States and ironically ended up infecting some US computer systems.[214] Based on interviews with American, European, and Israeli officials involved in the program, as well as several outside experts, the *New York Times* concluded that "from his first months in office, President Obama secretly ordered increasingly sophisticated attacks on the computer systems that run Iran's main nuclear enrichment facilities," including the release of the Stuxnet worm, and that "Mr. Obama decided to accelerate the attacks . . . even after an element of the program accidentally became public in the summer of 2010 because of a programming error that allowed it to escape Iran's Natanz plant and sent it around the world on the Internet."[215] Notably, "American officials have never confirmed they were part of the operation against Iran, codenamed 'Olympic Games.'"[216]

Furthermore, evidence quickly surfaced that Israel was also involved. For example, German cybersecurity expert Langner noted that Stuxnet "is a directed sabotage attack involving heavy insider knowledge," and his observation leads many to believe that "Israel is at it again, offering something blindingly new: a cyber weapon created to cross from the digital realm to the physical world—to destroy something."[217] Indeed,

> whoever designed Stuxnet and sent it to attack Iran's nuclear weapons facilities was building on—and extending and improving—Israel's IW [information warfare] capabilities as demonstrated on 6 September 2007. . . . The guess here is that Stuxnet was [Israeli Major] General [Amos] Yadlin's . . . farewell present to his successors. It is as if this indefatigable advocate of heavy investment in IW capabilities was eager to demonstrate to a new generation of military leaders how such capabilities allow a country to fight a war against an enemy thousands of miles away, and do so without firing a shot.[218]

By January 2011 there was "mounting evidence" that together "the United States and Israel created the virus specifically to hamper Iran's efforts to become a nuclear power."[219] Reportedly Israel had previously evaluated the effectiveness of the Stuxnet worm in the Negev on its Dimona complex, containing "nuclear centrifuges virtually identical to Iran's at Natanz," as a test run before using the virus in Iran. "The operations there [at Dimona], as well as related efforts in the United States, are among the newest and strongest clues suggesting that the virus was designed as an American-Israeli project to sabotage the Iranian program."[220] In April 2011 Gholam Reza Jalali, head of an Iranian military unit in charge of combating sabotage, said that independently "Iranian experts had determined that the United States and Israel were behind Stuxnet."[221]

Cyberattacks' Security Impact

Most analysts agree that Stuxnet significantly disrupted Iranian security. Initially Iranian experts minimized the damage done. In September 2010 the head of the Bushehr nuclear plant in Iran said that "the worm had affected only the personal computers of staff members," and Iran's telecommunications minister said the worm had not penetrated or caused "serious damage to government systems."[222] However, in late 2010, Iranian President Mahmoud Ahmadinejad, "after months of denials, admitted that the worm had penetrated Iran's nuclear sites, but he said it was detected and controlled."[223] Moreover, in April 2011 a senior Iranian official admitted that the Stuxnet malware had "inflicted serious damage on Iran's nuclear program, including large-scale accidents and loss of life."[224] Other sources reported that Stuxnet "caused Iranian uranium enrichment centrifuges to grind to a halt."[225] Ultimately, Stuxnet infected more than thirty thousand computers used in industrial control systems in Iran, caused between a thousand and two thousand centrifuges to be swapped out over just a few months, and delayed Iran's nuclear program by up to eighteen months.[226] Iran's nuclear enrichment program recovered within a year.[227]

Langner contended that launching the virus "was nearly as effective as a military strike, but even better since there are no fatalities and no full-blown war."[228] Stuxnet was "designed to take over the control systems and evade detection, and it apparently was very successful."[229] As one report observed, "The Stuxnet computer worm may have accomplished what five years of United Nations Security Council resolutions could not: disrupt Iran's pursuit of a nuclear bomb.... Moreover, Stuxnet may have been more effective than a conventional military attack and may have avoided a major international crisis over collateral damage."[230] Despite minority claims of Stuxnet's ineffectiveness, now few doubt that its impact was sizable; in retrospect, this impact appears to be both remarkable and unprecedented.[231]

The 2010 Stuxnet incident was not the first time a Middle Eastern nuclear program had suffered an effective outside disruption involving Israel. On September 6, 2007, in a surprise attack shortly after midnight, seven Israeli Air Force fighter jets executed Operation Orchard and destroyed a covert site of a future nuclear reactor near al-Kibar in northeast Syria. The operation was facilitated through sophisticated Israeli software attacks on Syria's electrical grid and represented "the first use of a combined software-hardware cyber-attack to blind a nation during a military operation."[232] After witnessing this Syrian disruption, Iran apparently had not adequately learned proper nuclear vulnerability lessons and failed to take adequate safety measures to protect its own nuclear program.

In the short run, Stuxnet inflicted limited collateral damage beyond its intended target. Indeed, "the most striking aspect of the fast-spreading malicious computer program—which has turned up in industrial programs around the world and which Iran said had appeared in the computers of workers in its nuclear project—may not have been how sophisticated it was, but rather how sloppy its creators were in letting a specifically aimed attack scatter randomly around the globe."[233] The worm ended up being "splattered on thousands of computer systems around the world," although indirectly affected systems were not subverted.[234] By September 2010 Stuxnet infected at least forty-five thousand computers worldwide, with most victim computers being in Iran, Pakistan, India, and Indonesia, although some machines in Germany, Canada, and the United States had been hit as well.[235] As a result, "global alarm over the deadly computer worm has come many months after the program was suspected of stealthily entering an Iranian nuclear enrichment plant."[236]

In the long run, Stuxnet "effectively legitimized the use of cyber-attacks outside the context of overt military conflict."[237] An Institute for Science and International Security report concludes with the following ominous warning:

> It is important for governments to approach the question of whether using a tool like Stuxnet could open the door to future national security risks or adversely and unintentionally affect U.S. allies. Countries hostile to the United States may feel justified in launching their own attacks against U.S. facilities, perhaps even using a modified Stuxnet code. Such an attack could shut down large portions of national power grids or other critical infrastructure using malware designed to target critical components inside a major system, causing a national emergency.[238]

Similarly, David Gewirtz, the cyberterrorism adviser for the International Association for Counterterrorism and Security Professionals, contends that "the Stuxnet virus has ushered in a new age of cyber warfare and potentially sparked a virtual arms race similar to how Hiroshima sparked the nuclear arms race."[239] It remains to be seen how many Stuxnet-like imitations will emerge in the future.

Response to the Cyberattacks

Iran apparently attempted quickly and quietly to manage the cyber disruption caused by the Stuxnet worm. Specifically, "rather than making public pronouncements and using the incident to incite its followers—typical behavior when dealing with the United States and Israel—the Iranian government focused on creating a new cyber warfare militia."[240] However, as of December 2010, cybersecurity experts in the United States and Europe reported that Iran's nuclear program was "still in chaos despite its leaders' claim that they have contained the computer worm that attacked their facilities. . . . [T]heir security Web sites, which deal with the computer worm known as Stuxnet, continue to be swamped with traffic from Tehran and other places in the Islamic Republic, an indication that the worm continues to infect the computers at Iran's two nuclear sites."[241] At this time, Iran still apparently had not "come to grips with the complexity of the malware that appears to be still infecting the systems at both Bashehr and Natanz."[242] Langner said he was not surprised by Iran's failure to eradicate Stuxnet quickly: "'The Iranians don't have the depth of knowledge to handle the worm or understand its complexity,' . . . raising the possibility that they may never succeed in eliminating it."[243]

A rather unexpected bump in the road in late 2010 helped to hamper a successful Iranian response to Stuxnet. In Tehran men on motorcycles attached magnetic bombs to the cars of two leading nuclear scientists, wounding one and killing the other. It turned out that "the murdered scientist was in charge of dealing with the Stuxnet virus at the nuclear plants."[244] Undoubtedly this event slowed the recovery.

Stuxnet triggered an action-reaction cycle between Iran and its Western adversaries. As fully discussed later, on August 15, 2012, Iran launched retaliatory cyberattacks on the information network of the Saudi Arabian state oil company Aramco. Furthermore, in the years since Stuxnet was unleashed, there has been a "striking acceleration of the use of cyberweapons by the United States and Iran against each other, both for spying and sabotage."[245]

Globally, this incident set in motion a wave of speedy reassessments of cybersecurity systems and how to plug holes against foreign cyberattacks. Industrial control specialists are alarmed because Stuxnet not only "laid bare significant vulnerabilities in industrial control systems" but also raised "fear of dangerous proliferation." Indeed, "the widespread availability of the attack techniques revealed by the software" led Melissa Hathaway, a former US national cybersecurity coordinator, to remark, "All of these guys are scared to death" that hackers will employ these techniques against them.[246]

Lessons for Improving Cyberdeterrence

A first lesson from the Stuxnet cyberintrusion is that cyberdeterrence seems most difficult to execute successfully when dealing with an innovative, sophisticated cyberattack. Even with cyberspace generally leveling the global playing field and empowering weaker states, countries such as Israel and the United States with superior time, money, intelligence, and resources can still hold an advantage. Because the Stuxnet worm was unprecedented, uncertainty existed about its scope and effects, and any cybertarget would have had difficulty anticipating it and preparing in advance to protect targeted data or systems. Stuxnet highlights the inherent limitations of tried-and-true protective cyberdeterrence mechanisms for safeguarding vital assets against every form of cyberthreat. Even with considerable cyber expertise, Iran found itself virtually helpless from a preemptive standpoint in terms of forestalling this cyberattack.

A second lesson is that once a virus as damaging as Stuxnet is unleashed, it may be difficult to control and contain; thus, it is important to promote "more extensive international cooperation for preventing the trafficking in perverse cyber threat technologies." Following the Stuxnet attack on Iran's nuclear facilities, "portions of its sophisticated digital code have been deciphered and emulated for secretive trafficking among prospective hackers and others. In view of the potency and unpredictability of this malware, a case exists for governmental regulation, and even international oversight, of the trade in potentially damaging cyber-code."[247] Because cyber expertise is distributed globally (albeit unevenly), and different experts rely on different tracking systems and software and hardware remedies, trying to recover and restore systems and data on one's own after such an attack seems imprudent. Once the Stuxnet worm hit, Iran could have perhaps recovered more quickly had it possessed sophisticated international allies willing and able to help it recover from this devastating cyberattack.

A third lesson is cyberdeterrence becomes more difficult when targets keep cyberattacks and responses too secret. Iranian government officials were slow to acknowledge the Stuxnet attack and even slower and less credible in revealing their response to the attack, and despite indications that Iran "accelerated its cyber programs after the attack," there has been little concrete indication of increased Iranian capacity for effective cyber responses afterward.[248] So future cyberattackers seem unlikely to hesitate or be deterred from launching another cyber salvo against the country.[249] In other words, after being hit by a major cyberattack that inflicts tangible damage, noncommunication can invite further cyberintrusions.

A fourth lesson concerns the question of accountability for cyberattack collateral damage. In cases such as Stuxnet, where there is some collateral damage to unintended civilian targets, perhaps there needs to be some form of outside encouragement for perpetrators, once they are informally identified, to take some responsibility for repairing the damage. The involvement of neutral international organizations might prove useful to stimulate this kind of perpetrator responsibility.

Cyberattacks on the International Monetary Fund

Cyberattacks' Description

On June 11, 2011, the International Monetary Fund—a United Nations international economic organization in Washington, DC, that manages global financial crises and promotes international monetary cooperation so as to expand international commerce—publicly announced it had been the target of an extensive cyberattack. It was discovered that the international organization, "which has been orchestrating the sensitive bailouts of European governments and dealing with the fallout from an attempted rape charge against its former boss, had been under assault for several months."[250] These attacks were likely facilitated by a technique known as spear phishing, "in which an individual is fooled into clicking on a malicious Web link or running a program that allows open access to the recipient's network."[251] Over the years, "the IMF has faced repeated cyber attacks," for "it routinely collects sensitive information about the financial conditions of its 187 member nations."[252]

The 2011 cyberattacks on the International Monetary Fund constituted cyberespionage. Mohan Koo, a cybersecurity expert who runs Dtex Systems, stated that "the IMF attack was clearly designed to infiltrate the IMF with the intention of gaining sensitive 'insider privileged information.'"[253] The attack is particularly troubling because it was "targeted, well organised and well executed."[254] In an internal memo issued on June 8, IMF chief information officer Jonathan Palmer said that "we detected some suspicious file transfers, and the subsequent investigation established that a Fund desktop computer had been compromised and used to access some Fund systems. At this point, we have no reason to believe that any personal information was sought for fraud purposes."[255]

More specifically, Tom Kellerman, a cybersecurity expert who has worked for both the IMF and the World Bank and served on the board of a group known as the International Cyber Security Protection Alliance, said that "the intruders had aimed to install software that would give a nation state a 'digital insider presence' on the IMF network."[256] He pointed out that "the intrusion could have yielded a treasure trove of non-public economic data used by the IMF to promote exchange rate stability, support balanced international trade, and provide resources to remedy members' balance-of-payments crises."[257] The attackers could also gain "visibility into IMF plans, particularly as it relates to bailing out the economies of countries on shaky financial footing."[258]

Cyberattacks' Attribution

Regarding the attribution for the IMF cyberattack, a probable suspect was not definitively confirmed because "security experts said it would be difficult for investigators to prove which nation was behind the attack."[259] IMF officials themselves "declined to say where they believe the attack originated—a delicate subject because most nations are members of the fund."[260] Nonetheless, there is very strong reason to believe that the IMF cyberattack emerged from the international hacktivist group Anonymous, the loosely affiliated international network of cyberattackers (originating in 2003) that over several years has engaged in cyberintrusions against businesses, governments, and international organizations. On June 1, 2011, the *Wall Street Journal* reported that the International Monetary Fund acknowledged that it knew of a threat from Anonymous, quoting spokesman William Murray as stating, "We are aware of the threat, and have taken appropriate action."[261] It turns out that a post linked to an Anonymous Twitter account "suggested hackers would target the IMF's website in relation to the fund's work with Greece."[262] The group specifically sent a tweet on June 1 "urging followers to set their sights on the IMF website" as part of "#OperationGreece."[263]

A few observers speculated that a state might be behind the International Monetary Fund cyberattacks. Bloomberg reporters suggested that the hackers' data theft from IMF computers was "linked to a foreign government."[264] A cybersecurity expert who is a member of the Department of Homeland Security Advisory Council believed "the IMF attack could have been conducted on behalf of a nation-state looking to either steal sensitive information about key IMF strategies or embarrass the organisation to undermine its clout."[265] The far stronger attribution evidence, however, points to Anonymous as the culprit.

The motives of Anonymous appeared to be political retribution for the International Monetary Fund's role in approving the Greek bailout, which required a severe austerity program for Greek citizens. The International Monetary Fund had been involved in negotiations to help stabilize Greece's economy and had approved a $40 billion loan to Greece as a part of a $140 billion bailout package that also called for severe cutbacks in public services.[266] On May 25, 2011, Anonymous had released a message "condemning the Greek Government and the IMF for accepting the loan without letting citizens vote on the agreement, and for subjecting the people of the country to 'prolonged poverty and a dramatic decrease in their standards of living.'" The message continued, "The people of Greece have been left with no other option than to take to the streets in a peaceful revolution against the economic tyrants that are the IMF."[267]

The backdrop to this Anonymous response began on April 23, 2010, when to address increasing concern about a sovereign default on debt, the Greek government had requested the activation of a bailout package from the European Union and the International Monetary Fund. In 2011 (and later in 2012), Greeks protested the austerity measures associated with the bailout and clashed violently with the government police. The reaction of government police was particularly brutal, involving shock grenades and chemical gases.[268] Outside observers sympathized with these protests given the severity of the government's economic cuts, and even an IMF official expressed understanding for the intensity of the protests.[269] Contributing to outside frustration with the International Monetary Fund was the trouble that befell its managing director Dominique Strauss-Kahn. In New York on May 14, 2011, he was charged with the attempted sexual assault of a hotel maid and placed under house arrest, thus forcing him to resign his post.

Cyberattacks' Security Impact

Although the International Monetary Fund was relatively closemouthed about the extent of the cyberattacks' damage, publicly saying only that—in the words of IMF spokesman David Hawley—"the Fund is fully functional," outside observers concluded that it had "become the latest, and potentially the most serious, victim of an attack by computer hackers."[270] Moreover, "several senior officials with knowledge of the attack said it was both sophisticated and serious," calling it "a very major breach."[271] As a demonstration of these apprehensions, a security expert who was familiar with the incident but declined to be identified claimed that the cyberattack on the fund "resulted in the loss of a 'large quantity' of data, including documents and e-mails."[272]

A devastating security impact could have ensued, affecting agreements that one IMF official called "political dynamite in many countries." Given that the fund is involved "at the center of economic bailout programs for Portugal,

Greece and Ireland—and possesses sensitive data on other countries that may be on the brink of crisis—its database contains potentially market-moving information. It also includes communications with national leaders as they negotiate, often behind the scenes, on the terms of international bailouts."[273] Discovery of the cyberattack immediately "caused concern that sensitive information about the finances of governments might have fallen into the wrong hands." More specifically, "speculators trading currencies or government bonds on the global financial markets could make profitable use of such stolen information, while political opponents and foreign intelligence services could also find explosive information about government dealings with the fund."[274]

The security vulnerability implications of the IMF cyberattack were quite wide. According to cybersecurity expert Koo, "Perhaps most frightening of all is the fact that these type of attacks could quite easily be directed toward Critical National Infrastructure (CNI) organizations, for example Energy and Water, where the impact of such a breach would have severe, immediate and potentially life-threatening consequences for everyday citizens."[275] Cybersecurity expert Jeff Moss worried that the success of the IMF intrusion "could inspire attacks on other large institutions."[276] Most broadly, the IMF attack globally served to "increase concerns over low-level cyberwarfare waged by governments for economic and industrial espionage purposes."[277]

Response to the Cyberattacks

At the time Anonymous initially issued its threat, the International Monetary Fund had stated that it was "taking action to strengthen its systems against hackers."[278] However, clearly these preemptive steps were inadequate, for even with advance warning the IMF had not anticipated the scope and nature of the cyberattack. Nonetheless, in the cyberattack's aftermath, the fund worked to increase the vigilance of its employees and to improve its cyberdefenses.[279]

In response to the IMF cyberattack, outsiders provided assistance. "The World Bank, an international agency focused on economic development, whose headquarters is across the street from the I.M.F. in downtown Washington, cut the computer link that allows the two institutions to share information. A World Bank spokesman said the step had been taken out of 'an abundance of caution' until the severity and nature of the cyberattack on the I.M.F. is understood."[280] In addition, the World Bank also "briefly shut down external access to its most sensitive systems, for fear that the stolen information could make it a target. But it quickly resumed its normal operations and says it has seen no evidence of any attacks."[281] In the long run, World Bank spokesperson Rich Mills said, "The World Bank Group, like any other large organisation, is increasingly aware of potential threats to the security of our information system, and we are constantly working to improve our defences."[282] Overall, this significant preemptive response from the World Bank shows the depth of concern among international organizations about uncontained cyberattack contagion.

Because the IMF cyberattack occurred in the United States, the US government also quickly responded. In the wake of this breach (along with several others on the US government), in 2011 the Obama administration introduced several cybersecurity proposals "to knit together a 'security infrastructure' to encompass the public and private sectors." It put forward "a new national data-breach reporting policy that would require private institutions to report security breaches to the affected individuals and the Federal Trade Commission (FTC)," with the Department of Homeland Security having "a regulatory role over the cybersecurity of critical infrastructure." The proposal also sought "to introduce mandatory minimum sentences for cyber criminals" and "to work with 'like-minded states' to create an international standard for cyber security."[283] In addition, the FBI helped with the investigation of the International Monetary Fund cyberattack.[284]

Lessons for Improving Cyberdeterrence

As with Stuxnet, a first cyberdeterrence lesson emerging from the IMF cyberattack is that complete non-transparency and secrecy about a breach not only stymie the efforts of other potentially vulnerable targets to protect themselves from similar breaches but also prevent outside groups and governments from providing much useful assistance. A second lesson is that international organizations, which many observers assume are not involved in major cyberspace confrontations, can become prime targets of cyberattack, particularly when they either possess sensitive data of great value on the international marketplace or involve themselves in undertaking or supporting controversial international actions, such as economic bailout efforts that involve stern austerity measures.

Because international organizations are highly vulnerable to cyberattacks, they need to focus on developing new ways to promote robust cyberdeterrence. The changes suggested by the IMF case are greatly improving security intelligence information sharing among member states of international organizations about potentially dangerous cyberattackers (such as Anonymous) and preparing and announcing in advance better sanctions, which might prevent intrusion from any outside party engaging in cyberespionage. International organizations such as the IMF should be especially vigilant when they have undertaken globally unpopular actions. Such efforts would help to promote "elaborate cooperation on threat perceptions, attack detection, and identification/apprehension of those responsible for attacks" in cyberspace.[285]

Iranian Cyberattacks on Saudi Arabian Oil Company Aramco

Cyberattacks' Description

On August 15, 2012, cyberattacks occurred on the information network of Saudi Arabian state oil company Aramco. As the world's largest oil company, it exports and supplies a tenth of the world's oil and generates about 80–90 percent of total Saudi revenues and over 40 percent of the country's gross domestic product.[286] The result of the cyberintrusion was devastating. "The data on three-quarters of the machines on the main computer network of Saudi Aramco had been destroyed," and "as a kind of calling card, the hackers lit up the screen of each machine they wiped with a single image, of an American flag on fire."[287]

The cyberattack method was a self-replicating virus named Shamoon (after a word in its code) that infected more than thirty thousand Microsoft Windows–based computers. This virus deleted files on randomly selected Aramco computers and overwrote their master boot records (necessary for the machines to start functioning), "rendering the machines unusable."[288] Shamoon's code included a kill switch, or a timer set to activate a computer disruption through an erasing mechanism named Wiper at 11:08 a.m., the exact time of the Aramco cyberattacks.[289] The virus erased documents, spreadsheets, emails, and other assorted files. A Saudi consultant working with government and telecom Internet-security efforts anonymously said that, as with the Stuxnet worm, "the virus was introduced by a hand-carried USB memory stick."[290]

By August 26, 2012, Aramco was able to restore its internal network services, "reporting that it had cleaned all affected workstations and resumed normal business."[291] However, its public website still experienced significant downtime even after the company announced its recovery. Moreover, more than two months after the Aramco attack, Aramco employees were unable "to gain access to their corporate e-mail and internal network for several days," and they could no longer "access Aramco's internal network remotely" until the company's executives were assured the system was secure.[292]

Cyberattacks Attribution

The attribution for the Aramco cyberattacks is a bit controversial. A spokesman for the Saudi Arabian Interior Ministry said that the ministry and Aramco investigated the attack and found that "the attackers were an organized group operating from countries on four continents."[293] A previously unknown "anti-oppression" hacking group called the Cutting Sword of Justice claimed responsibility for the Shamoon attacks and said its members were motivated because they were "fed up of crimes and atrocities taking place in various countries around the world, especially in the neighboring countries such as Syria, Bahrain, Yemen, Lebanon, Egypt."[294] In 2011 Saudi Arabia had sent troops into Bahrain to support its fellow Sunni Muslim rulers against Shi'ite-led protesters, and Saudi Arabia was sympathetic to the mainly Sunni rebels fighting against the Syrian regime.[295] Given that inside knowledge and inside privileges were required for this cyberattack on Aramco to occur, "one or more insiders with high-level access are suspected of assisting the hackers."[296]

However, Iran was immediately suspected as covertly sponsoring this hacking group because it had just been a victim of the Stuxnet cyberattacks from the United States and Israel, it had the necessary cyberoffense capabilities to launch such an attack, and the Shamoon virus was quite similar to the Flame virus, which was found earlier on Iranian Ministry of Energy computers.[297] Immediately following the Aramco attack, "officials gathered at the White House could not help wondering if the attack was payback from Iran, using America's Saudi ally as a proxy, for the ongoing program of cyber-warfare waged by the U.S. and Israel, and probably other Western governments, against the Iranian nuclear program."[298] Iran would necessarily have been aware that such a major cyberattack had emerged from within its boundaries because the attack had consumed so much bandwidth.[299] Indeed, "infecting the company's machines with Shamoon required the kind of coordination typical of state-sponsored attacks, and the virus' targeting of infrastructure critical to the Saudi and global economies, as well as international security, significantly shortens the list of suspects.... Iran's grievances against much of the international community for imposing sanctions on it, coupled with its possession of the wiper code, make it the prime suspect."[300]

American intelligence officials explicitly asserted that "the attack's real perpetrator was Iran."[301] One American official said that "U.S. intelligence has observed and tracked the attacks coming from Iran" and, without offering details, stated that "there is a belief that those involved were surrogates working with the Iranian government. 'We strongly believe there is a relationship between the people typing the code and people running the government.'"³⁰² Not surprisingly, Iran "officially denied any part in the programming or deployment of Shamoon."³⁰³

Cyberattacks' Security Impact

The Shamoon virus was a major short-term shock, causing "significant disruption to the world's largest oil producer" and "effectively destroying all the information on the system."³⁰⁴ US secretary of defense Leon Panetta stated that the Aramco hack was "probably the most destructive attack that the private sector has seen to date."³⁰⁵ The attack had a minimal financial impact, though: "By Aramco's own estimation, the losses amounted to just $15 million—a drop in the ocean for an organisation that turned over $311 billion in 2012."³⁰⁶ However, the Aramco cyberattack was not only "the most severe cyber attack ever reported on Saudi Arabia, wiping out what Aramco said was the hardware on 85% of the oil giant's devices," but also "one of the most destructive cyber strikes conducted against a single business" in history.³⁰⁷ Abdullah al-Saadan, Aramco's vice president for corporate planning, noted that the breach's principal aim "was to stop the flow of oil and gas to local and international markets and thank God they were not able to achieve their goals."³⁰⁸ While the company also avoided having an oil spill, its business operations were significantly disrupted, and some critical drilling and production data were lost, affecting "risk assessment of key infrastructure worldwide."³⁰⁹

Shamoon also spread to the networks of other oil and gas firms. Two weeks later it hit ResGas, the Qatari natural gas firm, which is "the second largest producer of liquefied natural gas in the world."³¹⁰ American intelligence officials also hold Iran responsible for that attack.³¹¹

The regular Aramco backup system had been insufficient to prevent calamitous consequences. Specifically, "drilling produces enormous volumes of data, which is then transferred to a Saudi Aramco database center and filtered, with other data discarded. The filtered data is supposed to be manually backed up twice a day but, perhaps because it was Ramadan, there were no backups carried out for either drilling or production data. It's the filtered data that's important . . . and it's the filtered data that was lost."³¹² The hackers had "picked the one day of the year they knew they could inflict the most damage on the world's most valuable company, Saudi Aramco," because on August 15 "more than 55,000 Saudi Aramco employees stayed home from work to prepare for one of Islam's holiest nights of the year—Lailat al Qadr, or the Night of Power—celebrating the revelation of the Koran to Muhammad."³¹³

Even partially disrupted Saudi Arabian oil production can severely impact global oil supplies and prices, hurting the entire global economy.[314] Thus, it was precisely "the kind of cyberattack that most alarms national security specialists."[315] In the wake of the Aramco cyberattacks, Bulent Teksoz, Symantec's Dubai-based chief security strategist for emerging markets, said, "Everybody saw it's not just one company under attack. What we saw was the world economy [under attack].... Everybody started panicking."[316] US secretary of defense Panetta described the Shamoon virus as "very sophisticated" and expressed "tremendous concern" about its security impact.[317] He argued that among the viruses, "Shamoon was one of the first that can actually take down and destroy computers ... to the point where they had to be replaced."[318]

Response to the Cyberattacks

Aramco took quick defensive steps in response to the cyberattacks. Immediately afterward, "the company announced it had cut off its electronic systems off from the outside world to prevent further attacks."[319] Aramco chief executive officer Khalid al-Falih stated that "all of our core operations continued smoothly. Not a single drop of oil was lost. No critical service or business transaction was directly impacted by the virus."[320] He also noted, "We addressed the threat immediately, and our precautionary procedures, which have been in place to counter such threats, and our multiple protective systems, have helped to mitigate these deplorable cyber threats from spiraling."[321] He added that "Saudi Aramco is not the only company that became a target for such attempts, and this was not the first nor will it be the last illegal attempt to intrude into our systems.... We will ensure that we will further reinforce our systems with all available means to protect against a recurrence of this type of cyberattack."[322]

As soon as key Aramco executives "were assured that only the internal communications network had been hit and that not a drop of oil had been spilled, they set to work replacing the hard drives of tens of thousands of its PCs and tracking down the parties responsible."[323] After Aramco flew in about a dozen American cybersecurity experts, "within hours of the attack researchers at Symantec, a Silicon Valley security company, began analyzing a sample of the virus."[324] The executives' concern about Aramco's cybersecurity had originally emerged on February 24, 2006, after a failed terrorist attack on its petroleum-processing complex in Abqaiq.[325] Because of this earlier attack, Aramco "was well protected against break-in attempts over the Internet," but its "protections could not prevent an attack by an insider with high-level access."[326]

In the long run, Saudi Arabia and its Western allies have focused on preventing future similar cyberattacks. A year after the breach, "Saudi Arabia telecoms and Western IT companies have stepped up online-security offerings to deal with what they say is a surge of Saudi interest—and ongoing attacks on Saudi data."[327] Along with Saudi banks and other businesses, "government bodies ranging from the stock-market regulating Capital Markets Authority to Riyadh city government say they also have launched in-house, or contracted, efforts to protect their data against hacking since the Aramco attack."[328] This increased preparedness occurred because in several countries "many current and former government officials took account of the brute force on display and shuddered to think what might have happened if the target had been different."[329] The US government capitalized "on the fear created by those attacks to build on the de facto alliance against Iran that it has constructed in the region."[330] Nonetheless, regarding countermeasures against the perpetrator, "nothing was politically done or said by Saudi Arabia despite the massive expenses."[331]

Lessons for Improving Cyberdeterrence

Taking steps to isolate key operational components in private energy companies is a key lesson from the Aramco cyberattacks. Because "politically motivated cyber attacks that specifically target infrastructure occur more and more frequently and are increasingly costly for affected companies, Shamoon is a reminder that firms need to be alert to the possibility of such attacks."[332] More specifically, because no reports indicated Shamoon had reached industrial control system computers involved in drilling or refining operations, an "important lesson" for cyberdeterrence is underscored for energy companies "about the need to separate computer systems used for general business operations and those monitoring and controlling upstream and downstream operations."[333]

The Aramco cyberattacks also provided the lesson that seemingly vulnerable cybertargets can still often find ways to retaliate:

> The finger-pointing demonstrates the growing concern in the United States among government officials and private industry that other countries have the technology and skill to initiate attacks. "The Iranians were faster in developing an attack capability and bolder in using it than we had expected," said James A. Lewis, a former diplomat and cybersecurity expert at the Center for Strategic and International Studies. "Both sides are going through a dance to figure out how much they want to turn this into a fight."[334]

The danger of an escalating, pernicious, future cyber action-reaction cycle between Iran and the West appears to be quite high. Richard Clarke, a former counterterrorism official at the National Security Council, concluded that from Iran's standpoint "the attacks were intended to say, 'If you mess with us, you can expect retaliation.'"[335] Most broadly, for the foreseeable future, threat intelligence firm Recorded Future suggests that "Iran and Saudi Arabia, regional rivals in the Middle East, may be engaged in cyber warfare," using Yemen as a proxy.[336]

Syrian Electronic Army Cyberattacks on United States and Europe

Cyberattacks' Description

The Syrian civil war began in March 2011, when as part of popular Arab Spring uprisings in the Middle East, resentment bubbled up against Syrian president Bashar al-Assad.[337] Boosted by the collapse of Muammar al-Qaddafi's regime, in October 2011 protests erupted across Syria, with protesters chanting bold slogans such as "Qaddafi is dead; prepare yourself Bashar."[338] The Syrian government quickly engaged in massive retaliation "on a no-holds-barred basis."[339] "As opposed to Egypt and Tunisia, in which security forces largely held back from overt or widespread violent tactics, there seems to be little restraint from direct action against protests" by the Syria regime.[340] Moreover, "the Syrian government expelled foreign journalists and prevented international news networks like CNN and Al-Jazeera from broadcasting live coverage of the protests."[341]

As of June 2015 the Syrian Observatory for Human Rights reported that more than 320,000 people, including at least 11,493 children, died in the Syrian civil war and over 1.5 million people were wounded.[342] MercyCorps International reported that as of May 2015 over 4 million Syrian refugees had fled to Turkey, Jordan, Lebanon, and Iraq, and more than half of Syria's 23 million people needed urgent humanitarian assistance.[343]

The pro-Assad Syrian Electronic Army launched a series of cyberattacks on news websites and social media platforms, and it damaged information infrastructure in Syria, Europe, and the United States. In April 2013 the group "hacked the Associated Press's Twitter account . . . to falsely report an attack on the White House, which caused the Dow Jones to drop by 150 points."[344] Later that same month, the group broke into the British newspaper *The Guardian* (which was accused of "spreading 'lies and slander about Syria'") and corrupted its Twitter feeds after having targeted the BBC, France 24 TV, and

National Public Radio in the United States.³⁴⁵ In May 2013 Syrian citizens were denied access to the Internet for two prolonged periods.³⁴⁶ On August 27, 2013, the Syrian Electronic Army hacked the computer networks of major American media outlets, "knocking the *New York Times* website offline for 20 hours" by penetrating the company that handles the paper's Internet domain.³⁴⁷ Since 2013 the Syrian Electronic Army also has hacked the websites or social media accounts of CNN, *Huffington Post, Forbes, Washington Post*, and even Facebook.³⁴⁸ On January 1, 2014, the group broke into Skype's social media accounts, with the stated aim of exposing the video-call service's vulnerabilities to spy agencies.³⁴⁹ On January 19, 2014, the army hacked and defaced sixteen Saudi Arabian government websites, posting messages accusing Saudi Arabia of terrorism and forcing all of them to go offline.³⁵⁰ On February 28, 2014, the group "threatened to launch a cyberattack on U.S. Central Command" if the United States engaged in cyberattacks on Syria.³⁵¹ On June 8, 2015, the Syrian Electronic Army claimed on Twitter to have hacked into the website of the US Army.³⁵² Overall, the cyber group had broken into more than one hundred twenty websites as of 2014.³⁵³

The Syrian Electronic Army's methods include distributed denial-of-service attacks, spear phishing, pro-Assad defacements of websites, and spamming campaigns against governments, online services, and media hostile to the Syrian government.³⁵⁴ The group focuses primarily on very basic "gateway attacks" on publicly exposed Internet Web pages.³⁵⁵ Some bogus tweets in the SEA cyberattacks included anti-Israel sentiments and the slogans "Long Live Syria" and the "Syrian Electronic Army Was Here."³⁵⁶ Most actions carried out by the Syrian Electronic Army, which "American intelligence officials suspect is actually Iranian," have been characterized simply as "cybervandalism."³⁵⁷

In a key cyberinitiative supporting the Syrian Electronic Army's pro-Assad ends, it stole the rebels' documents and plans. According to FireEye, a California-based computer security firm, "between November 2013 and January 2014 . . . pro-government hackers stole hundreds of documents and thousands of Skype conversations containing battle plans, supply route details, and personal information from opposition forces in and around Syria."³⁵⁸ To accomplish this, the perpetrators used the "honey trap" ruse, in which "a hacker, using a fake Skype or Facebook profile, would strike up a conversation with a target and invite him to swap photos. The hacker's photo, invariably that of an attractive woman, would contain malware that once downloaded by the target would copy chat logs, tactical strategies, and contact details from the target's device."³⁵⁹

Cyberattacks' Attribution

While "hackers can relatively easily hide their tracks from all but the most extensive and time-consuming forensic efforts," the Syrian Electronic Army admitted responsibility for its major global cyberattacks.[360] However, the internal cyberattacks against Syrian citizens lacked accountability. "While the Assad regime claims the lapses were the result of a faulty network link, the evidence suggests that they were deliberate efforts by the government to hamper the opposition's ability to communicate inside the country and with the outside world."[361]

The Syrian Electronic Army is a decentralized group of young political hacktivists.[362] The group emerged in 2011, has its servers in Russia, and moved from Syria to a secret office in Dubai.[363] As the first public Internet army for an Arab country, it has "historic links to a computer society founded years ago by Syrian President Bashar Assad," and "the group is funded by Rami Makhlouf, a cousin of Mr. Assad's and the owner of SyriaTel, a telecommunications and Internet service provider."[364]

The Syrian Electronic Army's aim was "to cause disruption and spread support for President Bashar al-Assad's regime."[365] A group spokesperson said that "military intervention in Syria has many consequences and will affect the whole world. Our main mission is to spread truth about Syria and what is really happening."[366] In online postings, the hacktivists claimed "to be motivated by Syrian patriotism and to act independently of the regime in Damascus."[367] Cybersecurity experts contended that the SEA cyberattacks were "designed to disrupt and embarrass, and the group will likely target any site that might give it an opportunity to spread propaganda for Assad."[368]

A key SEA goal was preempting the US military's intervention in Syria, as the Syrian Electronic Army shut down American media websites in August 2013 only "a few hours after US officials indicated the US may launch missile strikes against the Syrian government."[369] Michael Chertoff, former head of the US Department of Homeland Security, called the Syrian Electronic Army a typical front group, saying, "Front groups such as the Syrian Electronic Army still provide states with so-called plausible deniability. Even if it is evident that Syria is behind an attack, they can deny it."[370] Western intelligence agencies believed that the Syrian Electronic Army was "essentially a proxy for an administration that has been widely condemned over its brutal efforts to quell an internal uprising," as the Syrian government publicly distanced itself from the group while privately supporting it.[371]

Cyberattacks' Security Impact

The Syrian Electronic Army's security impact was significant given the important role that a free and open access to the Internet was in Arab Spring uprisings. The February 2011 Egyptian uprising serves as a good illustration: "After the fall of Hosni Mubarak's government, as Salafists sought control by spreading propaganda through traditional media outlets, an Egyptian cardiologist-turned-satirist, Bassem Youssef, began broadcasting YouTube clips to expose their baseless claims... and... for Egyptians to question poor governance and radical theology."[372] The Syrian conflict has seemed particularly sensitive to possible cyber manipulation by both sides.

Although the Syrian Electronic Army's curtailing cyber access in Syria was temporary and intermittent, it handicapped opposition groups both in waging internal anti-government operations and in attracting external Internet-based support. Indeed, "throughout the conflict in Syria, rebels have used YouTube to foment outrage and to tell their stories. A sentence can tell you that blood flows in the streets, but a handheld camera can show it. Hactivists everywhere have rallied to the cause."[373] However, the rebels' resiliency and funding were decidedly inadequate without substantial outside assistance.

Despite its hacking feats, observers doubted that the Syrian Electronic Army had the kind of advanced capacity to seriously disrupt Western power, transportation, or basic needs infrastructure.[374] Indeed, the SEA breaches were considered just "annoying but not potential game-changers on the battlefield."[375] Others agree that "while SEA cyber attacks cause paralysis and disruption, they rarely cause substantial, irreversible, or lasting damage, and hacks remain more embarrassing than destructive."[376] Nonetheless, among several cybersecurity experts who believe the group's cyberspace threat "should not be dismissed," Bob Gourley, a former chief technology officer for the US Defense Intelligence Agency, for example, has asserted that "this is a very capable group that has done some very significant things against well-defended targets."[377] Timothy Sample, a cybersecurity consultant for US intelligence and defense agencies, argued that "the barriers to entry for these kinds of capabilities are very low" given that "it is easy to buy cyberattack tools and hire hackers on the black market. It would be dangerous to rely on the proposition that any given attacker lacks a particular skill."[378]

Response to the Cyberattacks

The West's verbal cyberattack response was speedy. It readily considered employing a form of tit-for-tat cyber retaliation that would minimize collateral damage and chances for perceived global illegitimacy. Some observers asserted that "cyber attacks could provide a bloodless, non-military alternative to the airstrikes being considered in response to the Assad regime's use of chemical weapons" and could "take down Syrian civilian and military critical infrastructures, such as the electrical grid, military command and control, and air defense systems," while others contended that "the use of offensive cyber attacks against Syria could help to repair the United States' image in the wake of almost daily revelations about its efforts to surveil and militarize cyberspace."[379] In another argument for cyberattacks, Jason Healey of the Atlantic Council stated that "the world is increasingly seeing U.S. cyber power as a force for evil in the world. A cyber operation against Syria might help to reverse this view."[380] Advocates of cyber retaliation suggested that American policymakers "should consider a military cybercampaign to give Syrians the ability to communicate freely online. Doing so would serve our strategic interests, while also demonstrating a principled commitment to Internet freedom."[381]

Such a response could entail US monitoring of Syrian rebel networks. The US military's Cyber Command "could create a digital 'safe haven,' akin to physical safe havens for refugees, by deploying long-distance Wi-Fi technologies along Syria's borders and in rebel-held areas in coordination with vetted opposition groups," thus allowing these groups "to link their terrestrial and wireless networks with those of like-minded groups" and "enable them to reach deeper into the country, giving broad sections of the Syrian populace Internet access."[382] This arrangement would allow the United States to monitor those networks and make them beneficial to moderate opposition elements. In theory, this kind of cyber response sounded quite promising.

However, despite intermittent Western military aid going to Syrian rebels, bold Western rhetoric was not followed up by decisive cyberspace action at least in part because "Syria and its ally Iran have been building cyberattack capabilities for years" and because the Syrian Electronic Army, having already demonstrated its capacity to attack American cybertargets, left no doubt that the group "could retaliate against anticipated Western military strikes."[383] Nonetheless, covert US cyber action might still be possible. As cybersecurity expert Adam Segal of the Council on Foreign Relations notes, "Any U.S. response to a Syrian attack might well not be visible," for the US Cyber Command can "reach back into attackers' networks and 'prevent these attacks from their source, . . . essentially doing defense through offense."[384]

Full-blown Western cyber retaliation could lead to conflict escalation. If the United States launched "a precision strike on Syrian chemical facilities . . . [it] might cause the SEA, perhaps in conjunction with some allies, to join forces and launch a wide scale cyber attack on U.S. media, e-commerce sites and financial institutions."³⁸⁵ For example, Frank Cilluffo, director of the Homeland Security Policy Institute at George Washington University, believes SEA members could readily launch another strike and with outside help: "If they did work with some of their allies—with Iran, if they were to get some support from China and Russia—then the game changes quickly."³⁸⁶ Moreover, should the United States strike first, "a cyber attack launched by U.S. military personnel of precisely the kind that the United States has said it would consider an act of war is unlikely to be seen as a humanitarian, non-military alternative to war. Instead, it will be seen as a contradiction at best, hypocrisy at worst."³⁸⁷ Notably, "if the United States attacks Syria, it will be the first time it strikes a country that is capable of waging retaliatory cyberspace attacks on American targets."³⁸⁸

Lessons for Improving Cyberdeterrence

Key cyberdeterrence lessons emerge from the Syrian Electronic Army's cyberattacks on the United States and Europe. Each highlights the West's inadequate preparation for this kind of breach. Part of the reason for its failure, however, is the atypical nature of SEA operations.

One lesson is that potential targets should never underestimate the ability of any group to engage in international cyberattacks. Although the Syrian Electronic Army is purported to have "only basic skills," it "could use its ties to Russian and Iranian hackers to improve."³⁸⁹ With the global availability of cyberweapons and cybertechnology, it does not take much for anyone to quickly develop requisite expertise for more sophisticated cyber aggression.

A second, closely related lesson is targets always need to be prepared for cyber retaliation when undertaking cyberdeterrence against a cybercapable country or group. Even when technologically superior targets such as the United States and western Europe undertake cyberdeterrence, a cyberattacker such as Syria could ask its allies to step in and help it to retaliate effectively. If the United States were to "engage in open cyber warfare and, say, knock Syria off the Internet," then it could trigger dangerous reactions from Russia and China.³⁹⁰

A third lesson revolves around the need for cybertargets to be more versatile in preparing for unorthodox attacks. For example, given the Syrian Electronic Army's disruption to the social media that the Syrian rebels used to attract and communicate with fighters and financial supporters in the war against Assad's regime, there should have been more inside and outside efforts to keep those channels open. According to George Tubin, senior security strategist at cybersecurity firm Trusteer, "enterprises need to constantly rethink their cyber defence strategy and deploy technologies that are capable of stopping these continuously advancing threats" because when the Syrian Electronic Army employs "advanced spear-phishing and malware attacks, . . . the current defenses in place at the compromised companies, and most organisations for that matter, are not enough to block such a resourceful foe."[391]

The Syrian Electronic Army's cyberattacks on the United States and western Europe convey some more specific technical cyberdeterrence lessons. If you are a target with highly valuable assets and ongoing vulnerability, you need to engage in "securing your servers, firewalls and patching your applications."[392] Perhaps "the two most critical technical countermeasures that people can use to prevent attacks by the SEA and similar groups are multifactor authentication and domain locking."[393] Multifactor authentication requires those accessing a targeted system to present multiple means of verification, such as both entering a password and identifying a picture or personal information, and domain locking prevents unauthorized third-party transfers of your Web domain to other parties. However, because the group learns through experience and thus morphs its attacks over time, resting secure even with these specific cyber protection improvements appears unwise.

Russian Cyberattacks on Ukraine

Cyberattacks' Description

Months of protest, including clashes from February 18 to February 20, 2014, involving about twenty-five thousand rioters with at least eighty people killed in forty-eight hours, rocked Ukraine.[394] On February 22, 2014, violent Ukrainian protesters ousted President Viktor Yanukovych and seized control of presidential administration buildings. A few days later the parliament named Olexander Turchynov as interim president. Even after the Ukrainian Parliament removed Yanukovych from power and he fled the country, he refused to resign, and politicians from the east and south (including Crimea) declared their continued loyalty to him. Russia also refused to recognize the new interim government. On February 27, special police units named Berkut—using armored personnel carriers, grenade launchers, assault rifles, and machine guns—seized key checkpoints and gained control of all land traffic between Crimea and continental Ukraine. Unmarked uniformed armed forces (later identified as Russian Special Forces) in the Crimean capital, Simferopol, seized the parliamentary building and the Council of Ministers building, replaced the Ukrainian flag with the Russian flag, and installed Sergey Aksyonov, a pro-Russia politician, as Crimea's prime minister.

With the Russian Parliament's approval, Russian military units began moving into Crimea almost immediately after former president Yanukovych on February 28 called for Russian president Vladimir Putin to restore order in Ukraine. In response to the Russians' presence, on March 3 Ukraine mobilized its armed forces and reserves. After the Crimean Parliament voted to join Russia on March 6, a controversial referendum on March 16 saw 97 percent of the voters choosing to join Russia, but on March 27 a United Nations General Assembly resolution declared the Crimean referendum invalid. Internationally, the United States, United Kingdom, France, Germany, Italy, Poland, Canada, Japan, the Netherlands, South Korea, Georgia, Moldova, Turkey, Australia, and the European Union as a whole criticized Russia for violating Ukrainian sovereignty, and several countries implemented sanctions against Russia. On June 7, Petro Poroshenko was sworn in as president of Ukraine, vowing to bring "peace to a united and free Ukraine."[395] In June Russia finally announced the temporary withdrawal of regular combat troops from the border.[396] In the end, "Russia's occupation and annexation of the Crimean Peninsula in February and March have plunged Europe into ones of its gravest crises since the end of the Cold War."[397]

In this wartime context, on March 7, 2014, Ukrainian security officials complained that "attackers are interfering with the mobile phone services of members of Ukraine's parliament," increasing the difficulty of reaching political decisions about how to respond to Russia's incursion into Crimea.[398] Around the same time, the communications channels of Ukraine's National Security Council and Defense Council, as well as the state news agency, suffered a "massive" denial-of-service attack that overwhelmed servers for several hours.[399] Initially the conflict in Ukraine experienced "only limited cyberconfrontation, with some small attacks from Russia on Ukrainian communications and media targets."[400] As the conflict progressed, however, the Russians "used a more traditional path of propaganda, misinformation, physical destruction and modification of telecommunications equipment, and cyber attacks, all integrated into a single campaign."[401] The alleged military goal of these cyber disruptions was "to isolate the region," and Russian naval vessels carrying jamming equipment blocked radio communications directed to the port at Sevastopol, reinforcing the Internet website attacks.[402]

Cyberattacks' Attribution

Cyber Berkut, a pro-Russia hacktivist group, claimed that it was responsible for blocking "the phones of more than 700 Ukrainian government officials, whom it describes as 'political traitors,'" and it attacked and vandalized over forty "websites belonging to government agencies and to protest groups that helped oust former President Viktor Yanukovych."[403] Cyber Berkut also said that it was responsible for DDoS attacks on an unsecured email server, that it "pelted NATO websites with online nuisance attacks designed to knock the pages offline," and that it sent several websites "into darkness for several hours" during the March 16 referendum on secession from Ukraine.[404] Some attacks against Ukraine "could be tied to two large criminal botnets—millions of computers worldwide that are infected and controlled by malware from cyber criminal gangs"—and on March 14 DirtJumper, a group of eastern European criminal botnets, included on its DDoS target lists "numerous pro-Ukrainian government websites, including Ukrainian news media outlets."[405] Director of security for Arbor Networks Dan Holden argued that the DirtJumper network of computers used in DDoS attacks "was created in Russia."[406]

The Russian government appeared to bear considerable responsibility for the cyberattacks on Ukraine. In April 2015 the Cyber Threat Intelligence Group of Virginia-based cybersecurity firm LookingGlass Cyber Solutions released a report claiming that a Russian cyberespionage campaign called Operation Armageddon has been in place since at least mid-2013 and was designed to provide Russian leadership a strategic advantage by targeting Ukrainian government law enforcement and military officials and coordinating cyber warfare and espionage "with kinetic warfare, battlefield planning, and troop movement."[407] In 2014 British defense firm BAE Systems reported that sophisticated Russian malware known as Snake, potentially linked to Russian intelligence, had been infecting dozens of Ukrainian computer systems for eight years. "Evading host defences and providing the attackers covert communication channels," it had the ability "to take control of computers, shut down programmes, steal vast amounts of data, and smuggle it out via the Internet."[408] The Snake malware, which appeared fourteen times in Ukraine in 2014 (far more than in previous years), was "a highly sophisticated espionage tool—after it has infected a computer, it buries itself deep within the existing system, concealing itself from all but the most sophisticated scanning systems. It can exfiltrate whatever information its operators desire, from personal emails to military plans."[409]

Notably, "many markers point to Russia as the malware source—time stamps left in the code and Russian names, for example"; and "western intelligence experts are quick to corroborate what the markers indicate. . . . Military sources say there is little doubt that Russia is using such malware to obtain up-to-the-minute operational intelligence about what is going on in Ukraine and that it is using it effectively."[410] Thus, both data corruption and cyberespionage were goals of the cyberattacks on Ukraine, as "Russia appears to be having a fine time covertly sabotaging Ukrainian networks" of communication.[411]

Cyberattacks' Security Impact

The cyberattacks on Ukraine were severe, but they could have been a lot worse in terms of their immediate short-run security impact. John Bumgarner, a former intelligence officer working for the nonprofit US Cyber Consequences Unit, argued that Russian cyber actions looked "mainly like skirmishing for propaganda advantage" and that "if Russia really wanted to deal a devastating blow, they could have definitely done it."[412] No serious damage was done, most cybertargets got their service restored in a matter of hours, and no critical Ukrainian state secrets were revealed through cyberespionage.[413] Russian moderation in cyberattacks on Ukraine can be linked to fear of cyber retaliation. As noted by senior expert Doug Madory of New Hampshire–based cybersecurity firm Renesys, doubtlessly helping in this regard was Ukraine's lower cyber vulnerability to a national blackout because it "is not like Syria or Sudan with just a few Internet lines. It is served by many ISPs [Internet service providers] with many independent land connections to neighboring countries."[414]

However, the long-run security consequences seemed more ominous. In Ukraine, "Russia's (re)annexation of the Crimea in April 2014 is a fait accompli and unlikely to be revised anytime, and the on-going support of separatist groups in the eastern parts of the Ukraine where the Russian-speaking minority is in the majority, such as Donetsk and Luhansk, has seen an increase in open military combat."[415] Moreover, the Ukrainians' long-term sense of security was shattered. Outside of Ukraine, the Snake virus's disruptive security impact was not confined; the malware also reared its ugly head in Lithuania, Britain, and Georgia, among other places.[416]

Response to the Cyberattacks

Given the earlier cyberattacks on Estonia and Georgia, according to Kurt Baumgartner, the principal security researcher at cybersecurity firm Kaspersky

Lab, the malware detections in Ukraine had "'maintained a heightened level on a weekly basis' since early 2014 when the crisis in Ukraine erupted."[417] However, these advanced preparations proved insufficient to ward off the wave of cyberattacks experienced later that year. Moreover, Vitaly Naida, director of information security counterintelligence for Ukraine's Security Service, admitted in June 2015 that "when undercover Russian troops first invaded Crimea last year, the Ukrainian government and military were wholly unprepared for the new brand of hybrid warfare they launched."[418]

Since the outbreak of hostilities, the West's response to Russia has been tepid. The United States imposed economic sanctions on Russia and "provided millions of dollars in non-lethal military assistance to Ukraine, but has stopped short, so far, of offering up weapons and other lethal aid."[419] Although NATO provided "trust funds" to help Ukraine "reform and modernize its defense capabilities," it refrained from responding robustly to the Russian assault at least partly owing to Europe's dependence on Russian gas pipelines.[420]

Even more than the earlier Russian hacker attacks on Estonia and Georgia, the cyberattacks on Ukraine precipitated a debilitating action-reaction cycle. Although before the Russia-Ukraine confrontation the two sides mostly had refrained from mutual sniping, "so far, the Ukraine cyber conflict appears to have pitted the strong hacker communities in each nation against each other in hundreds of attacks that have disrupted websites or e-mail systems, notably at government agencies such as Ukraine's parliament and the Russian central bank and foreign ministry."[421] When Ukrainians retaliated by hitting Russian government sites with denial-of-service attacks, then on February 28, 2014, "unidentified men seized several control centers in Crimea run by Ukrtelecom JSC, Ukraine's telecommunications provider, essentially cutting off the peninsula from mobile, landline and Internet services" and "RT (formerly known as Russia Today) was hacked by unknown assailants."[422] On March 17, the day after the disputed Crimea vote, "Russian government sites were hit with a powerful wave of denial-of-service attacks, apparently in response to cyberattacks on official Ukrainian sites," with "132 separate DDoS blasts slamming Russian sites," including "one that was 148 times more powerful than anything Russia did in Georgia in 2008."[423]

Although Ukraine is much weaker militarily than Russia, former assistant secretary of policy at the Department of Homeland Security Stewart Baker noted that Ukraine "has some talented hackers," and "if there's an area they can punch above their weight, it's cyber crime." Ukraine "is well known for harboring a large number of talented cyber criminals working for various organized crime syndicates. 'They've learned how to buy protection with the government,' Baker said, 'and the connections are pretty tight.'"[424] It is globally recognized that although Ukraine "is inferior in conventional warfare, they have phenomenal hackers who can steal intelligence from the Russians, intelligence that could become very valuable as the Ukraine reaches out for help from the international community."[425] Security experts noted that "much of Ukraine and Russia's cyberattack capability lies with criminal gangs, as well as so-called patriotic hackers willing to work for each country's respective cause," and they warned "that Kiev and Moscow are locked in a cyber stand-off."[426]

Lessons for Improving Cyberdeterrence

One lesson from the Ukrainian cyberattacks is that over time cyber aggression may be getting more complicated to deter. With regard to Russia, its cyberinitiatives seem bolder as time progresses. "The Putin regime cares far more about the future of Ukraine than it does about Serbia [1999], Estonia or even Georgia. Six years after those latter campaigns, the technical means and proxies used this time are likely to be similar, though more dangerous."[427] Since launching the 2007 Estonia cyberattacks and the 2008 Georgia cyberattacks, "Russia has invested considerable resources into building more sophisticated and potent offensive cyber capabilities, which would likely be deployed" in the future.[428] A cyberattacker may experiment with more refined cyberintrusion techniques and gradually find some that work, gaining confidence over time about putting them into practice against adversaries in a wider variety of circumstances. This gradual evolution of cyber sophistication in this case points to an upward slope in "how organized and well-funded adversaries are using highly sophisticated tools and techniques to target legitimate organizations on a massive scale."[429]

A second lesson is that outside cyber restraint can be encouraged through the external highlighting of target cyberattack resiliency. For example, "Ukraine hosts a decentralized critical information infrastructure network and is served by many Internet Service Providers." Its diverse Internet has "more than 200 domestic autonomous systems purchasing direct international transit" and "a well-developed set of at least eight regional Internet exchanges, as well as direct connections over diverse physical paths to the major Western European exchanges."[430] If a smaller state vividly showcases this kind of multipronged and redundant system of global network connections through compelling measures to a neighboring larger and more powerful state, it could possibly cause the larger state to hesitate before initiating a cyber disruption due to lower confidence that such cyberattacks would succeed in accomplishing their security-disrupting objectives.

A third lesson is that "'blowback fear' by cyberattackers is not as farfetched as it seems," for anticipated negative boomerang effects can indeed sometimes help to deter severe cyber disruptions. Because "a 'cyber knockout blow' will certainly have repercussions in Russia and other parts of the world, ... for now, both Russia and Ukraine appear to be limiting their cybercampaigns to minor exchanges mostly consisting of patriotic propaganda, low-key hacks, as well as physical protection and seizure of network infrastructures."[431] Russia could devastate Ukraine through cyberattacks, but it would then also suffer some negative security consequences. Fears about hurting themselves, unintended negative consequences, and escalating action-reaction cycles can lead to restraint by even powerful aggressors who find themselves enmeshed in cyberconfrontations and who possess huge kinetic advantages in the military sphere.

A fourth broader lesson from the Ukraine conflict, derived from earlier insights, is that cyberspace can help level the global playing field. Despite the huge military power disparity between Russia and Ukraine, throughout the conflict Ukraine's formidable cyberhacking capabilities managed to force Russia to experience pain at every turn. Having vastly superior military power may force a target into conventional kinetic military submission, as with Ukraine, but it may do little to restrain a tech-savvy target's strong and effective cyber retaliation. So countries such as Russia (and the United States) with large military capabilities that are used to winning coercive confrontations may find themselves facing a far greater challenge in the future when enmeshed in cyberspace conflicts involving adversaries with full cyber retaliation capabilities.

North Korean Cyberattacks on Sony Pictures Entertainment

Cyberattacks' Description

Triggering the November 24, 2014, cyberattack on Sony Pictures Entertainment (SPE) was its planned US release of the movie *The Interview*, "a crude and poorly reviewed comedy about a C.I.A. effort to hire two bumbling journalists to knock off Kim Jong-un, the North Korean leader."[432] In the summer of 2014, the North Korean government had publicly announced that the movie's release would constitute an "act of war."[433] Following the cyberattack, which was "routed from command-and-control centers across the world," Sony Pictures Entertainment confirmed that the perpetrators had "destroyed systems and stole large quantities of personal and commercial data."[434]

Given previous massive spear phishing of key Sony administrators, the cyberintrusion involved "the deployment of destructive malware and the theft of proprietary information as well as employees' personally identifiable information and confidential communications," and it "rendered thousands of SPE's computers inoperable, forced SPE to take its entire computer network offline, and significantly disrupted the company's business operations."[435] More than a hundred terabytes of documents were stolen, as no key components of the company's operations were protected.[436] The cyberhackers responsible, calling themselves Guardians of the Peace, demanded that the film's release be canceled or else violent terrorist acts would ensue. Responding to the threat, on December 17 Sony cancelled the theatrical release. After the cyberattack, the Guardians of Peace leaked some unreleased Sony films and confidential data to attract the attention of social media sites and to maximize their coverage of the embarrassing inside information. On December 19 President Obama rebuked Sony for its action, arguing that it should not have cancelled the movie and should not be intimidated by the threat.[437] On December 23 Sony reversed its course and, besides paid online viewing, allowed about three hundred mostly independent theaters to show *The Interview*.[438]

Cyberattacks' Attribution

The US government eventually concluded that the North Korean government was behind the Sony cyberattack.[439] "It took three weeks for Mr. Obama to take the extraordinarily rare step of publicly identifying North Korea, and its leadership, as the culprit; and even now, the F.B.I. refuses to release much of its evidence, presumably because it could reveal the degree to which the United States had penetrated North Korea's networks and the Chinese systems through which they are routed."[440] Cybersecurity expert Bruce Schneier argued that the National Security Agency "has been trying to eavesdrop on North Korea's government communications since the Korean War, and it's reasonable to assume that its analysts are in pretty deep."[441] The attack's motives may have included extortion, for on November 30, 2014, a message from the email address used to leak Sony Pictures' data demanded that the firm stop its "terrible racial discrimination and human rights violation" and "pay proper monetary compensation to the victims."[442] In response to accusations, the North Korean government completely "denied orchestrating the breach."[443]

The US government's pronouncement of the identity of a foreign state cyberattacker was "unprecedented, marking the first time a government agency has formally blamed another nation for a cyber attack."[444] This open accusation was, however, consistent with its actions earlier in 2014 when the Justice Department filed indictments against alleged Russian cybercriminals and accused five Chinese army officers of stealing trade secrets. "The increased finger pointing is part of a broad new U.S. plan for responding to cyberattacks, setting the stage for retaliation such as sanctions or trade complaints, according to current and former government officials."[445] John Carlin, head of the Justice Department's National Security Division, explained these actions by saying, "We need to improve our defences, but we also need to make clear the consequences."[446]

However, others disagreed with the US government's conclusion. "When President Obama laid blame for the Sony hack squarely at North Korea's door, some cyber-security experts were skeptical, and remain so."[447] For example, Marc Rogers, principal cybersecurity researcher at CloudFlare, argued that "if you look at the evidence that the FBI passed out in its notice, on its own, it's largely speculative and it's not backed up by any really solid evidence.... [U]ntil I see some tangible stuff myself, things more than just correlations between certain pieces of malware, I'm going to remain skeptical."[448] Similarly, Chief Executive Officer of Errata Security Robert Graham, openly "a vocal skeptic of the government's attribution," argued that "the government is divided on the issue, but that certain parties forced a public statement."[449] Reportedly, "intelligence officers initially wanted more proof of North Korea's involvement before going public."[450]

Furthermore, some cybersecurity experts believed that the cyberattack on Sony was an "inside job," implicating current or former Sony Pictures employees. Kurt Stammberger, senior vice president at cybersecurity firm Norse, strongly contended that "Sony was not just hacked, this is a company that was essentially nuked from the inside.... We are very confident that this was not an attack master-minded by North Korea." He observed, "There are certainly North Korean fingerprints on this but when we run all those leads to ground they turn out to be decoys or red herrings." He believes instead that "insiders were key to the implementation of one of the most devastating attacks in history."[451] Even senior US government officials admit that "there are still differences of opinion over whether North Korea was aided by Sony insiders with knowledge of the company's computer systems."[452]

Nonetheless, the evidence appears to be strongest that North Koreans were behind the cyberattack (possibly with insider assistance) owing to independent verification by outside experts. Dmitri Alperovitch, cofounder and chief technology officer at CrowdStrike, has tracked the cyberattack back to a North Korean group (active since 2006) that had previously launched DDoS and espionage cyberattacks against South Korean military networks, US armed forces in South Korea, and related US military installations while using some of the same infrastructure, IP addresses, and malicious code.[453] Steven Bellovin, Columbia University computer science professor, affirmed this view and contended that the US government reached its conclusion by carefully building a profile of North Korean cyberintrusions based on multiple pieces of evidence.[454] Regardless of the exact identity of the cyberattacker, Sony is "still trying to figure out whether its attackers had inside knowledge or just got lucky."[455]

Cyberattacks' Security Impact

Compared with previous cyberattacks on American businesses, "what made the attack on Sony different was its destructive nature. By some accounts, it wiped out roughly two-thirds of the studio's computer systems and servers," making it "one of the most destructive cyberattacks on American soil."[456] As the chief executive officer of cybersecurity firm Red E-Digital noted, this was the first time hackers "threatened large-scale physical violence."[457] Ultimately, the hacking of Sony Pictures became "an international crisis, the cyberattack that put Americans' vulnerability on display, a free speech cause, an Oval Office gut-check, and a cautionary tale for the future of warfare."[458]

The cyberattack's debilitating impact on Sony was significant. The company's computer network still had not been "fully restored" even eight weeks after the breach, and it had to allocate in the first quarter of 2015 $15 million to deal with cyberattack damage.[459] The impact has been even greater, however, on escalating public fears. "Many Americans were left wondering why their government was unable to detect and stop this foreign threat, and whether it can prevent others that may be even more serious."[460] Concerns about freedom of artistic expression proliferated, as "other countries or hacking groups could try similar tactics over movies, books or television broadcasts that they find offensive."[461] While "Sony's abysmal levels of network security" were partially to blame, the cyberattack on Sony triggered in many observers' minds the specter of "a shadow war of nearly constant, low-level digital conflict, somewhere in the netherworld between what President Obama called 'cybervandalism' and what others might call digital terrorism."[462]

As to the security impact on North Korean foreign relations, some analysts concluded that "this confrontation with the least predictable of the nine nations possessing nuclear weapons may not yet be over."[463] Indeed, "there may be legitimate reasons for the US, UK and others to be concerned about the rise of North Korea as a cyber power," for North Korea "clearly views its cyber capability as a key national resource perhaps gradually approaching the level of its nuclear aspirations."[464] Regarding relations between North Korea and Japan, it did not help that "Sony is the only studio currently owned by the Japanese, whom the North Koreans have hated since the Japanese occupation of Korea from 1910 to 1945."[465]

Response to the Cyberattacks

Until late December 2014, the United States appeared very hesitant to respond to the Sony cyberattack. "The president's temptation has been to refrain from responding at all; but the combination of the destructive attack, the effort to silence American criticism of a brutal regime and the threats of attacks on American theaters made this one different."[466] Outrage in the United States was quite high, for "North Korea's actions were intended to inflict significant harm on a U.S. business and suppress the right of American citizens to express themselves. Such acts of intimidation fall outside the bounds of acceptable state behavior."[467] US government officials said the policy change from inaction to a strong response was due to "continuing, serious intrusions; improved ability to pinpoint those responsible; and a desire to educate the public and companies about the problem's seriousness."[468]

Within hours of discovering the breach, Sony reported it to the Federal Bureau of Investigation and received its help in reacting to it.[469] Sony also sought and received assistance from the American private security firm FireEye. The goals of this aid were to identify the cyberhackers, repair the damage to Sony systems, and protect compromised Sony employees.[470]

At the same time North Korea was identified as the culprit, President Obama warned that the United States would "respond proportionately and in a place and time and manner that we choose."[471] Then within days, in what could have been direct cyber retaliation, the "North Korean Internet connection sputtered and went dead."[472] Although this disruption's source was never definitely identified, and thus the United States may not have been involved, "it is possible that to deter future attacks, the [American] administration was not looking for subtlety," and "instead it might have simply wanted to remind Mr. Kim that the United States is training 6,000 'cyberwarriors' among its military units, and they all have North Korea's Internet Protocol address."[473] However, given that North Korea's networks were "largely isolated from the outside world" and its electric grid was "not thought to be able to support a large technological infrastructure," the impact of this outage was minimal.[474]

Doug Madory, director of Internet analysis at Dyn Research, asserted that "it would make no difference to the country to just ignore the outage and leave the networks down for six months."[475]

In early 2015 the US Department of Justice began considering if it could initiate criminal indictments for the Sony attack.[476] Former FBI cybercrime chief Shawn Henry (now an executive at private security firm CrowdStrike) described this initiative and the comments by President Obama and other American officials about the Sony cyberattack as constituting "an attempt to define the 'red lines' in cyberspace. 'The destruction of physical property is not acceptable, and the U.S. can take steps to demonstrate what the response is going to be,'" said Henry.[477]

Finally, the US government imposed retaliatory economic sanctions on North Korea. On January 2, 2015, in direct response to the Sony breach, the Obama administration announced "new, if largely symbolic, economic sanctions against 10 senior North Korean officials and the intelligence agency it said was the source of 'many of North Korea's major cyberoperations.'"[478] However, as with the disruption of North Korea's Internet, most outside analysts agreed that the impact of these sanctions was low. "Obama's public response [to the Sony cyberattack] so far has been to slap sanctions on North Korea that appear unlikely to have much effect on the insular country," for "the sanctions imposed against North Korea are not going to change its regime nor improve its international behavior to any significant degree."[479]

Overall, the Sony cyberattack caught the United States without a carefully thought-out advance plan about how to protect a private company by providing secure protection of vital operational components. James Lewis, a cybersecurity expert at the Center for Strategic and International Studies, contends that "if there's a lesson from this, it's that we're long overdue" for a national discussion about how to respond to cyberattacks and about how to use America's own growing arsenal of cyberweapons.[480] For this type of cyberattack to constitute the trigger for probing reconsideration of American cyberthreat responses seems odd. Indeed, as one senior US defense official colorfully declared, "If you had told me that it would take a Seth Rogen movie to get our government to really confront these issues, I would have said you are crazy . . . but then again, this whole thing has been crazy."[481]

Lessons for Improving Cyberdeterrence

The North Korean cyberattack on Sony reinforces an increasingly widely accepted lesson that even in cyberspace, adversaries deemed dormant can awaken and pose significant threats. Frank Cilluffo, noted cybersecurity expert currently with the Homeland Security Policy Institute, argues that "precisely because North Korea has fewer constraints, I would underscore that it poses an important 'wildcard' threat, not only to the United States but also to the region and broader international stability."[482] Even a poor, distant country appears to be able to launch a cyberattack that effectively hits within the borders of the richest and most powerful state in the world without fear of certain painful retaliation.

Another lesson is that the global legitimacy of cyberattack responses may depend on transparency in the attribution processes of identifying perpetrators. The US government did not release enough convincing evidence to persuade key observers—including some prominent cybersecurity experts—that the North Korean government was the culprit in this case. After the US government made its case, several sources, including the *Christian Science Monitor*, advocated for increased transparency in the cyberattacker attribution process and claimed that "the US cannot create the global norms it wants by keeping information classified and only discussing the issues behind closed doors with diplomats, generals and spies. . . . Transparency of all sorts, and especially a public investigation, would be a strong step to prove that attribution is possible and help create stronger international norms."[483]

A key strategic lesson concerns the potential value of indirect pressure on supporters, sponsors, or patrons of cyberattackers compared with direct pressure on the cyberattacker itself. Although North Korea is inherently hard for the United States to restrain, China appears to be in a better position to do so given its close ties to North Korea. As Jason Healey points out, "When it comes to preventing the regime of Kim Jong Un from lashing out with cyberattacks, the path must begin not in Pyongyang but Beijing." Thus, the US government should "re-engage the Chinese to rein in their unruly ally. China could probably stop this directly and immediately if they wanted, as many if not most North Korean hackers work from inside China."[484]

The United States unambiguously intended that its response to North Korea for the Sony cyberattack would deter future cyberattacks. In addition to the economic sanctions and other measures, "the president's decision to also mention the Chinese during a news conference" about the Sony attack was "'itself part of the effort to create some deterrence,' one administration official said, 'by making it clear we can cut through the fog.'"[485] However, within the elusive cyberspace realm, this case illustrates the difficulties of such subtle cyberattack responses:

In that murky world, the attacks are carefully calibrated to be well short of war. The attackers are hard to identify with certainty, and the evidence cannot be made public. The counterstrike, if there is one, is equally hard to discern and often unsatisfying. The damage is largely economic and psychological. Deterrence is hard to establish. And because there are no international treaties or norms about how to use digital weapons—indeed, no acknowledgment by the United States government that it has ever used them itself—there are no rules about how to fight this kind of conflict.[486]

As cybersecurity expert Cilluffo notes, when it comes to the North Koreans, "like Iran, they are difficult to deter, perhaps even more so, since any form of cyber retaliation would have limited effect, given they are not a wired country and would have less to lose."[487] Moreover, "the effects of the 'name and shame' campaign remain unclear," and such a strategy "could also prompt other states to point the finger at Washington for hacks in their own countries."[488] Thus, the type of cyberdeterrence efforts that the United States initiated against North Korea may not restrain future cyberattacks.

Isis Cyberattacks on US Central Command

Cyberattacks' Description

On January 12, 2015, US Central Command, headquartered in Tampa, Florida, and overseeing US military operations in Iraq and Syria, had its social media Twitter accounts and YouTube videos hacked. Inserted into the Twitter pages were slogans expressing support for ISIS, the jihadi group that has "transfixed the world with its ultraviolent ideology as it swept through Syria and Iraq in a frenzy of bloodshed and destruction."[489] As early as September 2014, warnings from the technology security company FireEye and from NSA director Michael Rogers indicated that "ISIS's adroit use of modern technology is raising a new specter: cyberterrorism." They pointed to "signs that rebel terrorist organizations are attempting to gain access to cyber weaponry" and cautioned that "the U.S. needs to bolster its defenses against digital attacks from terrorist groups like ISIS."[490]

Similar cyberattacks supporting ISIS occurred before and after this incursion. A week prior to the CENTCOM disruption, ISIS hacked the websites of WBOC-TV, a Maryland television station, and of the New Mexico daily newspaper *Albuquerque Journal*.[491] On February 10, 2015, the same perpetrator hacked into the Twitter account of the magazine *Newsweek* and posted threatening tweets against First Lady Michelle Obama and women in the group Military Spouses of Strength.⁴⁹² In March 2015 the "Islamic State Hacking Division" published a "hit list" of a hundred US military personnel, including names, photographs, and addresses, accompanied by death threats.⁴⁹³ The following month ISIS released a propaganda video threatening to "burn America" in another atrocity like 9/11 and behead President Obama.⁴⁹⁴ In May 2015 the "Islamic State's Defenders in the Internet" released a video in which it threatened "crippling cyber attacks" against Europe and Australia as well as the United States.⁴⁹⁵ ISIS has launched cyberattacks against news organizations in France (taking over the French TV network TV5Monde for twenty-four hours in April 2015), the United Kingdom, the United States, and Iran in "attempts to eliminate the freedom of the press and manipulate the views shared by the media."⁴⁹⁶

The CENTCOM cyberattack allowed the hackers to control the CENTCOM Twitter account for about thirty minutes. During that time, the perpetrators posted "I Love you ISIS" atop CENTCOM's Twitter page, "tweets with lists and charts containing office phone numbers of current Army officers and email and mailing addresses of retired officers," and "what the hackers said were military scenarios for a conflict with North Korea and China."⁴⁹⁷ The perpetrators also issued threats against military officials. For example, one tweet read, "American soldiers, we are coming, watch your back. ISIS."⁴⁹⁸

Cyberattacks' Attribution

The initiator of the CENTCOM cyberattack was a group calling itself the Cyber Caliphate. Although most analysts believe that this group was directly linked to ISIS, a minority (including some US defense officials) doubt that the Cyber Caliphate had any genuine connections to ISIS.⁴⁹⁹ The reasons for their skepticism include the hackers' reference on Twitter to the acronym "ISIS"—which the United States uses but the group's members or supporters rarely do—and the obscure folk-punk band Andrew Jackson Jihad from the southwestern United States.⁵⁰⁰

The primary individual suspect for having led the CENTCOM cyberattack was Junaid Hussain, a Briton from Birmingham in his early twenties who was believed to be in Syria and to have aligned himself with ISIS.⁵⁰¹ In 2012 he had pleaded guilty and afterward spent time in prison for breaching former British prime minister Tony Blair's personal accounts, publishing Blair's address book, and initiating nuisance calls to a British counterterrorist hotline. Hussain also was believed to have "tweeted under the pseudonym Abu Hussain al Britani, posting tweets calling for violent attacks against Israeli diplomats and encouraging more recruits to travel to join ISIS."[502] Alex Kassirer, an analyst with a private company named Flashpoint Global Partners that monitors extremist Internet postings, reported specifically that "Hussain led efforts by ISIS to recruit hackers to the CyberCaliphate."[503]

Attracting such tech-savvy recruits to ISIS has long been part of the group's larger plan, and it has successfully drawn to its ranks elite hackers, "a group that often thrives on a challenge."[504] Some recruits became "virtual collaborators," while others moved directly to the battle zone in the Middle East.[505] Overall, "the dangers posed by ISIS may be more acute because of its embrace of modern technology, mastery of the difficult art of online propaganda and its appeal to young, computer-literate foreigners, including known hackers."[506]

Cyberattacks' Security Impact

Regarding the cyberattack's tangible, physical defense implications, the security impact was minimal. CENTCOM described it as "embarrassing but not a security risk."[507] Several outside analysts disparaged the cyberattack's long-term security significance, as affected networks were "civilian controlled and hosted, not Pentagon owned or run. No critical command and control networks were touched, nor, for that matter, were any of the military's internal or external computer networks that are used to move classified or even run-of-the-mill information."[508] Overall, the cyberattack seemed "more like the digital equivalent of graffiti in an entrance hall than a theft of sensitive files from the Pentagon. The information shared was widely available and non-official, and Central Command said that no classified information was divulged or operational networks affected, and it viewed the hack as 'purely an act of vandalism.'"[509] If in the future ISIS attempted more devastating cyber disruption, such skeptics contend that "ISIS hackers would likely find attacking a specific physical target more challenging than the propaganda hits that have been their focus so far . . . because they require more time and skills."[510]

However, the psychological damage wrought by ISIS's CENTCOM attack was significant, constituting for ISIS "perhaps its most dramatic publicity coup."[511] The cyberattack "handed the militants a public relations victory in a fight against the West taking place on battlefields and online." Ben Fitzgerald, director of the Technology and National Security Program at the Center for New American Security, said, "It makes the US military look silly. The Cyber Caliphate looks more technologically savvy than Centcom, which isn't the case."[512] US Central Command represents a pivotal cyberattack target for ISIS.

"While hitting sites and social accounts for small media outfits might not give the Islamic militants or their supporters much credibility, defacing Centcom is a different story. After all, this is the military command post from which the US oversees operations in the Middle East, where American forces have been battling IS [Islamic State] militants."[513] Even though the action was probably not linked to ISIS's core strategy, it constituted a "valuable propaganda moment" for the organization.[514]

The global attention generated by this cyberattack underscores the growing role of social media. As compared to physical action primarily on the Middle Eastern battlefield, "the ISIS flag got waved in a medium that more people in the West both notice and care about—the social media environment."[515]

> Just as social media plays a role in shaping real wars, politics, and business today, so does a hack like this signify more than bluster. This hack was highly embarrassing for US Central Command, all the more so for taking place at the very moment the President was speaking on the importance of cybersecurity. In addition, the likely low-level way the hackers got in is very embarrassing and likely consequential to whoever had the keys to the CENTCOM accounts (one imagines them now awaiting reassignment to the Arctic).[516]

Social media has become a vital tool in recruiting fighters to militant extremist movements. Matthew Olsen, director of the National Counterterrorism Center, said ISIS "views itself as the now-leader of a global jihadist movement . . . and . . . uses social media to secure a widespread following."[517] Indeed, ISIS leaders' "enthusiasm for medieval barbarity is matched by an equally fervent embrace of modern technology. They know that a hacker like Hussain, behind his laptop, is as intimidating to some of their distant enemies as the gunmen terrorising people on the ground."[518] Using Twitter accounts "controlled and operated from within Syria and Iraq and a huge network of supporters and propagandists further afield," the Islamic State's "skill at manipulating social media, for recruitment and projection of power, has been acknowledged even by enemies and rivals, who have poured resources into trying to dismantle, defuse—or in the case of other jihadi groups, emulate—its online success."[519]

The future security implications of the ISIS cyberattack seem ominous. Although this attack "reflects a wider online strategy apparently focused more on publicity than damage so far" and ISIS members had "not yet been extremely visible carrying out more sophisticated activities such as high-level cybercrime or more destructive attacks," their implementing these actions may be "just a matter of time" because they represent "a very low-cost way to publicise their cause and harass their enemies."[520] The CENTCOM cyberattack raised ISIS's viability as a prominent globally disruptive player. It succeeded in enhancing "ISIS's fight with its competitors in the terrorism game for funding, recruits, and attention," given that it is "a rival to al Qaida and rose to prominence as much due to its savvy use of social media as by its actual operations on the ground."[521]

The group's one notable constraint appears to be funding. ISIS has been "reportedly struggling with the expensive business of trying to run a state. . . . [I]ts coffers were flush with cash from oil wells, looting and hostage ransoms, but the oil price has crashed, the rapid expansion that made looting so profitable has slowed, and the captives are mostly dead or gone now."[522] Overall, however, the broad symbolism of "a big organization being shown up by the little guy is powerful, and resonates all the more when that organization is the US military, which has already spent $1.2 billion in the fight against ISIS."[523]

Response to the Cyberattacks

In response to this cyberattack, while publicly the US military shrugged off its significance, political concern and call for action led to renewed defensive efforts. For example, Rep. Michael McCaul (R-TX), chairman of the Homeland Security Committee, asserted that the CENTCOM attack was "severely disturbing" and warned that "assaults from cyber-jihadists will become more common unless the administration develops a strategy for appropriately responding to these cyberattacks."[524] Similarly, Senator Lindsey Graham (R-SC) said, "I don't think it compromises our national security but it should be a wakeup call for all of us."[525]

As a result, the Federal Bureau of Investigation launched a detailed probe of the cyberattack.[526] Former assistant secretary for policy at the Department of Homeland Security Stewart Baker notes that "security wasn't a high enough priority across the command," but now as US defenses against such attacks are likely to improve, "we should see less of these attacks because people should be more aware" and because companies such as Twitter and Google are offering two-party authentication tools to help prevent such attacks in the future.[527] Furthermore, during at least three occasions in early 2015, US military members were strongly urged to limit their social media use to keep ISIS-linked terrorists from tracking down their personal information and location.[528]

In addition to taking defensive moves to harden targeted assets, offensive cyber retaliation also commenced. Both Western governments, which created the social media platforms that ISIS uses, and Anonymous hacktivists have declared war on ISIS's digital presence.[529] Outside of the United States, in June 2015, a Europe-wide police force was formed to track down and block social media accounts linked to ISIS after an American study found that at least forty-six thousand Twitter accounts were linked to ISIS recruitment efforts.[530] In November 2015 the British also announced the formation of an "elite cyber-offensive force" to join the digital war on ISIS.[531] These aggressive responses to the ISIS cyberattack may actually have made some headway, for "after months of rampaging through cyberspace as they swept through Iraq and Syria," ISIS members have been "lamenting the devastating impact of these efforts to shut down their propaganda machine."[532]

Lessons for Improving Cyberdeterrence

One lesson from the ISIS cyberattack is that cybertargets need to guard against not just their adversaries' tangible security disruptions but also their successful social media propaganda. Although social media attacks do not directly damage critical infrastructure or directly degrade vital assets, corrupt vital data or systems, and hurt people or property, they do indirectly strengthen the attackers by expanding successful recruiting and by tarnishing the targets' image, making them look vulnerable. Social media has become "a vital channel for terrorist groups to share news and seduce new members. The recent, notable successes of ISIS in the United States and Europe have demonstrated that terror groups can successfully use this approach to further their agenda of violence."[533] Meanwhile, cybertargets rarely prioritize social media protection. For example, in the United States, "while the military spends billions of dollars a year to defend its computer networks against intruders, many of its social media accounts appear to lack basic security measures."[534] Certainly the Islamic State's effective use of social media suggests the need to raise this security priority.

A second lesson is a familiar one—the need for planning to prevent cyberattacks instead of relying on after-the-fact reactions. As is typical in cyberspace, the ISIS attack highlighted that "far too little is being done to analyse and prepare for the threat, by governments or the companies that run our power and our water, our transport, our banks."[535] Because cybersecurity improvements do not happen "until something goes wrong," the nimbleness of ISIS supporters makes this a dangerous waiting game.[536]

A third lesson from the ISIS cyberattack concerns how accumulating tech-savvy recruits and cyberweapons extends the reach of transnational terrorists beyond the otherwise predictable limits of physical operations on the ground. Although the May 2015 ISIS video threat that "soon you will see how we control your electronic world" doubtlessly goes too far, it shows that the digital scope of cyber disruption is expansive and hard to contain.[537] While many digital threats from ISIS have not yet been carried out, "its enemies should not be complacent about its capacities or intent."[538]

Notes

1. Schneier, *Beyond Fear*, 47.
2. Posner, "China's Secret Cyberterrorism," 2.
3. Thornburgh, "Invasion of the Chinese Cyberspies," 34.
4. Graham, "Hackers Attack."
5. Norton-Taylor, "Titan Rain."
6. Thornburgh, "Invasion of the Chinese Cyberspies," 35.
7. Krepinevich, *Cyber Warfare*, 32.
8. Thornburgh, "Invasion of the Chinese Cyberspies," 36.
9. "Lesson of Titan Rain," *Homeland Security News Wire*.
10. Thornburgh, "Invasion of the Chinese Cyberspies," 35.
11. Graham, "Hackers Attack."
12. Thornburgh, "Invasion of the Chinese Cyberspies," 35.
13. Wan, "China Continues to Deny."
14. Harris, "China Reveals."
15. Lindsay, "Impact of China," 44; and Graham, "Hackers Attack."
16. Thornburgh, "Invasion of the Chinese Cyberspies," 36.
17. Richards, "Denial-of-Service."
18. Thornburgh, "Invasion of the Chinese Cyberspies," 36.
19. Ibid.
20. Norton-Taylor, "Titan Rain."
21. Arthur, "US Accusations."
22. "Twelve Chinese Hacker Groups," *Homeland Security News Wire*.
23. "Chinese Government Hackers," *Homeland Security News Wire*.
24. Davidson, "China Accuses U.S."
25. Gross, "Enter the Cyber-Dragon"; Krepinevich, *Cyber Warfare*, 32–34; and Finkle, "Hacker Group."
26. Krepinevich, *Cyber Warfare*, 34; and McAfee Foundstone Professional Services, *Global Energy Cyberattacks*, 3.
27. Gorman, Cole, and Dreazen, "Computer Spies."
28. Arthur, "US Accusations."
29. "Chinese Government Orchestrates," *Homeland Security News Wire*.
30. Geers et al., *World War C*, 6.
31. "President Obama Upbraids China," BBC News.
32. Sanger, "U.S. Blames China's Military."
33. Mimoso, "NetTraveler Espionage Malware."
34. Arthur, "US Accusations."
35. Graham, "Hackers Attack."

36. Ibid.
37. Norton-Taylor, "Titan Rain."
38. Graham, "Hackers Attack."
39. "China's Sustained Cyberattacks," *Homeland Security News Wire*.
40. Ackerman and Kaiman, "Chinese Military Officials."
41. Nakashima, "Following U.S. Indictments"; and Stahl, "Great Brain Robbery."
42. Gross, "Enter the Cyber-Dragon."
43. Estes, "China Can't Stop."
44. Ibid.
45. Lindsay, "Impact of China," 9, 46.
46. "Lesson of Titan Rain," *Homeland Security News Wire*.
47. Ibid. Brackets in original.
48. Lewis, *Computer Espionage*, 2.
49. Ibid., 2.
50. Alperovitch, *Revealed: Operation Shady RAT*, 4.
51. Ibid., 5.
52. Masters, "Operation Shady Rat."
53. Gross, "Operation Shady RAT."
54. Ibid.
55. Alperovitch, *Revealed: Operation Shady RAT*, 6.
56. Sterling, "Operation Shady RAT."
57. Masters, "Operation Shady Rat."
58. Ibid.
59. Alperovitch, *Revealed: Operation Shady RAT*, 3.
60. Ibid., 2.
61. "Cyber Experts Dispute," *Homeland Security News Wire*.
62. Masters, "Operation Shady Rat."
63. Ibid.
64. Alperovitch, *Revealed: Operation Shady RAT*, 6.
65. Masters, "Operation Shady Rat."
66. "Cyber Experts Dispute," *Homeland Security News Wire*.
67. "'Operation Shady Rat,'" *Daily Mail*.
68. Gross, "Operation Shady RAT."
69. Ibid.
70. Masters, "Operation Shady Rat Reveals."
71. Gross, "Operation Shady RAT."
72. Ibid.
73. Masters, "Operation Shady Rat."
74. Alperovitch, *Revealed: Operation Shady RAT*, 2, 17.
75. "'Operation Shady Rat,'" *Daily Mail*.
76. Richards, "Denial-of-Service."
77. Ruus, "Cyber War I."
78. Herzog, "Estonian Cyber Attacks," 50.
79. Ibid., 50–51.
80. Jackson, "Estonian Cyber Policy," 2.
81. Holden, "Estonia, Six Years Later."
82. Ruus, "Cyber War I."
83. Traynor, "Russia Accused."

84. Richards, "Denial-of-Service."
85. Herzog, "Estonian Cyber Attacks," 52.
86. Richards, "Denial-of-Service."
87. Ruus, "Cyber War I."
88. Ibid.
89. Ibid.
90. Richards, "Denial-of-Service."
91. Ruus, "Cyber War I."
92. Shachtman, "Kremlin Kids."
93. Associated Press, "Look at Estonia's Cyber Attack."
94. Richards, "Denial-of-Service."
95. Ibid.
96. Herzog, "Estonian Cyber Attacks," 53.
97. Richards, "Denial-of-Service."
98. Herzog, "Estonian Cyber Attacks," 51.
99. Jackson, "Estonian Cyber Policy," 5.
100. Ibid., 3.
101. Greenemeier, "Estonian Attacks."
102. Ruus, "Cyber War I."
103. Kramer, "Cyberpower and National Security," in Kramer, Starr, and Wentz, *Cyberpower and National Security*, 14.
104. Davis, "Hackers Take Down."
105. Ruus, "Cyber War I."
106. Jackson, "Estonian Cyber Policy," 4.
107. Herzog, "Estonian Cyber Attacks," 54.
108. Hughes, "NATO and Cyber Defence."
109. Jackson, "Estonian Cyber Policy," 8.
110. Ibid., 2, 6, 8–9.
111. Ibid., 10.
112. McCluskey, "Estonia Redefines."
113. Tiirmaa-Klaar, "Cyber Security Threats," 2.
114. Richards, "Denial-of-Service."
115. Ruus, "Cyber War I."
116. Davis, "Hackers Take Down."
117. Nichol, *Russia-Georgia Conflict*, 3.
118. Cornell, Popjanevski, and Nilsson, *Russia's War in Georgia*, 5–13.
119. King, "Five-Day War," 2.
120. "Five Years On," BBC News; and Nichol, *Russia-Georgia Conflict*, 15.
121. Adair, "Georgian Attacks."
122. Hollis, "Cyberwar Case Study," 2.
123. Nazario, "Politically Motivated," 5.
124. Menn, "Cyber-attacks on Georgia."
125. Deibert, Rohozinski, and Crete-Nishihata, "Cyclones in Cyberspace," 18.
126. AFCEA, *Russo-Georgian War, 2008*.
127. Tikk et al., *Cyber Attacks against Georgia*, 9.
128. Markoff, "Before the Gunfire."
129. Oltsik, "Russian Cyber Attack."
130. Shachtman, "Top Georgian Official."

131. Claburn, "Cyber Attack against Georgia."
132. Tikk et al., *Cyber Attacks against Georgia*, 13.
133. Ibid., 12.
134. Morozov, "Army of Ones and Zeroes."
135. "Who Is behind Cyber Attacks?," *Homeland Security News Wire*.
136. Swaine, "Russia 'Conducting Cyber War.'"
137. Tikk et al. *Cyber Attacks against Georgia*, 13.
138. Deibert, Rohozinski, and Crete-Nishihata, "Cyclones in Cyberspace," 4.
139. Tikk et al. *Cyber Attacks against Georgia*, 5.
140. Hollis, "Cyberwar Case Study," 2; Oltsik, "Russian Cyber Attack"; and Lomidze, *Cyber Attacks against Georgia*.
141. Tikk et al. *Cyber Attacks against Georgia*, 15.
142. Ibid., 16.
143. Ibid.
144. Oltsik, "Russian Cyber Attack."
145. Tikk et al. *Cyber Attacks against Georgia*, 15.
146. Ibid., 16.
147. Weitz, "Russia Refines."
148. Hart, "Longtime Battle Lines."
149. Tikk et al. *Cyber Attacks against Georgia*, 14.
150. Libicki, *Cyberdeterrence and Cyberwar*, 105.
151. "War, Redefined," *Los Angeles Times*.
152. Nazario, "'Cyberwar' Emerges."
153. Kirk, "Estonia, Poland."
154. "Who Is behind Cyber Attacks," *Homeland Security News Wire*.
155. Keizer, "Russian Hacker 'Militia.'"
156. Hollis, "Cyberwar Case Study," 3.
157. Arnoldy, "Cyberspace: New Frontier."
158. Ibid.
159. Nazario, "Politically Motivated," 16.
160. Deibert, Rohozinski, and Crete-Nishihata, "Cyclones in Cyberspace," 18.
161. Hollis, "Cyberwar Case Study," 6.
162. Hart, "Longtime Battle Lines."
163. Otte, "Cyberspace and Propaganda."
164. "Hamas, Hezbollah," *Homeland Security News Wire*.
165. Pfeffer, "Israel Suffered."
166. Stoil and Goldstein, "One if by Land."
167. Lukasik, "Framework for Thinking," 103.
168. Pfeffer, "Israel Suffered."
169. Nazario, "Politically Motivated," 8.
170. Nazario, "Effects of War."
171. "Cyber War," *Alray Palestinian Media Agency*.
172. Otte, "Cyberspace and Propaganda," 6.
173. Fowler, "Hamas and Israel."
174. Pfeffer, "Israel Suffered"; and "Hamas, Hezbollah," *Homeland Security News Wire*.
175. Rudner, "Cyber-Threats to Critical," 458.
176. "Hamas, Hezbollah," *Homeland Security News Wire*.
177. "Israel Hit by Cyber Terrorism," *Israel National News*.

178. Cohen and Levin, "Cyber Infiltration."
179. "Anonymous Hacker Attack," *The Guardian*; and Cohen and Levin, "Cyber Infiltration."
180. "Cyber War," *Alray Palestinian Media Agency*.
181. "Anonymous Hacker Attack," *The Guardian*.
182. "Cyber War," *Alray Palestinian Media Agency*.
183. Dearden, "Anonymous Vows"; and Winer, "Annual Cyber-Attack."
184. Ackerman, "Israeli Troops."
185. "Cyber War," *Alray Palestinian Media Agency*.
186. Dearden, "Anonymous Vows."
187. "Anonymous Hacker Attack," *The Guardian*.
188. Kaplan, "Cyber Warfare."
189. "Cyber War," *Alray Palestinian Media Agency*.
190. Brewster, "Persian Paranoia."
191. Moskowitz, "Cyberattack Tied to Hezbollah."
192. "Hamas, Hezbollah," *Homeland Security News Wire*.
193. Rudner, "Cyber-Threats to Critical," 460.
194. Greenhouse, "Tweets of War."
195. Bryant, "Israel Establishes Cyberdefense."
196. Ginsburg, "Army to Establish."
197. Libicki, *Cyberdeterrence and Cyberwar*, 93–94.
198. Fitzpatrick, "Cyberattacks in Israel."
199. Libicki, *Cyberdeterrence and Cyberwar*, 114–15.
200. Zetter, "Report Strengthens."
201. "Stuxnet Worm," *Homeland Security News Wire*.
202. Zetter, "Unprecedented Look." See also Zetter, *Countdown to Zero Day*.
203. Krepinevich, *Cyber Warfare*, 62.
204. Zetter, "Report Strengthens."
205. Zetter, "Unprecedented Look."
206. Schneier, "Story behind the Stuxnet Virus."
207. Neuman, "As the Worm Turns."
208. Markoff, "Silent Attack."
209. Fildes, "Stuxnet Worm."
210. "DHS Official," *Homeland Security News Wire*.
211. Raymond, "Paradoxes of (Cyber) Counterinsurgency."
212. Clayton, "Stuxnet Malware"; and "Stuxnet Worm," *Homeland Security News Wire*.
213. Schneier, "Story behind the Stuxnet Virus."
214. Neuman, "As the Worm Turns."
215. Sanger, "Obama Order Sped Up."
216. Sanger and Erlanger, "Suspicion Falls on Russia."
217. "Israel Used Cyber Weapon," *Homeland Security News Wire*.
218. Frankel, "Skullduggery on a Massive Scale."
219. "Stuxnet Heralds Age," *Homeland Security News Wire*.
220. Broad, Markoff, and Sanger, "Israeli Test on Worm."
221. "Iran Admits Stuxnet's Damage," *Homeland Security News Wire*.
222. Markoff, "Silent Attack."
223. "Stuxnet Worm," *Homeland Security News Wire*.
224. "Iran Admits Stuxnet's Damage," *Homeland Security News Wire*.
225. Neuman, "As the Worm Turns."

226. "Iran: Stuxnet Infected," *Homeland Security News Wire*; Zetter "How Digital Detectives"; and Ball, "Secrecy Surrounding."
227. Lindsay, "Stuxnet and the Limits," 366.
228. "Stuxnet Virus," *Homeland Security News Wire*.
229. "Stuxnet Worm," *Homeland Security News Wire*.
230. Geers, *Strategic Cyber Security*, 13.
231. Barzashka, "Are Cyber-Weapons Effective?," 48–56.
232. "Israel Used Cyber Weapon," *Homeland Security News Wire*.
233. Markoff, "Silent Attack."
234. Ibid.
235. Clayton, "Stuxnet Malware."
236. Markoff, "Silent Attack."
237. Gross, "Silent War."
238. Albright, Brannan, and Walrond, *Did Stuxnet Take Out*, 7.
239. "Stuxnet Heralds Age," *Homeland Security News Wire*.
240. Lachow, "Stuxnet Enigma," 122–23.
241. "Stuxnet Worm," *Homeland Security News Wire*.
242. Ibid.
243. Ibid.
244. Ibid.
245. Sanger, "Document Reveals."
246. Markoff, "Silent Attack."
247. Rudner, "Cyber-Threats to Critical," 472.
248. Negroponte, Palmisano, and Segal, *Defending an Open*, 35.
249. Rivera, "Deterrence in Cyberspace."
250. Foley, "Anti-Capitalist Hackers."
251. Sanger and Markoff, "I.M.F. Reports Cyberattack."
252. Reddy and Gorman, "IMF Hit by Cyber Attack."
253. Wolf and MacLean, "IMF Cyber Attack."
254. Arthur, "IMF Cyber-Attack."
255. Foley, "Anti-Capitalist Hackers."
256. Wolf and MacLean, "IMF Cyber Attack."
257. Arthur, "IMF Cyber-Attack."
258. Reddy and Gorman, "IMF Hit by Cyber Attack."
259. Arthur, "IMF Cyber-Attack."
260. Sanger and Markoff, "I.M.F. Reports Cyberattack."
261. Crittenden, "IMF: Taking Steps."
262. Ibid.
263. Lee, "International Monetary Fund."
264. Riley and Rastello, "IMF State-Backed Cyber-Attack."
265. Foley, "Anti-Capitalist Hackers."
266. Lee, "International Monetary Fund."
267. Ibid.
268. Dalakoglou, "Crisis before 'The Crisis,'" 34.
269. Atkinson, "Transcript of a Press Briefing."
270. Sanger and Markoff, "I.M.F. Reports Cyberattack"; and Foley, "Anti-Capitalist Hackers."
271. Sanger and Markoff, "I.M.F. Reports Cyberattack."
272. Riley and Rastello, "IMF State-Backed Cyber-Attack."

273. Sanger and Markoff, "I.M.F. Reports Cyberattack."
274. Foley, "Anti-Capitalist Hackers."
275. Wolf and MacLean, "IMF Cyber Attack."
276. Foley, "Anti-Capitalist Hackers."
277. Arthur, "IMF Cyber-Attack."
278. Foley, "Anti-Capitalist Hackers."
279. "'Sophisticated Cyber Attack,'" *Al Jazeera*.
280. Sanger and Markoff, "I.M.F. Reports Cyberattack."
281. Ibid.
282. Arthur, "IMF Cyber-Attack."
283. Etzioni, "Cybersecurity in the Private Sector," 62.
284. Wolf and MacLean, "IMF Cyber Attack."
285. Morgan, "Applicability of Traditional Deterrence," 74.
286. Finkle, "Insiders Suspected."
287. Gross, "Silent War."
288. Bronk and Tikk-Ringas, "Cyber Attack on Saudi Aramco," 85.
289. Perlroth, "In Cyberattack on Saudi Firm."
290. Knickmeyer, "After Cyberattacks."
291. Bronk and Tikk-Ringas, "Cyber Attack on Saudi Aramco," 86.
292. Perlroth, "In Cyberattack on Saudi Firm."
293. Reuters, "Aramco Says Cyber Attack."
294. Rundle, "Hacking Group."
295. Finkle, "Insiders Suspected."
296. Ibid.
297. Bronk and Tikk-Ringas, "Cyber Attack on Saudi Aramco," 88.
298. Gross, "Silent War."
299. Agence France-Presse, "US Says Iran behind Cyber."
300. Bronk and Tikk-Ringas, "Cyber Attack on Saudi Aramco," 92.
301. Perlroth, "In Cyberattack on Saudi Firm."
302. Mount, "U.S. Officials Believe."
303. Bronk and Tikk-Ringas, "Cyber Attack on Saudi Aramco," 89.
304. Ibid., 81; and Waterman, "Obama Hits Pause."
305. Gross, "Silent War."
306. Lipscombe, "Fallout from the Saudi."
307. Knickmeyer, "After Cyberattacks"; and Finkle, "Insiders Suspected."
308. Reuters, "Aramco Says Cyber Attack."
309. Bronk and Tikk-Ringas, "Cyber Attack on Saudi Aramco," 81, 82.
310. Ibid., 81; and Mills, "Virus Knocks Out."
311. Perlroth, "In Cyberattack on Saudi Firm."
312. Roberts, "Cyber Threats."
313. Perlroth, "In Cyberattack on Saudi Firm."
314. Itzkowitz Shifrinson and Priebe, "Crude Threat."
315. Waterman, "Obama Hits Pause."
316. Knickmeyer, "After Cyberattacks."
317. Bronk and Tikk-Ringas, "Cyber Attack on Saudi Aramco," 82.
318. Panetta, "DOD News Briefing."
319. Fineren and Bakr, "Saudi Aramco Says."
320. Finkle, "Insiders Suspected."

321. "Saudi Aramco Investigating," *Al Arabiya News*.
322. Perlroth, "Connecting the Dots."
323. Perlroth, "In Cyberattack on Saudi Firm."
324. Ibid.
325. Bronk and Tikk-Ringas, "Cyber Attack on Saudi Aramco," 82.
326. Finkle, "Insiders Suspected."
327. Knickmeyer, "After Cyberattacks."
328. Ibid.
329. Gross, "Silent War."
330. Shanker and Sanger, "U.S. Helps Allies."
331. Nagraj, "Cyber War."
332. Bronk and Tikk-Ringas, "Cyber Attack on Saudi Aramco," 89–90.
333. Ibid., 86–87.
334. Perlroth, "In Cyberattack on Saudi Firm."
335. Ibid.
336. Blake, "Iran and Saudi Arabia."
337. Ziadeh, "Syrian Revolution," 43.
338. Blanford, "With Qaddafi's Death."
339. Jansen, "Syria Torn," 12.
340. Ziadeh, "Syrian Revolution," 44.
341. Ibid., 43.
342. Syrian Observatory for Human Rights. "320,000 People Killed."
343. MercyCorps, "Quick Facts."
344. Bergen and Maurer, "Cyberwar Hits Ukraine."
345. Hopkins and Harding, "Pro-Assad Syrian Hackers."
346. Finan, "Cyberattack Campaign for Syria."
347. Waterman, "Obama Hits Pause."
348. "Pro-Regime Syrian Hackers," *Homeland Security News Wire*; Waterman, "Syrian Hackers"; and Acohido, "Syria's Cyber Retaliation."
349. "Hackers Strike at Snapchat," *Al Jazeera America*.
350. Cohen and Levin, "SEA: How Real Is the Threat?," 2.
351. "Pro-Regime Syrian Hackers," *Homeland Security News Wire*.
352. Mosendz, "Syrian Electronic Army."
353. Cohen and Levin, "SEA: How Real Is the Threat?," 2.
354. Geers et al., *World War C*, 16.
355. Cohen and Levin, "SEA: How Real Is the Threat?," 2.
356. Hopkins and Harding, "Pro-Assad Syrian Hackers."
357. Sanger and Schmitt, "Hackers Use Old Lure."
358. Mendoza. "How Syrian Rebel Fighters."
359. Ibid.
360. Waterman, "Obama Hits Pause."
361. Finan, "Cyberattack Campaign for Syria."
362. Cohen and Levin, "SEA: How Real Is the Threat?," 2.
363. Hopkins and Harding, "Pro-Assad Syrian Hackers."
364. Waterman, "Obama Hits Pause."
365. Hopkins and Harding, "Pro-Assad Syrian Hackers."
366. Waterman, "Syrian Hackers."
367. Waterman, "Obama Hits Pause."

368. Hopkins and Harding, "Pro-Assad Syrian Hackers."
369. Acohido, "Syria's Cyber Retaliation."
370. Waterman, "Obama Hits Pause."
371. Hopkins and Harding, "Pro-Assad Syrian Hackers."
372. Finan, "Cyberattack Campaign for Syria."
373. Thompson, "Why Did Syria?"
374. Waterman, "Obama Hits Pause."
375. Sanger and Schmitt, "Hackers Use Old Lure."
376. Cohen and Levin, "SEA: How Real Is the Threat?," 2.
377. "Pro-Regime Syrian Hackers," *Homeland Security News Wire*.
378. Waterman, "Obama Hits Pause."
379. Lawson, "Overheated Rhetoric."
380. Ibid.
381. Finan, "Cyberattack Campaign for Syria."
382. Ibid.
383. Waterman, "Obama Hits Pause."
384. Ibid.
385. Acohido, "Syria's Cyber Retaliation."
386. Todd and Brown, "Syria's Cyberattack."
387. Lawson, "Overheated Rhetoric."
388. Menn, "Syria, Aided by Iran."
389. Lewis, "Arms Race in Cyberspace," A03.
390. Acohido, "Syria's Cyber Retaliation."
391. Winder, "Syrian Electronic Army."
392. Beilman, "Security Lessons."
393. Winkler, "My Run-In."
394. "Berkut Quick Response Unit," GlobalSecurity.org.
395. "Ukraine's Petro Poroshenko," BBC News.
396. Bachmann and Gunneriusson, "Hybrid Wars," 88.
397. Mankoff, "Russia's Latest," 60.
398. Bergen and Maurer, "Cyberwar Hits Ukraine."
399. Strasser, "Why Ukraine"; and Matlack, "Cyberwar in Ukraine."
400. Strasser, "Why Ukraine."
401. Healey, "Russia vs. Ukraine."
402. Paganini, "Crimea—Is Russia."
403. Matlack, "Cyberwar in Ukraine."
404. Bernard, "Russia-Ukraine Crisis."
405. Clayton, "Massive Cyberattacks."
406. "Russia May Launch," *Homeland Security News Wire*.
407. LookingGlass, "LookingGlass Cyber Threat."
408. "Russian Cyber Attacks," Channel 4 News.
409. "Ukrainian Computer Systems," *Homeland Security News Wire*; and Jones, "Kremlin Alleged."
410. Jones, "Kremlin Alleged."
411. Arnold, "Cyber War in Ukraine."
412. Matlack, "Cyberwar in Ukraine."
413. Ibid.
414. Clayton, "Where Are the Cyberattacks?"

CYBERATTACK CASE STUDIES   145

415. Bachmann and Gunneriusson, "Hybrid Wars," 87.
416. Sanger and Erlanger, "Suspicion Falls on Russia."
417. Strasser, "Why Ukraine."
418. Marks, "Ukraine's Intel Chief."
419. US Department of State, "Ukraine and Russia Sanctions"; and Marks, "Ukraine's Intel Chief."
420. Associated Press, "Romania Turns"; and Bachmann and Gunneriusson, "Hybrid Wars," 87.
421. Healey, "Russia vs. Ukraine."
422. Gady, "Cyberwar in the Crimea?"
423. Clayton, "Massive Cyberattacks."
424. Bernard, "Russia-Ukraine Crisis."
425. Rashid, "Hacktivists, Cyber-Spies."
426. Lee, "Russia and Ukraine."
427. Healey, "How to Beat."
428. Bernard, "Russia-Ukraine Crisis."
429. "BAE Report," *New York Times*.
430. Gady, "Cyberwar in the Crimea?"
431. Ibid.
432. Sanger, "Countering Cyberattacks," A3.
433. Alperovitch and Rogers, "Some Experts Question."
434. Sanger and Perlroth, "U.S. Said to Find"; and Federal Bureau of Investigation (FBI), "Update on Sony Investigation."
435. Kerner, "Sony Hackers"; and FBI, "Update on Sony Investigation."
436. Cook, "Sony Hackers."
437. "US President Barack Obama," BBC News.
438. Shaw, "Sony to Release."
439. Zetter, "Experts Are Still Divided."
440. Sanger, "Countering Cyberattacks."
441. Ibid. See also Zetter, "Experts Are Still Divided."
442. Zetter, "Experts Are Still Divided."
443. Viswanatha and Menn, "In Cyberattacks."
444. Zetter, "Experts Are Still Divided."
445. Viswanatha and Menn, "In Cyberattacks."
446. Ibid.
447. Alperovitch and Rogers, "Some Experts Question."
448. Ibid.
449. Zetter, "Experts Are Still Divided."
450. Viswanatha and Menn, "In Cyberattacks."
451. "Was FBI Wrong," CBS News.
452. Sanger and Perlroth, "U.S. Said to Find."
453. Alperovitch and Rogers, "Some Experts Question"; and Zetter, "Experts Are Still Divided."
454. Ibid.
455. Sanger, "Countering Cyberattacks."
456. Ibid.
457. Hamedy, "Sony Hackers."
458. Seal, "Exclusive Look."
459. Viswanatha and Menn, "In Cyberattacks"; and Frizell, "Sony Is Spending."
460. Kroll, "Cyber Conundrum," 9.

461. Sanger and Perlroth, "U.S. Said to Find."
462. Brewster, "Sony Needed"; and Sanger, "Countering Cyberattacks."
463. Sanger, "Countering Cyberattacks."
464. Brewster, "Sony Pictures Hack"; and Siers, "North Korea."
465. Seal, "Exclusive Look."
466. Sanger, "Countering Cyberattacks."
467. FBI, "Update on Sony Investigation."
468. Viswanatha and Menn, "In Cyberattacks."
469. FBI, "Update on Sony Investigation."
470. Seal, "Exclusive Look."
471. Healey, "In Response to Sony Hack."
472. Sanger, "Countering Cyberattacks."
473. Zetter, "Experts Are Still Divided"; and Sanger, "Countering Cyberattacks."
474. Brewster, "Sony Pictures Hack."
475. Zetter, "Experts Are Still Divided."
476. Viswanatha and Menn, "In Cyberattacks."
477. Ibid.
478. Sanger and Schmidt, "More Sanctions."
479. Viswanatha and Menn, "In Cyberattacks"; and Caulderwood, "Sony Hack."
480. Sanger, "Countering Cyberattacks."
481. Ibid.
482. Siers, "North Korea," 11.
483. Healey, "In Response to Sony Hack."
484. Ibid.
485. Sanger, "Countering Cyberattacks."
486. Ibid.
487. Brewster, "Sony Pictures Hack."
488. Viswanatha and Menn, "In Cyberattacks."
489. Graham-Harrison, "Could Isis's 'Cyber Caliphate.'"
490. Frizell, "Experts Doubt ISIS."
491. Maza, "Centcom Twitter Hack."
492. Martinez, "Cyberwar: CyberCaliphate."
493. "Islamic State Calls," Reuters.
494. Moore, "ISIS Threaten America."
495. Paganini, "ISIS—Cyber Caliphate."
496. Herberger, "Cyber Attacks."
497. Barnes and Yadron, "Islamic Hack," A1.
498. Ibid.
499. Ibid.
500. Siegel and Youssef, "No, the Pentagon Wasn't."
501. MacAskill, "Briton Lead Suspect."
502. Ibid.
503. Ibid.
504. Graham-Harrison, "Could Isis's 'Cyber Caliphate.'"
505. Ibid.
506. Ibid.
507. MacAskill, "Briton Lead Suspect."
508. Singer, "It Doesn't Really Matter."

509. Graham-Harrison, "Could Isis's 'Cyber Caliphate.'"
510. Ibid.
511. Ibid.
512. Maza, "Centcom Twitter Hack."
513. Ibid.
514. Singer, "It Doesn't Really Matter."
515. Ibid.
516. Ibid.
517. Maza, "Centcom Twitter Hack."
518. Graham-Harrison, "Could Isis's 'Cyber Caliphate.'"
519. "Islamic State Web Accounts," BBC News; and Graham-Harrison, "Could Isis's 'Cyber Caliphate.'"
520. Graham-Harrison, "Could Isis's 'Cyber Caliphate.'"
521. Singer, "It Doesn't Really Matter."
522. Graham-Harrison, "Could Isis's 'Cyber Caliphate.'"
523. Singer, "It Doesn't Really Matter."
524. Barnes and Yadron, "Islamic Hack."
525. Siegel and Youssef, "No, the Pentagon Wasn't."
526. Maza, "Centcom Twitter Hack."
527. Ibid.
528. Schuppe, "ISIS 'Hit List.'"
529. Graham-Harrison, "Could Isis's 'Cyber Caliphate.'"
530. "Islamic State Web Accounts," BBC News.
531. Condliffe, "British 'Elite Cyber.'"
532. Graham-Harrison, "Could Isis's 'Cyber Caliphate.'"
533. "Countering Extremist Groups," *Homeland Security News Wire*.
534. Barnes and Yadron, "Islamic Hack."
535. Graham-Harrison, "Could Isis's 'Cyber Caliphate.'"
536. Singer, "It Doesn't Really Matter."
537. Gander, "Pro-Isis 'Hackers.'"
538. Graham-Harrison, "Could Isis's 'Cyber Caliphate.'"

CHAPTER 5

Case Study Patterns

Isolating cyberdeterrence patterns in the case studies is challenging due to the sketchiness of some of the details and to the inappropriateness of many of the targets' responses. Nonetheless, this chapter identifies the most significant case insights relevant to cyberdeterrence. This discussion begins with direct, empirically derived conditions promoting cyberattack success, and then it moves to more indirect cyberdeterrence case lessons.

Tables 5.1, 5.2, 5.3, and 5.4 provide data for the twenty elements of the twelve case profiles, with patterns seeming generalizable because the cases are representative of twenty-first-century foreign cyberattacks with major security implications. For the cyberattack cases, the data is broken into four categories: (1) the *background attributes* of initiator identity, initiator type, target identity, target type, and disruption dates; (2) the *initiator stimuli* of security goal, confrontation trigger, attack method, attribution clarity, and violence presence; (3) the *target responses* of cyber capacity, power disadvantage (of targets compared to initiators), cyber dependence, long-run reaction, and outside aid; and (4) the *strategic outcomes* of attack indirectness, security impact (short-run), tit-for-tat cycle, conflict contagion, and threat persistence.

Notable case breach patterns emerged. For cyberattackers, while their attribution was consistently low, most appeared to be non-state groups—including two recognized terrorist groups—working alone or indirectly with the hidden complicity of ethnically connected authoritarian state sponsors. Russia chose mostly to pursue security influence through cyberespionage against political and military targets, while China at least in recent years has chosen to pursue economic gain through cybertheft of intellectual property and financial account information.[1] Although the attack methods were similar, the policy ends differed. Most initiator goals focused on cyberespionage, crippling government functioning, or reducing government autonomy. In terms of initiator attack methods, social media often played an important role as a facilitator, with denial of service (referred to by some as a "cyber blockade"[2]), data corruption or theft, and website defacement as the disruption modes of choice. Some initiators emphasized propaganda and recruitment, while others focused on

TABLE 5.1.
CYBERATTACK CASE BACKGROUND ATTRIBUTES

Case Name	Initiator Identity	Initiator Type	Target Identity	Target Type	Disruption Date
Aramco Attack	"Cutting Sword of Justice" Hacktivists	Non-state Group, Iranian Support	Saudi Arabian Oil Producer	Civilian Oil Company	August 2012
Estonia Attack	Russian Hackers Nashi Youth Group	Non-state Group, Russian Support	Estonia	Government Business	April–May 2007
Gaza Attack	Hamas/Hezbollah Hacktivists	Non-state Criminal Terrorist Groups	Israel	Government Internet Infrastructure	January 2009
Georgia Attack	Russian Hackers	Non-state Criminal Group, Russian Support	Georgia	Government Websites Network Infrastructure	Summer 2008
IMF Attack	Anonymous Hacktivists	Non-state Group	IMF	Intergovernmental Body Website	June 2011
ISIS Attack	"Cyber Caliphate" Hacktivists	Non-state Terrorist Group	US CENTCOM	Government Military Defense Infrastructure	January 2015
Shady RAT Attack	China	National Government	International Groups, Several States	Intergovernmental Bodies Governments/Businesses	Mid-2006
Sony Attack	"Guardians of the Peace" Hacktivists	Non-state Group, North Korean Support	Sony Pictures Entertainment	Civilian Movie Company	November 2014
Stuxnet Attack	United States, Israel	National Governments	Iran	Government Military Nuclear Program	July–August 2010
SEA Attack	Syrian Hacktivists	Non-state Group, Syrian Support	Syrian Opposition, US, Western Europe	News Websites, Social Media Platforms	April 2013– the present
Titan Rain Attack	Chinese Hacktivists	Non-state Group	United States	Government, Military Defense Contractors	2003–7
Ukraine Attack	Russian Hacktivists "Cyber Berkut"	Non-state Group, Russian Support	Ukraine	Government State News Agency	March 2014– the present

data acquisition or immobilization. For cyberdefenders, most exhibited little internal disagreement, did not have a reputation for successful retaliation, and were cyber dependent and associated with Western or Western-sympathizing states. Two targets were international organizations, and two others were businesses. The record of targets receiving effective outside aid was highly uneven, and targets differed in their internal and external openness regarding their cyberattacks and cyber vulnerabilities.

For strategic outcomes, most cases exhibited attack indirectness and follow-up action-reaction cycles, with a substantial number evidencing conflict contagion; and in all cases short-term cyber disruption occurred, even if long-run success was questionable. Half of the cyberattacks transpired at the same time as real-world physical violence between adversaries. Nobody died as a direct result of a cyberattack, and no property or even substantial data was permanently and irrevocably lost. So up to this point real "boots-on-the-ground" warfare involving shooting and killing has been considerably more devastating than cyberconflict. However, one caveat here is that in terms of human security effects on the mass public (as is particularly evident in the Estonia, Sony Pictures Entertainment, and ISIS cyberattacks), many of the cases suggest cyberattacks have the potential at least to cause the same widespread debilitating psychological effects regarding fear and loss of confidence—including crippling the ability of an entire country or system to function—as do more narrowly focused kinetic land, air, sea, and space attacks that heavily concentrate on government soldiers and military installations.

Case Circumstances Promoting Cyberattack Success

Intriguing patterns of cyberattack success directly derive from the cases. What determines the comparative credibility of threat in each case? How does the basis for credibility differ across the threat categories and across perceiving parties? What is the key to establishing long-term, consistent, credible deterrence in the face of cyberthreat? When is allied intervention most and least helpful in cyberdeterrence? In considering these questions, for particular targets the relative difficulty of cyberdeterrence is a function of the costs of cyber protection, the agility of the cyberattackers, and the severity and persistence of the outside cyberthreats. Figure 5.1 summarizes the direct empirically derived patterns of cyberattacker and cybertarget attributes associated with breach success.

TABLE 5.2.
CYBERATTACK CASE INITIATOR STIMULI

Case Name	Security Goal	Confrontation Trigger	Attack Method	Attribution Clarity	Violence Presence
Aramco Attack	Disrupt Western Oil Supply	Stuxnet Attack and Saudi Support of Bahraini Regime	Data Corruption or Erasure, Insert Virus	Medium	No
Estonia Attack	Cyberespionage, Lower Estonian Autonomy	Upset over Move of Russian War Hero Statue	Denial of Service via Hijacked Computers	Medium	Yes—Internal Rioting by Ethnic Russians
Gaza Attack	Cripple Israeli Government	Israeli Military Campaign in the Gaza Strip	Denial of Service, Website Defacement	Low	Yes—Israeli Palestinian Conflict over Gaza
Georgia Attack	Cyberespionage, Lower Georgian Autonomy	Georgia Pushes for Closer Ties with the West	Denial of Service, Stealing Data, Website Defacement	Medium	Yes—Russian Invasion of Georgia
IMF Attack	Cyberespionage, Cripple Organization	Controversial Greek Government Bailout	Data Corruption/Stealing via Spear Phishing	Low	No
ISIS Attack	Cripple US Military	US Military Support for Anti-ISIS Middle Eastern Fighters	Twitter Account Defacement	Medium	Yes—War to Maintain ISIS Territory Control
Shady RAT Attack	Cyberespionage	Desire to Uncover Political Secrets	Stealing Political and Military Data	Medium	No
Sony Attack	Prevent Subversive Film's Release	Scheduled Christmas Subversive Movie Showing	Malware Insertion and Data Theft	Medium	No
Stuxnet Attack	Slow Iranian Nuclear Development	Fear of Iranian Nuclear Dangers Being Realized	Data Corruption via Worm Insertion	Medium	No
SEA Attack	Defeat Internal Rebellion	Western Support for Syrian Rebels	Denial of Service, Stealing Data, Social Media Hacks	High	Yes—Syrian Civil War
Titan Rain Attack	Cyberespionage	Desire to Grab US Military Technology	Stealing Political and Military Data	Medium	No
Ukraine Attack	Cyberespionage, Lower Ukrainian Autonomy	Desire to Assert Russian Hegemony	Denial of Service, Disrupting Phones, Website Defacement	Medium	Yes—Russian Invasion of Ukraine

TABLE 5.3.
CYBERATTACK CASE TARGET RESPONSES

Case Name	Cyber Capacity	Power Disadvantage	Cyber Dependence	Long-Run Reaction	Outside Aid
Aramco Attack	High	Medium—Iran Slight Advantage	High	Recognition of Vulnerability	Yes—Saudi Arabian Government Help
Estonia Attack	Medium	High—Russia Advantage	Very High	Cyber Alliance Formation	Yes—NATO Help
Gaza Attack	High	Low—Israel Advantage	High	Increased Cyberoffensive Acts	No
Georgia Attack	Low	High—Russia Advantage	Medium	Desire to Link Up to the West	Yes—US, Estonia, and Poland Help
IMF Attack	Low	Unknown	High	Cyber Alliance Promotion	Yes—US and World Bank Help
ISIS Attack	High	Low—US Advantage	High	Vital Asset Hardening Offensive Interference	No—Others Respond Separately
Shady RAT Attack	High	Low—Targets' Advantage	High	Distrust and Vigilance	No
Sony Attack	Medium	Low—US Advantage	High	Cyber Retaliation and Economic Sanctions Increased	Yes—US
Stuxnet Attack	Medium	High—US and Israel Advantage	Medium	Cyber Protection	Yes—US Government Help
SEA Attack	High	Low—US and Europe Advantage	High	Increased Funding of Syrian Rebels	Yes—US Help to Syrian Rebels
Titan Rain Attack	High	Low—US Advantage	High	Distrust and Vigilance	No
Ukraine Attack	Medium	High—Russia Advantage	Medium	Increased Support from the West	Yes—US and NATO Help

TABLE 5.4.
CYBERATTACK CASE STRATEGIC OUTCOMES

Case Name	Attack Indirectness	Security Impact	Tit-for-Tat Cycle	Conflict Contagion	Threat Persistence
Aramco Attack	High—Iran Uses Aramco to Get Back at West	Medium	High	High—Virus Spread to Other Oil and Gas Firms	Low
Estonia Attack	Medium—Russia Uses Hackers to Get Back at Estonia	High	Medium	Medium—Georgia and Ukraine Hit Much Later	Medium
Gaza Attack	High—Hamas Uses Criminals to Get Back at Israel	Medium	High	Low	High
Georgia Attack	Medium—Russia Uses Hackers to Get Back at Georgia	High	Medium	Medium—Ukraine Hit Much Later	Medium
IMF Attack	High—Anonymous Attacks IMF to Protest Greek Bailout	Medium	Low	Low	Low
ISIS Attack	Low—ISIS Directly Defaces CENTCOM Twitter Account	Low	Medium	Medium—Threats to Europe and Australia	High
Shady RAT Attack	Low—Chinese Government Directly Steals American Data	Low	Low	High—Many Countries Hit	Low
Sony Attack	Medium—North Korea Uses Hackers to Get Back at Sony	Medium	Medium	Low	Low
Stuxnet Attack	Low—Israel and US Directly Disrupt Iran's Nuclear Program	High	High—Aramco Strike	High—Worldwide Spread of Virus	High
SEA Attack	Medium—Syria Uses Hackers to Get Back at Rebels	Medium	High	Medium—Saudi Arabian Websites Hit	High
Titan Rain Attack	Medium—China Uses Hackers to Steal US Data	Medium	High	High—US Allies Hit	High
Ukraine Attack	Medium—Russia Uses Hackers to Get Back at Ukraine	Medium	High	Low	High

FIGURE 5.1.
Circumstances Promoting Cyberattack Success

CYBERATTACKER ATTRIBUTES
Possess an asymmetrical cybertechnology advantage relative to target defenses
Have really high-quality intelligence on intended targets
Use strong ethnic ties to a loyal segment of the population inhabiting intended targets
Garner credible collaboration and support from several other state or non-state parties
Choose strategies that minimize chances of retaliation and mutual conflict escalation
Maintain high capacity for long-term persistence in cyberattacks against intended targets

CYBERTARGET ATTRIBUTES
Are totally dependent on externally controllable Internet links for their functioning
Have valued assets but are weak or cannot respond with real-world sanctions
Rely on static cyberdefenses
Have done little advanced planning or preparation for protecting against cyberattacks
Manifest sharp internal disagreements about how to respond
Are located within cyberattackers' established legitimate regional sphere of influence

Cyberattacker Attributes Promoting Cyberattack Success

Cyberattacks work best when the cyberattacker has the following attributes: (1) an asymmetrical advantage in terms of vastly superior offensive cybertechnology capabilities relative to target defenses, (2) really high-quality intelligence on intended cybertargets, (3) strong ethnic ties to a segment of the population living within a target, (4) credible collaboration and support from several other state or non-state parties, (5) prudent strategies that minimize chances of retaliation and mutual conflict escalation, and (6) a high capacity for long-term persistence in cyberattacks against intended targets. Each attribute highlights a dimension where the target's existing cyberdeterrence policies have proven to be inadequate, where considerable innovation is needed for improved cyberdeterrence, and where even its concerted cyberdefense efforts might be overcome.

In terms of asymmetrical advantage, an aggressor with vastly superior cybertechnology capabilities relative to target defenses is more likely to wage successful cyberattacks because its greater understanding of how cyberthreat, cyberattacks, and cyber reprisals work give the aggressor less reason to fear retaliation. This logic particularly applies to mobile, tech-savvy non-state groups confronting more powerful state targets. The cyberattacks by Anonymous on the International Monetary Fund vividly illustrate this pattern.

Next, a cyberattacker with really high-quality intelligence (based on external spying or insider information) on intended cybertargets is more likely to wage successful aggression. Such sensitive intelligence makes it possible to pinpoint areas within a target that are most closely tied to critical infrastructure functioning, most valuable in terms of assets that could be penetrated, and most vulnerable to cyberattack. "Diligent and persistent intelligence on the target" can really pay off here.[3] Three examples of quality intelligence facilitating successful cyber disruption are the Stuxnet case, in which Israel and the United States together developed considerable intelligence on Iranian nuclear facilities; the highly sophisticated Titan Rain operation, in which Chinese military hackers penetrated "systems without committing any keystroke errors or leaving digital fingerprints" and created "a clean backdoor exit, all in under 20 minutes," demonstrating competences that "are comparable to the best demonstrated by militaries or intelligence agencies with advanced cyber skills"; and the Sony cyberattack, in which the North Koreans' advanced spear phishing gave them all the access they needed.[4]

The probability of cyberattack success increases when a cyberattacker has strong ethnic ties to a segment of the population living within a target. The support that outside Russian hackers received from loyal ethnic Russian populations in Estonia, Georgia, and Ukraine illustrates this pattern. "When combined with satellite television, the wide availability of Russian-language publications, and a plethora of Internet forums, these elements of globalization have enabled the Russian ethnic identity to transcend geopolitical borders" in facilitating cyberattacks.[5] The initiators of the cyberattacks on Israel in the Gaza Strip confrontation were also able to take advantage of their ethnic and religious ties linked to Hamas.[6] Overall, in many international cyber disruptions, "the attacker is able to employ classic guerilla warfare tactics to grow their size and power through the use of propaganda that appeals to an ethnic or national base."[7]

As to credible collaboration and support from other parties, this outside involvement allows a cyberdisruptor to launch multipronged cyberattacks that are considerably more difficult for defenders to deflect. Regardless of whether these collaborative supportive parties are states or non-state groups, this situation complicates cyberattacker attribution and diffuses any resentment among victims of cyberattacks. The Syrian Electronic Army has successfully attracted this form of outside collaboration and assistance in its struggle in support of the Syrian ruling regime, as "hactivists everywhere have rallied to the cause."[8] It is indeed ironic that those who are interested in offensive cyber aggression frequently find it easier to collaborate than do those who are concerned about defensive cyberdeterrence.

Cyberattackers often figure out ways to minimize the potential for target retaliation after cyberintrusions. To pursue this end, prior to launching a cyberattack, an aggressor may disable a target's capacity to engage in cyber retaliation. Often "the target nation's patriot hackers/cyber militia will probably be targeted first (or at least early in combat) by an aggressor nation in order to preemptively remove retaliatory capability." For example, in the case of Russian hacker cyberattacks on Georgia, "Georgian hacker forums were targeted early-in [sic] the process to preempt, disrupt, and degrade retaliatory operations."[9] Furthermore, an aggressor may make tracing attribution more difficult through indirect attacks and third-party usage. Clever cyberattackers may also choose to manipulate internal or international public opinion so that target retaliation is less likely, or alternatively they may strive to demonstrate credibly to a cyberattack target contemplating a tit-for-tat retaliatory response that it has "a great deal to lose from such an action, thus throwing doubt on the viability of an 'in-kind' deterrence strategy."[10]

As with conventional kinetic military attacks, for cyberattackers the capacity and will for long-term persistence against intended targets is a huge plus for success. China and its hacking community in their acknowledged and unacknowledged foreign cyberattacks have exemplified this kind of dogged determination in obtaining the kind of data they wish to possess. Overall, "the greatest source of risk in cyberspace comes from groups with the resources and commitment to relentlessly target a company or government agency until they succeed in breaking in and then take value out."[11] Enhancing the chances for cyberattack success—and thwarting cyberdeterrence—is the continued and escalating dependence of targets on cybertechnology. As a result, "the adversary is not going away and their attraction to this weakness will increase," because in the end "this adversarial persistence yields a never-ending challenge."[12] Usually long-term cyberintrusion efforts have eventually overwhelmed any short-run cyberdefense measures they have encountered.

Beneficial and Detrimental Cyberattacker Attributes

The case studies reveal a couple of advantages for cyberattackers. A first advantage is the unbounded ingenuity and presence of clever hackers who can penetrate highly sophisticated cyberdefenses, as even the most advanced systems can be vulnerable to such breaches. The Titan Rain, Sony, and Israeli Gaza Strip cases illustrate this pattern. The growing availability of cyberattack tools, the increased sense of power derived from past successful cyber penetration, and the monetary rewards from such success—all can accelerate this cyber vulnerability. A second advantage is the cyberattackers' ability to avoid attribution. The Israeli Gaza Strip and International Monetary Fund cases best illustrate this pattern. In the vast majority of the examined cases, even in retrospect those responsible for the cyberattacks were not absolutely and definitively identified, and for political reasons some targets held off from naming initiators or from taking action against alleged cyberattackers, recognizing that they did not have absolute proof of culpability. Nonetheless, the cases also indicated that common attribution difficulties were not totally paralyzing, for although targets could not prove who was responsible, they had an awfully strong suspicion of the culprit.

The case studies also reveal a couple of disadvantages for cyberattackers. One key cyberattacker disadvantage is a decreased global legitimacy when others become aware of the aggressive actions undertaken. Classic case examples are the Chinese actions in Titan Rain and in Operation Shady RAT and the Russian actions in Estonia, Georgia, and Ukraine. Such lowered legitimacy can affect many areas of international political negotiation, and when cyberattacks generate especially high outside resentment, it can lead to economic sanctions. Another important cyberattacker disadvantage is the difficulty of avoiding undesired collateral damage, where unintended targets are accidentally hit. The Stuxnet cyberattack, which inadvertently spread well beyond its originally intended target of the Iranians' nuclear program, vividly illustrates this problem. Fear of unintended consequences could restrict a cyberattacker's freedom of action. Should a state sponsor become "concerned about possible undesirable or unintended second-order effects of a cyber attack, it could attempt to prevent its proxy from executing such attacks."[13] Those people and governing bodies unintentionally victimized by cyberattacks and their disruptive security consequences are not particularly tolerant or forgiving when and if they learn that damage was accidental.

Cybertarget Attributes Promoting Cyberattack Success

Cyberattacks also work best when the victim has (1) externally controllable Internet links and is totally dependent on them for its functioning; (2) valuable assets but is militarily, economically, or politically weak or lacks the capacity or will to combine cyber responses with real-world sanctions; (3) static cyberdefenses; (4) little planning or preparation for protecting against cyberattacks; (5) sharp internal disagreements about how to respond to cyberattacks; and (6) a geographical location within the initiator's established legitimate regional sphere of influence. Each attribute highlights a dimension where even flawed cyberattacks could succeed, pointing to deficient cyberdefenses.

If a country is totally dependent on externally controllable digital links for its critical infrastructure functioning, then its vulnerability to foreign cyberattacks could not be higher. Indeed, "as dependence on ICT [information and communication technology] for everyday services and communication correlates with the level of harm that could be caused by the attacks, generally, countries with a higher degree of ICT development are more exposed to cyber attacks and consequently face greater damage."[14] Among the most appealing cybertargets are countries with just a few highly externally controllable connections to the global Internet, where "there may be only one or two companies who hold official licenses to carry voice and Internet traffic to and from the outside world, and they are required by law to mediate access for everyone else." In those cases, a government can easily take down the Internet. "Make a few phone calls, or turn off power in a couple of central facilities, and you've (legally) disconnected the domestic Internet from the global Internet"; however, it also becomes harder "for the government to defend the nation's Internet infrastructure against a determined opponent, who knows they can do a lot of damage by hitting just a few targets."[15] Estonia provides a perfect example of a state that failed to diversify by rooting all key government, business, education, and critical infrastructure functions firmly in cyberspace with few external Internet links, making the country incredibly vulnerable to the attacks by Russian hackers. Greater numbers of "modern societies will have to increase their dependency on networks (and thus their vulnerability) even more for cyberattacks to be highly cost-effective."[16] Indeed, while "countries that are not as dependent on high technology within their military establishment consider such dependence a potential 'Achilles [sic] heel' for their enemies," others recognize that as future global cyber dependence surpasses present-day levels, it will likely result in greater cyberattack successes.[17]

If a country has valued assets but is militarily, economically, and politically weak or lacks the capacity or will to combine cyber responses with real-world kinetic sanctions, then it becomes a mighty inviting cybertarget. Although the revenge motive was involved, the cyberattacks on Saudi Aramco illustrate this pattern: because a private company rather than a national government was penetrated, the capacity of the target to retaliate with military force or negative economic sanctions was considerably lower. With such inadequate defenses, an advanced persistent threat attack can successfully penetrate and exfiltrate "data without the victim even noticing"; moreover, "weak governance compounds the problem of defending against" such attacks by making cooperation between companies and government agencies difficult. "Even unsophisticated attacks can succeed in this environment."[18]

When a target's cyberdefenses are static, cyberattackers can have a heyday. In this situation, cyberattackers know exactly what obstacles they face and have plenty of time to find the optimum ways to overcome or circumvent these impediments, to penetrate the system, and to reach the targeted data or assets. Once having infiltrated a system with static defenses, aggressors need not fear detection, because they know nothing new will be injected to interfere with their covert subversive activities. The inherent weakness of static cyberdefenses is their total predictability. Operation Shady RAT's success appears to be at least partially a function of its target's defensive deficiency. Indeed, "the cyber arena is never static—whatever defensive countermeasures are developed, one can rest assured there will be answers to those measures."[19] Precisely because threats are more fluid and morph more readily in cyberspace than in any other domain, static defenses present the best response for cyberattackers and the worst response for cyberdefenders.

Potential targets that are unprepared for cyberattacks are the equivalent of "sitting ducks" for disruption. The Russian hackers' cyberattack on Georgia highlighted this vulnerability as "the Georgian commercial and government digital infrastructure was completely unprepared to defend against an attack of this scale."[20] Similarly, the US military, while extensively protecting its physical military assets, was totally unprepared for the ISIS cyberattack on CENTCOM. However, target cyber preparedness is highly subjective. Although many information technology executives in private companies think their resources for network protection are adequate, "confidence about resources does not always translate into confidence about preparedness. About a third . . . say their sector is unprepared to deal with major attacks or stealthy infiltrations by high-level adversaries."[21]

If sharp internal disagreements exist within targets about the nature or significance of a cyberthreat, its likely consequences, or the appropriate responses to it, then the resulting hesitation and delayed action can provide real advantages to cyberattackers. The disagreement among the experts in the Operation Shady RAT case illustrates this pattern. Regarding the threat of Chinese cyberattack, "so long as there is disagreement between countries about the definition of cyber crime, there will be disputes about transnational lawsuits, penalties, and extradition relating to such crimes" that will inevitably delay effective responses.[22] Uncertainty-induced disagreements about outcomes clearly can incapacitate states involved in cyberconfrontations, and internal disagreements about who is culpable for a cyberattack can be truly paralyzing.[23] Strong contention within governments about ongoing cyber policies can ultimately become an "insider threat" that jeopardizes critical national infrastructure.[24]

Despite the usual irrelevance of geographical proximity in cyberspace, having a cybertarget located within a cyberattacker's sphere of influence—especially when the initiator and part of the target's population share ethnic ties—can contribute to cyberattack success. That location can not only simplify cutting off links between the target and the rest of the world but also raise the outsiders' perception of the attack's legitimacy. More than any other state, Russia has used this advantage in its quest to assert regional hegemony, and in the future most analysts "expect to see DDoS [distributed denial of service] attacks continue to be a political weapon in the Russian power sphere, particularly for former Soviet bloc nations."[25] Although generally the international community condemns cross-country cyberattacks, those occurring within an initiator's sphere of influence appear to receive less global criticism and to be more immune to any form of truly punishing international retaliation.

Beneficial and Detrimental Cybertarget Attributes

Cybertargets appear to possess a couple of key advantages. One advantage is the low barrier to entry for developing an effective retaliatory cyber capacity, with cyberspace capable of leveling the global playing field. The interrelationship between cyberspace and the current global security environment is conducive to a more even distribution of the instruments of power and influence, including cyberattack tools. A more balanced power distribution empowers weak cybertargets, which otherwise might have greater difficulty obtaining or using cyberweapons and thus would otherwise be confined to far less effective forms of cyber retaliation. The Ukrainian and ISIS cases illustrate this pattern. Regardless of the overall power ratio between cyberattackers and cybertargets, in cyberspace tangible political, economic, and military advantages can often be overcome by more intangible cyberoffense and cyberdefense capabilities. In other words, "dominance in cyberspace can improve the performance of operations in other domains, but the loss of dominance can negate or diminish capabilities in other domains as well."[26]

A closely related advantage for cybertargets is that seemingly vulnerable and isolated targets can still find ways to retaliate defensively. While global technological diffusion aids this retaliation potential, an awareness that such retaliation cannot render a totally crippling and paralyzing blow from cyberattackers afterward really helps cybertargets. In other words, within cyberspace nobody can possess a permanent advantage or long-term hegemony, nobody can deliver a decisive knockout blow, and nobody can be permanently incapable of effective countermeasures.

A key disadvantage for cybertargets is defensive overconfidence based on the perceived soundness of ongoing cybersecurity measures. Because conventional credibility of military power against land, sea, and air attacks often does not carry over to cyberspace, feeling superior can be delusional, especially given the global diffusion of cybertools and cyberskills. Israel's surprise at its vulnerability to cyberattacks in the Gaza Strip case illustrates this pattern. Possessing conventional military power still yields significant benefits in today's physical world but not in cyberspace confrontations, and as a result seeking superior coercive capabilities may not yield great cyberdeterrence benefits. For example, many citizens in the United States have trouble understanding why their military, the most powerful in the world, cannot successfully prevent any foreign cyberattacks. Although the United States commonly claims that in cyberconfrontations "demonstrating superior American capabilities . . . would also help deter those who may wish to conduct their own cyberattack against our homeland in the future," the actual positive, long-term impacts of security protection are much more uncertain.[27] Often in this cyber domain, strategic nimbleness and versatility are far more valuable than possessing large armies, tanks, and aircraft carriers.

A closely related disadvantage for cybertargets is overestimating self-sufficiency, not acknowledging vulnerabilities and high foreign reliance, and believing that frequent denial and secrecy about break-ins—even when there are major cyber disruptions—can prevent a needed overhaul of cyberdefenses. This pattern applies especially to highly cyber-dependent targets with few external connections to the global Internet. The Operation Shady RAT case, the Estonia case, and the Georgia case illustrate various facets of this pattern. Despite the dangers surrounding possibly tarnishing one's image through openly admitting cyber penetration, as mentioned in chapter 2, complete non-transparency and secrecy about such intrusions can stymie attempts not only by other vulnerable targets to undertake needed remedial steps to protect themselves from future cyberattacks but also by outside groups, governments, and international organizations to provide much useful assistance to restore the current victim's affected information systems quickly.

Cyberdeterrence Case Lessons

Emerging indirectly from the cases are three clusters of cyberdeterrence lessons, summarized in figure 5.2, concerning common characteristics, advantageous circumstances, and special challenges (relating to the nature of confrontations, cyberattackers, and cybertargets). Common characteristics are the universality of difficult cyberattacker attribution and high cyberdefender vulnerability. These two problem areas negate the usual prerequisites for appropriately fine-tuning effective and legitimate retaliation and protection, and they sharply contrast with other security domains where aggression attribution can be more easily identified and vulnerabilities can be more easily concretely patched. Advantageous circumstances for both cyberattackers and cyberdefenders are the pivotal roles of indirect measures, economic interdependence, and social media. These advantageous cyberdeterrence circumstances suggest means for improving protection that seem distinctively applicable to the cyber realm and are not as useful in other security domains. Special confrontation challenges are hybrid (physical-virtual) conflict and cyberespionage penetration. Specifically, special challenges for cyberattackers are authoritarian states and terrorist groups, and those for cybertargets are international organizations and private companies. These special challenges highlight distinctive existing deficiencies where cybersecurity experts particularly need to focus their efforts on developing improved, specially tailored cyberdeterrence solutions.

Considering the cases with the benefit of hindsight, it is painfully evident that significant improvements in cyberdeterrence planning and execution could have significantly lowered cybertarget vulnerability and raised cyberattack restraint through altering the adversaries' decision calculus. However, given the recency of the cases and of novel cyber response ideas, in some circumstances cybertargets may have done the best they could with the very limited information, technical tools, and protective methods they then had at their disposal. Significant cybersecurity learning has developed over time (even if many cybertargets have not yet found ways to take advantage of it), leading to cautious optimism that in the future potential victims of cyberattacks will be wiser in preparing themselves and in responding to the threat.

Common Characteristics
Universality of Difficult Cyberattacker Attribution

The cases highlight the universal difficulties of definitive cyberattacker attribution, which is often combined with the initiator's plausible deniability. Widespread disagreement existed on who was responsible—both the direct perpetrators and the hidden supporters—for the breaches. Even in the Syrian Electronic Army case, where attribution certainty was high for the external cyberattacks, it was low for the internal cyberattacks in Syria. As more investigators conduct extensive research on cyberattack attribution, they can inadvertently widen the range of interpretations about who is culpable. Cybertargets have clearly not yet found reliable ways to overcome attribution ambiguities in cyberspace.

FIGURE 5.2.
Cyberdeterrence Case Lessons

COMMON CHARACTERISTICS

Universality of Difficult Cyberattacker Attribution
Contending about Both Direct Perpetrators and Hidden Supporters
Multiplying Number of Culpable Parties through More Investigators

Universality of High Cyberdefender Vulnerability
Overwhelming Pervasive Cyber Dependence
Overestimating National Cyberdefense and Global Restraining Norm

ADVANTAGEOUS CIRCUMSTANCES

Pivotal Role of Indirect Measures
For Cyberattackers, Challenging to Detect/Thwart and Needing Subtler Responses
For Cyberdefenders, Empowering Information Flows and Virtual Relationships

Pivotal Role of Economic Interdependence
For Cyberattackers, Capping the Magnitude, Scope, and Severity of Intrusions
For Cyberdefenders, Promoting Deterrence and Limiting Retaliation

Pivotal Role of Social Media
For Cyberattackers, Mobilizing Support and Gaining Recruits for Intrusions
For Cyberdefenders, Undercutting Subversive Message and Invoking Restraint Norms

SPECIAL CHALLENGES

Special Confrontation Challenges
Hybrid (Physical-Virtual) Conflict
Cyberespionage Penetration

Special Cyberattacker Challenges
Authoritarian States
Terrorist Groups

Special Cyberdefender Challenges
International Organizations
Private Companies

Universality of High Cyberdefender Vulnerability

The cases' universal target vulnerability to cyberattack is exemplified in the worldwide disruptive effects of Operation Shady RAT, while the Estonia case demonstrates the pervasive cyber dependence at the root of this cyber vulnerability. Huge dangers surround underestimating the ability of any group or state—no matter how weak—to launch cyberattacks, as evidenced by the West's initial dismissal of the cyber capabilities of ISIS and of the Syrian Electronic

Army. Despite continuous cyberattacks, some targets persist in overoptimistic wishful thinking about cyber vulnerability. For example, tech-savvy Israel in the Gaza Strip case overestimated the adequacy of its cyberdefenses, and Georgia overestimated global restraining norms and the chances of external Western military intervention.

Advantageous Circumstances
Pivotal Role of Indirect Measures for Cyberattackers/Cyberdefenders

For both cyberattackers and cyberdefenders, the cases imply that successful measures today may often be indirect rather than direct. A key source for this pattern is "modern society's heavy reliance on interconnected information systems," where "the indirect secondary or tertiary effects of cyber-attacks may be much more consequential than the direct and immediate ones."[28] For cyberattackers, indirect offensive measures are harder to detect and thwart—amplifying definitive perpetrator attribution difficulties—and require more subtle responses. Examples of this circuitous means to achieve offensive ends abound: Iran used its Aramco cyberattack to get back at the West; Russia used private hackers to retaliate against Estonia, Georgia, and Ukraine; Hamas used criminals to fight Israel; and Anonymous used its IMF attack to protest a Greek bailout.

For cyberdefenders, operating indirectly "is a viable means of more effective deterrence in the cyber age; leveraging connectivity in ways never before considered empowers dynamic flows of information and virtual relationship-building."[29] While indirect defensive measures have been rare, abundant opportunities exist for their use. For example, the United States could have pressured China to restrain North Korea from initiating or persisting in its cyberattack on Sony. Operating indirectly for defensive purposes allows cyberthreat victims to use more fruitfully their web of allies and supporters to help them implement more imaginative ways to respond to cyberspace dangers.

Pivotal Role of Economic Interdependence for Cyberattackers/Cyberdefenders

The cases suggest that cross-national economic interdependence can moderate global cyberconfrontations by causing contending parties to realize the tangible mutual harm a truly debilitating cyberattack could produce. Private multinational corporations could be vital in reinforcing this cyber restraint through raising awareness of these interconnections and mutual harm. For cyberattackers, interdependence's net effect is not to eliminate their initiation of global digital breaches but to help cap their scope and severity, stressing espionage or theft rather than utter incapacitation. For instance, "while this global economic interdependence has proven insufficient to prevent these countries from using cyber means to steal large amounts of commercial and economic data from U.S. businesses, it undoubtedly disincentivizes both Russia and China to take actions that would significantly harm the U.S. economy and, in particular, the ability of U.S. citizens to conduct cyber commerce."[30] In the Titan Rain case, economic interdependence kept both China and the United States from launching devastating mutual cyberattacks.

For cyberdefenders, economic interdependence also enforces deterrence. Because "this interdependency increases the value of accurate [financial] information to all actors and increases the harm caused by inaccurate information," as "states connect further, the incentives of attack will gradually decrease, and disincentives will increase."[31] Such interdependence also limits offensive retaliation by cyberdefenders and their supporters. For example, NATO showed restraint in the Ukraine conflict given that country's dependence on the Russian gas pipeline.

Pivotal Role of Social Media for Cyberattackers/Cyberdefenders

The cases also reveal how social media plays vital roles for both cyberattackers and cyberdefenders. Especially popular with the younger generation, which relies on this means for information sharing, both cyberattackers and cyberdefenders can use social media to promote ideological views or spread false information about adversaries to a highly vulnerable and volatile demographic. For cyberattackers, Russian hackers collaborated over social media, the Syrian Electronic Army used social media attacks to damage Western information infrastructure, and ISIS in its cyberattack on CENTCOM employed social media—in this case Twitter but later on through WhatsApp and Telegram[32]—as the primary path to attract new recruits and to build a global reputation. Numerous other adversaries of the West are increasingly using social media to promote international disruption. For example, "Hizbollah is deftly exploiting social media tools such as Facebook to gain intelligence and information" for its nefarious operations.[33] Indeed, "the cyber strategy of international terrorist organizations currently emphasizes the use of social media, especially Facebook and Twitter, to mobilize support and gain recruits for militant jihadist groups."[34]

Cyberdefenders' effective use of social media has been less common, although if used skillfully, this approach could readily undercut cyberintruders' subversive messages. Additionally, the "unprecedented levels of global interconnectedness through ... social media provide common incentives for, and more effective means of, fostering international cooperation and shared norms of behavior."[35]

Special Confrontation Challenges
Hybrid Conflict

In today's global security setting, a virtual conflict in cyberspace can be just as significant—in achieving both military wartime victory and strategic postwar goals—as a real-world kinetic military battle being fought on the ground. If cyberattacks occur as part of a kinetic war initiative, as was the case in the Russian-Georgian war and the Israeli-Palestinian war over the Gaza Strip, then their effects could be just as devastating as those in the physical combat.

The cases identify special hybrid conflict difficulties. When a war is ongoing, sometimes the cessation of physical battle can mean an increase in cyber battle, operating in a kind of inverse relationship. While common, the pattern seems least likely to occur when a conflict involves multiple adversaries, such as when ISIS physically fights one set of foes in the battlefield and a different set of foes in its overseas cyberattacks. Furthermore, sometimes conventional military preparedness and cyber protection expenditures are not mutually reinforcing, as each can reflect a decidedly different—and sometimes opposing—mind-set. These hybrid confrontation complexities raise the question of which type of conflict—virtual or real world—has a more devastating impact from a human security, national security, and global security standpoint. An even broader security question emerges about how common military and civilian perceptions surrounding the norms of war and rules of engagement—including the viability of cease-fires—will evolve to incorporate the peculiarities of cyber conflict.

Cyberespionage Penetration

Compared with other kinds of cyberattack, such as cybertheft, the cases suggest that in deterring cyberespionage the limited range of a target's response options presents a special challenge. While still entailing a diverse, multipronged cyber response, a cyberespionage victim should stress defensive protection more through denial sanctions than through traditional offensive punishment or retaliation sanctions. As illustrated by the Titan Rain case, the logic behind this emphasis is that many observers believe "espionage as a legitimate function of the state," with national cyber spying attempts likely to persist over time, often constitutes a form of advanced persistent threat and is largely immune to restraint via intimidation.[36] Indeed, "espionage in any form is common among nation-states and imagining a sufficiently high cost-benefit ratio when this activity is ultimately deterred is difficult."[37] Furthermore, detection and definitive attribution of cyberattackers may be difficult with cyberespionage, and the potential for punishment sanctions triggering tit-for-tat retaliation between cyberattackers and cyberdefenders may be especially high. Within this classic spy-versus-spy confrontation in cyberspace, given its commonality, there would still be limits on the intensity of countermeasures. For example, although cyberespionage against the United States "evoked anger in Americans and a desire to retaliate, the refusal of the United States to reassure its potential adversaries that it will also forgo spying in cyberspace kept the government from hitting back aggressively."[38]

Special Cyberattacker Challenges
Authoritarian States

In twenty-first-century cyberconfrontations, it is quite common for authoritarian states to be involved in cyberattacks, albeit often behind the smokescreen of private hacking groups that covertly receive state support and encouragement, while national governments take advantage of plausible deniability to claim no involvement. Illustrating this challenge are various cases involving state support: Russia (Estonia, Georgia, and Ukraine cases), Iran (Aramco case), Syria (Syrian Electronic Army case), China (Shady RAT case), and North Korea (Sony Pictures Entertainment case). Special cyberdeterrence difficulties emerge here because authoritarian cyberattackers possess unique advantages in keeping operations secret, employing deception, defying and avoiding orthodox cyber restraints based on Western rational analysis, and using Internet filtering and censorship to keep citizens uninformed or misled. Although cyberspace "has enabled new, nimble and distributed challenges to these regimes, manifest in vigorous, mobilized opposition movements, protests, and in some cases, even revolutionary challenges to political authority," the domestic population in authoritarian states is still "more accustomed to the demands of security" and so seems less likely to question any government involvement in or support for rash foreign cyberattacks.[39] Regarding this kind of regime, cyberspace is a two-edged sword, for while the Internet "can help mobilize and empower dissidents under oppressive governments, it also can provide additional population control tools to authoritarian leaders."[40]

Terrorist Groups

In the future, more transnational terrorist groups that undertake physical acts of violence for political ends may come to realize that cyberspace can extend their projection of fear even farther. The ISIS case and Gaza Strip case (involving Hezbollah and Hamas) illustrate this challenge. Although up to this point truly damaging terrorist cyberattacks have been limited, "it would not be much of a stretch for terrorists to seek more bang for their buck by turning to digital means as a force multiplier for kinetic action."[41] Terrorists are adept at temporary collaboration with other malevolent groups to achieve desired ends, and "whatever difficulties a terrorist group might confront in launching a cyber-attack from abroad can be substantially overcome if the group recruits a local accomplice who is familiar with and has access to the system to be attacked."[42] The cases underscore that confronting cyberterrorists, given their political zeal, disregard for anticipated costs, and lack of assets that one could hold at risk, poses particular problems for cyberdeterrence. For these reasons, as with cyberespionage, offensive punishment or retaliation by targets may fail. Indeed, "a terrorist group might be hard to deter by retaliation because there are no good targets to hit in retaliation, and almost certainly no important cyber targets," thus reflecting the "familiar problem of threatening attacks that would inflict sufficiently high costs on a terrorist group."[43] Given that terrorist cyberattacks are among the hardest to deter, they deserve to be the recipients of some of the most creative and comprehensive countermeasures.[44]

Special Cyberdefender Challenges
International Organizations

International organizations, which are often assumed to be outside the cyberattackers' bull's-eye, tend to possess inferior cyberdefenses; thus, they can become prime targets due to their high visibility if they have data of great value on the global marketplace or if they undertake controversial actions globally. The International Monetary Fund and Operation Shady RAT cases illustrate this pattern. When such international organizations do become targets, the cases imply that cyberdefense can be more difficult than usual, as often they not only have lower-quality cybersecurity but also (given scarce resources) cannot protect organizational headquarters or provide substantial cyber protection assistance to member states. However, some hope exists that this deficiency can be remedied. For example, NATO has undertaken positive cybersecurity steps and developed a new strategic concept that constitutes the first time ever that an international organization has seriously declared that its members will coordinate their national cyberdefense capabilities.[45] Although consistently disadvantaged by their lack of agreement enforcement, one advantage that international organizations do have in cyberspace is that they can help spread global norms of cyber restraint. Providing cyber protection assistance "through an international organization would encourage less developed states to join the treaty regime, thereby advancing the objective of creating a uniform and effective set of agreed and binding commitments."[46]

Private Companies

Isolating and protecting key operational components are crucial steps for successful cyberdeterrence within private companies. The Iranian cyberattacks on Saudi Aramco and the North Korean cyberattack on Sony Pictures Entertainment illustrate the dangers when such safeguards are absent. Hacking into private companies' databases can accomplish several cyberattacker goals: "undermining the firm's competitiveness, embarrassing it, stealing its intellectual property, or simply robbing its finances."[47] In attempting cyberdeterrence, private companies face the dual threat of corporate competitors spying on them to steal their secrets to gain market advantage and of foreign governments' intelligence services engaging in industrial espionage for political gain.[48] Although the economically motivated breaches are more widely reported, the politically motivated breaches can be more devastating. Thus, patching areas of corporate vulnerability seems particularly crucial from a security standpoint when private companies control critical infrastructure, develop and supply military weapons (such as Lockheed Martin) or private security (such as Blackwater), and provide software vital to societal functioning.[49] However, even in these vital areas, when efforts to penetrate private companies in the cyber realm "are officially sanctioned, they are likely to be off the negotiating agenda" for national governments to address.[50] Huge controversy surrounds governments being "permitted to counterstrike on behalf of private companies" that become victims of cyberattacks.[51]

Overall Comments

In the end, it has been exceedingly difficult for cyberattackers, cybertargets, and even uninvolved outside observers to anticipate accurately the long-range security outcomes and impacts of transnational cyberattacks. So many unexpected elements, from zealous sympathetic third parties to tit-for-tat countermeasures, can enter the picture, and the incredibly rapid pace of change in both cyberattack and cyberdefense technologies amplifies this chaos. The case evidence underscores that the result of this uncertainty can manifest in two opposite reactions: cyberattackers and cyberdefenders can become more hesitant to undertake offensive or defensive actions because they lack any certainty about positive lasting outcomes, or alternatively each can be more eager to undertake offensive or defensive actions because they lack any certainty about negative lasting outcomes. Thus, uncertain security outcomes can readily complicate successful cyberdeterrence.

Notes

1. For independent confirmation of this case study pattern, see FireEye, *APT28*, 3.
2. Russell, *Cyber Blockades*, 7.
3. Libicki, *Cyberdeterrence and Cyberwar*, 6.
4. Krepinevich, *Cyber Warfare*, 32.
5. Herzog, "Estonian Cyber Attacks," 52.
6. Otte, "Cyberspace and Propaganda," 1.
7. Nazario, "Politically Motivated," 11.
8. Thompson, "Why Did Syria Shut?"
9. Hollis, "Cyberwar Case Study," 6, 8.
10. Lupovici, "Cyber Warfare," 52; and National Research Council, *Proceedings*, 356.
11. Lewis, *Cyber Threat and Response*, 2.
12. Defense Science Board, *Resilient Military Systems*, 30.
13. Krepinevich, *Cyber Warfare*, 44.
14. Tikk et al., *Cyber Attacks against Georgia*, 16.
15. Cowie, "Could It Happen?"
16. Giacomello, "Bangs for the Buck," 400.
17. Shimeall, Williams, and Dunlevy, "Countering Cyber War," 16–17.
18. Lewis, *Cyber Threat and Response*, 4–5.
19. Crosston, "World Gone Cyber MAD," 110.
20. Hemmer, *Deterrence and Cyber-Weapons*, 44.
21. Baker, Waterman, and Ivanov, *In the Crossfire*, 13.
22. Lan and Xin, "Can Cyber Deterrence Work?," 2.
23. Glaser, *Deterrence of Cyber Attacks*, 7; and Goodman, "Cyber Deterrence," 113.
24. Rudner, "Cyber-Threats," 467.
25. Nazario, "Politically Motivated," 18.
26. Russell, *Cyber Blockades*, 12.
27. Finan, "Cyberattack Campaign for Syria."
28. Waxman, "Cyber-Attacks," 438.
29. Hunt and Chesser, *Deterrence 2.0*, 7.
30. Jensen, "Cyber Deterrence," 822.
31. Goodman, "Cyber Deterrence," 121.
32. Marcius and McShane, "ISIS Posts Diagram."
33. Cilluffo, Cardash, and Salmoiroghi, "Blueprint for Cyber Deterrence," 9.
34. Rudner, "Cyber-Threats," 457.
35. US Department of Defense, *Quadrennial Defense Review, 2014*, 28.
36. Waxman, "Cyber-Attacks," 435n61.
37. Rivera, "Deterrence in Cyberspace," 11.
38. Goodman, "Cyber Deterrence," 104.
39. Deibert and Rohozinski, "Risking Security," 21; and Baker, Waterman, and Ivanov, *In the Crossfire*, 39.
40. Parker, "Utility of Cyberpower," 30.
41. Cilluffo, Cardash, and Salmoiroghi, "Blueprint for Cyber Deterrence," 14.

42. Brenner and Goodman, "In Defense of Cyberterrorism," 54.
43. Glaser, *Deterrence of Cyber Attacks*, 3.
44. Nye, "Power and National Security," 18.
45. Dogrul, Aslan, and Celik, "Developing an International Cooperation," in Czosseck, Tyugu, and Wingfield, *Proceedings*, 39.
46. Sofaer, Clark, and Diffie, "Cyber Security and International Agreements," in National Research Council, *Proceedings*, 201.
47. Sterner, "Deterrence in Cyberspace," 21.
48. Office of the National Counterintelligence Executive, *Foreign Spies Stealing*, 4.
49. Guinchard, "Between Hype and Understatement," 84.
50. Sofaer, Clark, and Diffie, "Cyber Security and International Agreements," in National Research Council, *Proceedings*, 194.
51. Kesan and Hayes, "Thinking through Active Defense," 329.

CHAPTER 6

Improving Cyberdeterrence Planning

Today much cybersecurity policy is reactive, where "people tend to focus on the problem of the moment" and rely on after-the-fact measures, such as "the patching of software or the detection of attacks that have already occurred, instead of proactive measures that prevent attacks in the first place."[1] Because such an approach "largely cedes the initiative to a challenger" and "is largely reactive to a specific attack or campaign," it is highly vulnerable to diverse breaches.[2] Typically cyberthreat awareness occurs in governments only after they are victims of cyberattacks and in businesses only after they have been hacked and "months after it happened, usually when a third-party tells them."[3] In 2015 an agency of the Office of the Director of National Intelligence admitted its methods "haven't adequately enabled cybersecurity practitioners to get ahead of these threats."[4] Consequently, "transitioning away from a reactive, signature-based security is critical to developing effective security architecture for the future."[5]

The consensus is that planning is "one of the most important aspects of security defense."[6] Thus, six target effectiveness and legitimacy planning needs, summarized in figure 6.1, emerge for cyberdeterrence: (1) collection of more sensitive cyberintelligence, (2) readiness for more bizarre cyberattacks, (3) development of more articulate cyberstrategy doctrine, (4) promotion of more coordinated cross-institution cyberpolicy, (5) harmonization of more binding cybersecurity standards, and (6) preparation for more concerted cyberthreat containment. Together they are prerequisites for more successful cyberdeterrence policy execution.

Collection of More Sensitive Cyberintelligence

Better cyberintelligence on potential cyberattackers is the cornerstone for improved target cyberdeterrence planning. This thrust has two underlying focal points—better advanced detection of the adversaries' intentions to penetrate digital assets and any resulting success in significant penetration of these assets.

FIGURE 6.1.
Improving Cyberdeterrence Planning

COLLECTION OF MORE SENSITIVE CYBERINTELLIGENCE
Improve information collection and analysis, accurate attribution, and early warning systems
Improve data integrity monitoring by perceptually differentiating between insignificant and significant changes, including through automated artificially intelligent sensors discriminating among data anomalies

READINESS FOR MORE BIZARRE CYBERATTACKS
Improve defense against the last observed form of cyberintrusion
Improve dynamic, flexible, and agile adjustment in preparation for new cyberattack forms and perpetrators, including culturally different, zealous, irrational, and impulsive cyberattackers

DEVELOPMENT OF MORE ARTICULATE CYBERSTRATEGY DOCTRINE
Improve cyberattack discrimination, response rationales, and consequence expectations
Improve internal identification of response thresholds about what kinds of cyberattacks and cyberattack impacts merit retaliation

PROMOTION OF MORE COORDINATED CROSS-INSTITUTION CYBERPOLICY
Improve within-government cooperation, communication, and coordination of cyberpolicy
Improve cross-government (and outside of government) cooperation, communication, and coordination of cyberpolicy, including through international organizations

HARMONIZATION OF MORE BINDING CYBERSECURITY STANDARDS
Improve interest-based cyberdeterrence, demonstrating that cyberattacks lack strategic advantage
Improve norms-based cyberdeterrence, fostering a global cybersecurity culture, "rules of the road" for offensive cyberspace use, and ability of responsible parties to take corrective action

PREPARATION FOR MORE CONCERTED CYBERTHREAT CONTAINMENT
Improve the short-term goal of achieving a temporary lull in cyberattacks or ending an intrusion quickly
Improve the long-term goal of forestalling pernicious downstream cyberattack consequences, action-reaction cycles, and third-party contagion

To improve cyberintelligence along these lines, policymakers need to increase precise attribution and promote accurate cyberthreat early warning systems. The Intelligence and National Security Alliance is adamant that "the U.S. must develop strategies beyond the current 'patch and pray' procedures, create cyberintelligence policies, coordinate and share intelligence better among government agencies and businesses, and increase research on attack attribution and warnings."[7]

Regarding precise attribution planning, cybertargets need to improve methods of isolating and identifying perpetrators through better backward traffic tracing, anomaly analysis, potential beneficiary discovery, and information correlation across attacks.[8] More specifically, targets should "refocus intelligence collection and analysis to understand adversarial cyber capabilities, plans and intentions, and to enable counterstrategies." The intelligence collected "must include the identification and understanding of adversarial cyber weapon development organizations, tools, leadership, and intentions, and the development of targeting information to support initiatives to counter cyber weaponization."[9] Rapid reaction capability is crucial "to mitigate attacks, prevent escalation and derive lessons learned in order to advance best practices."[10]

Because the primary objective of intelligence is "to contribute to warning" to ward off threat, seize an opportunity, or provide the necessary lead time to formulate responses, improving early warning systems is imperative.[11] These systems should focus on improving the means "to monitor cyberspace, identify intrusions and locate the source of attacks with a trail of evidence that can support diplomatic, military and legal options—and we must be able to do this in milliseconds."[12] Such warning also needs to avoid the common foible of adversaries "feeding false information into a state's early warning system to spoof operators into believing their country is under attack when in fact it is not."[13] After cyberthreat detection, cybertargets should share any "warning of an attack to various interested parties so that they can provide assessments of what the threat means to them specifically."[14]

A couple of early warning efforts in 2010 illustrate the possibilities of preemptive detection. The US government "quietly launched" Perfect Citizen, an NSA digital surveillance project designed "to detect cyber attacks on private companies and government agencies running critical infrastructure . . . ; the program would rely on a set of sensors deployed in computer networks for critical infrastructure that would be triggered by unusual activity suggesting an impending cyber attack."[15] In addition, the Pentagon announced a strategy of "active defense," where "America's closest allies would be drawn into an early-warning network of collective cybersecurity; private industry would be mobilized in a kind of civil defense against attackers; and military commanders would be given authority to respond automatically to electronic invaders."[16]

Affecting both attribution and early warning, target cybersecurity officials need to improve the monitoring and evaluation of the integrity of valuable data and communication systems while paying special attention to changes in the frequency and severity of cyberintrusions. They also need to establish a clearer idea of what kinds of stolen, corrupted, or blocked data are likely to be most debilitating. This goal is difficult because usually data changes so rapidly over time and is so interconnected that it is hard to isolate which system elements deserve the closest attention.

System administrators within cybertargets need not only to track changes in data and systems but also to manage the highly challenging task of differentiating between major and minor changes to determine security priorities. These administrators should "focus on unusual activity, avoid false positives, more rapidly identify anomalies, and prevent overwhelming analysts with insignificant alerts."[17] For this discrimination, an unusual approach is to augment human sensitivity with automated artificially intelligent sensors using differentiation algorithms (somewhat parallel to but different from spam filters) to trigger anomaly awareness. One of Edward Snowden's NSA revelations illustrates this issue:

> Snowden was ... disturbed to discover a new, Strangelovian cyberwarfare program in the works, codenamed MonsterMind. The program ... would automate the process of hunting for the beginnings of a foreign cyberattack.... When it detected an attack, MonsterMind would automatically block it from entering the country—a "kill" in cyber terminology.
>
> Programs like this had existed for decades, but ... instead of simply detecting and killing the malware at the point of entry, MonsterMind would automatically fire back, with no human involvement.[18]

However, even if such automated artificial intelligence algorithms could be perfected by cybertargets, key trade-offs exist in their application, especially if they alone control the initiation of countermeasures. "On the one hand, automation can enhance cyber security dramatically by increasing the speed, reliability and accuracy of defensive systems. On the other hand, it will become harder to control the initiation, conduct and termination of cyber operations as human beings become increasingly divorced from direct operational involvement.... [A]rtificial intelligence could erode traditional notions of military command and control."[19] Given how many vital assets require cyber protection, developing accurate artificially intelligent sensors for this kind of anomaly discrimination appears to be quite difficult. As Snowden himself notes, because cyberattacks "are often routed through computers in innocent third countries," automated retaliatory responses might be unwise since "these attacks can be spoofed" (for example, a Chinese hacker could make it appear that an attack originated in Russia, leading to retaliation against the wrong target).[20] Nonetheless, employing artificial intelligence as purely a defensive means to assist in isolating significant breaches could potentially be of great value in cases where a target is overwhelmed at a given moment by a diverse flood of cyberattacks.

Readiness for More Bizarre Cyberattacks

Cyberspace seems to be unique among combat realms in the speedy emergence of vast numbers of new cyberattackers, attack methods, cybertools, and cybertargets. The cyberthreat possibilities are so varied that victims frequently feel unable to try to keep pace. Yet resting secure and complacent is an absolute curse in cyberspace, so improved readiness for novel breaches is crucial.

Expanding cyberdeterrence preparedness necessitates overcoming long-standing bureaucratic inertia–laden "satisficing" tendencies, where preparing for the familiar—that is, shielding vulnerable vital assets hit by previous cyberattackers using known attack tools—always seems easiest.[21] To surmount this obstacle, wider readiness is essential. Moving beyond what is currently in vogue, it entails developing deterrence against a broader and more diverse spectrum of potential adversaries, ranging from individuals to groups to states, and of potential incursions, ranging from "small invasions into computer systems to large scale 'attacks' that produce significant kinetic effects."[22]

Improved target planning entails engaging in "dynamic, flexible, and agile" adaptations to handle future cyberattacks, which "will be more sophisticated, more difficult to detect, and more capable of wreaking untold damage on the nation's computer systems."[23] Deterrence planning requires a versatile fluid tool kit because in the future "new and unforeseen threats are certain to emerge."[24] Such planning needs not only to consider unforeseen cyberspace dangers and threat sources but also to analyze changing, long-term security implications of these cyberthreats and to develop contingencies for how targets might effectively and legitimately respond to them. The aforementioned improvements in collecting more sensitive cyberintelligence, constantly updated over time and across areas, should guide the selection of contingencies emphasized in improving preparations for deviations from past cyberattack patterns.

Looking at highly unorthodox attackers, they include newly emerging, unruly, global "'irrational' cyber actors such as extremist groups, rogue nations or hacker activists."[25] These dangerous, malicious perpetrators fall into three categories: culturally different cyberattackers whose beliefs challenge those of targets, zealous cyberattackers who are willing to suffer heavy costs or even die for their cause, and impulsive cyberattackers who ignore consequences or who engage in disruptions for kicks or as virility tests "just to see if they can do it."[26] The target planning necessary to restrain these kinds of adversaries is complex, for stopping cyberattackers who are highly emotional or who eschew conventional cost-benefit analysis can require incredibly versatile, multifaceted countermeasures.[27] Cyberdeterrence success against such atypical attackers depends on targets scrutinizing in advance the attackers' ways of thinking to identify what they care about most; who their supporters, sponsors, and patrons are; and how potential pressure points could be used to increase restraint compliance. In this effort, it becomes important for targets to pinpoint beforehand what kinds of digital links, networks, relationships, and assets are both highly valued by attackers and very susceptible to penetration.

Turning to greatly unorthodox attack modes, a variety of new cyberattack technologies deserve careful tracking in order "to detect an emerging threat of attack well in advance, gaining time to assess it, design and implement appropriate deterrence threats, see how they are working, and make adjustments if needed," even if there is little "palpable evidence of an impending attack" and thus "little inducement to mount a specifically targeted deterrence."[28] Among the most potentially devastating is an electromagnetic pulse (EMP) attack, which is "not usually considered a cyber threat in Western doctrine" but is "in the playbooks for an Information Warfare Operation of Russia, China, North Korea, and Iran. These potential adversaries in their military doctrines include as part of cyber warfare a wide spectrum of operations beyond computer viruses, including sabotage and kinetic attacks, up to and including nuclear EMP attack."[29] Although EMP is electromagnetic rather than cyber, it poses a major cybersecurity threat and merits both attention and advanced preparation by potential targets because EMP attacks directly incapacitate all virtual networks, electronic control systems, and computerized digital devices. While unorthodox cyberattack planning could cause targets to develop more lethal cyberattack systems to preempt threats, potentially leading to intensified attacker-defender action-reaction cycles, one need not invent new malware or viruses to improve cyberdefenses. Within continuing system "stress tests," more imaginative preparation is needed for the largest range of future cyberattacks not yet encountered, and "when weaknesses are found, they must be fixed—and fixed fast."[30]

Development of More Articulate Cyberstrategy Doctrine

For targets with the capacity and will to respond to cyberattacks, cyberstrategy policy articulation can raise their reputation for resolve, credibility, effectiveness, and legitimacy.[31] Aggressors would anticipate retribution yet be vulnerable due to secrecy about exact target responses.

Former US Homeland Security secretary Michael Chertoff stresses the need for a well-articulated cyberdeterrence doctrine because "everyone needs to understand to rules of the game."[32] Cybersecurity intelligence and defense consultant Timothy Sample also defends taking this position "to let others know where we are going, what we stand for in the era, and the consequences of actions taken against us."[33] Such a doctrine has to be firm and decisive:

> The declaratory policy should provide a credible, convincing explanation of why the United States takes cyber threats seriously, why it would regard a major cyber attack as potentially an act of war against it, and the intention of the United States to respond with decisive actions, possibly including force. The declaratory policy should leave no doubt in the minds of potential adversaries that any cyber attacks on the United States would fail to achieve their goals and that the attackers would suffer unacceptable costs, damages, and risks in return. A U.S. declaratory policy for cyber deterrence needs to be firm, but it also needs to be balanced, sending the right messages regarding possible responses to cyber attack and avoiding inflammatory statements that could contribute to escalation of cyber conflicts.[34]

The doctrine should clarify distinctions between low-level and high-level cyberattacks, explain the justification behind responses to cyberattacks and behind treating some as acts of war, make known in advance the extreme weapons and tactics that might be part of a cyberthreat response, and shape consequence expectations by communicating to adversaries the improbability of meeting their goals through cyberattacks and by detailing the unacceptable costs, damages, and risks adversaries would suffer if they launched cyberattacks. This doctrine needs to avoid emotional overreactions and eschew inflammatory statements that could escalate antagonisms. Instead, it should signal tailored, proportional cyberthreat responses, even if ironclad attribution—which often inappropriately "wholly paralyzes any attempt to think fruitfully about a cyber deterrence strategy"[35]—is impossible.

Barriers to effective Western cybersecurity doctrine include domestic political pressures, technical expertise gaps, and inchoate cyberattack response thresholds about what cyberattacks merit retaliation. Domestic political pressures "to respond forcefully and promptly" to cyberattacks and technical expertise gaps between tech-savvy non-state groups and tech-ignorant security policymakers may distort cybersecurity doctrine as such doctrine may fail to recognize what most needs protecting, what is most vulnerable, or what integrates well with other security priorities.[36] Response thresholds must be set appropriately: if too low, then thresholds can risk widespread paranoia, resource waste, or needless aggression; and if too high, thresholds can leave a society unprepared for external disruption.[37] Political leaders need doctrinal guidance about when and how to respond to cyberthreat, including how to confront an aggressor, how to urge an attacker to declare its responsibility for cyberattacks, and how to impose penalties. Because the high frequency of cyberthreats makes reacting to each and every one of them foolhardy, "choosing a zero-tolerance policy is asking for trouble."[38]

Improving response threshold identification can be particularly helpful for cyberdeterrence, for "without a strategy in place where thresholds are developed to measure a given attack, deterrence would not exist."[39] First, thresholds should be flexible and conditional instead of fixed and formulaic. For example, "rather than drawing specific redlines, the United States needs to consider a range of retaliatory options to use against a range of threats that it may not be able to rank hierarchically, given the speed with which threats might change."[40] Second, thresholds should distinguish carefully among differing types of cyberthreats—for example, separating cyberespionage from cybertheft and separating those making military or financial systems inoperative from those misappropriating private citizens' identity data.[41] Third, thresholds for kinetic military responses to cyberthreat ought to be higher than for cyber responses at least in part because "one can expect the risk of unwanted escalation from cyber to other military domains to deter both sides from resorting to more destructive forms of computer network attack in most situations."[42] Furthermore, "in the case of political and economic retaliation, the threshold needed to justify imposing sanctions should be lower" than that for military sanctions.[43] Fourth, thresholds should be higher when cyberdeterrence success is most uncertain, and it should be "highest in the global arena, where the collateral effects are the least predictable."[44] Fifth, while specific thresholds should be confidential, the general capability and will to respond should be more transparent and credible than it is today.[45] Although exact cyberthreat response thresholds for each cybertarget "should not be public in nature as they would articulate what an actor may be able to get away with, . . . a nation's intent to respond to a given attack via cyberspace must be publicly known through its national security policy."[46]

Promotion of More Coordinated Cross-Institution Cyberpolicy

Targets need improved planning for better cyberpolicy communication, coordination, and cooperation within and among relevant agencies and within and across national governments (and relevant parties outside of government).

Although democratic governments pride themselves on consultation, cyberdeterrence decision making has traditionally often been both unilateral and cloaked in secrecy. Information-sharing improvements need to encompass an understanding of how systems fail as well as specific threat information.[47]

Within national governments, both civilian and military officials ought to play key cyberdeterrence roles. Cyberdeterrence responsibility in government often is too diffuse and compartmentalized. In the United States, for example, there is "a continuing lack of adequate coordination at the Federal level in our cyber resilience and, particularly, defense activities," accompanied by "continuing conflict over control of the cyber defense mission."[48] A 2010 US Government Accountability Office study found that "federal agencies have overlapping and uncoordinated responsibilities for cybersecurity, and it is unclear where the full responsibility for coordination lies."[49] Interagency task forces need better incentives for cross-agency cyberdeterrence cooperation.

For cross-governmental collaboration, cyberdefenses can be enhanced by "leveraging the capabilities, knowledge, and experience of a broader community."[50] Sharing attribution intelligence, thus widening the use of interoperable attribution technologies, seems especially crucial.[51] In 2010 the Government Accountability Office also determined that "the federal government does not have a formal strategy for coordinating outreach to international partners for the purposes of standards setting, law enforcement, and information sharing."[52] For restraining cyberthreat, cross-state public and private cooperation is especially vital because "it is rather hard to cope with the threat by means of merely 'national' cyber defense policies and strategies, since the cyberspace spans worldwide and [an] attack's origin can even be overseas."[53] Among national governments, coordinating pre-cyberattack outreach and bridge building to global partners (including identifying potential sources of aid) needs refinement for better standards setting, law enforcement, and information sharing.

Pragmatic steps promoting cross-institution cooperation include sharing effective early warning systems to help friendly states improve their cyberdetection and enhancing the ability of needy foreign governments to manage cyberthreats before they seep abroad. The United States and its other "Five Eyes" intelligence partners (Australia, Canada, United Kingdom, and New Zealand) are working together to improve cyberdefenses, "but the highly sensitive nature of the technology means there has been little collaboration on cyber weapons . . . partly because countries are unwilling to reveal exactly how much—or how little—they can do."[54] More "successful cooperation may well compel governments to accept constraints on their cyber activities within or traversing each other's national network infrastructures. Such assurances will largely be built on trust and bounded transparency, as countries will understandably be reluctant to allow scrutiny of their most-sensitive network infrastructures and activities by even their closest allies."[55]

Harmonization of More Binding Cybersecurity Standards

Without overarching global standards of acceptable cyberspace behavior, "states cannot rest assured that they will not be targeted by cyber attacks if they refrain from targeting others"; thus, this lack incentivizes "hitting first in cyberspace so states can victimize others before they become victims themselves."[56] As former US secretary of state Hillary Clinton states, "In an Internet-connected world, an attack on one nation's networks can be an attack on all."[57] Although standards alone certainly cannot stop cyberattacks, they can help to discourage severe breaches. While the Internet "is governed by consensual practices among the network's providers and operators that have their basis in norms without which the Internet could not function," cybercrime and cyberespionage "remain underregulated domains that so far have resisted attempts at global agreement."[58]

Universal standards are worthwhile given the failure of unilateral sanctions to deter cyberattacks and the wide variance in targets' cyberattack preparation.[59] A 2011 survey showed that the United States, United Kingdom, and Estonia were best prepared for cyberattacks, and Albania, Mexico, and Romania were least prepared.[60] Such so-called weak-link countries, lacking cyberdefense resources and expertise, are likely not only to attract cyberattacks but also to create "havens for cyber-criminals."[61] Establishing global standards could help to deny transnational hackers safe havens in such states by inducing compliance with foreign law enforcement and negotiating credible extradition agreements.

The normal route for targets to promote the harmonization of cybersecurity standards is through interests-based cyberdeterrence. With this approach, cybertargets assume a shared defensive stance, demonstrating to aggressors that their attacks lack strategic purpose. An underlying premise is that given core national interests, where states "purely maximize or optimize their given preferences," multiple countries would recognize the shared value in taking common restraining action.[62] This mode also assumes that adversaries would be far more likely to refrain from cyber aggression if they faced a tangibly unacceptable cost-benefit ratio due to such common multistate opposition than if they faced a conglomeration of international values and laws that prohibit such activity.[63]

A more uncommon way to promote global cyberdeterrence standards is with norms-based cyberdeterrence, which relies on rather different perceptual premises. This method employs "stigmatization," or signaling through a credible global norm that some forms of cyberattack "run counter to accepted international behavior."[64] The goal of this approach "is to nurture a variety of normative concepts intent on increasing global stability in cyberspace, to instigate a global culture of cybersecurity, and to develop 'rules of the road' for military and offensive uses of cyberspace" so as "to deliver deterrent effect where an 'interests-based approach' has thus far struggled on its own."[65] Existing "evolving rudimentary norms" already support restrained cyberbehavior.[66] Indeed, "even in light of claims of Internet anarchy, the cyber realm does not appear to be altogether free of broad and widely accepted principles of governance."[67]

Such norms might allow a variety of cyberspace actions to take place as long as "total offensive operations"—defined as "direct and malicious incidents that might lead to the destruction of the energy infrastructure of a state, or incidents meant to take control of army units or facilities"—are banned.[68] Promoting global cybernorms could increase "stability and predictability" and could enable international responsible parties "to take any required corrective measures" that would "increase openness, interoperability, security, and reliability."[69] Cyberspace policies should also promote "exercising proportionality and restraint in response to cyber attack" and uphold key freedoms (including Internet freedom), property rights, privacy, and protection from harm (including collateral damage).[70] Then-colonel. Sharon Afek, international cyberlaw expert and former Israeli deputy military advocate general, argues that "countries would benefit from developing an ethics code to govern cyber warfare operations," noting that "existing law already prohibits cyber operations which would directly lead to loss of life, injury, or property damage, such as causing a train to derail or undermining a dam."[71]

Many planning benefits could result from spreading cybersecurity norms. They can stimulate "responsible behavior in cyberspace," "common laws and policies among different nations," better control of advanced persistent threats, "clear rules that allow for mutual cooperation," and protection of "basic values like the rights of free speech, privacy, and access to information."[72] However, a persistent obstacle is that "the actors least in need of the norm are the first to adopt; actors who most need to adopt are often the recalcitrant."[73]

Preparation for More Concerted Cyberthreat Containment

Improved target cyberdeterrence planning requires explicit preparation for temporal and spatial cyberattack containment, or "the process of limiting the effects of a hostile action once it occurs."⁷⁴ Policymakers often ignore future interactive spirals involving cyber arms races or other players escalating cyber instability contagion. Compared to other cyberdeterrence planning needs, containment preparation receives the least concerted advanced attention.

Policymakers need to move beyond stressing short-term, temporary cyberattack lulls or the quick cessation of breaches (oriented toward immediate crisis deterrence rather than general deterrence) to focus on long-term cybersecurity. Preventing cyberattacks from escalating over time or spreading across countries is centrally important to minimize the overall security threat. Such durable cyberthreat containment is more likely than temporary stopgap measures to achieve meaningful regional and global stability.

Cyberthreat containment focuses on lowering the chances of two key components of cyberattacks—the entrance of undesired third parties in cyberattacks and the pernicious downstream consequences and action-reaction cycles resulting from cyberattacks. These uncontrolled cyberattack consequences are equally dangerous. Action-reaction cycles can lead to endless cyberoffense and cyberdefense expenditures with no significant advantage gained and no resolution in sight, and unwanted third-party contagion can lead to such a widespread diffusion of cyberthreat that as soon as it is managed in one area it rears its ugly head in another.

For military officers involved in cybersecurity, the war colleges and military higher education institutions need to emphasize downstream cyber consequences. It is essential to recruit and better train defense strategists who can creatively and realistically think several moves ahead, game things out, and anticipate how the other side will respond to one's moves while simultaneously determining their own next countermoves. Professional war games and military simulations of projected confrontations need to underscore unanticipated second-order and third-order force consequences.⁷⁵ Strategists should spend more time trying "to 'game out' possible scenarios—however unlikely"—to aid in identifying security holes and preparing for unexpected assaults.⁷⁶

Exemplifying this thrust is the annual Cyber Defense Exercise, which began in 2001. This four-day contest tests cybersecurity skills between senior cadets from the five service academies—the US Air Force Academy, Coast Guard Academy, Military Academy, Naval Academy, and Merchant Marine Academy—and the National Security Agency's top information assurance professionals.⁷⁷ In another illustration, the US European Command has sponsored a Combined Endeavor workshop since 1995. Meeting at a US military base in Germany on September 18, 2013, troops from the United States, Poland, Lithuania, Latvia, and Bulgaria participated in the Combined Endeavor exercise, probing for weaknesses in computer networks of allied countries.⁷⁸

Outside of the military sphere, civilian initiatives could help with cyberthreat containment. Private businesses could develop and use similar exercises—competing with each other to improve cyberdefenses—to get vulnerable company sectors thinking much further in advance about long-run cyberattack consequences and speedier countermeasures to isolate better any damaging financial impacts. For the public, better training exercises about containing digital breaches in a wide variety of settings might help, as well as increased encouragement to think ahead about the unintended long-run dangers of communicating private information via social media and leaving vital personal information unattended in highly vulnerable digital locations.

Regarding action-reaction cycles, given the global spread of cyberattack tools, cyber protection efforts—particularly those viewed as offensive rather than defensive—often trigger tit-for-tat cyber retaliation. A defiant willingness to escalate indefinitely may emerge, threatening critical infrastructure. Eric Byres, a cybersecurity expert who cofounded Torino Security, contends that in this "arms race," "every time a cyberattack is launched, you risk handing ammunition to the enemy. . . . 'It's like the first guy to throw a bronze spear. He might have won, but if his enemies survived and pulled it out of the ground, the first thing they'd say is, 'we've got to make one like this.'"[79] With improper cyberdeterrence implementation, the "age-old cycle of action and reaction between offense and defense" can resurface.[80] In cyberspace, "retaliation in kind is more attractive" since it "raises fewer issues of proportionality," ultimately legitimizing a form of dangerous enduring conflict.[81] Such a cyber arms race "consumes extensive resources, yet fails to produce an enduring or definitive outcome."[82] Ultimately, the result can be a stalemate. For example, "the more the United States uses cybertechnology as a weapon, the more it exposes itself to cyber-attack by foreign governments, free-lance hacker/terrorists and clever cyber-criminals."[83]

Certain situations maximize the chances of action-reaction cycles. When "states embroiled in irregular conflicts are confronted by a range of difficult-to-deter actors struggling in a dynamic strategic landscape in which escalation thresholds are fluid and difficult to ascertain" and when cyberattackers "face internal pressures to respond" or "believe they will lose in a cyber tit-for-tat but can counter in domains where they enjoy superiority."[84] The 2014 conflict between Russia and Ukraine shows the dangers when action-reaction cycles occur and spiral out of the cyber realm into the real world.

To minimize cyber action-reaction cycles, targets need to avoid responses that lead to adversaries escalating their threats and launching more cyberattacks.[85] There are two ways to accomplish this end—undertaking a "knockout blow" that disables the hackers' ability to launch more cyberattacks, or selecting "measures of the sort that are less likely to attract countermeasures" and are still capable of restraining adversaries but eschew approaches that overreact to existing provocations and that seem likely to provoke emotional responses.[86] In light of escalation fears, such responses need to be "incisive, surgical, and clear." Cyberdeterrence "is not a game of 'taking down' the adversary; it is demonstrating our capability and intention to dissuade them from further damage to our national security and economy."[87] Before responding to an adversary, both assessing its retaliation capacity and will and knowing its sensitivities seem essential in order to minimize the chances of unwittingly angering it into a cycle of retaliation. Decision makers need to gain a deeper understanding of how these cycles work in today's world and learn to identify the points early in the cycle where the hostile, entrapping interactive pattern can be most easily broken and the pressures that keep opposing parties from extricating themselves from this cycle even when one or both wish to do so.

Regarding cyberthreat contagion, uncontrolled third-party involvement can impede cyberdeterrence. First, such involvement can complicate cyber crisis management. Non-state groups, which often directly initiate cyberattacks, can escalate crises at the same time national governments are mutually attempting to diffuse or manage them.[88] Some third parties also intentionally disguise their actions to create or worsen a political crisis between two other parties.[89] Second, a third party's presence can be highly unpredictable and can complicate a cybertarget's efforts to return to normalcy following a cyberattack. For instance, when a target attempts to restrain potential aggressors by signaling to them likely negative consequences from a cyberattack, third-party involvement could interfere with this signal and "make it difficult to understand the relationships among attack, retaliation, and counterretaliation."[90] Third, third-party involvement can make cyberthreat attribution more problematic as "the trail of evidence often runs through countries with which the victim's government has poor diplomatic relations or no law enforcement cooperation. . . . This dynamic encourages 'false flagging' operations—where the attacker tries to pin the blame on a third party—and creates an environment in which even terrorists can find a home on the Internet."[91] Finally, like action-reaction cycles, third-party contagion can nullify gains derived from cyberdeterrence expenditures, when even after restraining efforts have thwarted a cyberthreat, new variants pop up in other places. Cyberthreat contagion creates fears about unanticipated "active external participants spoiling for an excuse to fight," making conflict more uncontrolled, unpredictable, undetermined, and unmanageable.[92]

Speedy cybertechnology diffusion often promotes ominous third-party contagion. For example, "the diffusion of U.S.-initiated technologies and strategies may allow opponents to deploy similar technologies but in dissimilar ways" that counter US national interests.[93] The result enables "new modes of cooperation between state and non-state players who share certain goals and adversaries" but often with dire consequences: "Once released, many malware agents will eventually replicate to third parties," ultimately making even well-intentioned, narrowly focused software an unwitting accomplice in eviscerating cybersecurity in unintended places.[94] Such rapid diffusion is highly unpredictable and decidedly not controllable by the cyberattacker, as "diffusion can take on a life of its own quickly through the neurocomputational mutations that can occur in cyberspace."[95]

Thus, cybertargets enmeshed in confrontations need to take steps prior to cyberattacks to minimize any disruptive third-party role. Such efforts need to focus on "changing the behavior of third parties, in particular making them less willing to cooperate with cyberattackers."[96] For example, there could have been efforts to persuade China to avoid any form of tacit cooperation with North Korea in its cyberattack on Sony Pictures Entertainment. As part of this preparation against third-party involvement, cybertargets should be hypervigilant about the possibility that adversaries will achieve technological breakthroughs. Furthermore, cybertargets need to expand their communication with and their moderating influence on those third parties that might join ongoing cyberattacks. Especially with extremist third parties that could enter the fray, the cybertargets' "capacity to develop relationships and continue to foster them over long distances represents a unique opportunity to establish relations which may contain the seeds of moderation."[97] Given the frequency of third-party complicity in cyberattacks, it is critical for targets "to develop cross-border relationships before an international crisis occurs."[98]

However, minimizing the role of third parties in cyberconfrontations is not always desirable or feasible for cybertargets. Those third parties that are sympathetic to cybertargets and share cultural, political, or economic commonalities with cyberattackers may prove useful on occasion and help deter the aggressors from initiating cyberattacks. Moreover, even when considering disruptive third parties, persuading them to refrain from involvement in cyberconfrontations is not always possible. Their involvement in cyberattacks may be unwitting, as private hackers within their territories can participate in cyberattacks without their government's knowledge or express permission.

Overall Comments

Although some of these suggested improvements in cyberdeterrence planning may appear to be self-evident, cybersecurity officials so far have not been able to implement them in a patently successful way. Aside from its generally reactive orientation, the fragmentary nature of cyberdeterrence decision making has contributed to this pattern of planning futility. For all types of cyberspace threats, each of these planning needs plays an important role, but perhaps the most difficult and crucial one is to focus more on coping with novel, as yet unseen dangers.

Notes

1. Schneier, *Beyond Fear*, 115; and Saadawi and Jordan, eds., *Cyber Infrastructure Protection*, v.
2. Sterner, "Retaliatory Deterrence in Cyberspace," 69.
3. Timberg and Rein, "Senate Cybersecurity Report"; and Lewis, *Cyber Threat and Response*, 4.
4. "Cyber Researchers," *Homeland Security News Wire*.
5. Lewis, *Cyber Threat and Response*, 8.
6. Schneier, *Beyond Fear*, 227.
7. "Study Warns US," Fox News.
8. Rowe, "Attribution of Cyber Warfare," in Green, *Cyber Warfare*, 64–67.
9. Defense Science Board, *Resilient Military Systems*, 8–9.
10. Rudner, "Cyber-Threats," 473.
11. Belden, "Indications, Warning," 181; and Ofri, "Crisis and Opportunity Forecasting," 821.
12. McConnell, "How to Win."
13. Krepinevich, *Cyber Warfare*, 74.
14. Homeland Security Policy Institute, *Cyber Deterrence Symposium*, 11.
15. "U.S. Quietly Launches Protection," *Homeland Security News Wire*.
16. Ignatius, "Pentagon's Cybersecurity Plans."
17. Gilligan and Skoudis, *Twenty Critical Controls*, 23.
18. Bamford, "Most Wanted Man."
19. Lord and Sharp, *America's Cyber Future*, 1:30.
20. Bamford, "Most Wanted Man."
21. Simon, "Rational Choice," 129–38.
22. Jensen, "Cyber Deterrence," 782.
23. US Department of Defense, *DoD Cyber Strategy*, 10, 33; and "Thwarting the Next Generation," *Homeland Security News Wire*.
24. Hunt and Chesser, *Deterrence 2.0*, 12.
25. Finkle, "'Irrational' Hackers."
26. Gallington, "U.S. Can't Wait."
27. Schneier, *Beyond Fear*, 64–65, 176.
28. Morgan, "Applicability of Traditional Deterrence," in National Research Council, *Proceedings*, 64.

29. Woolsey and Pry, "EMP Blackout."
30. Gallington, "U.S. Can't Wait."
31. Cilluffo and Siers, "Cyber Deterrence."
32. "Chertoff Calls for Cyber-Deterrence," *Homeland Security News Wire*.
33. Acohido, "Syria's Cyber Retaliation."
34. Kugler, "Deterrence of Cyber Attacks," 332.
35. Ibid., 309, 332.
36. Krepinevich, *Cyber Warfare*, 50; and Libicki, Ablon, and Webb, *Defender's Dilemma*, xxi. See also Mandel, "What Are We Protecting?," 335–55.
37. Buzan, *People, States and Fear*, 115.
38. Libicki, *Cyberdeterrence and Cyberwar*, 65.
39. Moore, "Prospects for Cyber Deterrence," 55.
40. Sterner, "Retaliatory Deterrence in Cyberspace," 75.
41. Kramer, "Cyberpower and National Security," in Kramer, Starr, and Wentz, *Cyberpower and National Security*, 15–16.
42. Lindsay, "Impact of China," 46.
43. Sterner, "Retaliatory Deterrence in Cyberspace," 71–72.
44. Nakashima, "List of Cyber-Weapons."
45. Moore, "Prospects for Cyber Deterrence," 71.
46. Ibid., 56.
47. Libicki, Ablon, and Webb, *Defender's Dilemma*, 106.
48. Rosenzweig, "Achieving Cyber Deterrence," in National Research Council, *Proceedings*, 261.
49. "GAO: U.S. Government," *Homeland Security News Wire*.
50. Zheng and Lewis, *Cyber Threat Information Sharing*, 1.
51. Solomon, "Cyberdeterrence between Nation-States," 7.
52. "GAO: U.S. Government," *Homeland Security News Wire*.
53. Dogrul, Aslan, and Celik, "Developing an International Cooperation," 29.
54. "Russian Cyber Attacks," Channel 4 News.
55. Solomon, "Cyberdeterrence between Nation-States," 7.
56. Goodman, "Cyber Deterrence," 120–21.
57. Clinton, "Remarks on Internet Freedom."
58. Deibert and Rohozinski, "Under Cover of the Net," in Clunan and Trinkunas, *Ungoverned Spaces*, 256; and Wittes and Blum, *Future of Violence*, 242.
59. Cilluffo and Siers, "Cyber Deterrence."
60. Security and Defence Agenda, *Cyber-Security*, 45.
61. Ibid., 19.
62. Stevens, "A Cyberwar of Ideas?," 156.
63. Ibid.
64. Lewis, *Cross-Domain Deterrence*, 4.
65. Stevens, "A Cyberwar of Ideas?," 149.
66. Nye, *Cyber Power*, 16–17.
67. Whetham and Lucas Jr., "Relevance of the Just War Tradition," in Green, *Cyber Warfare*, 171.
68. Valeriano and Maness, *Cyber War*, 62.
69. US Department of Defense, *Cyberspace Policy Report*, 5–6.
70. Lord and Sharp, *America's Cyber Future*, 1:8, 27; and Obama, *International Strategy for Cyberspace*, 10.
71. "Israeli Legal Expert," *Homeland Security News Wire*.
72. Lewis, *Cyber Threat and Response*, 7.

73. Finnemore, "Cultivating International Cyber Norms," 96.
74. Clark, Berson, and Lin, *At the Nexus*, 15.
75. See van Creveld, *Wargames*.
76. Gewirtz, "Russia, the Ukraine Invasion."
77. "West Point Wins," *Homeland Security News Wire*.
78. Healey, "Russia vs. Ukraine."
79. Neuman, "As the Worm Turns."
80. Arquilla and Ronfeldt, *Advent of Netwar*, 94.
81. Libicki, *Cyberdeterrence and Cyberwar*, 28.
82. Intelligence and National Security Alliance, *Cyber Intelligence*, 12.
83. Regan, "Wars of the Future," A1.
84. Morgan et al., *Dangerous Thresholds*, 132; and Libicki, *Cyberdeterrence and Cyberwar*, 69.
85. Gourley, "Towards a Cyber Deterrent."
86. Libicki, Ablon, and Webb, *Defender's Dilemma*, xxi.
87. Cilluffo and Siers, "Cyber Deterrence."
88. Libicki, *Cyberdeterrence and Cyberwar*, 63; and Gorman, "Georgia States Computers," A9.
89. Sterner, "Deterrence in Cyberspace, 74.
90. Libicki, *Cyberdeterrence and Cyberwar*, 62, 63.
91. Geers, *Strategic Cyber Security*, 157.
92. Valeriano and Maness, *Cyber War*, 63.
93. Gartzke and Lindsay, "Cross-Domain Deterrence," 24.
94. Kello, "Meaning of the Cyber Revolution," 37, 15.
95. McDermott, "Decision Making under Uncertainty," 240.
96. Cohen, "Targeting Third-Party Collaboration," in National Research Council, *Proceedings*, 313.
97. Hunt and Chesser, *Deterrence 2.0*, 45.
98. Geers, *Strategic Cyber Security*, 61, 114.

CHAPTER 7

Improving Cyberdeterrence Execution

Perfect cyberdeterrence is illusory. Even with multilayered defenses, every cyberattack cannot be foiled because "the attacker's task is to find or develop a single vulnerability, while the defenders must ensure they protect against any weakness, known or unknown, technological or user-driven."[1] From a policymaker's perspective, the strategic cybersecurity problem is that "we are attacked every day by an imaginative, highly motivated, and anonymous adversary. We can prevail only if we mount near-perfect defenses. And, since there's no penalty for mounting an attack, the adversary simply tries again and again until something works."[2] Thwarting all cyberattackers is not feasible due to the rising global digital dependence and the cyberthreat's scope having outstripped defense resources, leading to tight finances, limited trained personnel, and other pressing security issues. In cyberspace, "if someone is violently bent or fundamentally fixated, they may not be deterrable."[3]

Nonetheless, more effective and legitimate restraint of major cyberattacks is possible in today's global security setting through improved target cyberdeterrence execution that combines maximizing cyberattacker certainty about high costs via credible offensive retaliation/punishment sanctions and minimizing cyberattacker certainty about high benefits via credible defensive denial/resiliency measures (see figure 7.1). In cyberspace, "if the biggest and most dangerous attacks could be prevented, this alone would be an important accomplishment."[4] Given that in the cyber realm "there is simply no such thing as a completely secure system," then "the goal for defenders is to make attacks expensive, rather than impossible."[5] Cyberdeterrence thus entails managing the risks associated with cyberattacks so that both their frequency and the costs they incur do not exceed acceptable levels.[6]

Cost and Benefit Optimizations Mix

An April 2015 US Department of Defense cyberstrategy report highlighted that cyberdeterrence works "by convincing a potential adversary that it will suffer unacceptable costs if it conducts an attack on the United States, and

FIGURE 7.1.
Improving Cyberdeterrence Execution

MAXIMIZING CYBERATTACKER CERTAINTY ABOUT HIGH COSTS

Goals
High Certainty that Cyberattacker Will Suffer Unacceptable Multifaceted, Damaging Consequences
High Credibility of Offensive Retaliation/Punishment Sanctions

Direct, Tangible Orthodox Means
Use cyber retaliation: covertly snoop on cyberattackers, hack into their sites, and steal or corrupt their information
Expand coercive real-world military and economic retaliation against cyberattackers

Indirect, Intangible Unorthodox Means
Employ subtle political and diplomatic pressure on cyberattackers and their sponsors, supporters, and patrons
Increase cyberattacker perceptual awareness of globalization-induced negative blowback

MINIMIZING CYBERATTACKER CERTAINTY ABOUT HIGH BENEFITS

Goals
High Certainty that Cyberattacker Will Fail to Achieve Desired Outcomes
High Credibility of Defensive Denial/Resiliency Measures

Direct, Tangible Orthodox Means
Harden vital assets and expand data redundancy, remote dispersed backups, and system resiliency
Avoid single-system reliance and put in place basic comprehensive cyber-hygiene

Indirect, Intangible Unorthodox Means
Expand cyberattacker diversionary mechanisms using honeypots and honeynets
Increase cyberattacker distorted outcome assessment by reverse spoofing, imminent attack feints, and false damage reports

---

by decreasing the likelihood that a potential adversary's attack will succeed."[7] Promoting cyberattacker hesitation thus is a two-pronged process that maximizes cyberattacker high-cost certainty by emphasizing the idea that attacks would yield unacceptable consequences, which are linked to offensive punishment, and minimizes cyberattacker high-benefit certainty by promoting the idea that attacks would not achieve desired outcomes, due to defensive denial. Each target needs to move from largely focusing on increasing cyberattackers' losses to include decreasing prospects of cyberattackers' gains, thus altering their decision calculus in the direction of restraint. Specifically, to thwart cyber aggressors "we must make the cost so high and decrease their payoff so significantly that the advantages of cyber attack activity will be greatly reduced."[8]

These two strands require tight coordination. Maximizing cyberattacker high-cost certainty by offensive punishment and minimizing high-benefit cyberattacker certainty by defensive denial must occur in supportive ways so that "deterrence by punishment and deterrence by denial may in theory be mutually reinforcing."[9] Neither approach can do the job alone, so it becomes absolutely vital "to integrate denial and punishment strategies, combining the ability to defeat attack with the threat to retaliate."[10]

On the surface, major problems appear to surround heavy reliance on cost-benefit analysis for successful cyberdeterrence. Around the world, states and non-state groups with differing cultural values exhibit marked differences in how each assesses relevant costs (including risks and threats[11]) and benefits both for cyberoffense and for cyberdefense. Moreover, cost-benefit analysis reflects a particular type of Western rationality, one that differs from the prevalent mode of analysis of many groups and states around the world. Because of this difference, even if potential opponents possess some level of "instrumental rationality," they "may misinterpret deterrent threats while others may not feel threatened."[12] Such misinterpretation can be amplified by the distinctive cognitive style, history, and culture of each target as well.[13] Thus, gauging perceived costs and benefits among diverse cyberattackers with low attribution, high dispersal, and morphing membership may be challenging.

However, despite these cultural obstacles, maximizing adversary high-cost certainty and minimizing adversary high-benefit certainty are valuable because even the most malicious extremist hackers are to some degree "sensitive to costs and benefits."[14] Despite pronounced cultural value differences, distinctive ways of processing risk, and idiosyncratic decision-making processes, sufficient global commonality exists about signals, gains, and losses as to make this framework widely useful. Nonetheless, exceptionally high target sensitivity to different cyberattacker orientations seems essential to cyberdeterrence success.

Public and Private Initiatives Mix

Target states should broaden their participation in cyberdeterrence. In moving from having primarily national governments attempt to restrain cyberattackers to incorporating more input of the private sector—that is, combining state officials' input with that of private businesses and citizens—"governments need to recognize the limits of their own credibility and partner with non-state actors who are often more trusted by Internet users."[15] Because "more than 80% of information infrastructure belongs to the private sector in democratic countries, new crises management frameworks and public-private partnerships should be developed as a response to a new threat landscape."[16] Private business involvement is important because "commercial network operators, software developers and equipment manufacturers have detailed firsthand knowledge of and influence over the nature and extent of cyber threats in real time."[17] Indeed, frequently in cyberspace "the best change agents when it comes to flipping non-state actors (potential or realized) are other non-state actors."[18] Given that "the most valuable target for cyberattacks is a country's critical infrastructure, ... the challenge now is to develop strong enough private-public partnership to secure these systems and to convince people to make that investment."[19]

Public partnering with governments in cyberdeterrence, where private citizens play a key role in protecting themselves prior to cyberattacks, deserves more policy attention.[20] Cyberthreat has the potential to hurt human security, as breaches can interfere with the provision of basic needs. In stressing individual responsibility for cyber protection, great sensitivity when incorporating differing public understandings and response capacities is essential. There is a pressing need for the population to acknowledge that "security must become everyone's business."[21] In other words, people must recognize that "cybersecurity isn't a military problem, or even a government problem—it's a universal problem."[22] Citizen accountability, preparedness, and vigilance need heightening because "a mobilized, aware citizenry is an extremely powerful security instrument" to enhance cyberattack resiliency.[23] Justifying public involvement is the knowledge that "each new wave of technological advance creates more freedom for individuals, not less, and more systematic capacity for self-governance and resilience, not less."[24] Growing public exposure to cyberattacks—in May 2014, almost half of American adults had their data hacked over the preceding twelve months[25]—raises general public concern about digital protection and gives citizens a direct stake in improved cyberdeterrence. This exposure should lead to greater citizen receptivity to shouldering cyberdeterrence burdens and sacrifices derived from government partnerships.

Private sector inputs and responsibilities need to be carefully integrated with those of governments, with better public-private cooperation incentives based on comparative advantage for cyberdeterrence.[26] In accommodating inevitable opinion differences, they can develop various solutions in disparate areas for assorted kinds of cyber dangers. For successful integration, cyberthreat communication must be two-way, with governments and private sector participants both disseminating and collecting relevant information.

Orthodox and Unorthodox Restraints Mix

Targets should move from mainly perfecting past and ongoing standard, straightforward cyberattacker countermeasures to include developing alternative cyberattacker countermeasures that combine direct, tangible orthodox restraints and indirect, intangible unorthodox restraints. Differing cyberattackers may elicit varied responses. For example, "while we need unifying principles, the specific strategies must be tailored to key state and non-state actors; the strategy to deter Russia will not work for China or Iran or North Korea and certainly not for non-state actors such as criminal enterprises."[27] The legacy of cyberdeterrence failure shows the futility of relying solely on predetermined, uniform tried-and-true measures.

Direct, tangible measures normally attract more policymaker interest and public support than an indirect, intangible approach because they are more visible and understandable to outsiders and thus seem more likely to generate short-term change in cyberattackers' behavior. These direct, tangible measures rely not on subtle understandings or multifaceted relationships to stop aggression but on frontally confronting potential cyberattackers with the specter of immediate, concrete offensive target retaliation against aggressors or defensive shielding of vital target assets. The simplicity and straightforwardness of this approach enhance its wide appeal.

Nonetheless, indirect, intangible responses to cyberthreat are becoming more critical in a world where intangible power elements are increasingly influential and where indirect outside pressures are progressively eroding states' sovereign rights and transnational groups' autonomous rights to behave as they please. Indeed, in light of "a greatly expanded number and variety of mobile, fleeting and/or unknown adversaries operating within a variety of cyberspaces," classic narrow direct deterrence seems "too restrictive to serve as the basis of policy."[28] In part because "secondary or tertiary effects of cyberattacks may be much more consequential than the direct and immediate ones," cyberdeterrence can greatly benefit from indirect strategies such as undermining the support system for those engaged in cyber disruption rather than undermining the cyberattackers themselves.[29] Indirect deterrence is usually subtler than direct deterrence, entailing nuanced approaches to third parties (often adversaries' supporters, sponsors, and patrons) in addition to attack initiators. Because a key criticism of cyberdeterrence is that "the adversary must have something of value for a pre-emptive/retaliatory strike" and that if it does not (such as with highly dispersed non-state groups) "the threat of cyber deterrence becomes inconsequential," broad inclusive cyberdeterrence suggests using a wider range of methods on a wider array of parties.[30] Moreover, if state governments refuse to take responsibility for cyberattacks emanating from within their borders, then such an expanded deterrence scope can help thwart this plausible deniability.[31] Because what matters most is cyberdeterrence's long-term impact on human, state, and global security, cybertargets need to move well beyond reliance on past ways of dealing with cyberthreat—and on short-run quick fixes and Band-Aids—to address intangibly and indirectly enduring cybersecurity challenges.

Cyberspace and Real-World Responses Mix

Improved cyberdeterrence requires that targets be prepared to use a mix of cyberspace and real-world responses, moving from principally responding to cyberattackers in kind on the same playing field to responses that include different methods on other playing fields. This cross-domain deterrence removes the need to respond in kind to cyberattacks; instead, it looks outside of cyberspace and hits aggressors with many different options, including unexpected ones, at once. State targets should "demonstrate credible willingness to respond through a variety of measures, including economic sanctions, seizure of state resources, diplomatic and political maneuvers, or even military attack."[32] Private companies and international organizations also can impose real-world restrictions on aggressors. Cyber and other kinds of security are inextricably linked. Because cyberattack impacts emerge from the cyber realm, it is hard to differentiate defenses of cyberspace from those of real-world people and structures or to differentiate responses to cyberattacks from those to real-world attacks. Targets must properly integrate and synchronize cyber and kinetic components when preparing to launch cyberdeterrence, as the right mix may differ for each attacker, depending on its capabilities and vulnerabilities.

Some observers argue that cyberattack retaliation ought to be strictly limited to cyberspace, where confrontations presumably generate minimal real-world harm, because many see targets' cyber retaliation as the most logical eye-for-an-eye response to cyberthreat. However, responding only in cyberspace is often inadequate, as cyber retaliation in itself has difficulty restraining all cyberthreat. Cyber retaliation often works best when combined with "other measures such as presence, force movements (e.g., movement into theater; call up of reserves), and other direct deterrent actions that serve as a demonstration of will."[33] To alter an adversary's decision calculus, if a defender is not a great deal weaker than an aggressor in real-world capabilities, "the 'credible threat' against cyberattack needs to go beyond the cyber realm," as illustrated by "the Pentagon's plan for a mixed cyber- and real-world retaliatory force."[34] The "scant empirical record" suggests "the greatest benefit of cyber-weapons may be using them in conjunction with conventional or covert military strikes."[35]

Recently a two-way convergence between cyber and real-world retaliatory sanctions has emerged, with hybrid conflict on the rise. During "all-out conflict, digital attacks would not occur in a vacuum," for "a basic military law is that all weapons are most effective when used in incisive combinations with others," wreaking "virtual destruction with actual destruction."[36] In 2014 the North Korean hacking of Sony Pictures Entertainment led the United States to impose real-world negative economic sanctions against North Korea, and the real-world Russian invasion of Ukraine led Ukrainians to hack the Russian government. Although cyberattacks are situated in cyberspace, they often have "an effect in the natural world," as "we now face the prospect of cyber attacks that destroy real things, like perhaps the electric grid."[37] So today cyber battles may not be confined to cyberspace, and real-world battles may not completely avoid cyberspace, thus reducing any fixed strategic divide between the two.

Fear-Based Prevention and Hope-Based Persuasion Mix

Targets need to expand their orientation for altering adversaries' decision calculus. They need to move from mostly engaging in draconian intimidation of cyberattackers and find sensible ways to convince cyberattackers to restrain themselves by combining fear-based physical prevention and hope-based perceptual persuasion. Some analysts assume that hope-based persuasion is not part of deterrence, but broad inclusive cyberdeterrence embraces all means of preemptively compelling adversaries to cease and desist from aggression. Although used alone neither approach is sufficient to restrain cyberattacks, together they complement each other nicely.

Fear-based prevention—that is, relying on the "stick" of threatened punishing attack losses—gives targets key cyberdeterrence advantages. First, such a response does not require absolute certainty about a cyberattacker's identity, for intimidation can be intentionally diffused to multiple parties. Second, targets get to choose here between ambiguity and clarity: ambiguity can prevent an aggressor from guarding against a particular response, while clarity can communicate devastating inevitable retaliation. Third, fear-based prevention may save a target from having to carry through with retaliation. "The fear component . . . is just as great with a pulled punch as with a fully formed punch—as long as the target understands that the punch was, in fact, pulled."[38]

Not carrying out embedded threats, however, can embolden cyberattackers. For example, should a cyberdefender believe that for cyberdeterrence it must inflict pain on an aggressor "disproportionate to the pain caused by the aggressor's original attack, the defender may be reluctant to retaliate out of fear of either appearing heavy-handed or provoking escalation. If this means the defender declines to fulfill its threat, the attacker may be encouraged to probe elsewhere and see if the defender is shaky on other deterrence commitments."[39] Moreover, the defender must consider, "are the short-term gains from this sort of intimidation, even if latent, worth the long-term discomfort from accelerating the evolution of a particular class of weaponry?"[40]

Hope-based persuasion—that is, relying on the "carrot" of promised valuable restraint gains—can open communication lines between cyberattackers and cyberdefenders rather than simply physically make cyberattacks harder to undertake successfully. Such communication allows adversaries to be verbally convinced that cyberattacks are not worth the effort. Persuasion in cyberspace can be incredibly advantageous. For example, "a would-be bad guy who is induced or persuaded in some way to refrain from intruding on a victim's computer systems or networks results in no harm to those systems or networks, and such an outcome is just as good as thwarting his hostile operation (and may be better if the user is persuaded to avoid conducting such operations in the future)."[41] However, given that for hope-based persuasion, "deterrence is essentially an exercise in psychological manipulation in order to modify, or prevent, modes of behavior, it is fraught with uncertainty."[42] Moreover, even when appropriately applied with a credible intent to fulfill promises, such an option is "never likely to persuade all who might have the capabilities to prosecute actions in cyberspace that constitute strategic threats."[43]

Maximizing Cyberattacker Certainty about High Costs

Direct, Tangible Orthodox Means

Traditionally, improving cyberdeterrence execution by maximizing cyberattacker high-cost certainty has targets take two direct, tangible offensive steps—cyber retaliation against cyberattackers by giving them a taste of their own medicine and covertly snooping on them, hacking into their sites, and stealing or corrupting their information, and coercive real-world military and economic retaliation against cyberattackers or their supporters. Looking first at direct cyber retaliation, in April 2015 the US Defense Department announced that "it should be able to use cyber tools to disrupt an enemy's command of networks, military-related critical infrastructure and weapons capabilities."[44] Effective cyber retaliation must demonstrate great will and capacity, which are often dependent on accurate cyberattacker attribution. Turning to real-world military sanctions, most cybersecurity officials today believe they are crucial. As former Homeland Security secretary Michael Chertoff notes, "In cases where you have a persistent attack on critical national infrastructures, incapacitating the platform used to attack is something you have to do," as retaliating militarily "with overwhelming force" induces cyberattackers "whose internet hygiene is poor to clean up their act."[45] Indeed, irrational adversaries may understand little else. For example, Israeli observers argue that "Arabs and Israelis only understand the language of violence."[46]

In June 2011 the Pentagon adopted a strategy for kinetic military retaliation that classifies "major cyber attacks as acts of war," and as one US military official said, "If you shut down our power grid, maybe we will put a missile down one of your smokestacks."[47] The military response to cyberattacks likely is linked to whether they are comparable in damage to a conventional military strike. In November 2011 the Department of Defense reported that in cyberattack responses, the US military had the right to launch a physical attack and retaliate with force: "When warranted, we will respond to hostile acts in cyberspace as we would to any other threat to our country. All states possess an inherent right to self-defense, and we reserve the right to use all necessary means ... to defend our Nation, our Allies, our partners, and our interests."[48]

Despite legitimacy concerns, exact proportionality is not always required in such military responses to cyberattacks, especially if aggressors hit a target's critical infrastructure but lack similar assets that can be held at risk. "Depending on the clarity of the evidence identifying the attacker, and the attendant international political costs of a disproportionate punitive response, there may also be occasions on which a kind of 'massive conventional retaliation' can be carried out" because "disproportionate responses may have lasting deterrent effects on both the attacker in question, and upon other potential attackers."[49] Cyberattackers may not anticipate such strong target responses given "the normative red lines that states have instituted."[50]

In addition, targets may choose to take tangible negative economic sanctions against cyberattackers or their supporters. For example, in response to cyberthreat, the US government is "not going to necessarily hack back in response" given its greater flexibility with economic sanctions.[51] Such negative economic sanctions include imposing tariffs, waging boycotts and embargoes, blacklisting products, and instituting financial and criminal punishments.[52]

Cyberdeterrence punishment sanctions of all types need substantial improvement, particularly in balancing overly timid and overly bold responses. Generally "the more unpleasant the punishment, the better the deterrent," but even powerful targets have difficulty credibly convincing cyberattackers about high attack costs.[53] For example, "although the United States must demonstrate that it has in its toolkit the requisite items for use against hostile parties when necessary, there has not been a clear cut public demonstration of cyber dominance to date for which the US has definitively taken and actively sought ownership."[54] Cyberdeterrence needs better demonstration of capacity and will, cyberattacker attribution and intelligence, and research and development on offensive options.

To attain more "speed, surprise, and maneuverability" and to clarify rules of cyber engagement, in May 2011 the Department of Defense made public a list of acceptable tools and protocols for cyberdefense, "including viruses that can sabotage an adversary's critical networks, to streamline how the United States engages in computer warfare.... The integration of cyber-technologies into a formal structure of approved capabilities is perhaps the most significant operational development in military cyber-doctrine in years" and affirms, for example, that "the military needs presidential authorization to penetrate a foreign computer network and leave a cyber-virus that can be activated later.... [It] does not need such approval . . . to penetrate foreign networks for a variety of other activities."[55]

Indirect, Intangible Unorthodox Means

Augmenting traditional ways to maximize cyberattacker high-cost certainty are two indirect, intangible offensive target deterrent options—enhancing subtle political and diplomatic pressure on cyberattackers or their supporters, sponsors, or patrons, and increasing cyberattackers' awareness of negative blowback in which, owing to globalization, their own cyberintrusions come back and inadvertently hurt themselves or their allies. As yet, neither of these two alternatives is adequately integrated into cyberdeterrence strategy.

Even if seemingly immune to retaliation owing to dispersal and attribution obstacles, subtle indirect, intangible means of applying political and diplomatic pressure on cyberattackers or their supporters, sponsors, or patrons can be restraining. For example, sometimes such pressure on the Russian, Chinese, or North Korean governments could potentially restrain the nefarious activities of otherwise untouchable private Russian, Chinese, or North

Korean hackers. Ferreting out those who have ethnic, religious, or ideological affiliations with cyberattackers but who live in other societies and have assimilated to other ways of thinking can be highly worthwhile in this regard. This pressure includes public exposure and shaming, diplomatic condemnation and embassy closures, and expulsion from international organizations.[56] Cyberdefenders could "attempt to publicly humiliate the attacker by sharing selective information about the cyber attack with independent computer security researchers and the international media" so as to promote "a wide international consensus regarding the aggressor's probable guilt," which "even if based solely on circumstantial evidence, could prove extremely damaging to the aggressor state's diplomatic and informational power. Such embarrassment might convince the attacker that the potential gain from similar future cyber attacks might not be worth widespread public diplomacy blowback."[57] In another instance, quiet diplomacy may also be vital. A target can "persuade the attacker to stop without making it obvious to others *why* the attacker stopped," a process that often entails deterrence-enhancing fence mending without any loss of face.[58] To punish cyberattackers politically, "national authorities can begin to use the tools developed for terrorism, nonproliferation, and transnational crime ... [by] denying visas, restricting the ability to use banks, and indicting those we know have been involved with or have profited from cyber espionage."[59]

Reinforcing political and diplomatic pressure promotes perceptual awareness of globalization-induced negative blowback, which is defined in cyberspace circles as unforeseen and unwanted repercussions "when malicious code (computer viruses) that one has planted in another person's computer system ends up infecting one's own computers."[60] This blowback can occur when corrupt information reenters "one's own decision-making process undetected," where "blowback will degrade one's own information, reducing one's own situational awareness."[61] Adversaries worry about circumstances when such blowback palpably threatens and limits their pursuit of their own interests and those of their supporters, sponsors, and patrons. Compared to bombs and missiles, cyberweapons seem more likely to create much more "severe and unpredictable" collateral damage that "can be orders of magnitude worse than the intended effect" and can easily backfire on globally interdependent initiators.[62] "Even when the source of an attack can be successfully disguised under a 'false flag,' other governments may find themselves sufficiently entangled in interdependent relationships that a major attack would be counterproductive.... China, for example, would itself lose from an attack that severely damaged the American economy, and vice versa."[63] Thus, foes need convincing that "what they do to us and to others will bounce back to hurt them."⁵⁴ Indeed, to keep from hurting themselves, "even the most cyber-capable states in the system (United States, China, and Russia) are restrained from utilizing their most potent cyber weapons during conflict."⁶⁵

Twenty-first-century examples of blowback concerns abound. In 2003 the US government worried that cyberattacks against Iraq would cause collateral damage, with financial disruption spreading from the Middle East to Europe and then back to the United States.⁶⁶ In 2011 after the discovery of the malware Duqu, which was allegedly created by the United States and Israel to steal industrial facility designs from Iran, criminal hackers copied its unheard-of hacking method and rolled it into "exploit kits." They then sold them to global hackers, who in 2012 attacked "16 out of every 1,000 U.S. computers and an even greater proportion in some other countries."⁶⁷ Owing to such boomerang effects, a *Washington Post* journalist quipped, "What should the United States expect in the wake of all these American military innovations? Prepare to defend against others doing the same thing."⁶⁸

Minimizing Cyberattacker Certainty about High Benefits

Direct, Tangible Orthodox Means

Typically, improving cyberdeterrence execution by minimizing cyberattacker high-benefit certainty has targets take two direct, tangible defensive steps—hardening vital assets while expanding data redundancy, remote dispersed backups, and system resiliency, and avoiding single-system reliance while putting in place basic, comprehensive "cyber-hygiene" to protect against cyberthreats.⁶⁹ Such "cyberdeterrence by denial emphasizes hardening systems against penetration, designing redundancy and graceful degradation capabilities into systems, avoiding complete doctrinal or operational reliance upon individual systems or capabilities, and developing adaptation skills of system administrators and users through education and exercises" while simultaneously possessing "fight-through resiliency to compensate for any losses of fighting potential on the margins."⁷⁰ To be effective, such asset protection must carefully prioritize areas of greatest peril.

Hardening valued assets entails "a combination of layered defenses, well trained and rehearsed incident handlers, user education, and 'hunt' activities to locate and eradicate adversaries that have already found their way into your network."⁷¹ It is crucial to conduct continuous monitoring of sensitive data, systems, and networks that affect transportation facilities; public utilities including electricity, water, natural gas, and waste treatment; and public and government facilities, symbolic sites, town halls, county buildings, police, fire, and school buildings, stadiums, museums, and monuments.[72] The goal is to use "a robust combination of hardware and software components intended to make unauthorized access nearly impossible."[73] The result could "dramatically reduce the attacking actor's perceived benefits—to wit, proving them illusory and meaningless"; and adversaries could find that "developing and deploying potentially destructive cyber-weapons against hardened targets will require significant resources, hard-to-get and highly specific target intelligence, and time to prepare, launch and execute an attack."[74] Decentralizing Internet providers (needed in the Estonia case) and separating computer components (needed in the Aramco case) are key components of this strategy.

Traditional cyberdefense denial measures need substantial improvement and must overcome complacent beliefs that cyber protection is adequate. The tendency to react immediately to detected intrusions may be unwise. Although "signs of a network intrusion bring an almost visceral response from incident handlers and network defenders," it often might be better first for targets "to observe and contain the attacker," thus giving targets time to modify protection and prevent further penetration.[75] Owing to attribution difficulties, defensive denial measures should rely more heavily on target-centered approaches to restrain foreign cyberthreat and focus on improving cyber-hygiene to protect vital assets in ways that do not require exact cyberattacker identification.[76] Signaling through such self-protective measures to aggressors that future intrusions will be futile can "help deter an unknown attacker."[77]

Hardening of vital assets should include protecting vulnerable target systems from data overload, for often data or communications are overwhelmed with noise (often part of denial-of-service attacks designed to incapacitate target websites) that disrupts proper functioning. Combining experienced network defenders and intelligence experts can improve training and result in "skilled, experienced professionals who understand what standard network conditions look like and are able to anticipate and identify intrusions, then handle them appropriately.... [Because] cyber terrain can change drastically over time, ... effective network defenders [must] constantly patch and update systems to eliminate existing vulnerabilities ... [and] must be able to function in an environment where attackers discover new vulnerabilities routinely."[78] Greater use of two-factor or multifactor authentication for users could restrict unwanted data or system access.

Resiliency for targets entails being able to recover fully and quickly from cyberattacks.[79] Ideally this process involves completely reversing any detrimental impacts and returning to the pre-disruption condition, restoring not only information systems but also trust in the network after data breaches. Resilient systems are dynamic and heterogeneous, with the ability to "respond to new threats and new attacks," and they "can withstand failures" so that a single one will not "cause a cascade of other failures."[30] Going beyond the focus on data recovery, such resiliency—and indeed vital asset hardening more generally—needs to be embedded in the design of critical organizations and systems with the goal of preserving critical functions.[81] However, these traditional denial approaches to hardening vital assets and increasing system resiliency by themselves are not sufficient to protect defensively against cyberthreat.

Indirect, Intangible Unorthodox Means

Two indirect, intangible, nonstandard defensive options augment standard target means to minimize cyberattacker high-benefit certainty—enhancing cyberattacker diversionary mechanisms, such as through "honeypots" and "honeynets," and increasing cyberattackers' distortions of outcome assessment (often facilitated by social media) through such measures as "reverse spoofing," imminent attack feints, and false damage reports. The goal is to maximize cyberattacker confusion by using deceptive distraction (refocusing cyberattackers away from valued assets) and obfuscation (making a valued asset seem worthless). Government law enforcement and intelligence agencies have long used cyber deception, which "has already begun to prove itself critical in the information age."[82] Recently, "as the costs of digital espionage soar," private companies that want to be more proactive against cyberattacks have adopted deception "to turn the tables on hackers" by "planting fake data in Web servers to lure hackers into 'rabbit holes' in the hopes of frustrating them into giving up" their attacks.[83] However, deception has not yet been sufficiently integrated into cyberdeterrence strategy.

Honeypot and honeynet mechanisms can not only divert cyberattackers from valued assets but also aid with cyberintelligence collection. To detect and track adversaries as they infiltrate one's networks, targets use a honeypot, or a trap using a deceptively realistic computer environment to attract cyberintruders. Targets can set one up and "watch to see which documents, if any, the adversary chooses to exfiltrate," providing "clues about the adversary's motives" and helping "to identify the adversary, especially if" the target "has been able to obtain strategic intelligence on the operational practices of different actors."[84] For example,

> a Northern Virginia cybersecurity firm that works closely with U.S. intelligence agencies and has been targeted by hackers in China has used honey

pots to collect data on intruders. The firm, whose director requested anonymity to avoid drawing attention to the company, has created encrypted data files labeled with the names of Chinese military systems and put them in folders ostensibly marked for sharing with the National Security Agency and the CIA [Central Intelligence Agency]. With such bait, the firm has been able to document how individual hackers work and has linked their pseudonyms, which are sometimes embedded in source code, to real people. The honey pot "has given us a lot of information about these guys," the director said. "It confounds them."[85]

A useless system or network can be made to "look interesting as a way of persuading offenders to waste their time rummaging through it, show their cyber techniques to the defender, befuddle them with erroneous information, and perhaps get them to leave the system (falsely) satisfied."[86] Complex honeynet systems, comprising multiple honeypots, provide even more extensive possibilities of inviting hacker penetration. Lately "engineers have even begun to experiment with 'fake honeypots' in which legitimate machines try to look like an obvious honeypot in order to scare attackers away."[87]

Through diversion, cyberattacks "can be foiled" by increasing the chances that breaches will harm aggressors. "If it is easy for a covert attacker to gain access to an organization's data, it is also easy for a network protector to feed the attacker data that are useless, misleading, even harmful."[88] Even if a cyberattacker is sophisticated enough to recognize honeypots and honeynets when it stumbles into them, these systems can provide early warning alerts about an imminent cyberintrusion. As Anup Ghosh of cybersecurity firm Invincea concludes, "We can change the game by collecting intel on our adversaries when they compromise our virtual environments rather than them collecting intel on us."[89]

Although appealing, the value of diversion techniques is limited due to trade-offs between their intelligence payoff and potential operational misuse. For example, to attract and monitor terrorist activities, the CIA and the Saudi Arabian government designed a honey pot jihadist website and collected data that intelligence analysts used to track jihadists and their operational plans. But because "the website also was reportedly being used to transmit operational plans for jihadists entering Iraq to conduct attacks on U.S. troops," representatives from various US intelligence agencies debated its use and, after determining "that the threat to troops in theater was greater than the intelligence value gained from monitoring the website," ordered the site dismantled.[90] The lesson is that such diversion techniques need to be used with great caution and skill, lest operational threats are enabled.

Turning from cyberattacker diversion to cyberattacker confusion, increasing aggressor outcome uncertainty about benefits can directly aid targets. As one military analyst quips, "When you're launching a computer attack against somebody, how do you know you've got them and haven't hurt yourself?"[91] The subjectivity of cyberattack payoffs makes deceiving adversaries about them easier. Because cyberattackers lack both physical access to targeted systems and detailed knowledge of such systems, they are relegated to "gazing at the vast cyberspace of their targets through a virtual peephole"; thus, "an agile defender can let them see only what is necessary to support the image that the defender wishes to project."[92]

Even if adversaries engage in random breaches of data and systems, not really caring about any particular asset but rather just exploring to find anything interesting, they can still be upset if they come away with nothing of value or realize that they have become victims of deception. Moreover, if an adversary works hard to break into a system with little perceived gain, then it is likely to refrain from doing so again. Salvatore Stolfo, a Columbia University computer science professor who created a popular decoy data technique, argues that "deception is a very powerful tool going back to Adam and Eve.... If the hackers have to expend a lot of energy and effort figuring out what's real and what's not, they'll go elsewhere."[93] The aim of such decoys is "to create a unique environment that an attacker has never seen before," one where attackers have to struggle to gain intelligence and are unsure whether stolen information is accurate and where they are "forced to lose time, wander into digital traps, and betray information regarding their identity and intentions."[94]

Several modes of target deception are available to promote cyberattacker outcome confusion. First, one could devise reverse spoofing, whereby targets deceive cyberattackers about attack outcomes (the value of what was hacked) instead of cyberattackers deceiving targets about attack origins (the identity of the intruder). Hackers could believe that they had acquired a treasure trove of important data, when in reality what they have is toxic. Thus, "as cyber spies vacuum up terabytes of data from a target's networks, what is to keep them from contracting a virus? As they open exfiltrated files, how can they be sure they have not installed malware that will subvert their own systems? Unable to distinguish between data that are useful and data that are harmful, adversaries can be lulled into a false sense of security, even impunity."[95] Adversaries could experience "a diminishing return on their cyber espionage investments" if a target "can hide its 'signal' in the midst of an overwhelming supply of 'noise,'" such as networks loaded "with meaningless files and disinformation" or through "fake networks with automated, human-simulated packet traffic to deceive cyber spies into wasting time with decoys."[96] A deceptively projected image of a network and its contents can distort a cyberattacker's view of both its accomplishments and its physical capabilities.[97]

Second, one could create "a feint in the cyberspace domain to lure opposing forces into believing an attack is imminent in another warfighting domain," where using "patriotic hackers and cyberspace militia" could act as a deception effort and detract attention from key data assets.[98] Eventually, this feint could cause hackers to "start to imagine that everything is a trap."[99] Third, targets could use deception to convince an adversary that cyberattack damage was "minimal and was being repaired quickly," that undetected data backups existed, and that hoped-for gains "were modest and short lived."[100] Such false reports could reap key cyberdeterrence gains.

Often social media can facilitate adversary outcome confusion, with the added advantage of thwarting opponents' own attempts to use social media to publicize their cause and attract new recruits. While extremist adversaries such as ISIS commonly use social media to spread their views and recruit new members, "social media is equally important for groups that are sharing and communicating information to counter extremist discourse," and a key challenge for moderating voices is to find ways to "leverage social media to limit the diffusion of extremist ideology" while fostering images more favorable to cybertargets.[101] Because cyberattackers' social media sites can be highly useful for gathering intelligence on hacker groups and their supporters, instead of trying to shut down these sites sometimes it is better for targets to launch counteroffensives through them to persuade the same disgruntled audience to doubt the credibility of cyberattacker propaganda or to go in a very different direction. Such methods, which are especially effective on highly susceptible young people, could include creating social media sites that promote an opposite message, undermining the logic and evidence supporting the cyberattackers' message; defacing adversaries' websites; or reducing the credibility of adversaries' claimed successful breaches. Even if a target's manipulative behavior led to tit-for-tat retaliation, a cycle of social media website hacking and manipulation seems far preferable to a debilitating, escalating action-reaction cycle of global cyberstrikes that could disrupt critical infrastructure and citizens' welfare. There is no inherent reason why cyberattackers should have a long-term advantage over cyberdefenders in social media use.

Whether implemented for adversary diversion or adversary confusion, digital deception is a type of active defense that is integral to both cyberoffense and cyberdefense.[102] Adept deception helps cyberdeterrence by reinforcing adversaries' sense of futility, by fostering their wariness about future cyberattacks, and by persuading them in advance that any cyberattack gains would be minimal. Such cyber deception seems available to most targets who depend more on cleverness than advanced technical skills or massive resources.

As with broader strategic deception, cyber deception's effectiveness as "a powerful security countermeasure" requires "the ability of those who know about the deception to keep quiet" and a high correspondence of projected images with "the preconceptions of the attacker."[103] As to cyber deception legitimacy, "most experts say deceptive tactics fall within legal boundaries, as long as fake data are planted only inside a company's network and do not damage a third party's computer system."[104] For example, wide tolerance exists for cyberspace ruses that create "dummy" target systems and transmit false data to mislead intruders, tricking them into trusting results when they should not.[105] The resulting psychological benefits of successful deception-induced outcome confusion, as aptly noted by Brown Printing Company's senior information technology officer Nathan Hosper, are that "you're no longer just having to sit passively by and take it. You have the ability to take control of the situation."[106]

Nonetheless, deception is not always an available option. Its use over time is difficult. Moreover, often deception may work only once, after which the deceived party figures out what happened. In cyberspace, one encounters the dizzying specter of "deception inside of deception inside of deception," much like the real-world spy-versus-spy probing with double agents.

Overall Comments

Although outside-the-box countermeasures are useful for protection in all strategic realms, in cyberspace they are particularly vital due to attack fluidity. For this reason, the underused indirect, unorthodox means suggested are particularly important for cyberdeterrence. For maximizing high-cost certainty, targets must use subtle political and diplomatic pressure on cyberattackers and their sponsors, supporters, and patrons; and they must increase cyberattacker awareness of negative blowback due to globalization. For minimizing high-benefit certainty, targets must also expand cyberattacker diversionary mechanisms, using honeypots and honeynets, and increase cyberattackers' distorted outcome assessment through reverse spoofing, imminent attack feints, and false damage reports. Together such wily indirect approaches can significantly improve cyberattack restraint.

Notes

1. Baker, Waterman, and Ivanov, *In the Crossfire*, 33; and Div, "Five Most Common."
2. Baker, *Skating on Stilts*, 228.

3. Hunt and Chesser, *Deterrence 2.0*, 7.
4. Kugler, "Deterrence of Cyber Attacks," 309.
5. Newitz, "9 Facts about Computer Security."
6. Libicki, *Cyberdeterrence and Cyberwar*, 32.
7. US Department of Defense, *DoD Cyber Strategy*, 11.
8. Cilluffo and Siers, "Cyber Deterrence."
9. Lupovici, "Cyber Warfare," 58–59.
10. Glaser, *Deterrence of Cyber Attacks*, 2.
11. Schneier, *Beyond Fear*, 17.
12. Libicki, *Cyberdeterrence and Cyberwar*, 118; and Lewis, *Cross-Domain Deterrence*, 1.
13. Stein, "Rational Deterrence," in Paul, Morgan, and Wirtz, *Complex Deterrence*, 74.
14. Libicki, Ablon, and Webb, *Defender's Dilemma*, xii.
15. Rattray and Healey, "Non-State Actors," in Lord and Sharp, *America's Cyber Future*, 2:80.
16. Tiirmaa-Klaar, "Cyber Security Threats," 6.
17. Gross et al., "Cyber Security Governance," in Lord and Sharp, *America's Cyber Future*, 2:117.
18. Hunt and Chesser, *Deterrence 2.0*, 26, 31.
19. Security and Defence Agenda, *Cyber-Security*, 9.
20. Raduege, "Fighting Weapons of Mass Disruption," in Nagorski, *Global Cyber Deterrence*, 4.
21. See Flynn, "The Brittle Superpower," in Auerswald et al., *Seeds of Disaster*, 32.
22. Schneier, "Who Should Be in Charge?"
23. Wittes and Blum, *Future of Violence*, 224, 227.
24. Hunt and Chesser, *Deterrence 2.0*, 27.
25. Pagliery, "Half of American Adults."
26. Singer and Friedman, *Cybersecurity and Cyberwar*, 205–11.
27. Cilluffo and Siers, "Cyber Deterrence."
28. Hunt and Chesser, *Deterrence 2.0*, 50.
29. Waxman, "Cyber-Attacks," 438; and Hunt and Chesser, *Deterrence 2.0*, 12.
30. Iasiello, "Is Cyber Deterrence," 64–65.
31. Rowe, "Attribution of Cyber Warfare," in Green, *Cyber Warfare*, 68.
32. Haley, "Theory of Cyber Deterrence."
33. Wheatley and Hayes, *Information Warfare and Deterrence*, chapter 3.
34. Singer and Friedman, *Cybersecurity and Cyberwar*, 146.
35. Rid and McBurney, "Cyber-Weapons," 12.
36. Peters, "Washington Ignores Cyberattack Threats."
37. Hodges and Creese, "Understanding Cyber-Attacks," 35; and Rosenzweig, *Cybersecurity and Public Goods*, 7.
38. Libicki, *Brandishing Cyberattack Capabilities*, 15.
39. Solomon, "Cyberdeterrence between Nation-States," 11.
40. Libicki, *Brandishing Cyberattack Capabilities*, 16.
41. Clark, Berson, and Lin, *At the Nexus*, 51.
42. Sheldon, "Space Power and Deterrence," 1.
43. Stevens, "Cyberwar of Ideas?," 165.
44. Stewart, "Pentagon's New Cyber Strategy."
45. "Chertoff Calls for Cyber-Deterrence," *Homeland Security News Wire*.
46. Follath and Stark, "Story of Operation Orchard."

47. "U.S. Will View," *Homeland Security News Wire*.
48. US Department of Defense, *Cyberspace Policy Report*, 2.
49. Arquilla and Ronfeldt, *Advent of Netwar*, 97.
50. Valeriano and Maness, *Cyber War*, 63, 163.
51. "U.S. Adopts," *Homeland Security News Wire*.
52. Rosenzweig, "Achieving Cyber Deterrence," 257–58.
53. Schneier, *Beyond Fear*, 176.
54. Cilluffo, Cardash, and Salmoiroghi, "Blueprint for Cyber Deterrence, 15.
55. Ibid., 16, 17; and Nakashima, "List of Cyber-Weapons."
56. Rosenzweig, "Achieving Cyber Deterrence," 257–58.
57. Solomon, "Cyberdeterrence between Nation-States," 13.
58. Libicki, "Pulling Punches in Cyberspace," 137.
59. Lewis, *Cyber Threat and Response*, 6.
60. Neuman, "As the Worm Turns"; and Feaver, "Blowback: Information Warfare" 90.
61. Ibid., 106, 111.
62. Raymond, "Paradoxes of (Cyber) Counterinsurgency."
63. Nye, "Power and National Security," 17.
64. Schwartz, "Scenarios for the Future," in Lord and Sharp, *America's Cyber Future*, 2:224.
65. Valeriano and Maness, *Cyber War*, 48, 64.
66. Ibid., 62; and Markoff and Shanker, "Halted '03 Iraqi Plan."
67. Menn, "U.S. Cyberwar Strategy."
68. Pincus, "Inevitable Blowback," A19.
69. Leson, *Assessing and Managing*, 5.
70. Solomon, "Cyberdeterrence between Nation-States," 20.
71. Raymond, "Paradoxes of (Cyber) Counterinsurgency."
72. Lewis, *Cyber Threat and Response*, 5; and Leson, *Assessing and Managing*, 5.
73. Haley, "Theory of Cyber Deterrence." See also Morgan, "Applicability of Traditional Deterrence," 58–59; and Kugler, "Deterrence of Cyber Attacks," 334.
74. Hunt and Chesser, *Deterrence 2.0*, 26; and Rid and McBurney, "Cyber-Weapons," 11.
75. Raymond, "Paradoxes of (Cyber) Counterinsurgency."
76. See Mandel, *Global Threat*, chapters 5 and 8.
77. Nye, *Cyber Power*, 5, 17.
78. Raymond, "Paradoxes of (Cyber) Counterinsurgency."
79. Hunt and Chesser, *Deterrence 2.0*, 1–2.
80. Schneier, *Beyond Fear*, 120–21.
81. Singer and Friedman, *Cybersecurity and Cyberwar*, 169–73.
82. Gartzke and Lindsay, "Weaving Tangled Webs," 318.
83. Nakashima, "To Thwart Hackers."
84. Lachow, *Active Cyber Defense*, 6.
85. Nakashima, "To Thwart Hackers."
86. Libicki, "Pulling Punches in Cyberspace," 125.
87. Gartzke and Lindsay, "Weaving Tangled Webs," 340.
88. Ibid., 336.
89. Masters, "Operation Shady Rat."
90. Theohary and Rollins, *Terrorist Use*, 13.
91. CNN, "Fierce Cyber War Predicted."
92. Libicki, *Cyberdeterrence and Cyberwar*, 172.
93. Nakashima, "To Thwart Hackers."

94. Geers, *Strategic Cyber Security*, 100.
95. Gartzke and Lindsay, "Weaving Tangled Webs," 338–39.
96. Goodman, "Cyber Deterrence," 123.
97. Libicki, *Cyberdeterrence and Cyberwar*, 172–73.
98. Hollis, "Cyberwar Case Study," 6.
99. Gartzke and Lindsay, "Weaving Tangled Webs," 339.
100. Libicki, *Cyberdeterrence and Cyberwar*, 84.
101. "Countering Extremist Groups," *Homeland Security News Wire*.
102. Nakashima, "To Thwart Hackers."
103. Schneier, *Beyond Fear*, 215.
104. Nakashima, "To Thwart Hackers."
105. Schmitt, *Tallinn Manual*, 184; and Clark, Berson, and Lin, *At the Nexus*, 35–36.
106. Nakashima, "To Thwart Hackers."

CHAPTER 8

When Cyberdeterrence Works Best

Although a growing global consensus exists that cyberattacks require "a more robust response" than in the past, so far little guidance has emerged about the conditions under which improved countermeasures would work best or are most needed.[1] Owing to the diversity of cyberthreats and the dangers from misapplying countermeasures, identifying innovative ways to promote cyberdeterrence seems valuable only if they are simultaneously accompanied by the conditions of when to apply them. Assuming their full commitment to take necessary action when it is most advantageous, responsible security decision makers need better situational guidance about when and how to apply this book's broad inclusive mix of cyberattack-restraining elements.

Certain circumstances promote successful target cyberdeterrence. Beyond generally exploring when broad inclusive cyberdeterrence is most vital, this study identifies the conditions when cost versus benefit optimizations, public versus private initiatives, orthodox versus unorthodox restraints, cyberspace versus real-world responses, and fear-based prevention versus hope-based persuasion appear to be most crucial. It also discusses when cyberdeterrence neglect can lead to worst-case scenarios. Given the inescapably limited security resources possessed by targets wishing to apply cyberdeterrence strategies, isolating propitious circumstances is critical to help establish cybersecurity policy priorities.

When Broad Inclusive Cyberdeterrence Is Most Vital

The conditions when broad inclusive cyberdeterrence is most vital are summarized in figure 8.1. These circumstances identify different cyberattacker and cybertarget attributes affecting cyberconfrontation outcomes. Together these insights suggest when it is most important to consider the recommended improvements in cyberdeterrence planning and execution.

FIGURE 8.1.
When Broad Inclusive Cyberdeterrence Is Most Vital

CYBERATTACKER ATTRIBUTES

Ambiguity
If cyberattackers have low attribution and unclear initiator-target power ratios

Danger
If cyberattackers threaten critical national infrastructure (beyond cybertheft of intellectual property)

Support
If cyberattackers have outside support from and ties to other parties

Cleverness
If cyberattackers are technologically sophisticated with fluid attack techniques

Vulnerability
If cyberattackers are not cyber dependent but have high physical/financial vulnerability

Persistence
If cyberattackers have both the capacity and will for sustained cyberattacks

Resolve
If cyberattackers have a legacy of past cyberattack success

CYBERTARGET ATTRIBUTES

Dependence
If cybertargets have high dependence on technology and on other states

Dissension
If cybertargets have internal public-private cybersecurity disagreements

Isolation
If cybertargets are located inside cyberattackers' legitimate regional sphere of influence

Duality
If cybertargets engage in both cyberoffense and cyberdefense initiatives

Transparency
If cybertargets are unable to hide the scope of cyberattack damage

Manipulability
If cybertargets possess few easily internationally controllable Internet connections

Inflexibility
If cybertargets rely on static predictable, formulaic, single-option cyberattack responses

Cyberattacker Attributes

Broad inclusive cyberdeterrence seems most vital when cyberattackers have the following attributes: (1) attacker ambiguity, pertaining to those having low attribution and unclear initiator-target power ratios; (2) attacker danger, aiming to disrupt critical national infrastructure rather than stealing intellectual property; (3) attacker support, having outside support from and ties to other parties; (4) attacker cleverness, possessing technological sophistication and fluid attack techniques; (5) attacker vulnerability, maintaining low cyber dependence but having high physical and financial vulnerabilities; (6) attacker persistence, having both the capacity and will to carry out sustained cyberattacks; and (7) attacker resolve, boasting a legacy of past cyberattack success. These attributes highlight areas where it is most dangerous for targets to stand pat with existing cyberdefenses.

More specifically, if both cyberattacker identity and the initiator-target power ratio are unknown, then better cyberdeterrence contingency planning can help with this decision making under uncertainty. Cyberattacks on critical infrastructure require better overall cyberdeterrence execution given the society-wide security dangers. If an aggressor has support from other parties, then targets benefit from expanded cyberdefense participation because cyberthreat is likely to be multipronged, making it difficult for any single deterrer to stop. If a tech-savvy initiator launches a cyberattack, then targets need to seek an expanded array of expertise from supporters, sponsors, or patrons. If an aggressor has low cyber vulnerability—perhaps due to low cyber dependence or high cyber protection—combined with high physical or financial vulnerabilities, then targets need to use integrated real-world and cyberspace strategies. If an aggressor has both the capacity and the will to carry out sustained cyberattacks, possibly linked to ethnic antagonisms and real-world conflict, then cybertargets would benefit from adaptive and flexible strategic thinking about unorthodox options to avoid prolonged and futile action-reaction cycles. If an aggressor has a legacy of past cyberattack success, then a mix of fear-based prevention and hope-based persuasion may be useful to introduce unexpected cyberdeterrence countermeasures.

Cybertarget Attributes

Broad inclusive cyberdeterrence seems most vital if cybertargets have the following attributes: (1) target dependence, being highly dependent on technology and on other states; (2) target dissension, having internal public-private disagreements over cyberthreat responses; (3) target isolation, being located inside cyberattackers' legitimate regional sphere of influence; (4) target duality, possessing both cyberoffense and cyberdefense initiatives; (5) target transparency, being unable to hide the scope of cyberattack damage; (6) target manipulability, having few easily, internationally controllable Internet connections; and (7) target inflexibility, relying on static predictable, formulaic, single-option cyberattack responses. These areas present the highest vulnerability to cyberattack.

More specifically, if a cybertarget is highly dependent on other states, then it can use its partners to promote pressure and persuasion on aggressors about the undesirability of cyberattack. If government-business disagreements exist within a cybertarget, then a fluid and integrated public-private mix of policy options seems crucial. If a cybertarget is located within a cyberattacker's sphere of influence, then defensive denial moves hardening targets, promoting resiliency, and avoiding single-system reliance are important. If a cybertarget engages in both offensive and defensive initiatives, its global image may be tarnished and its vulnerability heightened, requiring reputation-restoring cyber-hygiene and fence-mending political and diplomatic initiatives. If a cybertarget cannot hide the scope of devastating cyberattack damage, then it should seek outside aid. If a cybertarget is highly manipulable in cyberspace due to a few foreign Internet links—especially where cyberattacker access denial is easy "against a smaller country with fewer external cyber connections and a potentially less resilient system"—then integrated cyberspace and real-world sanctions (preferably aided by allies if a target is weak) seem imperative.[2] If a cybertarget's past cyberthreat reactions have been predictably static and formulaic, then employing indirect, intangible unorthodox cyberdeterrence strategies may keep opponents off-guard.

When Maximizing Costs and Minimizing Benefits Are Most Vital

Maximizing cyberattacker high-cost certainty and minimizing cyberattacker high-benefit certainty are the most important actions under certain conditions (see figure 8.2). Cost maximization seems most consequential when a cyberattacker thinks that it can evade punishment for its actions; when a cyberattacker perceives a cybertarget as being weak, "easy prey" with a history of cyber penetration and who does not retaliate or is unable to detect or launch effective countermeasures; and when the international community is not particularly vigilant or concerned about a target's cyber vulnerability. Benefit minimization seems most necessary when a cyberattacker appears overconfident about the probable success of its actions and about its concrete and image gains, when a cybertarget is highly capable of improving defenses and using outcome deception against a cyberattacker, and when a cyberattacker perceives a target's desired assets as invaluable.

Looking first at cost maximization, if cyberattackers think that they can evade punishment for their actions, then targets need to increase the certainty of severe negative offensive retribution, often by including real-world sanctions. If a cyberattacker sees targets as weak and vulnerable, then the targets need to seek assistance from allies to increase breach costs. If the international community is indifferent about targets' vulnerability, then they may need to amplify and diversify their cyber retaliation capabilities in the absence of a protective defense umbrella.

Asymmetric conflict—where smaller, weaker parties use cyberattacks against major powers—seems particularly propitious for targets seeking to maximize cyberattacker high-cost certainty.[3] While advanced industrial societies depend heavily on networked military, economic, political, and social infrastructure, a smaller and weaker cyberattacker may have few targetable assets because the assets it deems crucial may not be dependent on digital information or externally networked. As a result, this smaller cyberattacker can "do serious damage to a state that is richer and more high-tech but that is correspondingly more dependent on its information systems."[4] North Korea's cyberattack on Sony Pictures Entertainment in the United States illustrates how "cyberweapons are perfect for a failing state" in many ways: "unlike North Korea's small arsenal of six to 12 nuclear weapons, they can be used without risking an annihilating response," and "unlike North Korea's missile fleet, they are uncannily accurate."[5] In such cases, "the low price of entry, anonymity, and asymmetries in vulnerability means that smaller actors have more capacity to exercise hard and soft power in cyberspace than in many more traditional domains of world politics."[6]

In manipulating cyberspace technologies, "smaller countries that could never compete in a conventional military sense with their larger neighbours can develop a capability that gives them a strategic advantage."[7] Today "the Internet has become a powerful asymmetric tool for transnational groups who view themselves as disenfranchised and seek to intimidate the nation-states and other actors presumably responsible for their grievances."[8] Further, owing to low-cost computing devices, resource-starved adversaries need not purchase expensive weapons systems to threaten a militarily superior target. Indeed, "cyber attacks represent a perfect asymmetric weapon—by way of contrast to physical attacks, cyber attacks are relatively cheap to mount and

FIGURE 8.2.
When Cost and Benefit Optimizations Are Most Vital

When Maximizing Cyberattacker Costs Is Most Vital

General Conditions

Cyberattackers

If cyberattackers think that they can evade punishment for their actions

Cybertargets

If cyberattackers perceive cybertargets as being weak, "easy prey" with a history of failed countermeasures

International Community

If the international community is not particularly vigilant or concerned about a target's cyber vulnerability

Specific Conditions

Cyberattacker-Cybertarget Power Ratio

If smaller, weaker powers use cyberattacks in asymmetric confrontations with major powers

Cyberattacker Vulnerability

If cyberattackers lack assets of consequence worth retaliating against
If cyberattackers fear real-world sanctions against their supporters, sponsors, or patrons

When Minimizing Cyberattacker Benefits Is Most Vital

General Conditions

Cyberattackers

If cyberattackers seem overconfident about chances of success and about concrete and image gains

Cybertargets

If cybertargets are highly capable of quality defenses and using outcome deception against cyberattackers

Asset Value

If cyberattackers perceive the desired targeted assets as invaluable

Specific Conditions

Cyberattack Type

If targets use deception against cybertheft rather than cyberespionage

Cyberattacker Experience

If targets use deception against novices ("noobs" or "script kiddies") rather than experts

Cybertarget Regime

If targets use deception within authoritarian rather than democratic societies

Cybertarget Asset

If targets use deception to protect military rather than civilian assets their perpetrators are often difficult, if not impossible, to identify."[9] Within asymmetric cyberconflict, real-world sanctions against supporters, sponsors, or patrons may be necessary when massive cyber retaliation alone may be insufficient to increase cyberattack costs and to restrain zealous and resourceful cyberattackers with significant cyber capabilities, deep passions, ideological commitments, willingness to die, or troubles being "identified and located."[10]

Turning to benefit minimization, having cyberattackers supremely confident about their cyber aggression capabilities means that increasing offensive retaliation threats may not work well, so diversionary mechanisms such as honeypots or honeynets may be needed to prevent any breach gains. The value of this approach is increased if cybertargets are capable of staging quality defenses and of using a diverse array of outcome confusion techniques against attackers. If cyberattackers are convinced that a target has invaluable assets, then they may pursue them regardless of the cost; thus, using trickery about the identity or location of these assets could prove pivotal.

Certain circumstances appear especially conducive to deception's interfering with cyberattacker goal attainment. First, deception seems more useful for cybertheft than for cyberespionage by increasing the needed "time to analyze and assess the validity and utility of stolen information" and by decreasing "the benefits of the attack because of uncertainty about the value of the stolen data."[11] Because cyber thieves are exclusively concerned with monetary gain from cyberattacks, such uncertainty is a potent obstacle, and because their attack mode sometimes rests on quick in-and-out operations, this roadblock could deter them and persuade them to choose other easier, lucrative targets. Second, those without much experience in cyberhacking—conventionally called noobs or script kiddies—seem more vulnerable than expert hackers are to deception-induced outcome confusion. Even today "poorly executed cyber-attacks from unskilled or unresourced attackers" continue to occur, as novice initiators usually engage in simple unstructured cyberattacks and lack the training and resources to differentiate actual from projected outcomes involving deception.[12]

Third, authoritarian states seem more proficient than democratic states are at using cyber deception to promote cyberattack outcome confusion. Such non-transparency for targets assists attacker uncertainty, as "their adeptness at deception and manipulation of information" is "facilitated by the closed and secretive nature of their societies."[13] Fourth, cyber deception seems to work better in protecting military over civilian assets. "Military organizations necessarily have an interest in deception that goes beyond whatever help it provides in securing networks," as these organizations delight in misleading cyberattackers' leadership.[14] Because those military officials who are responsible for vulnerable assets are always expected to maintain high levels of confidentiality, their projecting a deceptive image of imperviousness, redundancy, and resiliency in cyberspace can be quite effective in aiding cyberdeterrence.

When Public and Private Initiatives Are Most Vital

Public and private initiatives are most vital under certain conditions (see figure 8.3). Public government countermeasures seem most important when a cyberattack hits many assets in many parts of a country simultaneously and changes rapidly, when a cyberattack involves cyberespionage and hits military and political assets, and when a cyberattack is covert and requires extraordinary intelligence to identify the initiator or the intrusion method or to determine the proper response mode. Private business or citizen countermeasures seem most crucial when a cyberattack hits just one local area or one corporation and is relatively static, when a cyberattack involves cybercrime and hits economic or cultural assets, and when a cyberattack is overt and requires little intelligence to identify the initiator or the intrusion method or to determine proper responses.

Looking first at public government initiatives, if a cyberattack has a far-flung and rapidly changing scope against key assets such as critical infrastructure for societal functioning, then having the national government lead the target response makes sense for a few reasons. It can standardize protection systems across different areas within countries—and across countries if undertaken through international organizations—and thus create highly predictable expectations concerning cyber protection; and it can fine-tune protection levels depending on changing government estimates about the magnitude, severity, and probability of incoming cyberthreats. In contrast, local or privatized responsibility for target cyberdefense can create large cybersecurity differentials. Thus, in this case, "a purely private regime . . . would be undesirable because the lack of uniformity in software and procedure for active defense indicates that a privately run active defense regime would be unpredictable at best."[15] If a cyberattack is aimed at cyberespionage and assaults sensitive political or military assets, including weapons or protection suppliers, then having the national government take the lead in target responses makes sense because, given its security focus, it understands best how to safeguard these assets from foreign spies.

If a cyberattack is covert and requires extraordinary intelligence for attribution, penetration isolation, or countermeasures, especially when involving

FIGURE 8.3.
When Public and Private Initiatives Are Most Vital

PUBLIC INITIATIVES
If cyberattacks hit many key assets in many parts of a country simultaneously and change rapidly
If cyberattacks involve cyberespionage and target military and political assets
If cyberattacks are covert and require great intelligence to identify the initiator, the intrusion method, or the preferred response

PRIVATE INITIATIVES
If cyberattacks hit just one local area or one corporation and are relatively static
If cyberattacks involve cybercrime and target economic or cultural assets
If cyberattacks are overt and require little intelligence to identify the initiator, intrusion method, or the preferred response

a state initiator, then the national government (unless it is weak, poor, or corrupt) should bear primary responsibility for the target response for two reasons: usually it has better intelligence capabilities than the private sector's, and it can marshal the necessary resources—given that security is a public good—to carefully monitor spillover effects and ensure that reducing one area's vulnerability does not increase that of others. Businesses and private citizens usually lack both the deep and wide intelligence context that government cyberintelligence officials possess about cyberthreats and the necessary resources to address them. "Currently companies big and small only know a piece of the cybersecurity puzzle. Right now, 'situational awareness' about cyber threats is fractured."[16]

Turning to private business or citizen initiatives, if a cyberattack's impact is highly localized and relatively static, especially if public-private differences exist, then the private sector should take the lead in target responses through globalization-related supply chain and private purchasing changes because it knows the hit assets well and has a better localized response capacity than the government does. Indeed, "commercial network operators, software developers and equipment manufacturers have detailed firsthand knowledge of and influence over the nature and extent of cyber threats in real time."[17] If a cyberattack is oriented toward cybercrime and hits economic or cultural assets, then relying heavily on the private sector for target responses makes sense because the people know the targeted assets or direct victims and suffer the pain of the losses. However, the government should play a role as well because, for example, "U.S. interests are harmed by intellectual property theft and U.S. citizens are directly hurt when their information is stolen from company databases."[18] If a cyberattack is overt with a clear initiator (especially non-state) and intrusion method, then the lead in target responses could go to the private sector because it will not need to worry about possibly hitting the wrong perpetrator or responding inappropriately.

For business protection, "the most reasonable option is to let private companies secure themselves, but [the government should] step in if a breach occurs to provide attribution and retaliation services," with the classification system streamlined to facilitate better information sharing and to clarify the support and protection provided.[19] For public protection, when vital data or networked systems are jeopardized, it is crucial to facilitate—often using social media—"public awareness of how individuals can protect their own internet data and promote cyber-security education and training."[20] Governments also should reinforce in citizens' minds the dangers of indiscriminately posting sensitive information online.

When Orthodox and Unorthodox Restraints Are Most Vital

Orthodox and unorthodox restraints are most vital under certain conditions (see figure 8.4). Direct, tangible orthodox countermeasures seem most imperative in these circumstances: if a cyberattack is severe and persists over time and if a cyberattack is barely noticed. Indirect, intangible unorthodox countermeasures seem key under these circumstances: if a capable and willing cyberattacker is opaque due to cultural differences or untouchable due to having few valued assets to lose, and if a cyberattack has exhibited low control and high unpredictability, while a target's responses have traditionally exhibited high predictability.

Looking first at direct, tangible orthodox restraints, if a cyberattack is severe and lasts over time, such as with advanced persistent threats, then targets should use cyber retaliation and coercive real-world negative military and economic sanctions.[21] Cyberattacker attribution seems more likely with this kind of enduring threat (given extra time and evidence to track down the perpetrator), and a cyberattacker needs to recognize that continuing its aggression would lead to its suffering the same kind of debilitating consequences as its target. Such frontal retaliation, possibly involving target allies, seems most likely to convince an adversary to stop its long-term penetration. Alternatively, if a cyberattack is so covert that a victim is unaware of its being perpetrated, then targets should harden valued assets; increase system redundancy, backups, and resiliency; and avoid single-system reliance because these steps could

FIGURE 8.4.
When Orthodox and Unorthodox Restraints Are Most Vital

ORTHODOX RESTRAINTS

Maximizing Cyberattacker High-Cost Certainty
If cyberattacks are severe and persist over time

Minimizing Cyberattacker High-Benefit Certainty
If cyberattacks are barely noticed

UNORTHODOX RESTRAINTS

Maximizing Cyberattacker High Cost-Certainty
If capable and willing cyberattackers are opaque or untouchable

Minimizing Cyberattacker High-Benefit Certainty
If cyberattacks have high unpredictability and target responses have had high predictability

---

minimize long-term damage from any and all unknown assailants and cyberintrusions.[22] The increased difficulty for adversaries to penetrate and disrupt such well-protected systems could cause attack initiation hesitation even when targets are oblivious to breaches.

Turning to indirect, intangible unorthodox restraints, if a target is aware of a breach by a capable and willing cyberattacker who is opaque due to cultural differences or is immune to direct retaliation due to having few valued assets to lose, then the target should promote subtle political and diplomatic pressures on the attacker's supporters, sponsors, and patrons as well as an awareness of negative blowback pressures associated with globalization.[23] Applying such outside pressures can isolate cyber aggressors and either bottleneck vital aggression resources or cause these aggressors to be more cautious due to apprehensions about undesired side effects from breaches. Alternatively, if a cyberattack is unpredictable with low initiator control (such as when it entails many interlocked steps or extensive outside coordination) and a target's past responses have been highly predictable, then a target should use deceptive diversionary mechanisms and outcome assessment error promotion because even before deception the attacker is already predisposed to overconfidence about the nature of target countermeasures but uncertain about breach outcomes.[24] The resulting cyberattacker confusion, combined with the increased ability to gather incriminating information on the cyberattacker, could cause it to question payoffs from continued aggression.

When Cyberspace and Real-World Responses Are Most Vital

Cyberspace and real-world responses are most significant under certain conditions (see figure 8.5). Cyberspace countermeasures appear to be most vital when real-world military and economic retaliation seems likely to generate massive devastation, when a cyberattacker is at a relative disadvantage in terms of its capacity and will to use sophisticated cyberweapons, and when a cyberattacker is extremely geographically distant or physically inaccessible. Real-world countermeasures seem most paramount when cyber retaliation appears escalatory due to low attacker or high target cyber vulnerability, when a cyberattacker is at a relative disadvantage in terms of its capacity and will to use real-world military and economic sanctions, and when a cyberattacker is very geographically close or easily physically accessible.

Looking first at cyberspace responses, if a target's use of real-world military and economic countermeasures looks highly likely to generate massive devastation to persons and property (including collateral damage to unintended civilian targets) either directly as a result of these countermeasures or indirectly as a result of cyberattacker retaliation to these countermeasures, then real-world responses ought to be avoided and cyber retaliation should be employed instead. The rationale here is that cyberdeterrence should ideally strive for the greatest cyberattack restraint with the lowest long-term devastation. Because cyberattacks "can achieve goals that used to require conventional force" and the weapons involved "are unlikely to cause collateral damage in the same way conventional weapons do, . . . in many situations the use of computers would be ethically preferable to the use of conventional weapons." Indeed, "a cyberattack might be less violent, less traumatizing, and more limited."[25] If a target has the advantage in terms of the capacity and the will to use sophisticated cyberweapons over a cyberattacker, then cyber retaliation is preferable over real-world countermeasures. The underlying principle here is that targets ought to go with their relative advantage when responding to cyberattackers, although "the distribution of emerging cyber-capabilities and vulnerabilities—vulnerabilities defined not only by the defensive capacity to block actions but also by the ability to tolerate and withstand attacks—is unlikely to correspond to the status quo distribution of power built on traditional measures like military and economic might."[26] Targets should also consider that this distribution of power is likely to change in volatile ways over time.

If a cyberattacker is extremely physically distant from a target or physically inaccessible to a target, then cyber retaliation—"not constrained by geographic

FIGURE 8.5.
When Cyberspace and Real-World Responses Are Most Vital

CYBERSPACE RESPONSES
If real-world military and economic retaliation seems likely to generate massive devastation
If cyberattackers are at a relative disadvantage in terms of their capacity and will to use sophisticated cyberweapons
If cyberattackers are geographically distant or physically inaccessible

REAL-WORLD RESPONSES
If cyber retaliation seems escalatory due to low attacker or high target cyber vulnerability
If cyberattackers are at a relative disadvantage in terms of their capacity and will to use real-world military and economic sanctions
If cyberattackers are very geographically close or easily physically accessible

---

location or distance (though the manmade infrastructure supporting cyberspace is so constrained)"—may be the most sensible option. "When combined with the attribution challenge, cyberspace's speed and collapse of distance present a formidable security challenge. . . . Geographic distance imposes significant time and maneuverability constraints on military operations on land, in the air, at sea and in outer space. In these domains, temporal and physical distance often enables a target to prepare and/or preempt when it sees an attack coming."[27] Indeed, in cyberconfrontations, "the terrestrial distance between adversaries can be irrelevant because everyone is a next-door neighbor in cyberspace."[28]

Turning to real-world responses, if target retaliation exclusively in cyberspace seems escalatory in terms of constraining an adversary's response—perhaps owing to low attacker or high target cyber vulnerability—then "cross-domain deterrence" incorporating real-world military and economic countermeasures is preferred, especially when an attacker is vulnerable physically or financially. This response has the potential to reduce action-reaction cycles because in many circumstances even the most devastating cyberattacks cannot prevent targets from undertaking cyber retaliation.[29] If a cyberattacker is proficient in cyberweapons but is deficient relative to a target in conventional real-world military and economic capabilities, then a target should use real-world military and economic retaliation because vast target superiority in conventional real-world power—where the target had credibly shown both the capability and the will to use such force effectively—could discourage a cyberattacker from retaliating. If a cyberattacker is physically proximate or easily physically accessible—preferably within a target's sphere of influence—then a target's use of real-world military and economic retaliation could be warranted. The justification relates to both the effectiveness and legitimacy of the response: for effectiveness, a target's real-world military sanctions are easier to apply logistically to proximate cyberattackers, and for legitimacy, just as the international community sees greater legitimacy for a cyberthreat initiated within rather than outside one's regional sphere of influence, so it might see greater legitimacy for the target's real-world retaliation initiated within rather than outside its sphere of influence.

When Fearful Prevention and Hopeful Persuasion Are Most Vital

Fear-based physical prevention and hope-based perceptual persuasion are most consequential under certain conditions (see figure 8.6). Fear-based prevention countermeasures appear to be most important when a cyberattack involves an initiator whose attribution seems especially difficult, when a cybertarget has a past reputation for successful retaliation, and when a cyberattack seems to present a low probability of a tit-for-tat arms race. Hope-based persuasion countermeasures seem most vital when a cyberattack involves an initiator whose attribution is certain, when a cyberattacker has a reputation for success and the cyberdefender has a reputation for failure, and when a cyberattack seems to present a high probability of a tit-for-tat arms race.

Looking first at fear-based physical prevention, if cyberattacker attribution seems especially difficult, then target-initiated hope-based persuasion becomes next to impossible due to the uncertainty about exactly which initiator one would negotiate with or attempt to influence. In contrast, a target's projection of a broad, global intimidating image with a perceived high probability of painful retaliation for any cyberattack could restrain several adversaries without having to know which one was the culprit for a particular aggressive incident. Thus, "ironclad attribution is not necessary for deterrence as long as attackers can be persuaded that their actions may provoke retaliation."[30] If from past cyberconfrontations a target is known as a successful, committed, and credible cyber retaliator, then even when facing obstacles, the target's use of fear-based prevention can succeed due to its reputation for resolve. Such intimidating approaches may work best "when they arise from the past record of interactions between the same deterrer and aggressor."[31] If a cyberconfrontation presents a particularly low probability of tit-for-tat mutual arms races, because of either a power imbalance between the two sides or one side's unwillingness/

FIGURE 8.6.
When Fearful Prevention and Hopeful Persuasion Are Most Vital

FEAR-BASED PHYSICAL PREVENTION
If cyberattacks involve initiators whose attribution seems especially difficult
If cybertargets have a past reputation for successful retaliation
If cyberattacks seem to present a low probability of a tit-for-tat arms race

HOPE-BASED PERCEPTUAL PERSUASION
If cyberattacks involve initiators whose attribution seems certain
If cyberattackers have a reputation for success and cyberdefenders have a reputation for failure
If cyberattacks seem to present a high probability of a tit-for-tat arms race

---

incapacitation to keep responding over time, then it seems advantageous for targets to employ fear-based physical prevention in cyberdeterrence. However, judging this low probability for action-reaction cycles would need to be done very carefully because of the high chances for misperception and misestimation.

> Conflict in cyberspace is uniquely predisposed to escalation given uncertainties about what constitutes an act of war and the growing number of state and non-state actors seeking offensive capabilities. Actors are more likely to misperceive or miscalculate actions in cyberspace, where there is no widely understood strategic language for signaling intent, capability and resolve. Uncertainty will encourage states to prepare for worst-case contingencies, a condition that could fuel escalation. Furthermore, "false flag" attacks, in which an actor purposefully makes an attack look like it came from a third party, could also ignite a conflict.[32]

If targets misinterpret the chances of ensuing arms races or they mishandle fear-based prevention, then such high-risk responses could backfire and lead to endless conflict or strategic stalemate.

Turning to hope-based perceptual persuasion, if a target seems reasonably sure about the attribution of a cyberattacker, then—parallel to the earlier discussion of fear-based prevention—it is presented with a great opportunity to respond not by intimidating a cyberattacker but by engaging in a concerted effort to persuade the culprit non-coercively not to carry through with its intended cyberintrusions. Given that today the "Internet will increasingly be used during the conflicts as the medium to influence international public opinion," it can also assist in altering an adversary's decision calculus when a cyberattacker can be readily identified.³³ If a cyberattacker has a reputation for success and a target lacks a reputation for resolve in its coercive responses to past cyberthreat, then hope-based persuasion seems to give it the best chance for a successful outcome. Even if cyberattacker attribution is not ironclad, "a great deal depends on how risk-averse the target is. If the target fears the consequences of not retaliating against the true attacker (the wimp factor) more than it fears the consequences of retaliating against an innocent state (the blunder factor), it does not need much confidence in its attribution to convince itself" to respond.³⁴ Manipulating social media to emphasize the logic of restraint can aid these target persuasion efforts, for cyberattackers of all stripes appear to be highly attentive to what is on the Internet. If an endless cyber arms race seems inevitable due to the substantial capabilities and determined will of both cyberattackers and cyberdefenders, then fear-based retaliation would be self-defeating. In this case, hope-based persuasion—that is, by demonstrating the interminable futility of continued confrontation—seems to be the only option (other than non-response) that could defuse the tense and volatile situation. The ensuing interactive communication appears most likely to produce a stable outcome once the two sides recognize the high costs of failure.

When Cyberdeterrence Neglect Leads to Worst-Case Scenarios

If these propitious conditions are ignored and cyberdeterrence is neglected, then the likely security consequences seem quite ominous (see figure 8.7). None of the goals for a smoothly operating, globally interconnected data network—access, freedom, privacy, or security—would be attained. The resulting cyberattacks could unpredictably control or crash global information networks in a terrifying manner. For instance, "if they take over a network, cyber warriors could steal all of its information or send out instructions that move money, spill oil, vent gas, blow up generators, derail trains, crash airplanes, send a platoon into an ambush, or cause a missile to detonate in the wrong place." Alternatively, "if cyber warriors crash networks, wipe out data, and turn computers into door stops, then a financial system could collapse, a supply chain could halt, a satellite could spin out of orbit into space, an airline could be grounded."³⁵

The consequences of such attacks could be devastating to both human and state security. Indeed, "the impact of a destructive cyber attack on the civilian population would be even greater with no electricity, money, communications, TV, radio, or fuel (electrically pumped). In a short time, food and medicine

FIGURE 8.7.
When Cyberdeterrence Neglect Leads to Worst-Case Scenarios

DESTRUCTION OF GLOBAL INFORMATION SYSTEM
None of the goals for a smoothly operating, internationally interconnected data network—access, freedom, privacy, or security—would be attained
Cyberintruders would crash networks, wipe out data, and turn computers into doorstops

DESTRUCTION OF GLOBAL POWER/COMMUNICATIONS/
TRANSPORTATION SYSTEM
Basic societal survival—relying on continuing power sources and transportation and communications systems—would be jeopardized
Cyberintruders would spill oil, vent gas, blow up generators, derail trains, and crash/ground airplanes

DESTRUCTION OF GLOBAL MILITARY SYSTEM
Cyberintruders would send a platoon into an ambush, cause a missile to detonate in the wrong place, or cause a satellite to spin out of orbit and into space
Military command and control during wartime and peacetime would be haphazard at best

DESTRUCTION OF GLOBAL POLITICAL SYSTEM
Both human and state security would be substantially degraded, with critical national infrastructure ceasing to function under adverse conditions
The world could easily descend into total cyber anarchy, with no effective governance

DESTRUCTION OF GLOBAL ECONOMIC SYSTEM
Cyberintruders would steal all existing financial information, send out instructions that move money at will, and bring supply chains to a halt
The global financial system could collapse, causing rampant cybercrime and corporate cyberespionage

DESTRUCTION OF GLOBAL SOCIAL SYSTEM
Nobody's information would be secure, and nobody would know what to believe because no reliable source would exist for cross-checking information
Mutual distrust among parties dependent on cyberspace would escalate

distribution systems would be ineffective; transportation would fail or become so chaotic as to be useless. Law enforcement, medical staff, and emergency personnel capabilities could be expected to be barely functional in the short term and dysfunctional over sustained periods."[36] Because "defense, the police, banking, trade transportation, scientific work, and a large percentage of the government's and the private sector's transactions are online," the result could expose "enormous vital areas of national life to mischief or sabotage by any computer hacker, and concerted sabotage could render a country unable to function."³⁷ Besides data contamination and property damage, cyberattacks may then cause "even the loss of human life."³⁸ Total global anarchy could eventually ensue.

The specter of a completely interpenetrated and vulnerable world, where the capacity for and susceptibility to cyberattacks are both maximized, is a true nightmare. There would be constant cyberconflict, cyberespionage, cyberterrorism, and cybercrime, with virtually no cybersecurity.³⁹ Nobody's information—no matter how important or protected—would be secure, proprietary, or private. Moreover, nobody would know what to believe—thus escalating mutual distrust—because no source would be reliable. Critical national infrastructure would become dysfunctional, interrupting power sources, transportation, and communications. Military command and control during wartime and peacetime would be haphazard at best.

Developing policy responses based exclusively on worst-case analysis is always unwarranted, and much of this dire scenario may derive from highly subjective fatalistic fears rather than from reality. Nonetheless, owing to growing publicity surrounding seemingly ever more devastating cyberattacks, the public may become increasingly terrified of foreign cyberthreat and buy into this worst-case nightmare scenario, because in cyberspace, as in the real-world, "people still seek protection from states, organizations, and individuals who would harm them."⁴⁰ As a result, public and private cybersecurity decision makers must strive to resist the temptation of giving in to calls for immediate drastic retaliation in response to any cyberintrusion and instead prudently and dispassionately assess what should be done to promote global restraint.

Overall Comments

The quest to identify the circumstances under which cyberdeterrence works best or worst and is most or least necessary is inescapably more tentative than doing so for the deterrence of most other kinds of strategic threats. This tentativeness is due to the recency of cyberthreat's emergence, the difficulties in objectively determining attribution or attack details, the rapidly changing nature of the perpetrators and attack methods, and the scarcity of situations where preventive policies were implemented that could be deemed successful. Nonetheless, the conditions identified here qualify the utility of cyberdeterrence in ways that could guide security policy and clarify how countermeasures that might work in one circumstance would fail in others, thus preventing a universal, one-size-fits-all mentality from prevailing.

Notes

1. Brenner, *Glass Houses*, xi.
2. Russell, *Cyber Blockades*, 145.
3. See Carter, "Asymmetric Cyberwarfare"; and Phillips, "Asymmetric Nature."
4. Libicki, *Cyberdeterrence and Cyberwar*, 70, 122.
5. Sanger, "Countering Cyberattacks."
6. Nye, *Cyber Power*, 1.
7. Shimeall, Williams, and Dunlevy, "Countering Cyber War," 16.
8. Herzog, "Estonian Cyber Attacks," 52.
9. Rudner, "Cyber-Threats," 458.
10. Kay, *Global Security*, 247; and Caldwell and Williams, *Seeking Security*, 174–75.
11. Lachow, *Active Cyber Defense*, 6.
12. Hodges and Creese, "Understanding Cyber-Attacks," 58–59; and Giampiero, *Information Society*, 1531.
13. Coll, "Unconventional Warfare," 17.
14. Libicki, *Cyberdeterrence and Cyberwar*, 171–72.
15. Kesan and Hayes, "Thinking through Active Defense," 337.
16. Lewis, *Cyber Threat and Response*, 7.
17. Gross et al., "Cyber Security Governance," in Lord and Sharp, *America's Cyber Future*, 2:117.
18. Haley, "Theory of Cyber Deterrence."
19. Ibid.; and Lord and Sharp, *America's Cyber Future*, 1:8.
20. Security and Defence Agenda, *Cyber-Security*, 5.
21. Hodges and Creese, "Understanding Cyber-Attacks," 46–47.
22. Ibid., 50.
23. Caldwell and Williams, *Seeking Security*, 174–75.
24. Hodges and Creese, "Understanding Cyber-Attacks," 46.
25. Rid, "Cyberwar and Peace," 85.
26. Waxman, "Cyber-Attacks," 450.
27. Lord and Sharp, *America's Cyber Future*, 1:24.
28. Geers, *Strategic Cyber Security*, 10.
29. Libicki, *Cyberdeterrence and Cyberwar*, 163.
30. Ibid., xvi.
31. Rekasius, *Unconventional Deterrence Strategy*, 32; and Huth, "Deterrence and International Conflicts," 25–48.
32. Lord and Sharp, *America's Cyber Future*, 1:28, 30.
33. Tiirmaa-Klaar, "Cyber Security Threats," 7.
34. Libicki, *Brandishing Cyberattack Capabilities*, 14.
35. Clarke and Knake, *Cyber War*, 70.
36. Defense Science Board, *Resilient Military Systems*, 5.
37. Laqueur, "Postmodern Terrorism," 35.
38. Lord and Sharp, *America's Cyber Future*, 1:7.
39. Schwartz, "Scenarios for the Future," 225–26.
40. Wittes and Blum, *Future of Violence*, 261.

Conclusion

This conclusion discusses how to (1) integrate and stabilize cyberdeterrence elements, (2) consider critical cyberdeterrence legitimacy and ethics dilemmas, (3) address the cyberdeterrence paradoxes, and (4) project realistic future cyberdeterrence prospects. This discussion ties together earlier insights and places in an interpretive context policy recommendations about broad inclusive cyberdeterrence elements (see figure C.1).

Integrating and Stabilizing Cyberdeterrence

For success, the multifaceted strategies embedded in broad inclusive cyberdeterrence when applied globally require both integration and stabilization. If integration and stabilization efforts fail, the countermeasures that cybertargets undertake could fall flat or undercut one another. The principal ways to integrate and stabilize cyberdeterrence, as shown in figure C.2, emphasize improving (1) cyber burden sharing, (2) cyber arsenal broadening, (3) cyber protection equalization, and (4) cyber outcome evaluation.

Cyber Burden Sharing

For enhanced cyber burden sharing, a target should reduce multilateral barriers and foster collective responsibility. To accomplish both ends, it needs to take advantage of existing globalization and interdependent relationships by spreading common cybersecurity norms and common cross-national defense practices among affected public and private parties. Spreading such norms and practices in the short run could help address the obstacles to forward progress that are presented in chapter 3. These dispersed norms and practices could create a foundation for more meaningful and binding international cybersecurity agreements and for smoother paths to dealing with seemingly disruptive global power shifts caused by cyberspace developments. Such norm diffusion could also help affected states, transnational groups, and international organizations adjust better to the global sea change discussed in chapter 2 that deals

FIGURE C.1.
Broad Inclusive Cyberdeterrence Elements

COST AND BENEFIT OPTIMIZATIONS MIX
Moving from largely increasing cyberattackers' losses to include decreasing prospects of cyberattackers' gains, combining maximizing certainty about high costs and minimizing certainty about high benefits

PUBLIC AND PRIVATE INITIATIVES MIX
Moving from primarily national governments making decisions about restraining cyberattackers to include the private sector, combining state officials' input with that of private businesspeople and citizens

ORTHODOX AND UNORTHODOX RESTRAINTS MIX
Moving from mainly perfecting past and ongoing standard, straightforward cyberattacker countermeasures to include developing alternative cyberattacker countermeasures, combining direct, tangible orthodox restraints and indirect, intangible unorthodox restraints

CYBERSPACE AND REAL-WORLD RESPONSES MIX
Moving from principally responding to cyberattackers in kind on the same playing field to include responding via different methods on other playing fields, combining cyberspace and real-world responses

FEAR-BASED PREVENTION AND HOPE-BASED PERSUASION MIX
Moving from mostly engaging in draconian intimidation of cyberattackers to include finding sensible ways to convince cyberattackers to restrain themselves, combining fear-based physical prevention and hope-based perceptual persuasion

---

with reduced sovereignty and authority and the resulting lower confidence in traditional sources of power.

To reduce multilateral barriers, potential targets need specifically and clearly to delineate cyber duties among multiple parties, to identify who has final cyber authority, to restrict decision compartmentalization, to use multilateral tracking and monitoring of illicit cybertool sales, and to incentivize coherent, common cyberthreat intelligence sharing. Mutual distrust must be overcome within and across national governments, between government and business, and between government and the public. Clarifying the roles and duties of the different parties is facilitated by participating in advance joint cyberdefense exercises, and restricting compartmentalization and incentivizing information sharing is enabled by comprehensively reevaluating the security

FIGURE C.2.
How to Integrate and Stabilize Cyberdeterrence Elements

CYBER BURDEN SHARING

Reduce Multilateral Barriers

Delineate clearly cyber duties among multiple parties and identify who has final authority
Restrict decision compartmentalization and incentivize coherent, common cyberthreat intelligence sharing

Foster Collective Responsibility

Let private companies secure themselves but have the government step in if a breach occurs
Promote cybersecurity education and training to increase public awareness of how to protect data

CYBER ARSENAL BROADENING

Set Acceptable Parameters

Induce ways for everyone to harden cybertargets and agree on acceptable retaliation means
Ensure that responses to cyberthreats are an outgrowth of overarching deterrence doctrine

Expand Credible Options

Make cyberdeterrence planning and execution strategies more mutually reinforcing
Accentuate more speed, surprise, and maneuverability in denial/resiliency and retaliation/punishment strategies

CYBER PROTECTION EQUALIZATION

Limit Safety Disparities

Enhance system administrator and user skills and reduce technician-strategist and attacker-defender knowledge gaps
Spread cyber-hygiene and early warning systems universally to provide basic cyberthreat protection

Reinforce Security Balances

Help government, business, and the public balance cyberopenness with cybersecurity
Weigh one's security priorities in light of adversaries' goals, motives, cost-benefit calculations, and risk-taking propensities

CYBER OUTCOME EVALUATION

Multiply Adversary Hurdles

Judge whether adversaries are denied safe havens in other countries and are convinced of negative cyberattack blowback
Assess whether adversaries have to work hard for sensitive data, to question its value, and to wander into digital traps

Improve Integration Assessment

Evaluate regularly the adequacy of cyberdeterrence planning and execution strategies classification of cyberthreat information and, in the process, broadening what kinds of critical information and cyber protection technologies could be safely shared with allies.

A key component of reducing these multilateral barriers involves improving public-private sector cooperation in restraining cyberattacks, and doing so entails taking concrete steps to reduce existing public-private distrust in this area. These steps require national governments and multinational corporations to make significant compromises: governments need to be more willing in certain circumstances to lower their standards for granting security clearance for corporate executives so they can receive valuable intelligence about cyberthreats, and corporations need to be more willing in certain circumstances to lower their concerns about maintaining a competitive market advantage and to share information about breaches and countermeasures. To increase each party's willingness to make such sacrifices, they need to focus both on the common threats and high costs that cyberattacks pose and on the huge advantages in terms of speedy and effective responses that would likely result from such enhanced information sharing.

To foster collective responsibility, cybertargets need to let private companies secure themselves but allow the government step in if breaches occur, and they must promote cybersecurity education and training to increase the public's awareness of how to protect data. Forging a sense of being part of a team, where each component feels its complementary contribution to the collective cybersecurity is valued, enhances cooperation between government and business, and it allows each to operate with the comparative advantage in knowledge and capabilities. To increase the public's awareness and involvement in protecting sensitive data and to improve citizen compliance with government cybersecurity initiatives, the education and training offered needs to be directly relevant and connected to people's daily lives, presented in a clear and concise way, and designed to underscore the growing costs of cyberattacks and the sizable benefits reaped by more consistent and effective public self-protection.

Cyber Arsenal Broadening

For improved cyber arsenal broadening, a target needs to set acceptable parameters and to expand credible options. To set acceptable parameters, it should induce better ways for everyone to harden vital assets and agree on acceptable retaliation means (with technical details kept secret), and it should ensure that cyberthreat responses are an outgrowth of overarching deterrence doctrine. To improve globally the use of the best cyber protection methods, each cybertarget needs to learn each other's lessons about how to tailor cyber tool choices to a particular adversary's vulnerabilities and to a particular cyberattack threat. Keeping effective cyberdefense techniques secret and proprietary among allies makes little sense, although cybertargets must take care not to release details of all-important cyberintelligence weapons' secrets and cybertechnologies in a manner that could seep out to adversaries.

Targets need to ensure that cyberdeterrence fits in with overall strategic deterrence policy. For each target, cyberthreat responses should be "an outgrowth of its broader deterrence strategy relative to a given actor, meaning that the cyber-deterrence component should be consistent with and complementary to any preexisting, broader ... deterrence strategy."[1] Sometimes cyberdeterrence initiatives are considered so distinctive that they are isolated from—and even inconsistent with—broader deterrence policies, and that variance erodes security coherence. For maximum credibility and effectiveness, cyberdeterrence needs to be a well-integrated defense component that is in tune with non-cyber policy initiatives, and to accomplish this, policymakers need to juxtapose carefully cyberdeterrence means and ends to those involved in broader deterrence policies.

To expand credible options, cybertargets need to make cyberdeterrence improvements more mutually reinforcing and to accentuate more speed, surprise, and maneuverability in denial and punishment sanctions. For better mutual reinforcement, cybersecurity decision makers need to communicate more regularly with each other about what they are doing and to take steps to ensure that no countermeasure will function at cross-purposes with any of the others. For increased speed, surprise, and maneuverability, special emergency task force arrangements that allow cyberdeterrence officials to cut through red tape and to act quickly and decisively may be necessary to increase the chances of bypassing bureaucratic sluggishness in times of cyber crisis.

A key component of broadening one's arsenal in cyberspace is ensuring that one's choice of tool or tactic matches up well with each of a wide variety of potential cyberattackers. To achieve this end, targets need to learn as quickly as possible the vulnerabilities and sensitivities of each adversary and then evaluate carefully their available arsenal of responses to determine which is most appropriate. As suggested in chapter 6, variations of simulations and war games could serve the purpose of exploring in advance how well particular responses play out in the short run and the long run within hypothetical confrontations. Further, as noted in chapter 3, one prerequisite to success here is to avoid any response pattern that appears rigidly predictable when dealing with highly adaptive assailants.

Cyber Protection Equalization

For improved cyber protection equalization, a target needs to limit safety disparities and reinforce security balances. To accomplish the first goal, it should find ways to develop and improve common baseline system administrator and user adaptation skills, to reduce knowledge gaps between tech-savvy employees and strategic planners and between cyberattackers and cyberdefenders, and to spread cyber-hygiene and early warning systems universally to provide basic cyberthreat protection. Officials need to reexamine the bottlenecks restricting the free flow of cyberdefense techniques, for adjusting "regulations that constrict the flow of information" prevents "disparities among people's access to knowledge" and "a negative effect on the shape, architecture, safety, and resilience of the Internet."[2] The spread of cyber-hygiene requires a willingness to empower system administrators and users with the set of skills and influence necessary to promote robust resiliency—including keeping careful logs of ongoing cyber activity to help track down intrusions—when facing unforeseen modes of cyberattack. To function properly, early warning systems should seamlessly operate across national boundaries and be accompanied by concrete, well-publicized, and well-understood actions about necessary steps that should be undertaken once an alert occurs about an imminent cyberattack.

A key component in cyber protection equalization entails an altered emphasis by national governments and private corporations, moving from working toward achieving superiority in one's own cyber protection relative to that of the state or of corporate competitors to becoming concerned about improving the cyber protection of the most vulnerable global targets. This shift requires sharing the most viable and transportable ideas with others. Although on the surface this thrust seems contrary to self-interest, the high level of global interdependence means that a serious breach in one part of the world can easily affect politics or business in another part of the world. To motivate this emphasis switch, those with the best cybersecurity need to be more aware that eliminating weak links in the international system is an advantage to all cybertargets, and those with the worst cybersecurity need to recognize the advantages of requesting assistance from those who could help improve their protection against cyberattacks.

To reinforce security balances, cybertargets need to help governments, businesses, and the public balance cyberopenness with cybersecurity, and they need to weigh their security priorities in the context of the goals, motives, cost-benefit calculations, and risk-taking propensities of their adversaries. Balancing cyberopenness with cybersecurity requires more public-private dialogue within and across countries about strong, underlying emotional feelings on these issues, for a broad consensus needs to emerge about how to weigh competing values. In weighing their own security priorities in the context of their adversaries' inclinations, cybertargets must show a greater willingness to deviate from generic security formulas in those circumstances when a need emerges to defend against highly unorthodox cyber aggressors that requires nontraditional responses from single or multiple targets. Although making such assessments may seem cumbersome, this flexibility and nimbleness are central to cyberdeterrence success.

Cyber Outcome Evaluation

For improved cyber outcome evaluation, a target needs to multiply adversary hurdles and improve integration assessment. To multiply adversary hurdles, a target should judge the extent to which adversaries begin to find other countries are denying them safe havens and support; become convinced of self-interested, negative cyberattack blowback; start having to work harder for sensitive data and questioning its value; and increasingly wander into digital traps. This process of generating more obstacles for one's adversaries focuses on the psychology of cyberattackers, with the goal of significantly altering their decision calculus.

To improve integration assessment, cybertargets need to evaluate regularly the adequacy of their cyberdeterrence planning and execution outcomes and to monitor continually the sufficiency of emergency contingency options. Assessment is one of the trickiest cyberdeterrence elements because targets commonly tend to monitor and evaluate systems too sporadically or too incompletely and to assume that everything is working well unless blatant discrepancies or malfunctions occur. Instead, targets should strive for an atmosphere of nonstop wariness and vigilance, with outsider groups performing assessments to reduce tendencies that justify dysfunctional, ongoing standard operating procedures.

In considering cyberconfrontation outcome evaluation, it is difficult to judge if a lowered threat directly results from particular cyberdeterrence strategies, especially in a highly interconnected world. This dilemma is comparable to that of evaluating counterterrorism policy outcomes in the aftermath of the 9/11 attacks, when seemingly in response to defensive steps taken by the United States "the risk of further large-scale attacks on the U.S. mainland fell," but "no one knows by how much."[3] Security effectiveness is usually hard to gauge because "most of the time we hear about security only when it fails.... Security, when it is working, is often invisible not only to those being protected, but to those who plan, implement, and monitor security systems."[4] Moreover, judging cyberdeterrence success requires speculative calculation of opportunity costs—that is, what would have happened had the cyberdeterrence not occurred. Complicating metrics for cyberdeterrence is that it can follow security dilemma dynamics, with less for me meaning more for you and vice versa. Similarly, in cyberspace it is possible that "actions that are designed to deter one type of actor will only incentivize other actors," especially "if they could mask or spoof their operation to look like [that of] someone else."[5] Both cyberattackers and cyberdefenders often can spin cyberdeterrence outcomes in whatever direction they wish.

Demonstrating the scarcity of useful cyberdeterrence outcome measures, a 2013 Department of Defense study reported that it "unsuccessfully searched for cyber metrics in commercial, academic, and government spaces that directly determine or predict the cyber security or resilience of a given system."[6] A key deficiency is that although cyberdeterrence may be either direct or indirect and short term or long term, most existing outcome measures seem inappropriately biased toward direct short-term success and to favor immediate deterrence in crisis situations over general deterrence.[7]

The spectrum of possible options for measuring cyberdeterrence success can go from ensuring adversaries do not acquire the capacity to launch cyberattacks, to allowing adversaries to have that capacity but not use it, and to permitting cyberattack initiation but with limited frequency and severity. Perhaps the simplest cyberdeterrence success metric is "anything you (the enemy) can throw at me, I can counter faster and better," but this approach's logic appears to incorporate built-in incentives for escalating mutual cyber retaliation.[8] Given that the Internet "lacks any kind of sensible allocation of risk," some observers suggest that the key to this measurement is the extent to which risk is appropriately distributed across relevant parties (including both users and those introducing vulnerabilities).[9]

Cognizant that any outcome measurement system would be imperfect, targets still need to settle on an appropriate yardstick. Given this book's emphasis on having targets maximize their adversaries' high-cost certainty and minimize their high-benefit certainty, the recommended cyberdeterrence outcome assessment here is to reduce significantly over a substantial period the frequency and severity of cyberattacks on vital assets. This effort entails making major changes in the adversaries' decision calculus: "cyber deterrence, like all other deterrence, succeeds when an adversary decides not to act aggressively" because "the costs of cyber aggression outweigh its benefits" and "the benefits of restraint in cyberspace outweigh its costs."[10] Although such an approach may need to be combined with other assessment measures, it seems to provide a useful starting point.

Considering Cyberdeterrence Legitimacy and Ethics Dilemmas

Interrelated legitimacy and ethics concerns surround when and how to apply cyberdeterrence (see figure C.3). First, if legitimacy is considered too low and moral outrage too high, diplomacy can fail and trigger disruptive, negative economic sanctions. Second, in cyberspace, the lower legitimacy of target retaliation is associated with a greater probability of cyberattacker counterretaliation.[11] Third, "governments often have no more legitimacy or credibility about cyber security issues than any other group with a loud voice—and the Internet comes fully equipped with a multitude of loud voices."[12] Fourth, legitimacy worries affect both offense and defense: "Cyber defenders take great pains to distinguish legitimate from illegitimate or harmful traffic.... Cyber offenders, in turn, take comparable pains to elude these detection mechanisms by masquerading as legitimate traffic."[13] Together these concerns can limit the range of appropriate policy options, particularly with targets that are highly sensitive to domestic and international approval.

Separating legitimate from illegitimate—and ethical from unethical—cyber action is hard, given competing liberty, privacy, and security values.

> Meanwhile, various national governments hold different views about the legitimate uses of the Internet and are pushing hard for rules that reflect their preferred vision. For example, governments in Russia and China see internal dissent and anti-government writings disseminated on the Internet as a threat. Both have curtailed free speech and access to the Internet as part of their vision of "cyber security"—a view the United States is not likely to embrace. Without some basic "rules of the road," conflict between these competing values and visions will intensify.[14]

However, "this uncertainty does not mean cyber operations exist in a normative void."[15] For example, a ban on the unprovoked use of force against any state is widely accepted, but because cyberattacks blur the distinction between low-intensity and high-intensity conflict, controversy still prevails about whether this prohibition applies to cyberattacks and requires physical damage or violence for it to be in effect.[16] The most widely credited criteria for determining whether a cyberattack falls under this global ban are its severity, immediacy, directness, invasiveness, measurability, and presumptive legitimacy, although these measures are highly susceptible to subjective interpretation and to cyberspace attribution roadblocks.[17]

Such normative evaluation of cyberspace action may not be possible across the board and may differ depending on the observer and the context. Distinguishing between attack initiation and retaliation in cyberspace is important, even though the tenet that retaliation is more acceptable than initiation is violated by the reality that "sometimes a threat must be anticipated if it is to be successfully defended against."[18] In considering the general self-defense justification for target retaliation, global approval appears to follow two general principles: First, targets seeking to retaliate against the most extreme cyberattacks, which cause death and destruction, are more justified than targets retaliating against more common low-level cyber aggression.[19] Second, targets seeking to retaliate by cyber means are more justified than those preferring to retaliate by more traditional, kinetic military means.[20] However, even such overarching principles for justified target retaliation have exceptions, as both the initiator's low-level cyber aggression and the target's restrained cyber retaliation can sometimes indirectly lead to a significant rise in long-term human insecurity.

Cyberdeterrence Legitimacy Controversies

Traditionally, target retaliation legitimacy exists if collateral damage is low and response proportionality and respect for neutral party rights are high.[21] Its legitimacy is maximized when cyberattacks occur outside the initiators' sphere of influence and participation in the target's retaliation decision is wide, diverse, and linked to soft rather than hard power and to a well-articulated cyberdeterrence doctrine. However, the justifiability of foreign cyberintrusions (including offensive cyberdeterrence) remains shaky and not necessarily credible to internal and external audiences. "The attacking state may well deny everything and claim itself to be the victim of aggression (rather than retaliation) unless it chooses to boast of the attack to support a campaign of intimidation against the target state."[22]

Cyberattackers' stated goals influence the targets' decisions regarding the legitimacy and wisdom of retaliation versus alternative responses.[23] For example, the United States controversially sees state-sponsored cyberespionage for political security purposes as legitimate but views intellectual property theft for economic gain as illegitimate. The targets' response legitimacy may rise

FIGURE C.3.
Cyberdeterrence Legitimacy and Ethics Dilemmas

CYBERDETERRENCE LEGITIMACY CONTROVERSIES

Retaliation Legitimacy Concern about Traditional Shortfalls

Problems exist if collateral damage is high, response proportionality is low, attack is within initiator's sphere of influence, retaliation decision is narrowly based, or retaliation motives are secret or incoherent

Retaliation Legitimacy Concern about Cyberattacker Denial

Cyberattacker may well deny everything and claim to be a victim of aggression, making observers skeptical about the justifiability of target retaliation

Retaliation Legitimacy Concern about Outsider Ignorance

Very few people understand cyberspace well enough to evaluate the evidence of attribution and the danger of future cyberattacks in an objective manner, even if the information is all laid out

CYBERDETERRENCE ETHICS CONTROVERSIES

Ethical Concern about Advocacy for Outcome Deception

Promotion of lying to one's citizens and to the international community about motivations, expectations, and the extent of devastation on one's society could jeopardize long-term internal and external credibility

Ethical Concern about Advocacy for Private Empowerment

Empowerment of private companies and citizens unfairly encourages those not duly elected and not democratically accountable to play key roles in cyberdefense, allowing reckless self-interested vigilantism

Ethical Concern about Advocacy for Real-World Sanctions

Use of military force and economic sanctions in response to cyberattacks could ethically incense those who feel that cybersecurity confrontations ought to be contained exclusively within cyberspace

---

by stressing future cyberattack dangers (although purely fear-based logic is problematic) and by "convincing individuals that the government's cause is the right one and they personally need to take steps to help—that is, nurturing both their intent to be helpful (or at least not harmful) and their capability to do so."[24] In sum, legitimacy consensus entails "continued discussions with partners and potential adversaries about the laws of armed conflict in cyberspace, the definition of legitimate targets, and how states signal intentions and control escalation."[25]

Cyberdeterrence Ethics Controversies

Ethics controversies abound in cyberdeterrence planning and execution. First, advocacy for deception can promote targets' lying to their citizens and to the international community. If used too indiscriminately, then this could jeopardize credibility, alliances, and ultimately global survival. Domestic and international trust could completely evaporate, with disastrous security consequences for cooperation at all levels. As a remedy, a better balance requires more target transparency in determining whether to retaliate—and in communicating the means of determining cyberattacker attribution[26]—and more target deception in distorting cyberattack outcomes.

Second, advocacy for private company or private citizen involvement can lead to empowering those who are not elected by the people, and thus are less democratically accountable, and those who might exhibit reckless self-interested vigilantism—that is, safeguarding their own digital assets at the expense of others' security. As a solution, better norm development about the responsibilities and the limitations of those involved in cyber protection needs concerted, internal public-private discussion and monitoring.

Third, pushing for coercive, real-world negative military and economic retaliation to cyberattacks can incense those who feel that cyberconfrontations ought to be contained exclusively within cyberspace given ethical concerns about preserving human life or about kinetic measures that have the potential to tangibly degrade people and property. As a resolution, using physical force in response to cyberattacks needs better justification and well-articulated, prudent restraint that restricts its application to high-stakes, last-resort scenarios. Because so many countries—including those most intent on preserving the global status quo—possess cyberoffense capabilities that could potentially violate someone else's cybersecurity, making progress on these thorny ethical issues is handicapped by the absence of a moral high ground in cyberspace, reflecting its free-for-all, anarchic Wild West character.[27]

Addressing Cyberdeterrence Paradoxes

The legitimacy and ethics controversies presented here link with the cyberdeterrence paradoxes introduced in chapter 2. The global case studies vividly highlight the enduring nature of these troublesome paradoxes in the twenty-first century. Nonetheless, practical steps do exist that could address, if by no means completely overcome, the underlying dilemmas.

For the cyber-sophistication vulnerability paradox, although high global digital connectivity persists, those most dependent on cyberspace could be encouraged both to spend more time and money on figuring out ways to secure their sensitive data and critical infrastructure and to seek more outside aid and alliances to provide adequate cyber protection. The cyberattack on Estonia exemplified this paradox and the practical steps to address it.

For the cyber-restraint hypocrisy paradox, although global cyber actions that are widely deemed aggressive do persist, those engaged in both cyberdefense and cyberoffense initiatives could be encouraged to minimize apparent contradictions between the two by specifying and justifying the limited circumstances when offensive initiatives would be undertaken and by refraining from promoting any global cyberspace agreements they are not willing to honor in all of their actions. Israel and the United States as both cyberattackers and cybertargets illustrate this paradox, but up to this point they have not addressed it in a globally acceptable manner.

For the cyber-publicity muddle paradox, although targets want to maintain secrecy regarding their exact cyber capabilities and most of their cyberespionage exploits, those targets undertaking cyberattack responses could be encouraged to be more transparent in the strategic communication and public affairs announcements surrounding cyberattacks. In particular, the targets could be more open about the subsequent apprehension and trial of cybercriminals, thus ensuring that other aspiring cybercriminals would see the enormous risks involved and the difficulties in evading law enforcement and about the resulting incapacitation of the targets' public and private assets to promote their eligibility for outside aid. In striking a key balance, one would consider the rights of one's citizens and allies to know what is going on, the need to alert cyberattackers about the high costs of their cyberintrusions, and the dangers of cyberattackers learning too much about the details of protective measures and discovering the weak spots in one's cybersecurity. The International Monetary Fund as a cybertarget exemplified this paradox, as its non-transparency about its cyber penetration impeded remedial action.

Finally, for the cyber-liberty tension paradox, although the global spread of democratic values means clashes between public expectations and security realities still persist, those affected could be encouraged to do two things: first, to initiate more discussion between governments and citizens about appropriate balances "between allowing Internet freedom on one hand and maintaining adequate early warning and monitoring systems on the other," and second, to pursue consensus-building cybersecurity measures that minimize freedom-protection trade-offs.[28] Illustrating this paradox is North Korea's cyberattack on cybertarget Sony Pictures Entertainment. North Korea was able to interfere with American citizens' freedom of artistic expression because security measures that were acceptable to Sony (and the United States) proved inadequate to protect against the cyberthreat.

Projecting Future Cyberdeterrence Prospects

Figure C.4 projects a set of realistic future cyberdeterrence prospects, given the trajectory of current global trends. The emphasis is on elements that are likely to experience major changes over time rather than on those likely to remain relatively constant. Unlike worst-case scenarios, the projection here is mixed in terms of a secure and well-functioning global system.

Looking first at positive future trends, holes in cyberdefender knowledge and strategy may decrease. The cyberattacker-cyberdefender expertise gap seems likely to shrink in confrontations, for with globalization and as time passes, the proportion of the global population that feels at home in cyberspace and comfortable analyzing cybersecurity is likely to increase. Furthermore, cyberdeterrence seems likely to become better intertwined with other deterrence forms and overall security strategy, for with time cyberthreats will be considered less novel, idiosyncratic, and disconnected from conventional defense concerns.

Turning to mixed or neutral future trends, heterogeneity, utility, and ambiguity may increase in cyberspace tools and ties. First, both cyberattackers and cyberdefenders are likely to expand their use of social media as a means of influence and as a target for defacement owing to the rising global importance of this kind of communication in all forms of virtual interaction. Second, more diverse, imaginative, and dispersed cyberattack and cyberdefense tools seem likely to emerge, for the rate of technological innovation and diffusion will undoubtedly escalate in the future. Third, both cyberattackers and cyberdefenders seem likely to become more aware of unintended side effects of their actions as their experience in cyber repercussions deepens and as the unpredictability of long-term security impacts intensifies. Fourth, cross-national and cross-regional ties seem likely to become more vital to both cyberattackers and cyberdefenders as formal and informal ethnic, religious, and ideological marriages of convenience continue to proliferate worldwide under globalization pressures. Fifth, determining the exact ratio of cyber capabilities between adversaries—and thus their exact level of cyber vulnerability—seems likely to become harder for both cyberattackers and cyberdefenders given the growing diversity of cyberattack and cyberdefense tools and the increasing ambiguity

FIGURE C.4.
Future Cyberdeterrence Prospects

POSITIVE TRENDS

Decreasing Holes in Cyberdefender Knowledge and Strategy

Cyberattacker-cyberdefender cyber expertise gap seems likely to shrink in cyberconfrontations

Cyberdeterrence seems likely to be more intertwined with other deterrence forms and overall security strategy

MIXED/NEUTRAL TRENDS

Increasing Heterogeneity, Utility, and Ambiguity in Cyberspace Tools and Ties

Use of social media seems likely to expand as a means of influence and as a target for defacement

Development seems likely of more diverse, novel, and dispersed cyberattack and cyberdefense tools

Cyberattackers and cyberdefenders seem likely to become more aware of unintended side effects of actions

Cross-national/cross-regional ties seem likely to become more vital to cyberattackers and cyberdefenders

Determination of the exact ratio of cyber capabilities between adversaries seems likely to become harder

Value of indirect approaches to cyberdeterrence seems likely to grow

NEGATIVE TRENDS

Increasing Cyberdefender Susceptibility to Cyberattack

Cyber addiction and cyber dependence seem likely to escalate even more, increasing vulnerability

Internal cyberdefender disagreements about how to respond to cyberthreat seem likely to escalate

---

surrounding these tools' effectiveness in the context of rapidly changing cyberspace. Sixth, the value of indirect approaches to cyberdeterrence seems likely to escalate among cyberdefenders because of multiplying cross-national and cross-regional ties and the rising sophistication of deception, obfuscation, and diversion techniques.

Concluding with negative future trends, cyberdefender susceptibility to cyberattacks may increase. Cyber addiction and cyber dependence seem likely to escalate even more, and they will increase the vulnerability of potential cyberattack victims on two accounts: globally the tentacles of digital technology show no signs of relenting in their inexorable deepening penetration into everyone's way of life, and humans show no signs of developing increased patience during service interruptions. Furthermore, internal cyberdefender disagreements about responses to cyberthreat seem likely to grow given the rising importance, public awareness, and available options surrounding cyberthreat.

Concluding Thoughts

In reflecting on the relative importance of deterring foreign cyberthreat, a dual danger exists in underestimating and overestimating threats. On the one hand, it makes little sense to be complacent and think that existing cyberdefenses are sufficient and that foreign adversaries lack the will or the capability to instigate devastating cyberattacks. On the other hand, panicking and assuming that the world's critical infrastructure is on the brink of collapse due to devastating cyberintrusions do not make sense either. Somehow cybersecurity policymakers need to find a prudent middle ground between the two extremes while constantly reassessing the evolving predicament over time and then bringing along governments, international organizations, businesses, and members of the public to accept this balanced level of cybervigilance, freedom and privacy sacrifice, cyber expenditure, and mixed cyber and real-world countermeasures. In implementing this balance, these policymakers need to avoid cyber responses containing either hollow promises and threats or empty symbolic measures that do not actually increase government or societal protection against cyberthreat.

The global determination of the appropriate balance between the severity of cyberthreat and that of protective responses must be situated explicitly in a broader security framework outside of cyberspace. Cyberthreat does not exist in a vacuum, so responses should be formulated and implemented "in the context of larger global security affairs," explicitly connected to broader individual, local, national, regional, and global security policies affecting both state and human security.[29] To accomplish this end, both the academic and the policy communities need to abandon the tendency to treat cyberthreat as so special and distinct from other threats that it deserves in both concept and application to be separated, isolated, and compartmentalized from other security dangers. In particular, there is a pressing need for a better meshing of insights about threat both from the general international relations and strategic studies literature and from the cybersecurity literature, with areas of contradiction, trade-off, and mutual reinforcement carefully noted and analyzed. While especially important when combining orthodox and unorthodox cyber and non-cyber security threats and responses emanating from states and non-state groups, this dovetailing of insights can help to isolate the special security impact of leveling the greater playing field through the technological diffusion present in cyberspace compared to other domains.

Even with the greater uncertainties surrounding cyberthreat and cyberthreat responses when compared with other security threats and responses to them, a great deal remains to be learned from the explicit juxtaposition and integration of best practices regarding cyber and non-cyber threats and countermeasures. The ongoing tug-of-war in resource allocation between protecting cyberspace and protecting land, air, sea, and space domains should not be portrayed as a zero-sum effort, because in several cases expenditures can simultaneously assist in safeguarding against both real-world and virtual threats, especially given the utility of integrated cross-domain deterrence. With virtual cyberspace confrontations now as important as conventional kinetic military confrontations, neither one deserves to eclipse the other in its overall security priority.

The seemingly limitless global scope of vital assets needing cyberattack protection is daunting but not insuperable. Because "the number of potential targets in cyberspace is nearly boundless, and it is impossible to protect them all, . . . policymakers should adopt a risk management approach that endeavors to reduce aggregate cyber security risk through closely scrutinized investments" in areas where the chances of cyberattacks are greatest, vulnerability is highest, and "consequences of inaction are most grave."[30] The greatest challenge here remains how to prioritize properly what is most important to the state and society, especially when offensive and defensive cyberspace initiatives are undertaken simultaneously, but a coherent response to this challenge is possible, aided both by within-government and cross-government discourse for state security issues and by public-private discourse between governments and their private businesses and publics for human security issues.

Even with this cyber risk management strategy in place, the path to cyberdeterrence is not easy and entails considerable subtlety and sensitivity about globally diverse cyberthreats and cyber responses. Different combinations of measures are important depending on adversaries' security vulnerabilities, threat tolerance, willingness to compromise, risk propensities, physical and psychological resiliency, and political aspirations. Broad inclusive cyberdeterrence helps to facilitate this versatility by expanding the focus: (1) moving from increasing cyberattackers' losses to include decreasing prospects of their gains while combining maximizing certainty about high costs and minimizing certainty about high benefits; (2) moving from national governments making decisions about restraining cyberattackers to include the private sector's views by combining the input of state officials with that of private businesspeople and citizens; (3) moving from perfecting past and ongoing standard, straightforward cyberattacker countermeasures to include developing alternative cyberattacker countermeasures that combine direct, tangible orthodox restraints and indirect, intangible unorthodox restraints; (4) moving from responding to cyberattackers in kind on the same playing field to include responding via different methods on other playing fields by combining cyberspace and real-world tactics; and (5) moving from engaging in the draconian intimidation of cyberattackers to include finding sensible ways that combine fear-based physical prevention and hope-based perceptual persuasion to convince cyberattackers to restrain themselves. If implemented properly, cyberdeterrence planning and execution could induce even culturally different adversaries to perceive the risks of a mission's failure as higher than its value, thus increasing their reluctance to undertake cyberattacks, and it could address long-term stability through minimizing boomerang effects, action-reaction cycles, and conflict contagion.[31]

To improve the prospects for the global success of these multifaceted thrusts, responsible cybersecurity officials need more creative, innovative, outside-the-box thinking. Exemplifying this approach in the United States was the October 2008 launching of the Comprehensive National Cybersecurity Initiative, which solicited "the most promising game-changing ideas"—ones that would "'morph the gameboard,' 'change the rules' or 'raise the stakes'" and have "the potential to reduce vulnerabilities to cyber exploitations by altering the cybersecurity landscape."[32] Establishing a breeding ground for more refined, effective, and legitimate nontraditional cyberdeterrence ideas also requires more "cyber warriors," or "top-tier talent who can be certified to perform at the elite or extreme cyber conflict levels"; better training to develop skilled situational thinking for these recruits; and improved opportunities for the trainees to have an impact on the substance and priority of cyber policy.[33] Further, the skill set of public and private sector officials should include being adept at tracking non-transparent transnational transactions, including those involving plausible deniability; coping with ambiguous threat initiation and outcome identification; and thwarting adversaries' subtle means of transnational influence by taking advantage of economic interdependence, employing indirect leverage, and manipulating social media. With such an army of cybersecurity talent in place, there is absolutely no reason that many practitioners should perceive cyberdefense as lagging behind cyberoffense and cyberattackers as more agile and responsive than cyberdefenders.

Although there is some "low-hanging fruit" (where cyberdangers are easy to forestall) with quixotic cyberattack triggers, globally the greatest emerging cyberspace dangers involve advanced persistent threat by sophisticated cyberattackers—both profit-seeking criminals and state-sponsored spies—who have substantial resources and long-term commitments to target critical infrastructure in increasingly lethal ways that not only demolish the integrity of data, systems, and networks but also end up wreaking kinetic havoc by destroying physical equipment and private property. To respond to such relentless threats effectively, targets will inevitably have to consider undertaking countermeasures that are both counterintuitive and unpopular. They might challenge dominant, enlightened global values and norms and may highlight socially divisive trade-offs between openness and secrecy, freedom and stability, security and justice, fear and hope, and dependence and vulnerability. However, if done appropriately, "cyber defense is difficult, but should be sufficiently effective" and legitimate to make cyberattacks tougher to execute, less likely to yield positive payoffs, and consequently less frequent and damaging than they are today.[34]

Although cyberspace may at first seem utterly confounding—impeding effective countermeasures, negating deterrence possibilities, and thwarting overall global security—a more probing examination reveals that the vast worldwide cyber vulnerability can be circumscribed under the right conditions. While after-the-fact reactive stock responses to cyberthreat may be more natural, imaginative thinking could develop and apply better threat preemption options—involving different kinds of cyberdeterrence initiators, countermeasures, and targets—to operate within ethical bounds to forestall major transnational cyberattacks. Thus, concrete steps to improve urgently needed cyberdeterrence deserve immediate policy attention and substantial resource allocation that will increase secure, predictable protection of humanity from the ravages of cyberattacks.

Notes

1. Cilluffo, Cardash, and Salmoiroghi, "Blueprint for Cyber Deterrence," 13.
2. Negroponte, Palmisano, and Segal, *Defending an Open*, 15.
3. Posner, *Catastrophe*, 171.
4. Schneier, *Beyond Fear*, 5, 6.
5. Jensen, "Cyber Deterrence," 783, 784.
6. Defense Science Board, *Resilient Military Systems*, 12.
7. Hunt and Chesser, *Deterrence 2.0*, 7.
8. Ibid., 26.
9. Wittes and Blum, *Future of Violence*, 216.
10. Goodman, "Cyber Deterrence," 107.
11. Libicki, *Cyberdeterrence and Cyberwar*, 75.

12. Rattray and Healey, "Non-State Actors," in Lord and Sharp, *America's Cyber Future*, 2:80.
13. Libicki, "Pulling Punches in Cyberspace," 125.
14. Finnemore, "Cultivating International Cyber Norms," 89.
15. Schmitt, *Tallinn Manual*, 5.
16. Whetham and Lucas Jr., "Relevance of the Just War Tradition," in Green, *Cyber Warfare*, 168; Green, "Regulation of Cyber Warfare," in Green, *Cyber Warfare*, 98–99; and Dinstein, *War, Aggression*, 88.
17. Schmitt, "Cyber Operations," 576.
18. Whetham and Lucas Jr., "Relevance of the Just War Tradition," in Green, *Cyber Warfare*, 162.
19. Waxman, "Self-Defensive Force," 111; and Green, "Regulation of Cyber Warfare," in Green, *Cyber Warfare*, 115.
20. Harrison Dinness, "Regulation of Cyber Warfare," in Green, *Cyber Warfare*, 141.
21. Former US deputy secretary of defense William Lynn, quoted in Center for Strategic and International Studies, *Global Security Forum, 2012*, 5–6.
22. Libicki, "Pulling Punches in Cyberspace," 127, 132.
23. Libicki, *Cyberdeterrence and Cyberwar*, 75.
24. Rattray and Healey, "Non-State Actors," in Lord and Sharp, *America's Cyber Future*, 2:80.
25. Negroponte, Palmisano, and Segal, *Defending an Open*, 37.
26. Alperovitch and Rogers, "Some Experts."
27. Moens, Cushing, and Dowd, *Cybersecurity Challenges*, iii, 2.
28. Herzog, "Revisiting the Estonian Cyber Attacks," 56.
29. Kugler, "Deterrence of Cyber Attacks," 310.
30. Lord and Sharp, *America's Cyber Future*, 1:16.
31. For elaboration of this kind of balance, see Hodges and Creese, "Understanding Cyber-Attacks," 57.
32. "U.S. Government," *Homeland Security News Wire*.
33. Defense Science Board, *Resilient Military Systems*, 9.
34. Gray, *Making Strategic Sense*, 45.

Bibliography

Ackerman, Gwen. "Israeli Troops Swap Guns for Computers as Cyber Attacks Rise." *Bloomberg Business*, January 28, 2013. http://www.bloomberg.com/news/articles/2013-01-27/israeli-troops-swap-guns-for-computers-as-cyber-attacks-increase.

Ackerman, Spencer, and Jonathan Kaiman. "Chinese Military Officials Charged with Stealing US Data as Tensions Escalate." *The Guardian*, May 20, 2014. http://www.theguardian.com/technology/2014/may/19/us-chinese-military-officials-cyber-espionage.

Acohido, Byron. "Syria's Cyber Retaliation Signals New Era of Warfare." *USA Today*, August 30, 2013. http://www.usatoday.com/story/cybertruth/2013/08/30/syrias-cyber-retaliation-signals--new-era-of-warfare/2740457/.

Adair, Steven. "Georgian Attacks: Remember Estonia?" *Shadowserver Foundation*, August 13, 2008. https://www.shadowserver.org/wiki/pmwiki.php/Calendar/20080813.

AFCEA (Armed Forces Communications and Electronics Association). *The Russo-Georgian War, 2008: The Role of the Cyber Attacks in the Conflict*. Fairfax, VA: AFCEA, May 24, 2012. http://www.afcea.org/committees/cyber/documents/TheRusso-GeorgianWar2008.pdf.

Agence France-Presse. "US Says Iran behind Cyber Attack in Saudi Arabia." *Al Arabiya News*, October 13, 2012. https://english.alarabiya.net/articles/2012/10/13/243475.html.

AGT Intelligence. "Objectives of Cyber Attacks." http://www.agtintelligence.com/practices/corporate-clients/cyber-security/objectives-of-cyber-attacks/ (link no longer active).

Al Arabiya. "Saudi Aramco Investigating Origins of 'Shamoon' Virus Following Attack." August 26, 2012. https://english.alarabiya.net/articles/2012/09/12/237530.html.

Albright, David, Paul Brannan, and Christina Walrond. *Did Stuxnet Take Out 1,000 Centrifuges at the Natanz Enrichment Plant?* Washington, DC: Institute for Science and International Security, December 22, 2010.

Al Jazeera. "'Sophisticated Cyber Attack' Targets IMF." June 12, 2011. http://www.aljazeera.com/news/americas/2011/06/20116122232738960.html.

Al Jazeera America. "Hackers Strike at Snapchat and Skype." January 2, 2014. http://america.aljazeera.com/articles/2014/1/2/snapchat-skype-syrianelectronicarmy.html.

Alperovitch, Dmitri. *Revealed: Operation Shady RAT*. Santa Clara: McAfee, 2011.

———. "Towards Establishment of Cyberspace Deterrence Strategy." In *Proceedings of 3rd International Conference on Cyber Conflict*. Edited by C. Czosseck, E. Tyugu, and T. Wingfield, 87–94. Tallinn, Estonia: NATO Cooperative Cyber Defence Centre of Excellence, 2011.

Alperovitch, Dmitri, and Marc Rogers. "Some Experts Question Evidence North Korea Is behind the Sony Hack—Part 2." Interview by Gwen Ifill. *NewsHour*. PBS, December 23, 2014. http://www.pbs.org/newshour/bb/debating-north-koreas-involvement-sony-hack/.

Alray Palestinian Media Agency. "Cyber War against 'Israel' Escalates." October 28, 2013. http://alray.ps/en/index.php?act=post&id=312#.U21bStJdVqQ.

Andreas, Peter, and Ethan Nadelmann. *Policing the Globe: Criminalization and Crime Control in International Relations*. Oxford: Oxford University Press, 2006.

Arnold, Bruce Baer. "Cyber War in Ukraine—Business as Usual for the Russian Bear." *Homeland Security News Wire*, March 13, 2014. http://www.homelandsecuritynewswire.com/dr20140313-cyber-war-in-ukraine-business-as-usual-for-the-russian-bear.

Arnoldy, Ben. "Cyberspace: New Frontier in Conflicts." *Christian Science Monitor*, August 13, 2008. http://www.csmonitor.com/USA/Military/2008/0813/p01s05-usmi.html.

Arquilla, John, and David Ronfeldt. *The Advent of Netwar*. Santa Monica: RAND Corporation, 1996.

———. "Cyberwar Is Coming!" In *In Athena's Camp: Preparing for Conflict in the Information Age*. Edited by John Arquilla and David Ronfeldt, 23–60. Santa Monica: RAND Corporation, 1997.

———. "A New Epoch—and Spectrum—of Conflict." In *In Athena's Camp: Preparing for Conflict in the Information Age*. Edited by John Arquilla and David Ronfeldt, 1–22. Santa Monica: RAND Corporation, 1997.

Arthur, Charles. "IMF Cyber-Attack Led by Hackers Seeking 'Privileged Information.'" *The Guardian*, June 12, 2011. http://www.theguardian.com/business/2011/jun/12/imf-cyber-attack-hack.

———. "US Accusations of Chinese Hacking Point to Eight-Year Spying Campaign." *The Guardian*, May 19, 2014. http://www.theguardian.com/technology/2014/may/19/us-accusations-chinese-hacking-eight-years.

Associated Press. "Anonymous Hacker Attack on Israeli Websites 'Causes Little Real Damage.'" *The Guardian*, April 8, 2013. http://www.theguardian.com/technology/2013/apr/08/anonymous-hacker-attack-israeli-websites.

———. "A Look at Estonia's Cyber Attack in 2007." *NBC News*, July 8, 2009. http://www.nbcnews.com/id/31801246/ns/technology_and_science-security#.U21NGtJdVqQ.

———. "Romania Turns Hacking Crisis into Advantage, Helping Ukraine." *Daily Mail*, May 13, 2015. http://www.dailymail.co.uk/wires/ap/article-3079344/Romania-turns-hacking-crisis-advantage-helping-Ukraine.html.

Atkinson, Caroline. "Transcript of a Press Briefing by Caroline Atkinson, External Relations Department, International Monetary Fund." International Monetary Fund, Washington, DC, May 26, 2011. http://www.imf.org/external/np/tr/2011/tr052611.htm.

Bachmann, Sascha-Dominik, and Håkan Gunneriusson. "Hybrid Wars: 21st Century's New Threats to Global Peace and Security." *South African Journal of Military Studies* 43, no. 1 (2015): 77–98.

Baker, Stewart A. *Skating on Stilts: Why We Aren't Stopping Tomorrow's Terrorism*. Stanford: Hoover Institution Press, 2010.

Baker, Stewart, Shaun Waterman, and George Ivanov. *In the Crossfire: Critical Infrastructure in the Age of Cyber War*. Santa Clara: Center for Strategic and International Studies and McAfee, 2010.

Ball, James. "Secrecy Surrounding 'Zero-Day Exploits' Industry Spurs Call for Government Oversight." *Washington Post*, September 1, 2012. http://www.washingtonpost.com/world/national-security/secrecy-surrounding-zero-day-exploits-industry-spurs-calls-for-government-oversight/2012/09/01/46d664a6-edf7-11e1-afd6-f55f84bc0c41_story.html.

Bamford, James. "The Most Wanted Man in the World." *Wired*, August 13, 2014. http://www.wired.com/2014/08/edward-snowden/?mbid=social_gplus#ch-1.

Barnes, Julian E., and Danny Yadron. "Islamic Hack Hits Military Accounts." *Wall Street Journal*, January 13, 2015, A1.
Barzashka, Ivanka. "Are Cyber-Weapons Effective? Assessing Stuxnet's Impact on the Iranian Enrichment Programme." *RUSI (Royal United Services Institute) Journal* 158, no. 2 (2013): 48–56.
BBC News. "Five Years On, Georgia Makes Up with Russia." June 24, 2013. http://www.bbc.co.uk/news/world-europe-23010526.
———. "Islamic State Web Accounts to Be Blocked by New Police Team." June 22, 2015. http://www.bbc.com/news/world-europe-33220037.
———. "President Obama Upbraids China over Cyber Attacks." March 13, 2013. http://www.bbc.com/news/world-us-canada-21772596.
———. "Ukraine's Petro Poroshenko Pledges 'End to War.'" May 25, 2014. http://www.bbc.com/news/world-europe-27571612.
———. "US President Barack Obama Holds Last News Briefing of 2014." December 19, 2014. http://www.bbc.com/news/world-us-canada-30548747.
Beilman, Bryon D. "Security Lessons Learned from the Syrian Electronic Army." Iuvo Technologies, May 13, 2014. http://www.iuvotech.com/blog/security-lessons-learned-from-the-syrian-electronic-army/.
Belden, Thomas G. "Indications, Warning, and Crisis Operations." *International Studies Quarterly* 21, no. 1 (March 1977): 181–98.
Bergen, Peter, and Tim Maurer. "Cyberwar Hits Ukraine." CNN, March 7, 2014. http://www.cnn.com/2014/03/07/opinion/bergen-ukraine-cyber-attacks/.
Berkowitz, Bruce D. "Warfare in the Information Age." *Issues in Science and Technology* 12 (Fall 1995): 59–66.
Bernard, Doug. "Russia-Ukraine Crisis Could Trigger Cyber War." Voice of America, April 20, 2014. http://www.voanews.com/content/russia-ukraine-crisis-could-trigger-cyber-war/1894855.html.
Betz, David J., and Tim Stevens. *Cyberspace and the State: Toward a Strategy for Cyberpower*. London: International Institute for Strategic Studies, November 2011.
Blake, Eben. "Iran and Saudi Arabia Heading toward a Cyber War?" *International Business Times*, June 30, 2015. http://www.ibtimes.com/iran-saudi-arabia-heading-toward-cyber-war-1989789.
Blanford, Nicholas. "With Qaddafi's Death, World Attention Turns to Syria." *Christian Science Monitor*, October 21, 2011. http://www.csmonitor.com/World/Middle-East/2011/1021/With-Qaddafi-s-death-world-attention-turns-to-Syria.
Brenner, Joel. *Glass Houses: Privacy, Secrecy, and Cyber Insecurity in a Transparent World*. New York: Penguin Books, 2013.
Brenner, Susan W., and Marc D. Goodman. "In Defense of Cyberterrorism: An Argument for Anticipating Cyber-Attacks." *Journal of Law, Technology & Policy* no. 1 (2002): 1–57. http://illinoisjltp.com/journal/wp-content/uploads/2013/10/Brenner-Goodman.pdf.
Brewster, Tom. "Persian Paranoia: America's Fear of Iranian Cyber Power." *The Guardian*, August 29, 2014. http://www.theguardian.com/technology/2014/aug/29/iran-cyber-power-america-networks.
———. "Sony Needed to Have Basic Digital Protection. It Failed." *The Guardian*, December 20, 2014. http://www.theguardian.com/commentisfree/2014/dec/21/sony-hacking-north-korea-cyber-security.
———. "Sony Pictures Hack: How Much Damage Can North Korea's Cyber Army Do?" *The*

Guardian, December 5, 2014. https://www.theguardian.com/technology/2014/dec/05/sony-pictures-hack-north-korea-cyber-army.

Broad, William J., John Markoff, and David E. Sanger. "Israeli Test on Worm Called Crucial in Iran Nuclear Delay." *New York Times*, January 15, 2011. http://www.nytimes.com/2011/01/16/world/middleeast/16stuxnet.html?_r=3&.

Bronk, Chris. "Treasure Trove or Trouble: Cyber-Enabled Intelligence and International Politics." *American Intelligence Journal*, 28 (2010): 26–30.

Bronk, Christopher, and Eneken Tikk-Ringas. "The Cyber Attack on Saudi Aramco." *Survival*, 55 (April–May 2013): 81–96.

Bryant, Christa Case. "Israel Establishes Cyberdefense Authority to Fight Rise in Digital Attacks." *Christian Science Monitor*, February 20, 2015. http://www.csmonitor.com/World/Passcode/2015/0220/Israel-establishes-cyberdefense-authority-to-fight-rise-in-digital-attacks.

Burke, Adrienne. "Why Microsoft's Craig Mundie Worries about Weapons of Mass Disruption." *Forbes*, November 15, 2013. http://www.forbes.com/sites/techonomy/2013/11/15/why-microsofts-craig-mundie-worries-about-weapons-of-mass-disruption/.

Buzan, Barry. *People, States and Fear: An Agenda for International Security Studies in the Post–Cold War Era*. 2nd ed. Boulder: Lynne Rienner, 1991.

Caldwell, Dan, and Robert Williams Jr. *Seeking Security in an Insecure World*. 2nd ed. Lanham, MD: Rowman & Littlefield, 2012.

Carter, Jeff. "Asymmetric Cyberwarfare: Cyber-threats, Information Warfare and Critical Infrastructure Protection." January 25, 2012. http://www.hstoday.us/columns/best-practices/blog/asymmetric-cyberwarfare-cyber-threats-information-warfare-and-critical-infrastructure-protection/ca78009d7a39df4aeaf54dbc933ec569.html.

Caulderwood, Kathleen. "Sony Hack: Sanctions against North Korea Likely to Be Ineffective, Experts Say." *International Business Times*, January 11, 2015. http://www.ibtimes.com/sony-hack-sanctions-against-north-korea-likely-be-ineffective-experts-say-1776694.

CBS News. "Was FBI Wrong on North Korea?" December 23, 2014. http://www.cbsnews.com/news/did-the-fbi-get-it-wrong-on-north-korea/.

Center for Strategic and International Studies (CSIS). *Global Security Forum, 2012: Fighting a Cyber War*. Washington, DC: CSIS, April 11, 2012.

Channel 4 News. "Russian Cyber Attacks on Ukraine: The Georgia Template." May 3, 2014. http://www.channel4.com/news/ukraine-cyber-warfare-russia-attacks-georgia.

Cilluffo, Frank J., Sharon L. Cardash, and George C. Salmoiroghi. "A Blueprint for Cyber Deterrence: Building Stability through Strength." *Military and Strategic Affairs* 4, no. 3 (December 2012): 1–23.

Cilluffo, Frank J., and Rhea D. Siers. "Cyber Deterrence Is a Strategic Imperative." *Wall Street Journal*, April 28, 2015. http://blogs.wsj.com/cio/2015/04/28/cyber-deterrence-is-a-strategic-imperative/.

Claburn, Thomas. "Cyber Attack against Georgia Blurred Civilian and Military: Last Year's Cyber Assault against Georgia Represents a Template for Civilian Involvement in Military Action." *Information Week*, August 17, 2009. http://www.darkreading.com/risk-management/cyber-attack-against-georgia-blurred-civilian-and-military/d/d-id/1082322.

Clark, David, Thomas Berson, and Herbert S. Lin, eds. *At the Nexus of Cybersecurity and Public Policy: Some Basic Concepts and Issues*. Washington, DC: National Research Council of the National Academies Press, 2014.

Clarke, Richard A., and Robert K. Knake. *Cyber War: The Next Threat to National Security and What to Do about It*. New York: Ecco, 2010.
Clayton, Mark. "Massive Cyberattacks Slam Official Sites in Russia, Ukraine." *Christian Science Monitor*, March 18, 2014. http://www.csmonitor.com/World/Passcode/2014/0318/Massive-cyberattacks-slam-official-sites-in-Russia-Ukraine.
———. "Stuxnet Malware Is 'Weapon' out to Destroy . . . Iran's Bushehr Nuclear Plant?" *Christian Science Monitor*, September 21, 2010. http://www.csmonitor.com/USA/2010/0921/Stuxnet-malware-is-weapon-out-to-destroy-Iran-s-Bushehr-nuclear-plant.
———. "Where Are the Cyberattacks? Russia's Curious Forbearance in Ukraine." *Christian Science Monitor*, March 3, 2014. http://www.csmonitor.com/World/Security-Watch/2014/0303/Where-are-the-cyberattacks-Russia-s-curious-forbearance-in-Ukraine.-video.
Clinton, Hillary. "Remarks on Internet Freedom." Newseum, Washington, DC, January 21, 2010. http://www.state.gov/secretary/20092013clinton/rm/2010/01/135519.htm.
CNN. "Fierce Cyber War Predicted." March 3, 2003. http://www.cnn.com/2003/TECH/ptech/03/03/sprj.irc.info.war.ap/ (link no longer active).
Cohen, Daniel, and Danielle Levin. "Cyber Infiltration during Operation Protective Edge." *Forbes*, August 12, 2014. http://www.forbes.com/sites/realspin/2014/08/12/cyber-infiltration-during-operation-protective-edge/.
———. "SEA: How Real Is the Threat?" *Insight* no. 521. Tel Aviv: Institute for National Security Studies, February 26, 2014. http://www.inss.org.il/index.aspx?id=4538&articleid=6679.
Cohen, Geoff A. "Targeting Third-Party Collaboration." In *Proceedings of a Workshop on Deterring Cyberattacks: Informing Strategies and Developing Options for U.S. Policy*, edited by National Research Council, 313–36. Washington, DC: National Academies Press, 2010.
Coll, Alberto R. "Unconventional Warfare, Liberal Democracies, and International Order." *International Law Studies* 67, no. 3 (1992): 3–21.
Condliffe, Jamie. "A British 'Elite Cyber Offensive Force' Will Join the Digital War on ISIS." *Gizmodo*, November 18, 2015. http://gizmodo.com/a-british-elite-cyber-offensive-force-will-join-the-dig-1743218088.
Conklin, Wm. Arthur, Greg White, Roger Davis, and Chuck Cothren. *Principles of Computer Security*. 3rd ed. New York: McGraw-Hill, 2012.
Cook, James. "Sony Hackers Have over 100 Terabytes of Documents; Only Released 200 Gigabytes So Far." *Business Insider*, December 16, 2014. http://www.businessinsider.com/the-sony-hackers-still-have-a-massive-amount-of-data-that-hasnt-been-leaked-yet-2014-12.
Cooper, Jeffrey R. "A New Framework for Cyber Deterrence." In *Cyberspace and National Security: Threats, Opportunities and Power in a Virtual World*. Edited by Derek S. Reveron, 105–20. Washington DC: Georgetown University Press, 2012.
Cornell, Svante E., Johanna Popjanevski, and Niklas Nilsson. *Russia's War in Georgia: Causes and Implications for Georgia and the World*. Washington, DC and Stockholm: Central Asia–Caucasus Institute & Silk Road Studies Program Joint Center, August 2008.
Cowie, Jim. "Could It Happen in Your Country?" *Renesys*, November 30, 2012. http://research.dyn.com/2012/11/could-it-happen-in-your-countr/.
Crittenden, Michael R. "IMF: Taking Steps against Possible Hacking Threat." *Wall Street Journal*, June 1, 2011. http://blogs.wsj.com/economics/2011/06/01/imf-taking-steps-against-possible-hacking-threat/?mod=wsj_share_twitter.

Crosston, Matthew D. "World Gone Cyber MAD: How 'Mutually Assured Debilitation' Is the Best Hope for Cyber Deterrence." *Strategic Studies Quarterly* (Spring 2011): 100–16.

Czosseck, C., E. Tyugu, and T. Wingfield, eds. *Proceedings of 3rd International Conference on Cyber Conflict.* Tallinn, Estonia: NATO Cooperative Cyber Defence Centre of Excellence, 2011.

Daily Mail. "'Operation Shady Rat': Investigators Uncover Massive Cyber Attack on U.S. and UN 'by China.'" August 5, 2011. http://www.dailymail.co.uk/news/article-2022789/Operation-Shady-Rat-Investigators-uncover-massive-cyber-attack-U-S-UN-China.html.

Dalakoglou, Dimitris. "The Crisis before 'The Crisis': Violence and Urban Neoliberalization in Athens." *Social Justice,* 39 (March 2013): 2442.

Davidson, Jacob. "China Accuses U.S. of Hypocrisy on Cyberattacks." *Time,* July 1, 2013. http://world.time.com/2013/07/01/china-accuses-u-s-of-hypocrisy-on-cyberattacks/.

Davis, Joshua. "Hackers Take Down the Most Wired Country in Europe." *Wired* 15 (August 21, 2007). http://archive.wired.com/politics/security/magazine/15-09/ff_estonia?currentPage=all.

Davis, Paul K. "Deterrence, Influence, Cyber Attack and Cyberwar." *Journal of International Law and Politics* 47, no. 2 (Winter 2014): 327–55.

Dearden, Lizzie. "Anonymous Vows to Wreak 'Electronic Holocaust' on Israel for 'Crimes in the Palestinian Territories.'" *The Independent,* March 31, 2015. http://www.independent.co.uk/news/world/middle-east/anonymous-vows-to-wreak-electronic-holocaust-on-israel-for-crimes-in-the-palestinian-territories-10145175html?origin=internalSearch.

Defense Science Board. *Resilient Military Systems and the Advanced Cyber Threat.* Washington, DC: US Government Printing Office, January 2013.

Defense Security Service. *Targeting U.S. Technologies: A Trend Analysis of Reporting from Defense Industry.* Washington, DC: Defense Security Service Counterintelligence Directorate, November 29, 2012.

Deibert, Ronald J., and Rafal Rohozinski. "Risking Security: Policies and Paradoxes of Cyberspace Security." *International Political Sociology* 4 (2010): 15–32.

———. "Under Cover of the Net: The Hidden Governance Mechanisms of Cyberspace." In *Ungoverned Spaces: Alternatives to State Authority in an Era of Softened Sovereignty.* Edited by Anne L. Clunan and Harold A. Trinkunas, 275–94. Stanford: Stanford University Press, 2010.

Deibert, Ronald J., Rafal Rohozinski, and Masashi Crete-Nishihata. "Cyclones in Cyberspace: Information Shaping and Denial in the 2008 Russia–Georgia War." *Security Dialogue* 43 (2012): 3–24.

DiNardo, R. L., and Daniel J. Hughes. "Some Cautionary Thoughts on Information Warfare." *Airpower Journal,* Winter 1995. http://www.au.af.mil/au/afri/aspj/airchronicles/apj/apj95/win95_files/dinardo.htm.

Dinstein, Yoram. *War, Aggression, and Self-Defense.* New York: Cambridge University Press, 2011.

Div, Lior. "The Five Most Common Cyberattack Myths—Revealed." *Forbes,* September 11, 2014. http://www.forbes.com/sites/frontline/2014/09/11/the-five-most-common-cyber-attack-myths-revealed/.

Dogrul, Murat, Adil Aslan, and Eyyup Celik. "Developing an International Cooperation on Cyber Defense and Deterrence against Cyber Terrorism." In *Proceedings of 3rd International Conference on Cyber Conflict.* Edited by C. Czosseck, E. Tyugu, and T. Wingfield,

29–43. Tallinn, Estonia: NATO Cooperative Cyber Defence Centre of Excellence, 2011. http://www.ccdcoe.org/publications/2011proceedings/DevelopingAnInternationalCooperation...-M.%20Dogrul-Aslan-Celik.pdf.

Eriksson, E. Anders. "Information Warfare: Hype or Reality?" *Nonproliferation Review* 6 (Spring–Summer 1999): 57–64.

Ernst, Aaron. "Is This the Future of Cyberwarfare?" *Al Jazeera America*, February 5, 2015. http://america.aljazeera.com/watch/shows/america-tonight/articles/2015/2/5/black-energy-malware-cyberwarfare.html.

Estes, Adam Clark. "China Can't Stop Hacking the World's Only Superpower." *Gizmodo*, November 7, 2013. http://gizmodo.com/china-cant-stop-hacking-the-worlds-only-superpower-1460216761.

Etzioni, Amitai. "Cybersecurity in the Private Sector." *Issues in Science and Technology* 28, no. 1 (Fall 2011): 58–62.

Feaver, Peter D. "Blowback: Information Warfare and the Dynamics of Coercion." *Security Studies* 7, no. 4 (Summer 1998): 88–120.

Federal Bureau of Investigation (FBI). "Update on Sony Investigation." Press release. Washington, DC, December 19, 2014. https://www.fbi.gov/news/pressrel/press-releases/update-on-sony-investigation.

Fildes, Jonathan. "Stuxnet Worm 'Targeted High-Value Iranian Assets.'" BBC News, September 23, 2010. http://www.bbc.com/news/technology-11388018.

Finan, Chris. "A Cyberattack Campaign for Syria." *New York Times*, May 23, 2013. http://www.nytimes.com/2013/05/24/opinion/a-cyberattack-campaign-for-syria.html.

Fineren, Daniel, and Amena Bakr. "Saudi Aramco Says Most Damage from Computer Attack Fixed." Reuters, August 26, 2012. http://www.reuters.com/article/2012/08/26/net-us-saudi-aramco-hacking-idUSBRE87P0B020120826.

Finkle, Jim. "Hacker Group in China Linked to Big Cyber Attacks: Symantec." Reuters, September 17, 2013. http://www.reuters.com/article/2013/09/17/us-cyberattacks-china-idUSBRE98G0M720130917.

———. "Insiders Suspected in Saudi Cyber Attack." Reuters, September 7, 2012. http://www.reuters.com/article/2012/09/07/net-us-saudi-aramco-hack-idUSBRE8860CR20120907.

———. "'Irrational' Hackers Are Growing U.S. Security Fear." Reuters, May 22, 2013. http://www.reuters.com/article/2013/05/22/us-cybersecurity-usa-infrastructure-idUSBRE94L13R20130522.

Finnemore, Martha. "Cultivating International Cyber Norms." In *America's Cyber Future: Security and Prosperity in the Information Age*. Edited by Kristin Lord and Travis Sharp, 87–102. Vol. 2. Washington, DC: Center for a New American Security, June 2011.

FireEye. *APT28: A Window into Russia's Cyber Espionage Operations?* Milpitas, CA: FireEye, 2014.

Fitzpatrick, Alex. "Cyberattacks in Israel and Gaza Increased after Cease Fire Declared." Mashable, December 5, 2012. http://mashable.com/2012/12/05/cyberattacks-gaza-israel/.

Flynn, Stephen E. "The Brittle Superpower." In *Seeds of Disaster, Roots of Response: How Private Action Can Reduce Public Vulnerability*. Edited by Philip E. Auerswald, Lewis M. Branscomb, Todd M. La Porte, and Erwann O. Michel-Kerjan, 26–36. Cambridge: Cambridge University Press, 2006.

Foley, Stephen. "Anti-Capitalist Hackers in the Frame as IMF Reveals Cyber Attack." *The Independent*, June 13, 2011. http://www.independent.co.uk/news/world/politics/anticapitalist-hackers-in-the-frame-as-imf-reveals-cyber-attack-2296760.html?service=Print.

Follath, Erich, and Holger Stark. "The Story of 'Operation Orchard': How Israel Destroyed Syria's Al Kibar Nuclear Reactor." *Spiegel Online International*, November 2, 2009. http://www.spiegel.de/international/world/0,1518,658663,00.html.

Fontaine, Richard, and Will Rogers. "Internet Freedom and Its Discontents: Navigating the Tensions with Cyber Security." In *America's Cyber Future: Security and Prosperity in the Information Age*, edited by Kristin M. Lord and Travis Sharp, 143–64. Vol. 1. Washington, DC: Center for a New American Security, June 2011.

Fowler, Sarah. "Hamas and Israel Step Up Cyber Battle for Hearts and Minds." BBC News, July 15, 2014. http://www.bbc.com/news/world-middle-east-28292908.

Fox News. "Study Warns US Must Develop Cyber Intelligence." September 12, 2011. http://www.foxnews.com/us/2011/09/12/study-warns-us-must-develop-cyber-intelligence/.

Frankel, Ben. "Skullduggery on a Massive Scale." *Homeland Security News Wire*, October 11, 2010. http://www.homelandsecuritynewswire.com/skullduggery-massive-scale.

Frizell, Sam. "Experts Doubt ISIS Could Launch Major Cyberattack against the U.S." *Time*, September 19, 2014. http://time.com/3403769/isis-cyberattack/.

———. "Sony Is Spending $15 Million to Deal with the Big Hack." *Time*, February 4, 2015. http://time.com/3695118/sony-hack-the-interview-costs/.

Gady, Franz-Stefan. "Cyberwar in the Crimea?" *U.S. News & World Report*, March 7, 2014. http://www.usnews.com/opinion/blogs/world-report/2014/03/07/russias-cyberwar-restraint-in-ukraine.

Gallington, Daniel J. "U.S. Can't Wait for a 9/11-Scale Attack to Act on China Cyberspying." *U.S. News & World Report*, February 22, 2013. http://www.usnews.com/opinion/blogs/world-report/2013/02/22/us-cant-wait-for-a-911-scale-attack-to-act-on-china-espionage.

Gander, Kashmira. "Pro-Isis 'Hackers' Threaten to Carry Out Cyber Attacks against Europe, US and Australia in Propaganda Video." *The Independent*, May 12, 2015. http://www.independent.co.uk/news/world/middle-east/proisis-hackers-threaten-to-carry-out-cyber-attacks-against-europe-us-and-australia-in-propaganda-video-10245161.html.

Gartzke, Erik, and Jon Lindsay. "Cross-Domain Deterrence: Strategy in an Era of Complexity." Paper prepared for the Annual Meeting of the International Studies Association, Toronto, Canada, March 25–29, 2014. http://www.jonrlindsay.com/research/papers/CDDOverview_20140322.pdf (no longer active).

———. "Weaving Tangled Webs: Offense, Defense, and Deception in Cyberspace." *Security Studies* 24 (2015): 316–48.

Geers, Kenneth. *Strategic Cyber Security*. Tallinn, Estonia: NATO Cooperative Cyber Defence Centre of Excellence, June 2011.

Geers, Kenneth, Darien Kindlund, Ned Moran, and Rob Rachwald. *World War C: Understanding Nation-State Motives behind Today's Advanced Cyber Attacks*. Milpitas, CA: FireEye, 2014. https://www.fireeye.com/content/dam/fireeye-www/global/en/current-threats/pdfs/fireeye-wwc-report.pdf.

Gewirtz, David. "Russia, the Ukraine Invasion, and U.S. Cybersecurity Implications." *ZDNet*, March 3, 2014. http://www.zdnet.com/russia-the-ukraine-invasion-and-u-s-cybersecurity-implications-7000026915/.

Giacomello, Giampiero. "Bangs for the Buck: A Cost-Benefit Analysis of Cyberterrorism." *Studies in Conflict & Terrorism* 27 (2004): 387–408.

———. "The Information Society and the Danger of Cyberterrorism." In *Encyclopedia of Digital Government*. Edited by Ari-Veikko Anttiroiko and Matti Malkia. Hershey, PA: Idea Group, 2006.

Gilligan, John, and Ed Skoudis. *Twenty Critical Controls for Effective Cyber Defense: Consensus Audit Guidelines*. Washington, DC: CSIS, August 10, 2009. http://csis.org/files/publication/Twenty_Critical_Controls_for_Effective_Cyber_Defense_CAG.pdf.

Ginsburg, Mitch. "Army to Establish Unified Cyber Corps." *Times of Israel*, June 16, 2015. http://www.timesofisrael.com/army-to-establish-unified-cyber-corps/.

Glaser, Charles L. *Deterrence of Cyber Attacks and U.S. National Security*. Cyber Security Policy and Research Institute Report no. GW-CSPRI-2011-5. Washington, DC: George Washington University, June 1, 2011.

GlobalSecurity.org. "Berkut Quick Response Unit." http://www.globalsecurity.org/intell/world/ukraine/berkut.htm.

Goldsmith, Jack. "Cyber Paradox: Every Offensive Weapon Is a (Potential) Chink in Our Defense—and Vice Versa." *Lawfare*, April 12, 2014. http://www.lawfareblog.com/2014/04/cyber-paradox-every-offensive-weapon-is-a-potential-chink-in-our-defense-and-vice-versa/.

Goodman, Will. "Cyber Deterrence: Tougher in Theory than in Practice?" *Strategic Studies Quarterly* 4, no. 3 (Fall 2010): 102–35.

Gorman, Siobhan. "Georgia States Computers Hit by Cyberattack." *Wall Street Journal*, August 12, 2008, A9.

Gorman, Siobhan, August Cole, and Yochi Dreazen. "Computer Spies Breach Fighter-Jet Project." *Wall Street Journal*, April 21, 2009. http://www.wsj.com/news/articles/SB124027491029837401.

Gourley, Bob. "Towards a Cyber Deterrent." CCSA Cyber Conflict Studies Association, May 28, 2008. http://papers.ssrn.com/sol3/papers.cfm?abstract_id=1542565.

Graham, Bradley. "Hackers Attack via Chinese Web Sites." *Washington Post*, August 25, 2005. http://www.washingtonpost.com/wp-dyn/content/article/2005/08/24/AR2005082402318.html.

Graham-Harrison, Emma. "Could Isis's 'Cyber Caliphate' Unleash a Deadly Attack on Key Targets?" *The Guardian*, April 12, 2015. http://www.theguardian.com/world/2015/apr/12/isis-cyber-caliphate-hacking-technology-arms-race.

Gray, Colin S. *Making Strategic Sense of Cyber Power: Why the Sky Is Not Falling*. Carlisle, PA: Strategic Studies Institute, April 2013.

Green, James A., ed. *Cyber Warfare: A Multidisciplinary Analysis*. New York: Routledge, 2015.

———. "The Regulation of Cyber Warfare under the *Jus ad Bellum*." In *Cyber Warfare: A Multidisciplinary Analysis*. Edited by James A. Green, 96–124. New York: Routledge, 2015.

Greenemeier, Larry. "Estonian Attacks Raise Concern over Cyber 'Nuclear Winter.'" *Information Week*, May 24, 2007. http://www.informationweek.com/estonian-attacks-raise-concern-over-cyber-nuclear-winter/d/d-id/1055474.

Greenhouse, Emily. "The Tweets of War." *New Yorker*, November 19, 2012. http://www.newyorker.com/online/blogs/newsdesk/2012/11/the-tweets-of-war-israel-and-hamas-take-to-twitter.html.

Gross, David A., Nova J. Daly, M. Ethan Lucarelli, and Roger H. Miksad. "Cyber Security Governance: Existing Structures, International Approaches and the Private Sector." In *America's Cyber Future: Security and Prosperity in the Information Age*. Edited by Kristin M. Lord and Travis Sharp, 103–22. Vol. 2. Washington, DC: Center for a New American Security, June 2011.

Gross, Michael Joseph. "Enter the Cyber-Dragon." *Vanity Fair*, August 2, 2011. http://www.vanityfair.com/culture/features/2011/09/chinese-hacking-201109.

———. "Operation Shady RAT—Unprecedented Cyber-espionage Campaign and Intellectual-Property Bonanza." *Vanity Fair*, August 2, 2011. http://www.vanityfair.com/culture/features/2011/09/operation-shady-rat-201109.

———. "Silent War." *Vanity Fair*, June 6, 2013. http://www.vanityfair.com/news/2013/07/new-cyberwar-victims-american-business.

Grow, Brian, and Mark Hosenball. "Special Report: In Cyberspy vs. Cyberspy, China Has the Edge." *Reuters*, April 14, 2011. http://www.reuters.com/article/2011/04/14/ctech-us-china-usa-cyberespionage-idCATRE73D24220110414.

Guinchard, Audrey. "Between Hype and Understatement: Reassessing Cyber Risks as a Security Strategy." *Journal of Strategic Security* 4 (Summer 2011): 75–96.

Haley, Christopher. "A Theory of Cyber Deterrence." *Georgetown Journal of International Affairs*, February 6, 2013. http://journal.georgetown.edu/2013/02/06/a-theory-of-cyber-deterrence-christopher-haley/.

Hamedy, Saba. "Sony Hackers Issue Threat in Latest Message: 'The World Will Be Full of Fear.'" *Los Angeles Times*, December 16, 2014. http://www.latimes.com/entertainment/envelope/cotown/la-et-ct-sony-hackers-threat-christmas-the-interview-20141216-story.html.

Harris, Shane. "China Reveals Its Cyberwar Secrets." *Daily Beast*, March 18, 2015. http://www.thedailybeast.com/articles/2015/03/18/china-reveals-its-cyber-war-secrets.html.

Harrison Dinness, Heather A. "The Regulation of Cyber Warfare under the *Jus in Bello*." In *Cyber Warfare: A Multidisciplinary Analysis*. Edited by James A. Green, 125–59. New York: Routledge, 2015.

Hart, Kim. "Longtime Battle Lines Are Recast in Russia and Georgia's Cyberwar." *Washington Post*, August 14, 2008. http://www.washingtonpost.com/wp-dyn/content/article/2008/08/13/AR2008081303623.html.

Havely, Joe. "Why States Go to Cyber-War." February 16, 2000. http://news.bbc.co.uk/1/hi/sci/tech/642867.stm.

Healey, Jason. "How to Beat a Russian Cyber Assault on Ukraine." *Atlantic Council*, March 3, 2014. http://www.atlanticcouncil.org/blogs/new-atlanticist/how-to-beat-a-russian-cyber-assault-on-ukraine.

———. "In Response to Sony Hack, US Should Focus on China Not North Korea." *Christian Science Monitor*, December 19, 2014. http://www.csmonitor.com/World/Passcode/Passcode-Voices/2014/1219/Opinion-In-response-to-Sony-hack-US-should-focus-on-China-not-North-Korea.

———. "Russia vs. Ukraine: The Cyber Front Unfolds." *Atlantic Council*, April 2, 2014. http://www.atlanticcouncil.org/blogs/new-atlanticist/russia-vs-ukraine-the-cyber-front-unfolds.

HelpNet Security. "73% of Organizations Hacked in the Last 2 Years." February 8, 2011. http://www.net-security.org/secworld.php?id=10550.

Hemmer, Patrick T. *Deterrence and Cyber-Weapons*. Monterey, CA: US Naval Postgraduate School, March 2013.

Herberger, Carl. "Cyber Attacks on News Organizations: ISIS Changes Tactics to Win Mindshare." *Security Magazine*, May 12, 2015. http://www.securitymagazine.com/articles/86355-cyber-attacks-on-news-organizations-isis-changes-tactics-to-win-mindshare.

Hersh, Daniel. "Ukrainians Split on Military Aid from U.S." *Military Times*, March 13, 2015. http://www.militarytimes.com/story/military/capitol-hill/2015/03/13/ukrainians-aid-us/70221874/.

Herzog, Stephen. "Revisiting the Estonian Cyber Attacks: Digital Threats and Multinational Responses." *Journal of Strategic Security* 4 (Summer 2011): 49–60.

Hodges, Duncan, and Sadie Creese. "Understanding Cyber-Attacks." In Cyber Warfare Warfare: A Multidisciplinary Analysis. Edited by James A. Green, 33–60. New York: Routledge, 2015.

Holden, Dan. "Estonia, Six Years Later." *Arbor Networks*, May 16, 2013. http://www.arbornetworks.com/asert/2013/05/estonia-six-years-later/.

Hollis, David. "Cyberwar Case Study: Georgia 2008." *Small Wars Journal*, January 6, 2011. http://www.smallwarsjournal.com/blog/journal/docs-temp/639-hollis.pdf.

Homeland Security News Wire. "Chertoff Calls for Cyber-deterrence Doctrine." October 15, 2010. http://www.homelandsecuritynewswire.com/chertoff-calls-cyber-deterrence-doctrine.

———. "China's Sustained Cyberattacks on U.S. Are an Economic, Strategic Threat." June 16, 2011. http://www.homelandsecuritynewswire.com/chinas-sustained-cyberattacks-us-are-economic-strategic-threat.

———. "Chinese Government Hackers Steal Designs of Advanced U.S. Weapons Systems." May 29, 2013. http://www.homelandsecuritynewswire.com/dr20130529-chinese-government-hackers-steal-designs-of-advanced-u-s-weapons-systems.

———. "Chinese Government Orchestrates Cyberattacks on U.S." February 19, 2013. http://www.homelandsecuritynewswire.com/dr20130219-chinese-government-orchestrates-cyberattacks-on-u-s-experts.

———. "Contradictions in U.S. Cybersecurity Policy." February 28, 2011. http://www.homelandsecuritynewswire.com/contradictions-us-cybersecurity-policy.

———. "Countering Extremist Groups' Social Media Influence, Persuasion." July 8, 2015. http://www.homelandsecuritynewswire.com/dr20150708-countering-extremist-groups-social-media-influence-persuasion.

———. "Cyber Attacks on U.S. Are Becoming More Lethal." September 19, 2011. http://www.homelandsecuritynewswire.com/cyber-attacks-us-are-becoming-more-lethal.

———. "Cyber Experts Dispute McAfee's Shady RAT Report." August 22, 2011. http://www.homelandsecuritynewswire.com/cyber-experts-dispute-mcafees-shady-rat-report.

———. "Cyber Researchers Need to Predict, Not Merely Respond to, Cyberattacks: U.S. Intelligence." March 9, 2015. http://www.homelandsecuritynewswire.com/dr20150309-cyber-researchers-need-to-predict-not-merely-respond-to-cyberattacks-u-s-intelligence.

———. "DHS Official: Stuxnet a 'Game Changer.'" November 19, 2010. http://www.homelandsecuritynewswire.com/dhs-official-stuxnet-game-changer.

———. "Fighting Cyber Attacks Costs Pentagon $100 Million." April 8, 2009. http://www.homelandsecuritynewswire.com/fighting-cyber-attacks-costs-pentagon-100-million.

———. "US government Not Properly Coordinating Cybersecurity Efforts, Warns GAO." March 9, 2010. http://www.infosecurity-magazine.com/news/us-government-not-properly-coordinating/.

———. "Hamas, Hezbollah Employ Russian Hackers for Cyber Attacks on Israel." June 15, 2009. http://www.homelandsecuritynewswire.com/hamas-hezbollah-employ-russian-hackers-cyber-attacks-israel.

———. "House Approves $447 [Million] for Cyber Command." January 20, 2014. http://www.homelandsecuritynewswire.com/dr20140120-house-approves-447-for-cyber-command.

———. "Innovative U.S. Cybersecurity Initiative to Address Cyberthreats." May 2, 2014. http://www.homelandsecuritynewswire.com/dr20140502-innovative-u-s-cybersecurity-initiative-to-address-cyberthreats.

———. "Iran Admits Stuxnet's Damage." April 18, 2011. http://www.homelandsecuritynewswire.com/iran-admits-stuxnets-damage.

———. "Iran: Stuxnet Infected Industrial Computers Cleaned." October 5, 2010. http://www.homelandsecuritynewswire.com/iran-stuxnet-infected-industrial-computers-cleaned.

———. "Israeli Legal Expert Urges Development of Ethics Code for Cyberwarfare." February 11, 2014. http://www.homelandsecuritynewswire.com/dr20140211-israeli-legal-expert-urges-development-of-ethics-code-for-cyberwarfare.

———. "Israel Used Cyber Weapon to Disrupt Iran's Nuclear Reactor." September 23, 2010. http://www.homelandsecuritynewswire.com/experts-israel-used-cyber-weapon-disrupt-irans-nuclear-reactor.

———. "The Lesson of Titan Rain: Articulate the Dangers of Cyber Attack to Upper Management." December 14, 2005. http://www.homelandsecuritynewswire.com/lesson-titan-rain-articulate-dangers-cyber-attack-upper-management.

———. "Political Denial-of-Service Attacks on the Rise." March 23, 2009. http://www.homelandsecuritynewswire.com/political-denial-service-attacks-rise.

———. "Private Sector Responsible for Infrastructure Protection Planning." February 8, 2007. http://www.homelandsecuritynewswire.com/private-sector-responsible-infrastructure-protection-planning.

———. "Pro-Regime Syrian Hackers Threaten Cyberattacks on CENTCOM." March 6, 2014. http://www.homelandsecuritynewswire.com/dr20140306-proregime-syrian-hackers-threaten-cyberattacks-on-centcom.

———. "Russia May Launch Crippling Cyberattacks on U.S. in Retaliation for Ukraine Sanctions." May 2, 2014. http://www.homelandsecuritynewswire.com/dr20140502-russia-may-launch-crippling-cyberattacks-on-u-s-in-retaliation-for-ukraine-sanctions.

———. "Stuxnet Heralds Age of Cyber Weapons, Virtual Arms Race." January 27, 2011. http://www.homelandsecuritynewswire.com/stuxnet-heralds-age-cyber-weapons-virtual-arms-race.

———. "Stuxnet Virus Set Back Iran's Nuclear Weapons Program by Two Years." December 16, 2010. http://www.homelandsecuritynewswire.com/stuxnet-virus-set-back-irans-nuclear-weapons-program-two-years-langner.

———. "Stuxnet Worm Wreaks Havoc at Iran's Nuclear Sites," December 10, 2010. http://www.homelandsecuritynewswire.com/experts-stuxnet-worm-wreaks-havoc-irans-nuclear-sites.

———. "Thwarting the Next Generation of Cyberattacks." April 17, 2015. http://www.homelandsecuritynewswire.com/dr20150417-thwarting-the-next-generation-of-cyberattacks.

———. "Twelve Chinese Hacker Groups Responsible for Attacks on U.S." December 16, 2011. http://www.homelandsecuritynewswire.com/dr20111216-twelve-chinese-hacker-groups-responsible-for-attacks-on-u-s.

———. "Ukrainian Computer Systems Attacked by Sophisticated Malware with 'Russian Roots.'" March 10, 2014. http://www.homelandsecuritynewswire.com/dr20140310-ukrainian-computer-systems-attacked-by-sophisticated-malware-with-russian-roots.

———. "U.S. Adopts a More Assertive Cyber Defense Posture." April 29, 2015. http://www

.homelandsecuritynewswire.com/dr20150429-u-s-adopts-a-more-assertive-cyber-defense-posture.
———. "U.S. Government Looking for Game-Changing CybLerspace Ideas." October 15, 2008. http://www.homelandsecuritynewswire.com/us-government-looking-game-changing-cyberspace-ideas.
———. "U.S. Quietly Launches Protection Program against Cyber Attacks on Critical Infrastructure." July 8, 2010. http://www.homelandsecuritynewswire.com/us-quietly-launches-protection-program-against-cyber-attacks-critical-infrastructure.
———. "U.S. Slow to Pinpoint Source of Cyber Attacks." March 11, 2009. http://www.homelandsecuritynewswire.com/us-slow-pinpoint-source-cyber-attacks.
———. "U.S. Will 'View Major Cyber Attacks as Acts of War.'" June 1, 2011. http://www.homelandsecuritynewswire.com/us-will-view-major-cyber-attacks-acts-war.
———. "West Point Wins Cyber Defense Exercise, Launches Army Cyber Institute." April 14, 2014. http://www.homelandsecuritynewswire.com/dr20140415-west-point-wins-cyber-defense-exercise-launches-army-cyber-institute.
———. "Who Is behind Cyber Attacks on Georgia?" August 14, 2008. http://www.homelandsecuritynewswire.com/who-behind-cyber-attacks-georgia.
Homeland Security Policy Institute. *Cyber Deterrence Symposium: Proceedings Report*. Washington, DC: US Government Printing Office, November 2009.
Hopkins, Nick, and Luke Harding. "Pro-Assad Syrian Hackers Launching Cyber-Attacks on Western Media." *The Guardian*, April 29, 2013. http://www.theguardian.com/world/2013/apr/29/assad-syrian-hackers-cyber-attacks.
Hughes, Rex B. "NATO and Cyber Defence: Mission Accomplished?" *Atlantisch Perspectief* 8 (2008). http://www.atlcom.nl/site/english/nieuws/wp-content/Hughes.pdf.
Hundley, Richard O., and Robert H. Anderson. "Emerging Challenge: Security and Safety in Cyberspace." In *In Athena's Camp: Preparing for Conflict in the Information Age*. Edited by John Arquilla and David Ronfeldt, 231–52. Santa Monica: RAND Corporation, 1997.
Hunt, Carl, and Nancy Chesser, eds. *Deterrence 2.0: Deterring Violent Non-State Actors in Cyberspace*. Arlington, VA: Strategic Multi-Layer Analysis Team for the US Strategic Command Global Innovation and Strategy Center, January 9–10, 2008.
Huth, Paul K. "Deterrence and International Conflicts: Empirical Findings and Theoretical Debates." *Annual Review of Political Science* 2 (1999): 25–48.
Iasiello, Emilio. "Is Cyber Deterrence an Illusory Course of Action?" *Journal of Strategic Security* 7 (2013): 54–57.
Ignatius, David. "Pentagon's Cybersecurity Plans Have a Cold War Chill." *Washington Post*, August 26, 2010. http://www.washingtonpost.com/wp-dyn/content/article/2010/08/25/AR2010082505962.html.
Intelligence and National Security Alliance. *Cyber Intelligence: Setting the Landscape for an Emerging Discipline*. Arlington, VA: INSA, September 2011.
Israel National News. "Israel Hit by Cyber Terrorism during Gaza War." June 15, 2009. http://www.israelnationalnews.com/News/Flash.aspx/166479#.U21a3NJdVqQ.
Itzkowitz Shifrinson, Joshua R., and Miranda Priebe. "A Crude Threat: The Limits of an Iranian Missile Campaign against Saudi Arabian Oil." *International Security* 36 (Summer 2011): 167–201.
Jackson, Camille Marie. "Estonian Cyber Policy after the 2007 Attacks: Drivers of Change and Factors for Success." *New Voices in Public Policy* 7 (Spring 2013): 1–15.

Jansen, Michael. "Syria Torn between Armed and Peaceful Struggle." *Irish Times*, March 16, 2012. http://www.irishtimes.com/newspaper/world/2012/0316/1224313394428.html.

Jensen, Eric Talbot. "Cyber Deterrence." *Emory International Law Review* 26 (2012): 773–824.

Jones, Sam. "Kremlin Alleged to Wage Cyber Warfare on Kiev." *Financial Times*, June 5, 2014. http://www.ft.com/cms/s/0/e504e278-e29d-11e3-a829-00144feabdc0.html#axzz34AuqFZSb.

Kaplan, Rebecca. "Cyber Warfare: The Next Front in the Israel-Gaza Conflict?" CBS News, July 28, 2014. http://www.cbsnews.com/news/cyber-warfare-the-next-front-in-the-israel-gaza-conflict/.

Kay, Sean. *Global Security in the Twenty-First Century: The Quest for Power and the Search for Peace*. 2nd ed. New York: Rowman & Littlefield, 2012.

Keizer, Gregg. "Russian Hacker 'Militia' Mobilizes to Attack Georgia." *ComputerWorld*, August 12, 2008. http://www.computerworld.com/article/2532365/cybercrime-hacking/russian-hacker--militia--mobilizes-to-attack-georgia.html.

Kello, Lucas. "The Meaning of the Cyber Revolution: Perils to Theory and Statecraft." *International Security* 38 (Fall 2013): 7–40.

Kerner, Sean Michael. "Sony Hackers Used Apple ID Phishing Scheme, Researchers Claim at RSA." *EWeek*, April 21, 2015. http://www.eweek.com/security/sony-hackers-used-apple-id-phishing-scheme-researchers-claim-at-rsa.html.

Kerry, John. *The New War: The Web of Crime that Threatens America's Security*. New York: Simon & Schuster, 1997.

Kesan, Jay P., and Carol M. Hayes, "Thinking through Active Defense in Cyberspace." In *Proceedings of a Workshop on Deterring Cyberattacks: Informing Strategies and Developing Options for U.S. Policy*. Edited by National Research Council, 327–44. Washington, DC: National Academies Press, 2010.

King, Charles. "The Five-Day War: Managing Moscow after the Georgia Crisis." *Foreign Affairs* 87 (November/December 2009): 2–11.

Kirka, Danica. "BAE Report Says Ukraine Has Faced Cyberattacks." March 9, 2014. http://www.cnsnews.com/news/article/bae-report-says-ukraine-has-faced-cyberattacks.

Kirk, Jeremy. "Estonia, Poland Help Georgia Fight Cyberattacks." *Computerworld*, August 12, 2008. http://www.computerworld.com/s/article/9112399/Update_Estonia_Poland_help_Georgia_fight_cyberattacks?intsrc=hm_list.

Knickmeyer, Ellen. "After Cyberattacks, Saudi Steps Up Online Security." *Wall Street Journal*, August 26, 2013. http://blogs.wsj.com/middleeast/2013/08/26/after-cyberattacks-saudi-steps-up-online-security/.

Krahmann, Elke. "From State to Non-State Actors." In *New Threats and New Actors in International Security*. New York: Palgrave Macmillan, 2005.

———. *New Threats and New Actors in International Security*. New York: Palgrave Macmillan, 2005.

Kramer, Franklin D. "Cyberpower and National Security: Policy Recommendations for a Strategic Framework." In *Cyberpower and National Security*. Edited by Franklin D. Kramer, Stuart H. Starr, and Larry Wentz, 3–23. Washington, DC: National Defense University Press and Potomac Books, 2009.

Kramer, Franklin D., Stuart H. Starr, and Larry Wentz, eds. *Cyberpower and National Security*. Washington, DC: National Defense University Press and Potomac Books, 2009.

Kramer, Franklin D., and Melanie J. Teplinsky. "Cybersecurity and Tailored Deterrence." Issue Brief. Washington, DC: Atlantic Council, December 2013.

Krepinevich, Andrew F. *Cyber Warfare: A "Nuclear Option"?* Washington, DC: Center for Strategic and Budgetary Assessments, 2012.

Kroll, Joshua A. "The Cyber Conundrum: Why the Current Policy for National Cyber Defense Leaves Us Open to Attack." *The American Prospect*, June 1, 2015. http://prospect.org/article/cyber-conundrum.

Kugler, Richard L. "Deterrence of Cyber Attacks." In *Cyberpower and National Security*. Edited by Franklin D. Kramer, Stuart H. Starr, and Larry Wentz, 309–40. Washington, DC: National Defense University Press and Potomac Books, 2009.

Kuschner, Karl. "Legal and Practical Constraints on Information Warfare." Newport, RI: Naval War College, June 14, 1996.

Lachow, Irving. *Active Cyber Defense: A Framework for Policymakers.* Washington, DC: Center for a New American Security, February 2013.

———. "The Stuxnet Enigma: Implications for the Future of Cybersecurity." *Georgetown Journal of International Affairs* (2011): 118–26.

Lan, Tang, and Xhang Xin, "Can Cyber Deterrence Work?" In *Global Cyber Deterrence: Views from China, the U.S., Russia, India, and Norway*. Edited by Andrew Nagorski, 1–3. New York: EastWest Institute, April 2010.

Laqueur, Walter. "Postmodern Terrorism: New Rules for an Old Game." *Foreign Affairs*, 75 (September/October 1996): 24–36.

Lawson, Sean. "Overheated Rhetoric Undermines the Case for Syria Cyber Attacks." *Forbes*, September 10, 2013. http://www.forbes.com/sites/seanlawson/2013/09/10/overheated-cyber-rhetoric-undermines-the-case-for-syria-cyber-attacks/.

Lee, Amy. "International Monetary Fund Braces for Possible Hack Attack from Anonymous." *Huffington Post*, June 1, 2011. http://www.huffingtonpost.com/2011/06/01/anonymous-imf_n_869914.html.

Lee, Dave. "Russia and Ukraine in Cyber 'Stand-Off.'" BBC News, March 5, 2014. http://www.bbc.com/news/technology-26447200.

Leson, Joel. *Assessing and Managing the Terrorism Threat*. Washington, DC: Bureau of Justice Assistance, September 2005.

Lewis, Brian C. "Information Warfare." http://www.fas.org/irp/eprint/snyder/infowarfare.htm.

Lewis, James Andrew. "The Arms Race in Cyberspace." *Washington Post*, October 10, 2013, A03.

———. *Computer Espionage, Titan Rain and China*. Washington, DC: Center for Strategic and International Studies, December 2005.

———. *Cross-Domain Deterrence and Credible Threats*. Washington, DC: Center for Strategic and International Studies, July 2010.

———. "Cyber Deterrence" Washington, DC: Center for Strategic and International Studies, November 15, 2012. http://www.stimson.org/about/news/jim-lewis-of-csis-speaks-at-stimson-on-cyber-deterrence/ (link no longer active).

———. *Cyber Threat and Response: Combating Advanced Attacks and Cyber Espionage.* Washington, DC: Center for Strategic and International Studies, March 2014.

———. *Securing Cyberspace for the 44th Presidency.* Washington, DC: Center for Strategic and International Studies, December 2008.

———. "Truly Damaging Cyberattacks Are Rare." *Washington Post*, October 10, 2013. http://www.washingtonpost.com/postlive/truly-damaging-cyberattacks-are-rare/2013/10/09/ae628655-2d00-11e3-b139-029811dbb57f_story.html.

Libicki, Martin C. *Brandishing Cyberattack Capabilities*. Santa Monica: RAND Corporation, 2013.

———. *Cyberdeterrence and Cyberwar*. Santa Monica: RAND Corporation, 2009.
———. "Information War, Information Peace." *Journal of International Affairs* 51 (Spring 1998): 411–28.
———. "Pulling Punches in Cyberspace." In *Proceedings of a Workshop on Deterring Cyberattacks: Informing Strategies and Developing Options for U.S. Policy*. Edited by National Research Council, 123–50. Washington, DC: National Academies Press, 2010.
Libicki, Martin C., Lillian Ablon, and Tim Webb. *The Defender's Dilemma: Charting a Course toward Cybersecurity*. Santa Monica: RAND Corporation, 2015.
Lin, Herbert. "Operational Considerations in Cyber Attack and Cyber Exploitation." In *Cyberspace and National Security: Threats, Opportunities and Power in a Virtual World*. Edited by Derek S. Reveron, 37–56. Washington, DC: Georgetown University Press, 2012.
Lindsay, Jon R. "The Impact of China on Cybersecurity." *International Security* 39 (Winter 2014/2015): 7–47.
———. "Stuxnet and the Limits of Cyber Warfare." *Security Studies* 22 (2013): 365–404.
Lipscombe, Joe. "Fallout from the Saudi Arabia Breach Continues." *Bloomberg Businessweek*, April 8, 2014. https://www.joelipscombejournalism.com/2014/08/08/fallout-from-the-saudi-aramco-breach-continues/.
Lomidze, Irakli. *Cyber Attacks against Georgia*. Tbilisi: Ministry of Justice of Georgia, Data Exchange Agency, 2011. http://www.dea.gov.ge/uploads/GITI%202011/GITI2011_3.pdf.
LookingGlass. "Lookingglass Cyber Threat Intelligence Group Links Russia to Cyber Espionage Campaign Targeting Ukrainian Government and Military Officials." Reston, VA, April 28, 2015. https://www.lookingglasscyber.com/press-release/lookingglass-cyber-threat-intelligence-group-links-russia-to-cyber-espionage-campaign-targeting-ukrainian-government-and-military-officials/.
Lord, Kristin M., and Travis Sharp, eds. *America's Cyber Future: Security and Prosperity in the Information Age*. Vol. 1. Washington DC: Center for a New American Security, June 2011.
———, eds. *America's Cyber Future: Security and Prosperity in the Information Age*. Vol. 2. Washington, DC: Center for a New American Security, June 2011.
Los Angeles Times. "War, Redefined." August 17, 2008. http://articles.latimes.com/2008/aug/17/opinion/ed-cyberwar17.
Lukasik, Stephen J. "A Framework for Thinking about Cyber Conflict and Cyber Deterrence with Possible Declaratory Policies for These Domains." In *Proceedings of a Workshop on Deterring Cyber Attacks: Informing Strategies and Developing Options for U.S. Policy*. Edited by National Research Council, 99–122. Washington, DC: National Academies Press, 2010.
Lupovici, Amir. "Cyber Warfare and Deterrence: Trends and Challenges in Research." *Military and Strategic Affairs* 3 (December 2011): 49–62.
Lynn, William J. III. "Defending a New Domain: The Pentagon's Cyberstrategy." *Foreign Affairs* 89 (September/October 2010): 97–108.
MacAskill, Ewen. "Briton Lead Suspect after US Central Command's Twitter Account Is Hacked." *The Guardian*, January 14, 2015.
Mandel, Robert. *The Changing Face of National Security: A Conceptual Analysis*. Westport, CT: Greenwood, 1994.
———. *Coercing Compliance: State-Initiated Brute Force in Today's World*. Stanford: Stanford University Press, 2015.
———. *Dark Logic: Transnational Criminal Tactics and Global Security*. Stanford: Stanford University Press, 2011.

———. *Global Security Upheaval: Armed Non-State Groups Usurping State Stability Functions*. Stanford: Stanford University Press, 2013.
———. *Global Threat: Target-Centered Assessment and Management*. Westport, CT: Praeger Security International, 2008.
———. "What Are We Protecting?" *Armed Forces & Society* 22 (Spring 1996): 335–55.
Mankoff, Jeffrey. "Russia's Latest Land Grab: How Putin Won Crimea and Lost Ukraine." *Foreign Affairs* 93 (May/June 2014): 60–68.
Marcius, Chelsea Rose, and Larry McShane. "ISIS Posts Diagram of Best Apps for Terrorist Communication Online." *New York Daily News*, November 18, 2015. http://www.nydailynews.com/news/world/isis-rates-best-apps-terrorist-communications-online-article-1.2439192.
Markoff, John. "Before the Gunfire, Cyberattacks." *New York Times*, August 12, 2008. http://www.nytimes.com/2008/08/13/technology/13cyber.html?_r=2&.
———. "A Silent Attack, but Not a Subtle One." *New York Times*, September 26, 2010. http://www.nytimes.com/2010/09/27/technology/27virus.html.
Markoff, John, and Thom Shanker. "Halted '03 Iraqi Plan Illustrates U.S. Fear of Cyberwar Risk." *New York Times*, August 1, 2009. http://www.nytimes.com/2009/08/02/us/politics/02cyber.html.
Marks, Joseph. "Ukraine's Intel Chief: We Weren't Ready." *POLITICO*, June 22, 2015. http://www.politico.eu/article/ukraines-intel-chief-we-werent-ready.
Martinez, Michael. "Cyberwar: CyberCaliphate Targets U.S. Military Spouses; Anonymous Hits ISIS." CNN, February 11, 2015. http://www.cnn.com/2015/02/10/us/isis-cybercaliphate-attacks-cyber-battles/.
Masters, Greg. "Operation Shady Rat Reveals Vulnerability to Cyber Intrusion." *SC Magazine*, August 3, 2011. http://www.scmagazine.com/operation-shady-rat-reveals-vulnerability-to-cyber-intrusion/article/208997/.
Matlack, Carol. "Cyberwar in Ukraine Falls Far Short of Russia's Full Powers." *Bloomberg Businessweek*, March 10, 2014. http://www.businessweek.com/articles/2014-03-10/cyberwar-in-ukraine-falls-far-short-of-russias-full-powers.
Maza, Cristina. "Centcom Twitter Hack and the Rewards of Digital Vandalism." *Christian Science Monitor*, January 14, 2015. http://www.csmonitor.com/World/Passcode/2015/0114/Centcom-Twitter-hack-and-the-rewards-of-digital-vandalism-video.
McAfee Foundstone Professional Services. *Global Energy Cyberattacks: "Night Dragon."* Santa Clara: McAfee Labs, February 10, 2011.
McCluskey, Molly. "Estonia Redefines National Security in a Digital Age." *Al Jazeera*, March 20, 2015. http://www.aljazeera.com/indepth/features/2015/03/estonia-redefines-national-security-digital-age-150318065430514.html.
McConnell, Mike. "Cyber Insecurities: The 21st Century Threatscape." In *America's Cyber Future: Security and Prosperity in the Information Age*. Edited by Kristin M. Lord and Travis Sharp, 25–40. Vol. 2. Washington, DC: Center for a New American Security, June 2011.
———. "How to Win the Cyber-War We're Losing." *Washington Post*, February 28, 2010. http://www.washingtonpost.com/wp-dyn/content/article/2010/02/25/AR2010022502493.html.
———. "To Win the Cyber-War, Look to the Cold War." *Washington Post*, February 28, 2010, B1.
McDermott, Rose. "Decision Making under Uncertainty." In *Proceedings of a Workshop on Deterring Cyberattacks: Informing Strategies and Developing Options for U.S. Policy*.

Edited by National Research Council, 227–41. Washington, DC: National Academies Press, 2010.

Mendoza, Jessica. "How Syrian Rebel Fighters Fell for 'Honey Trap' Hackers." *Christian Science Monitor*, February 2, 2015. http://www.csmonitor.com/World/Global-News/2015/0202/How-Syrian-rebel-fighters-fell-for-honey-trap-hackers.

Menn, Joseph. "Cyber-attacks on Georgia Websites Tied to Mob, Russian Government." *Los Angeles Times*, August 13 2008. http://latimesblogs.latimes.com/technology/2008/08/experts-debate.html.

———. "Syria, Aided by Iran, Could Strike Back at U.S. in Cyberspace." Reuters, August 29, 2013. http://www.reuters.com/article/2013/08/29/us-syria-crisis-cyberspace-analysis-idUSBRE97S04Z20130829.

———. "U.S. Cyberwar Strategy Stokes Fear of Blowback." Reuters, May 10, 2013. http://www.reuters.com/article/2013/05/10/us-usa-cyberweapons-specialreport-idUSBRE9490EL20130510.

MercyCorps. "Quick Facts: What You Need to Know about the Syria Crisis." May 15, 2015. http://www.mercycorps.org/articles/turkey-iraq-jordan-lebanon-syria/quick-facts-what-you-need-know-about-syria-crisis.

Mills, Elinor. "Virus Knocks Out Computers at Qatari Gas Firm ResGas." CNET News, August 30, 2012. https://www.cnet.com/news/virus-knocks-out-computers-at-qatari-gas-firm-rasgas/.

Mimoso, Michael. "NetTraveler Espionage Malware Campaign Uncovered, Links to Ghost RAT, Titan Rain Found." ThreatPost, June 4, 2013. https://threatpost.com/net-traveler-espionage-campaign-uncovered-links-to-gh0st-rat-titan-rain-found/100865.

Minority Staff of the Homeland Security and Governmental Affairs Committee, Senate. *The Federal Government's Track Record on Cybersecurity and Critical Infrastructure*. Washington, DC: US Government Printing Office, February 4, 2014.

Moens, Alexander, Seychelle Cushing, and Alan W. Dowd. *Cybersecurity Challenges for Canada and the United States*. Vancouver, Canada: Fraser Institute, March 2015.

Molander, Roger C., and Sanyin Siang. "The Legitimization of Strategic Information Warfare: Ethical Considerations." *Professional Ethics Report* (American Academy for the Advancement of Science) 11, no. 4 (Fall 1998). http://www.aaas.org/sites/default/files/migrate/uploads/per15.pdf.

Moore, Jack. "ISIS Threaten America with Another 9/11." *Newsweek*, April 13, 2013. http://europe.newsweek.com/isis-release-propaganda-video-threatening-another-911-america-321837.

Moore, Ryan J. "Prospects for Cyber Deterrence." Thesis, US Naval Postgraduate School, Monterey, CA, December 2008. http://hdl.handle.net/10945/3740.

Morgan, Forrest E., Karl P. Mueller, Evan S. Medeiros, Kevin L. Pollpeter, and Roger Cliff. *Dangerous Thresholds: Managing Escalation in the 21st Century*. Santa Monica: RAND Corporation, 2008.

Morgan, Patrick M. "Applicability of Traditional Deterrence Concepts and Theory to the Cyber Realm." In *Proceedings of a Workshop on Deterring Cyberattacks: Informing Strategies and Developing Options for U.S. Policy*. Edited by National Research Council, 55–76. Washington, DC: National Academies Press, 2010.

———. *Deterrence Now*. Cambridge: Cambridge University Press, 2003.

Morozov, Evgeny. "An Army of Ones and Zeroes: How I Became a Soldier in the Georgia-Russia Cyberwar." *Slate*, August 14, 2008. http://www.slate.com/articles/technology/technology/2008/08/an_army_of_ones_and_zeroes.html.

Mosendz, Polly. "Syrian Electronic Army Claims to Have Hacked U.S. Army Website." *Newsweek*, June 8, 2015. http://www.newsweek.com/syrian-electronic-army-claims-have-hacked-us-army-website-340874.

Moskowitz, Jeff. "Cyberattack Tied to Hezbollah Ups the Ante for Israel's Digital Defenses." *Christian Science Monitor*, June 1, 2015. http://www.csmonitor.com/World/Passcode/2601/Cyberattack-tied-to-Hezbollah-ups-the-ante-for-Israel-s-digital-defenses.

Mount, Mike. "U.S. Officials Believe Iran behind Recent Cyber Attacks." CNN, October 16, 2012. http://www.cnn.com/2012/10/15/world/iran-cyber/.

Munro, Neil. "The Pentagon's New Nightmare: An Electronic Pearl Harbor." *Washington Post*, July 16, 1995, C3.

Nagorski, Andrew, ed. *Global Cyber Deterrence: Views from China, the U.S., Russia, India, and Norway*. New York: EastWest Institute, April 2010.

Nagraj, Aarti. "Cyber War: Is the Middle East Prepared?" *Gulf Business*, June 20, 2015. http://gulfbusiness.com/2015/06/cyber-war-middle-east-prepared/#.VZr-63pVhBc.

Nakashima, Ellen. "Following U.S. Indictments, Chinese Military Scaled Back Hacks on American Industry." *Washington Post*, November 30, 2015. https://www.washingtonpost.com/world/national-security/following-us-indictments-chinese-military-scaled-back-hacks-on-american-industry/2015/11/30/fcdb097a-9450-11e5-b5e4-279b4501e8a6_story.html?hpid=hp_rhp-more-top-stories_no-name%3Ahomepage%2Fstory.

———. "Large Worldwide Cyber Attack Uncovered." *Washington Post*, February 18, 2010, A3.

———. "List of Cyber-Weapons Developed by Pentagon to Streamline Computer Warfare." *Washington Post*, May 31, 2011. http://www.washingtonpost.com/national/list-of-cyber-weapons-developed-by-pentagon-to-streamline-computer-warfare/2011/05/31/AGSublFH_story.html?wpisrc=nl_politics.

———. "To Thwart Hackers, Firms Salting Their Servers with Fake Data." *Washington Post*, January 2, 2013. http://articles.washingtonpost.com/2013-01-02/world/36211654_1_hackers-servers-contract-negotiations.

———. "U.S. Cyberwarfare Force to Grow Significantly, Defense Secretary Says." *Washington Post*, March 28, 2014. http://www.washingtonpost.com/world/national-security/us-cyberwarfare-force-to-grow-significantly-defense-secretary-says/2014/03/28/0a1fa074-b680-11e3-b84e-897d3d12b816_story.html.

Nando Times. "U.S. Official Warns of Future Attacks on Vital Computer Systems," November 17, 2001. http://www.nando.net/technology/story/172635p-1669909c.html (link no longer active).

National Research Council. *Proceedings of a Workshop on Deterring Cyberattacks: Informing Strategies and Developing Options for U.S. Policy*. Washington, DC: National Academies Press, 2010.

Nazario, Jose. "'Cyberwar' Emerges amid Russia-Georgia Conflict." Interview by Jeffrey Brown. *NewsHour*. PBS. August 13, 2008. http://www.pbs.org/newshour/bb/europe-july-dec08-cyberwar_08-13/.

———. "The Effects of War: Gaza and Israel." Arbor Networks, January 5, 2009. https://www.arbornetworks.com/blog/asert/the-effects-of-war-gaza-and-israel/

———. "Politically Motivated Denial of Service Attacks." In *The Virtual Battlefield: Perspectives on Cyber Warfare*. Tallinn, Estonia: NATO Cooperative Cyber Defence Centre of Excellence, 2009. http://www.ccdcoe.org/publications/virtualbattlefield/12_NAZARIO%20Politically%20Motivated%20DDoS.pdf.

Negroponte, John D., Samuel J. Palmisano, and Adam Segal. *Defending an Open, Global,*

Secure, and Resilient Internet. Independent Task Force Report no. 70. New York: Council on Foreign Relations, 2013.

Neuman, Scott. "As the Worm Turns: Cybersecurity Expert Traces Blowback from Stuxnet." National Public Radio, June 1, 2012. http://www.npr.org/blogs/thetwo-way/2012/06/01/154162121/as-the-worm-turns-cybersecurity-expert-tracks-blowback-from-stuxnet.

Newitz, Annalee. "9 Facts about Computer Security that Experts Wish You Knew." *Gizmodo*, March 4, 2015. http://gizmodo.com/9-facts-about-computer-security-that-experts-wish-you-k-1686817774.

New York Times. "Daily Report: How Aramco Got Hacked." October 24, 2012. http://bits.blogs.nytimes.com/2012/10/24/daily-report-how-aramco-got-hacked/.

Nichiporuk, Brian, and Carl H. Builder, "Societal Implications." In *In Athena's Camp: Preparing for Conflict in the Information Age*. Edited by John Arquilla and David Ronfeldt, 295–314. Santa Monica: RAND Corporation, 1997.

Nichol, Jim. *Russia-Georgia Conflict in August 2008: Context and Implications for U.S. Interests*. Washington, DC: Congressional Research Service, March 3, 2009.

Norton-Taylor, Richard. "Titan Rain—How Chinese Hackers Targeted Whitehall." *The Guardian*, September 4, 2007. http://www.theguardian.com/technology/2007/sep/04/news.internet.

Nye, Joseph S., Jr. *Cyber Power*. Cambridge MA: Belfer Center for Science and International Affairs at the Harvard Kennedy School, May 2010.

———. "Power and National Security in Cyberspace." In *America's Cyber Future: Security and Prosperity in the Information Age*. Edited by Kristin M. Lord and Travis Sharp, 7–23. Vol. 2. Washington, DC: Center for a New American Security, June 2011.

Obama, Barack. *International Strategy for Cyberspace: Prosperity, Security, and Openness in a Networked World*. Washington DC: US Government Printing Office, May 2011.

———. "Remarks by the President on Securing Our Nation's Cyber Infrastructure." White House, Washington, DC, May 29, 2009. http://www.whitehouse.gov/the_press_office/Remarks-by-the-President-on-Securing-Our-Nations-Cyber-Infrastructure.

Office of the National Counterintelligence Executive. *Foreign Spies Stealing US Economic Secrets in Cyber Space: Report to Congress on Foreign Economic Collection and Industrial Espionage, 2009–2011*. October 2011. http://www.ncix.gov/publications/reports/fecie_all/Foreign_Economic_Collection_2011.pdf.

Office of the Under Secretary of Defense for Acquisition and Technology. "Report of the Defense Science Board Task Force on Information Warfare-Defense." Washington, DC: November 1996. http://jya.com/iwd.htm (link no longer active).

Ofri, Arie. "Crisis and Opportunity Forecasting." *Orbis* 27 (Winter 1983): 821–27.

Oltsik, Jon. "Russian Cyber Attack on Georgia: Lessons Learned?" *Network World*, August 17, 2009. http://www.networkworld.com/community/node/44448.

Otte, Jan Thomas. "Cyberspace and Propaganda: Israel and the War in Gaza." February 2009. http://lisd.princeton.edu/sites/lisd/files/commentary_february2009.pdf.

Paganini, Pierluigi. "Crimea—Is Russia Adopting the Same Cyber Strategy Used in Georgia?" *Security Affairs*, March 5, 2014. http://securityaffairs.co/wordpress/22781/cyber-warfare-2/crimea-russia-cyber-strategy.html.

———. "ISIS—Cyber Caliphate Hackers Are Threatening Electronic War." *Security Affairs*, May 17, 2015. http://securityaffairs.co/wordpress/36883/cyber-crime/cyber-caliphate-electronic-war.html.

Pagliery, Jose. "Half of American Adults Hacked This Year." CNN Money, May 28, 2014. http://money.cnn.com/2014/05/28/technology/security/hack-data-breach/.

Panetta, Leon. "DOD News Briefing with Secretary Panetta and General Dempsey from the Pentagon." US Department of Defense News Transcript, October 25, 2012. http://www.defense.gov/transcripts/transcript.aspx?transcriptid=5143 (link no longer active).

Parker, Kevin L. "The Utility of Cyberpower." *Military Review* (May–June 2014): 26–33.

Perlroth, Nicole. "Connecting the Dots after Cyberattack on Saudi Aramco." *New York Times*, August 27, 2012. http://bits.blogs.nytimes.com/2012/08/27/connecting-the-dots-after-cyberattack-on-saudi-aramco/?_php=true&_type=blogs&_r=0.

———. "In Cyberattack on Saudi Firm, U.S. Sees Iran Firing Back." *New York Times*, October 23, 2012. http://www.nytimes.com/2012/10/24/business/global/cyberattack-on-saudi-oil-firm-disquiets-us.html?pagewanted=all.

Peters, Ralph. "Washington Ignores Cyberattack Threats, Putting Us All at Peril." *Wired*, August 23, 2007. http://archive.wired.com/politics/security/magazine/15-09/ff_estonia_america.

Pfeffer, Anshel. "Israel Suffered Massive Cyber Attack during Gaza Offensive." *Haaretz*, June 15, 2009. http://www.haaretz.com/news/israel-suffered-massive-cyber-attack-during-gaza-offensive-1.278094.

Phillips, Andrew. "The Asymmetric Nature of Cyber Warfare." *USNI News*, October 14, 2012. http://news.usni.org/2012/10/14/asymmetric-nature-cyber-warfare.

Pincus, Walter. "The Inevitable Blowback to High-Tech Warfare." *Washington Post*, October 16, 2012, A19.

Posner, Gerald. "China's Secret Cyberterrorism." *Daily Beast*, January 12, 2010, 2. http://www.thedailybeast.com/articles/2010/01/13/chinas-secret-cyber-terrorism.html.

Posner, Richard A. *Catastrophe: Risk and Response*. New York: Oxford University Press, 2005.

Raduege Jr., Harry D. "Fighting Weapons of Mass Disruption: Why America Needs a 'Cyber Triad.'" In *Global Cyber Deterrence: Views from China, the U.S., Russia, India, and Norway*. Edited by Andrew Nagorski, 3–5. New York: EastWest Institute, April 2010.

Rashid, Fahmida Y. "Hacktivists, Cyber-Spies at War in Ukraine, Russia Conflict." *PC Magazine*, March 3, 2014. http://securitywatch.pcmag.com/none/321274-hacktivists-cyber-spies-at-war-in-ukraine-russia-conflict.

Rattray, Gregory J. *Strategic Warfare in Cyberspace*. Cambridge, MA: MIT Press, 2001.

Rattray, Gregory J., and Jason Healey. "Non-State Actors and Cyber Conflict." In *America's Cyber Future: Security and Prosperity in the Information Age*. Edited by Kristin M. Lord and Travis Sharp, 65–86. Vol. 2. Washington, DC: Center for a New American Security, June 2011.

Raymond, David. "Paradoxes of (Cyber) Counterinsurgency." *Cyber Defense Review*, February 9, 2015. http://www.cyberdefensereview.org/2015/02/09/490/.

Reddy, Sudeep, and Siobhan Gorman. "IMF Hit by Cyber Attack." *Wall Street Journal*, June 11, 2011. http://online.wsj.com/news/articles/SB10001424052702304259304576380034225081432.

Regan, Tom. "Wars of the Future . . . Today." *Christian Science Monitor*, June 24, 1999, A1.

Rekasius, Mindaugas. *Unconventional Deterrence Strategy*. Monterey, CA: US Naval Postgraduate School, June 2005.

Reuters. "Aramco Says Cyber Attack Was Aimed at Production." *New York Times*, December 9, 2012. http://www.nytimes.com/2012/12/10/business/global/saudi-aramco-says-hackers-took-aim-at-its-production.html.

———. "Islamic State Calls on Hackers to Kill 100 U.S. Military Personnel." March 21, 2015. http://www.reuters.com/article/2015/03/21/us-mideast-crisis-threat-idUSKBN0MH0QQ20150321.

Reveron, Derek S., ed. *Cyberspace and National Security: Threats, Opportunities and Power in a Virtual World*. Washington, DC: Georgetown University Press, 2012.

———. "An Introduction to National Security and Cyberspace." In *Cyberspace and National Security: Threats, Opportunities and Power in a Virtual World*. Edited by Derek S. Reveron, 3–20. Washington, DC: Georgetown University Press, 2012.

Richards, Jason. "Denial-of-Service: The Estonian Cyberwar and Its Implications for U.S. National Security." *International Affairs Review* 18, no. 2 (2009). http://www.iar-gwu.org/node/65.

Rid, Thomas. "Cyberwar and Peace: Hacking Can Reduce Real-World Violence." *Foreign Affairs* 92 (November/December 2013): 77–87.

Rid, Thomas, and Peter McBurney. "Cyber-Weapons." *RUSI (Royal United Services Institute) Journal*, 157 (2012): 6–13.

Riley, Michael, and Sandrine Rastello. "IMF State-Backed Cyber-Attack Follows Hacks of Lab, G-20." *Bloomberg*, June 13, 2011. http://www.bloomberg.com/news/2011-06-11/imf-computer-system-infiltrated-by-hackers-said-to-work-for-foreign-state.html.

Rivera, Matthew. "Deterrence in Cyberspace." Thesis, Joint Forces Staff College, Joint Advanced Warfighting School, Norfolk, VA, June 13, 2012. http://www.dtic.mil/cgi-bin/GetTRDoc?Location=U2&doc=GetTRDoc.pdf&AD=ADA562428.

Roberts, John. "Cyber Threats to Energy Security, as Experienced by Saudi Arabia." *Platts*, November 27, 2012. http://blogs.platts.com/2012/11/27/virus_threats/.

Rosenzweig, Paul. *Cybersecurity and Public Goods: The Public/Private "Partnership."* Stanford: Stanford University, Hoover Institution Koret-Taube Task Force on National Security and Law, 2011.

———. "The Organization of the United States Government and Private Sector for Achieving Cyber Deterrence." In *Proceedings of a Workshop on Deterring CyberAttacks: Informing Strategies and Developing Options for U.S. Policy*. Edited by National Research Council, 245–72. Washington, DC: National Academies Press, 2010.

Rowe, Neil C. "The Attribution of Cyber Warfare." In *Cyber Warfare: A Multidisciplinary Analysis*. Edited by James A. Green, ch. 3. New York: Routledge, 2015.

Rudner, Martin. "Cyber-Threats to Critical National Infrastructure: An Intelligence Challenge." *International Journal of Intelligence and Counterintelligence* 26 (2013): 453–81.

Rundle, Michael. "Hacking Group Claims Massive Attack on Oil Giant Saudi Aramco, Threatens Fresh Assault." *Huffington Post*, August 24, 2012. http://www.huffingtonpost.co.uk/2012/08/24/hacking-group-claims-massive-saudi-aramco-attack_n_1826910.html.

Russell, Alison Lawlor. *Cyber Blockades*. Washington, DC: Georgetown University Press, 2014.

Ruus, Kertu. "Cyber War I: Estonia Attacked from Russia." *European Affairs* 9 (Winter/Spring 2008). http://www.europeaninstitute.org/index.php/component/content/article?id=67:cyber-war-i-estonia-attacked-from-russia.

Saadawi, Tarek, and Louis Jordan, Jr., eds. *Cyber Infrastructure Protection*. Carlisle, PA: Strategic Studies Institute, May 2011.

Sanger, David E. "Countering Cyberattacks without a Playbook." *New York Times*, December 24, 2014, A3. http://www.nytimes.com/2014/12/24/world/asia/countering-cyberattacks-without-a-playbook.html.

———. "Document Reveals Growth of Cyberwarfare between the U.S. and Iran." *New York Times*, February 22, 2015. http://www.nytimes.com/2015/02/23/us/document-reveals-growth-of-cyberwarfare-between-the-us-and-iran.html?hp&action=click

&pgtype=Homepage&module=first-column-region&region=top-news&WT.nav=top-news&_r=0.
———. "Obama Order Sped Up Wave of Cyberattacks against Iran." *New York Times*, June 1, 2012. http://www.nytimes.com/2012/06/01/world/middleeast/obama-ordered-wave-of-cyberattacks-against-iran.html?_r=2&hp&.
———. "U.S. Blames China's Military Directly for Cyberattacks." *New York Times*, May 6, 2013. http://www.nytimes.com/2013/05/07/world/asia/us-accuses-chinas-military-in-cyberattacks.html?_r=0.
Sanger, David E., and Steven Erlanger. "Suspicion Falls on Russia as 'Snake' Cyberattacks Target Ukraine's Government." *New York Times*, March 8, 2014. http://www.nytimes.com/2014/03/09/world/europe/suspicion-falls-on-russia-as-snake-cyberattacks-target-ukraines-government.html?_r=0.
Sanger, David E., and John Markoff. "I.M.F. Reports Cyberattack Led to 'Very Major Breach.'" *New York Times*, June 11, 2011. http://www.nytimes.com/2011/06/12/world/12imf.html.
Sanger, David E., and Nicole Perlroth. "U.S. Denies It Knew of Heartbleed Bug on the Web." *New York Times*, April 11, 2014. http://www.nytimes.com/2014/04/12/us/us-denies-knowledge-of-heartbleed-bug-on-the-web.html?_r=2.
———. "U.S. Said to Find North Korea Ordered Cyberattack on Sony." *New York Times*, December 17, 2014. http://www.nytimes.com/2014/12/18/world/asia/us-links-north-korea-to-sony-hacking.html?_r=0.
Sanger, David E., and Michael S. Schmidt. "More Sanctions on North Korea after Sony Case." *New York Times*, January 2, 2015. http://www.nytimes.com/2015/01/03/us/in-response-to-sony-attack-us-levies-sanctions-on-10-north-koreans.html?_r=0.
Sanger, David E., and Eric Schmitt. "Hackers Use Old Lure on Web to Help Syrian Government." *New York Times*, February 1, 2015. http://www.nytimes.com/2015/02/02/world/middleeast/hackers-use-old-web-lure-to-aid-assad.html.
Schmitt, Michael N. "Cyber Operations and the *Jus ad Bellum* Revisited." *Villanova Law Review* 56 (2011): 569–605.
———. "New Interest in Hacking as Threat to Security." *New York Times*, March 13, 2012. http://www.nytimes.com/2012/03/14/us/new-interest-in-hacking-as-threat-to-us-security.html?_r=2&ref=fb.
———, ed. *Tallinn Manual on the International Law Applicable to Cyber Warfare*. New York: Cambridge University Press, 2013.
Schneider, Barry R., and Lawrence E. Grinter, eds. *Battlefield of the Future: A 21st Century Warfare Issue*. Studies in National Security no. 3. Maxwell Air Force Base, AL: Air War College, September 1995.
Schneier, Bruce. *Beyond Fear: Thinking Sensibly about Security in an Uncertain World*. New York: Copernicus Books, 2003.
———. "The Story behind the Stuxnet Virus." *Forbes*, October 6, 2010. http://www.forbes.com/2010/10/06/iran-nuclear-computer-technology-security-stuxnet-worm.html.
———. "Who Should Be in Charge of Cybersecurity?" *Wall Street Journal*, March 31, 2009. http://online.wsj.com/news/articles/SB123844579753370907?mg=reno64-wsj&url=http%3A%2F%2Fonline.wsj.com%2Farticle%2FSB123844579753370907.html.
Schuppe, Jon. "ISIS 'Hit List' Fuels Concerns Over Tech-Savvy Terrorists." *NBC News*, May 23, 2015. http://www.nbcnews.com/news/us-news/isis-hit-list-fuels-concerns-over-tech-savvy-terrorists-n328781.
Schwartz, Peter. "Scenarios for the Future of Cyber Security." In *America's Cyber Future: Security and Prosperity in the Information Age*. Edited by Kristin M. Lord and

Travis Sharp, 217–28. Vol. 2. Washington, DC: Center for a New American Security, June 2011.

Scott, Andrew M. *The Revolution in Statecraft: Informal Penetration.* New York: Random House, 1965.

Seal, Mark. "An Exclusive Look at Sony's Hacking Saga." *Vanity Fair*, February 4, 2015. http://www.vanityfair.com/hollywood/2015/02/sony-hacking-seth-rogen-evan-goldberg.

Security and Defence Agenda. *Cyber-Security: The Vexed Question of Global Rules.* Brussels: Security and Defence Agenda and McAfee, February 2012.

Shachtman, Noah. "Kremlin Kids: We Launched the Estonian Cyber War." *Wired*, March 11, 2009. http://www.wired.com/2009/03/pro-kremlin-gro/.

———. "Top Georgian Official: Moscow Cyber Attacked Us—We Just Can't Prove It." *Wired*, March 11, 2009. http://www.wired.com/dangerroom/2009/03/georgia-blames/.

Shanker, Thom, and David E. Sanger. "U.S. Helps Allies Trying to Battle Iranian Hackers." *New York Times*, June 8, 2013. http://www.nytimes.com/2013/06/09/world/middleeast/us-helps-allies-trying-to-battle-iranian-hackers.html?_r=0.

Shaw, Lucas. "Sony to Release 'The Interview' in More than 300 Cinemas." *Bloomberg Business*, December 23, 2014. http://www.bloomberg.com/news/articles/2014-12-23/sony-to-release-the-interview-on-dec-25-theaters-say.

Sheldon, John B. "Space Power and Deterrence: Are We Serious?" *Policy Outlook*. Washington, DC: George C. Marshall Institute, November 2008. http://marshall.org/wp-content/uploads/2013/08/616.pdf.

Shimeall, Tim, Phil Williams, and Casey Dunlevy. "Countering Cyber War." *NATO Review* (Winter 2001/2002): 16–18.

Siegel, Jacob, and Nancy A. Youssef. "No, the Pentagon Wasn't Hacked by ISIS." *Daily Beast*, January 13, 2015. http://www.thedailybeast.com/articles/2015/01/12/isis-hackers-love-american-folk-punk-don-t-know-the-name-of-their-own-terror-group.html.

Siers, Rhea. "North Korea: The Cyber Wild Card." *Journal of Law and Cyber Warfare* 1 (2014): 1–12.

Silverstein, Ken. "Buck Rogers Rides Again: A 'Revolution' in High-Tech Systems Promises Big Profits and for the U.S. Risk-Free War." *Nation* 269 (October 25, 1999): 23–32.

Simon, Herbert A. "Rational Choice and the Structure of the Environment." *Psychological Review* 63 (1966): 129–38.

Singer, Peter W. "It Doesn't Really Matter if ISIS Sympathizers Hacked Central Command's Twitter." *Wired*, January 13, 2015. http://www.wired.com/2015/01/doesnt-really-matter-isis-sympathizers-hacked-central-commands-twitter.

Singer, Peter W., and Allan Friedman. *Cybersecurity and Cyberwar: What Everyone Needs to Know.* New York: Oxford University Press, 2014.

Sofaer, Abraham D., David Clark, and Whitfield Diffie. "Cyber Security and International Agreements." In *Proceedings of a Workshop on Deterring CyberAttacks: Informing Strategies and Developing Options for U.S. Policy.* Edited by National Research Council, 179–206. Washington, DC: National Academies Press, 2010.

Solomon, Jonathan. "Cyberdeterrence between Nation-States: Plausible Strategy or a Pipe Dream?" *Strategic Studies Quarterly* (Spring 2011): 1–25.

SPAMfighter News. "Most Web Hacks Found to Be Profit-Oriented." February 18, 2008. http://www.spamfighter.com/News-9841-Most-Web-Hacks-Found-to-be-Profit-oriented.htm.

Stahl, Lesley. "The Great Brain Robbery." *60 Minutes*. CBS News, January 17, 2016. http://www.cbsnews.com/news/60-minutes-great-brain-robbery-china-cyber-espionage/.

Stein, George J. "Information War—Cyberwar—Netwar." In *Battlefield of the Future: A 21st Century Warfare Issue*. Edited by Barry R. Schneider and Lawrence E. Grinter, 153–70. Studies in National Security no. 3. Maxwell Air Force Base, AL: Air War College, September 1995.

Stein, Janice Gross. "Rational Deterrence against 'Irrational' Adversaries? No Common Knowledge." In *Complex Deterrence: Strategy in the Global Age*. Edited by T. V. Paul, Patrick M. Morgan, and James J. Wirtz, 58–84. Chicago: University of Chicago Press, 2009.

Sterling, Bruce. "Operation Shady RAT." *Wired*, August 3, 2011. http://www.wired.com/2011/08/operation-shady-rat/.

Sterner, Eric. "Deterrence in Cyberspace: Yes, No, Maybe?" In *Returning to Fundamentals: Deterrence and U.S. National Security in the 21st Century*. Edited by Robert Butterworth, Peter Marquez, John B. Sheldon, and Eric Sterner, 20–27. Washington, DC: George C. Marshall Institute, 2011.

———. "Retaliatory Deterrence in Cyberspace." *Strategic Studies Quarterly* (Spring 2011): 62–80.

Stevens, Tim. "A Cyberwar of Ideas? Deterrence and Norms in Cyberspace." *Contemporary Security Policy* 33 (April 2012): 148–70.

Stewart, Phil. "Pentagon's New Cyber Strategy Cites U.S. Ability to Retaliate." Reuters, April 23, 2015. http://www.reuters.com/article/2015/04/23/us-usa-pentagon-cyber-idUSKBN0NE0AS20150423.

Stoil, Rebecca Anna, and James Goldstein. "One if by Land, Two if by Modem." *The Jerusalem Post*, June 28, 2006. http://www.jpost.com/Israel/One-if-by-land-two-if-by-modem.

Stokes, Bruce. "'Extremists, Cyber-attacks Top Americans' Security Threat List." Pew Research Center, January 2, 2014. http://www.pewresearch.org/fact-tank/2014/01/02/americans-see-extremists-cyber-attacks-as-major-threats-to-the-u-s/.

Strasser, Max. "Why Ukraine Hasn't Sparked a Big Cyberwar, So Far." *Newsweek*, March 18, 2014. http://www.newsweek.com/why-ukraine-hasnt-sparked-big-cyberwar-so-far-232175.

Swaine, Jon. "Georgia: Russia 'Conducting Cyber War.'" *The Telegraph*, August 11, 2008. http://www.telegraph.co.uk/news/worldnews/europe/georgia/2539157/Georgia-Russia-conducting-cyber-war.html.

Syrian Observatory for Human Rights. "320,000 People Killed since the Beginning of the Syrian Revolution." June 5, 2015. http://web.archive.org/web/20150626152105/http://www.syriahr.com/en/2015/06/320000-people-killed-since-the-beginning-of-the-syrian-revolution/.

Theohary, Catherine A., and John Rollins. *Terrorist Use of the Internet: Information Operations in Cyberspace*. Washington, DC: Congressional Research Service, March 8, 2011.

Thomas, Douglas. *Hacker Culture*. Minneapolis: University of Minnesota Press, 2003.

Thompson, Nicholas. "Why Did Syria Shut Down the Internet?" *New Yorker*, May 8, 2013.

Thomson, Janice E. *Mercenaries, Pirates, and Sovereigns: State-Building and Extraterritorial Violence in Early Modern Europe*. Princeton, NJ: Princeton University Press, 1994.

Thornburgh, Nathan. "The Invasion of the Chinese Cyberspies (and the Man Who Tried to Stop Them)." *Time*, September 5, 2005. http://content.time.com/time/magazine/article/0,9171,1098961,00.html.

Tiirmaa-Klaar, Heli. "Cyber Security Threats and Responses at Global, Nation-State, Industry and Individual Levels." Paris: Sciences Po, March 2011. http://www.sciencespo.fr/ceri/sites/sciencespo.fr.ceri/files/art_htk.pdf.

Tikk, Enekin, Kadri Kaska, Kristel Rünnimeri, Mari Kert, Anna-Maria Talihärm, and Liis Vihul. *Cyber Attacks against Georgia: Legal Lessons Identified.* Tallinn, Estonia: NATO Cooperative Cyber Defence Centre of Excellence, November 2008.

Timberg, Craig, and Lisa Rein. "Senate Cybersecurity Report Finds Agencies Often Fail to Take Basic Preventive Measures." *Washington Post,* February 3, 2014. http://www.washingtonpost.com/business/technology/senate-cybersecurity-report-finds-agencies-often-fail-to-take-basic-preventive-measures/2014/02/03/493390c2-8ab6-11e3-833c-33098f9e5267_story.html.

Todd, Brian, and Forrest Brown. "Syria's Cyberattack: First Wave of a Bigger War?" CNN News, August 30, 2013. http://www.cnn.com/2013/08/30/tech/syria-cyberattacks/.

Traynor, Ian. "Russia Accused of Unleashing Cyberwar to Disable Estonia." *The Guardian,* May 16, 2007. http://www.theguardian.com/world/2007/may/17/topstories3.russia.

Umbach, Frank. "Cyber Threats Are Growing in Size, Volume and Sophistication." *World Review,* May 23, 2013. http://www.worldreview.info/content/cyber-threats-are-growing-size-volume-and-sophistication (link no longer active).

US Army Training and Doctrine Command (TRADOC). *Critical Infrastructure Threats and Terrorism.* DCSINT Handbook no. 1.02. Fort Leavenworth: TRADOC, August 10, 2006.

US Department of Defense. *Cyberspace Policy Report: A Report to Congress Pursuant to the National Defense Authorization Act for Fiscal Year 2011, Section 934.* Washington, DC: US Government Printing Office, November 2011.

———. *The DoD Cyber Strategy.* Washington, DC: US Government Printing Office, April 2015.

———. *Quadrennial Defense Review, 2014.* Washington, DC: US Government Printing Office, March 2014.

US Department of State. "Ukraine and Russia Sanctions, Department of the Treasury," March 2014. http://www.state.gov/e/eb/tfs/spi/ukrainerussia/.

US Government Accountability Office. Statement for the Record to the Subcommittee on Terrorism and Homeland Security, Committee on the Judiciary, US Senate. *Cybersecurity: Continued Efforts Are Needed to Protect Information Systems from Evolving Threats.* Washington DC: US Government Printing Office, November 17, 2009.

Valeriano, Brandon, and Ryan C. Maness. *Cyber War versus Cyber Realities: Cyber Conflict in the International System.* New York: Oxford University Press, 2015.

———. "Persistent Enemies and Cyberwar." In *Cyberspace and National Security: Threats, Opportunities and Power in a Virtual World.* Edited by Derek S. Reveron, 139–58. Washington, DC: Georgetown University Press, 2012.

Van Creveld, Martin. *Wargames: From Gladiators to Gigabytes.* Cambridge: Cambridge University Press, 2013.

Vincent, James. "Russian Nuclear Power Plant Infected by Stuxnet Malware Says Cyber-Security Expert." *The Independent,* November 12, 2013. http://www.independent.co.uk/life-style/gadgets-and-tech/news/russian-nuclear-power-plant-infected-by-stuxnet-malware-says-cybersecurity-expert-8935529.html.

Viswanatha, Aruna, and Joseph Menn. "In Cyberattacks such as Sony Strike, Obama Turns to 'Name and Shame.'" Reuters, January 14, 2015. http://www.reuters.com/article/2015/01/14/uk-usa-cybersecurity-idUSKBN0KN2E520150114.

Wan, William. "China Continues to Deny Carrying Out Cyberattacks against U.S." *Washington Post,* May 29, 2013. http://www.washingtonpost.com/world/asia_pacific/china

-continues-to-deny-us-cyber-attack-accusations/2013/05/29/a131780e-c85e-11e2-9245-773c0123c027_story.html.

Washington Post. "Leon Panetta Warns of 'Cyber Pearl Harbor.'" October 13, 2012. http://www.washingtonpost.com/posttv/leon-panetta-warns-of-cyber-pearl-harbor/2012/10/13/6cdcbd5e-14c9-11e2-9a39-1f5a7f6fe945_video.html (link no longer active).

Waterman, Shaun. "Obama Hits Pause on U.S. Action in Face of Crippling Cyber Strikes from Syria, Iran." *Washington Times*, August 28, 2013. http://www.washingtontimes.com/news/2013/aug/28/syria-iran-capable-of-launching-a-cyberwar/?page=all.

———. "Syrian Hackers Threaten Retaliation for Any U.S. Strike." *Washington Times*, August 30, 2013. http://www.washingtontimes.com/news/2013/aug/30/syrian-hackers-threaten-retaliation-any-us-strike/.

Waxman, Matthew C. "Cyber-Attacks and the Use of Force: Back to the Future." *Yale Journal of International Law* 36 (2011): 421–59.

———. "Self-Defensive Force against Cyber Attacks: Legal, Strategic and Political Dimensions." *International Legal Studies* 89 (2013): 109–22.

Weber, Tim. "Cybercrime Threat Rising Sharply." BBC News, January 31, 2009. http://news.bbc.co.uk/2/hi/business/davos/7862549.stm.

Weiner, Sarah. "Searching for Cyber-Deterrence." Washington, DC: Center for Strategic and International Studies, November 26, 2012. http://csis.org/blog/searching-cyber-deterrence (link no longer active).

Weinschenk, Matthew. "Cyber Security's New Face: Growing Threats and Growing Profits." *Wall Street Daily*, February 22, 2012. http://www.wallstreetdaily.com/2012/02/22/cyber-security-growing-threats-and-profits/.

Weise, Elizabeth. "Average Cost of Computer Breach Is $3.79 Million." *USA Today*, May 27, 2015. http://www.usatoday.com/story/tech/2015/05/27/ponemon-ibm-computer-breach/27977657/.

———. "Computer Security Has Failed, Says Keynote a Giant Security Gathering." *USA Today*, April 21, 2015. http://www.usatoday.com/story/tech/2015/04/21/rsa-amit-yoran-computer-security-failed/26139927/.

Weitz, Richard. "Russia Refines Cyber Warfare Strategies." *CNN*, August 26, 2009. http://ireport.cnn.com/docs/DOC-320195 (link no longer active).

Wheatley, Gary F., and Richard E. Hayes. *Information Warfare and Deterrence*. Washington, DC: National Defense University Press, December 1996.

Whetham, David, and George R. Lucas Jr. "The Relevance of the Just War Tradition to Cyber Warfare." In *Cyber Warfare: A Multidisciplinary Analysis*. Edited by James A. Green, ch. 7. New York: Routledge, 2015.

Williams, Phil. "Combating Transnational Organized Crime." In *Transnational Threats: Blending Law Enforcement and Military Strategies*. Edited by Carolyn W. Pumphrey, 185–202. Carlisle, PA: Strategic Studies Institute, November 2000.

Winder, Davey. "The Syrian Electronic Army: Lessons to Be Learned." *ITPro*, September 30, 2013. http://www.itpro.co.uk/hacking/21403/the-syrian-electronic-army-lessons-to-be-learned.

Winer, Stuart. "Annual Cyber-Attack on Israel Targets MK's Website." *Times of Israel*, April 7, 2015. http://www.timesofisrael.com/annual-cyber-attack-on-israel-hits-mks-website/.

Winkler, Ira. "My Run-In with the Syrian Electronic Army." *ComputerWorld*, May 13, 2014.

http://www.computerworld.com/s/article/9248299/Ira_Winkler_My_run_in_with_the_Syrian_Electronic_Army?taxonomyId=82&pageNumber=1.

Wittes, Benjamin, and Gabriella Blum. *The Future of Violence: Robots and Germs, Hackers and Drones—Confronting a New Age of Threat*. New York: Basic Books, 2015.

Wolf, Jim, and William MacLean. "IMF Cyber Attack Aimed to Steal Insider Information." Reuters, June 12, 2011. http://www.reuters.com/article/2011/06/12/us-imf-cyberattack-idUSTRE75A20720110612.

Woolsey, R. James, and Peter V. Pry. "EMP Blackout Could Be Closer than You Think." *Israel National News*, November 7, 2013. http://www.israelnationalnews.com/Articles/Article.aspx/14076#.UuF9gdLTnmE.

WorldPublicOpinion.org. "International Public Opinion Says Government Should Not Limit Internet Access." April 30, 2009. http://worldpublicopinion.org/pipa/articles/btjusticehuman_rightsra/477.php?lb=bthr&pnt=477&nid=&id=.

Zetter, Kim. *Countdown to Zero Day: Stuxnet and the Launch of the World's First Digital Weapon*. New York: Crown, 2014.

———. "Experts Are Still Divided on Whether North Korea Is behind Sony Attack." *Wired*, December 23, 2014. http://www.wired.com/2014/12/sony-north-korea-hack-experts-disagree/.

———. "How Digital Detectives Deciphered Stuxnet, the Most Menacing Malware in History." *Wired*, July 11, 2011. http://www.wired.com/2011/07/how-digital-detectives-deciphered-stuxnet/.

———. "Report Strengthens Suspicions that Stuxnet Sabotaged Iran's Nuclear Plant." *Wired*, December 27, 2010. http://www.wired.com/2010/12/isis-report-on-stuxnet/.

———. "An Unprecedented Look at Stuxnet, the World's First Digital Weapon." *Wired*, November 3, 2014. http://www.wired.com/2014/11/countdown-to-zero-day-stuxnet/.

Zheng, Denise E., and James A. Lewis. *Cyber Threat Information Sharing: Recommendations for Congress and the Administration*. Washington, DC: Center for Strategic and International Studies, March 2015.

Ziadeh, Radwan. "The Syrian Revolution: The Role of the 'Emerging Leaders.'" In *Revolution and Political Transformation in the Middle East*. Vol. 1, *Agents of Change*. Edited by Middle East Institute, 43–45. Washington, DC: Middle East Institute, August 2011.

Index

Aaviksoo, Jaak, 80
action-reaction cycles, 2, 87, 121, 183, 184
Adobe, 69
Afek, Sharon, 182
Ahmadinejad, Mahmoud, 97
Air Force Academy (US), 183
Aksyonov, Sergey, 118
Albania, cybersecurity strategy in, 181
Albuquerque Journal targeted by cyberattacks, 130
Alperovitch, Dmitri, 22–23, 72–75, 76, 126
Andrew Jackson Jihad, 131
anomaly analysis, 174
Anonymous (hacktivist group), 91, 92, 102–3, 135
Anthem targeted for cyberattacks, 10
antivirus software, 47
Aramco targeted by Iranian cyberattacks, 17, 99, 106–11; attribution, 107–8; description of attacks, 106; lessons learned, 110–11; response to, 109–10; security impact, 108–9
Arbor Networks, 57, 87
al-Assad, Bashar, 111, 113
Associated Press, 111
Association of Southeast Asian Nations (ASEAN), 72, 73
asymmetric conflict, 154–55, 215
attribution: as challenge, 5, 55–56, 162; and cyberthreat contagion, 185; and intelligence collection, 174; International Monetary Fund cyberattacks, 102–3; Iranian cyberattacks on Aramco, 107–8; ISIS cyberattacks on US Central Command, 131–32; Israel and US cyberattack on Iran (Stuxnet), 96–97; North Korean cyberattacks on Sony Pictures Entertainment 124–26; Russian cyberattacks on Estonia, 79–80; Russian

cyberattacks on Georgia, 84–85; Russian cyberattacks on Ukraine, 119–20; Shady RAT (Chinese cyberattack on US), 73–74; Syrian Electronic Army cyberattacks on US and Europe, 113; Titan Rain (Chinese cyberattack on US), 67–68
Aurora (Chinese cyberattacks on US), 69
Australia: Chinese cyberattacks against, 68; in Five Eyes partnership, 180–81; and Ukraine crisis, 118
authoritarian states, 167, 217

BAE Systems, 119
Baker, Stewart, 121–22
Bank of Jerusalem, 91
barriers. *See* obstacles to progress
Baumgartner, Kurt, 120–21
BBC, 111
Bell, Sandra, 70
Bellovin, Steven, 126
benefit minimization: cyberdeterrence best practices for, 214–18, 216f; cyberdeterrence execution, 1, 190–92, 201–7
best practices. *See* cyberdeterrence best practices
BlackEnergy (malware), 20–21, 46
Blackwater (security firm), 169
Blair, Dennis, 55
Blair, Tony, 131
blowback, 200–201, 207
boomerang effects, 2, 58–59, 201
botnets, 21, 79, 80, 119
Britain. *See* United Kingdom
Bulgaria, 183
Bumgarner, John, 120
burden sharing for cyberdeterrence, 230–33
Bush, George W., 70
Byres, Eric, 184

279

Canada: Chinese cyberattacks against, 68, 72; in Five Eyes partnership, 180–81; Stuxent infected computers in, 98; and Ukraine crisis, 118
Capital Markets Authority (Saudi Arabia), 110
Carlin, John, 125
Carney, Jay, 75
Cartwright, James, 24–25, 33
case studies: Chinese cyberattacks on US, 66–77; International Monetary Fund targeted by cyberattacks, 101–6; Iranian cyberattacks on Aramco, 106–11; ISIS cyberattacks on US Central Command, 130–36; Israel targeted by cyberattacks, 88–94; North Korean cyberattacks on Sony Pictures Entertainment, 123–30; patterns of, 148–71, 149t, 151–53t; Russian cyberattacks on Estonia, 77–83; Russian cyberattacks on Georgia, 83–88; Russian cyberattacks on Ukraine, 117–23; Syrian Electronic Army cyberattacks on US and Europe, 111–17; US and Israeli cyberattacks on Iran (Stuxnet), 94–101
Caucasus Network, 86
Center for New American Security, 132
Center for Strategic and International Studies, 45, 73, 128
Central Command. *See* US Central Command
Central Intelligence Agency (CIA), 204
CERT (Computer Emergency Response Team), 81, 87
challenges. *See* obstacles to progress
Chertoff, Michael, 56, 113, 178, 198
China: and Cold War deterrence model, 3; cyberattacks on US, 66–77; and cyber-restraint hypocrisy, 37–38; Google targeted for cyberattacks by, 10; Shady RAT cyberattack, 72–77; Titan Rain cyberattack, 66–72
Christian Science Monitor on cyberattacker attribution process, 129
CIA (Central Intelligence Agency), 204
Cilluffo, Frank, 116, 129, 130
Cisco, 69
citizen attitudes as challenge, 52–53, 193
Citizen Lab at University of Toronto, 88
civil liberties, 53
Clarke, Richard, 70, 111
Clinton, Bill, 70
Clinton, Hillary, 181
Clinton, Larry, 51
CloudFlare, 125
CNI (Critical National Infrastructure) organizations, 104
CNN targeted by cyberattacks, 112
Coast Guard Academy (US), 183
Cold War deterrence model, 2–3, 4, 57
collateral damage, 101, 114–15, 182, 194, 200–201
collective responsibility, 233
Combined Endeavor workshop, 183
command, control, communications, and intelligence (C^3I) networks, 20, 22, 47–48
Commerce Department (US), 12
Commission on the Theft of American Intellectual Property, 13
Commodity Futures Trading Commission (US), 13
Comprehensive National Cybersecurity Initiative (US), 247
Computer Emergency Response Team (CERT), 81, 87
conflict contagion, 2, 185
Cooperative Cyber Defence Centre of Excellence, 81
coordination of cyberpolicy, 179–81
cost maximization: cyberdeterrence best practices for, 214–18, 216f; cyberdeterrence execution, 1, 190–92, 197–201; and cyberdeterrence paradoxes, 33
Critical National Infrastructure (CNI) organizations, 104
CrowdStrike, 126
Cutting Sword of Justice (hacking group), 107
cyberattack containment, 182–86
cyberattackers, 14–17; attributes promoting cyberattack success, 154–57, 154f, 213; defiance of, 25–28, 27f; goals of, 17–20, 19f; initiator-target cyber expertise imbalance, 45–46; motivations of, 17–20, 19f; patterns of case studies, 150–61, 154f; styles, 20–23. *See also specific case studies*
Cyber Berkut (hacktivist group), 119
Cyber Caliphate, 131, 132

Cyber Command. *See* US Cyber Command
Cyber Defence Management Authority (NATO), 81
Cyber Defense Exercise, 183
Cyber Defense League, 82
cyberdeterrence: arsenal expansion, 233–34; burden sharing for, 230–33; ethics dilemmas, 238–39, 240*f*, 241; future of, 243–45, 244*f*; integrating and stabilizing, 230–38, 231–32*f*; land, air, and sea deterrence contrasted with, 4–6, 9*f*; legitimacy of, 238–41, 240*f*; narrow vs. broad deterrence, 2–3, 8*f*; outcome evaluations, 236–38; protection equalization, 235–36. *See also* case studies; *headings below starting with "cyberdeterrence"*
cyberdeterrence best practices, 211–29, 212*f*; for cost maximization vs. benefit minimization, 214–18, 216*f*; for cyberattacker attributes, 213; for cyberspace vs. real-world responses, 222–24, 223*f*; for cybertarget attributes, 213–14; for fearful prevention vs. hopeful persuasion, 224–26, 225*f*; for orthodox vs. unorthodox restraints, 220–21, 221*f*; for public vs. private initiatives, 218–20, 219*f*; worst-case scenarios when neglected, 226–28, 227*f*
cyberdeterrence execution, 190–210, 191*f*; cost and benefit optimization, 190–92, 197–207; cyberspace vs. real-world responses mix, 195–96; fear-based prevention, 196–97; hope-based persuasion, 196–97; orthodox vs. unorthodox restraints mix, 194–95; public vs. private initiatives, 192–93
cyberdeterrence paradoxes, 32–42, 36*f*; addressing, 241–43; cyber-liberty tension, 40–41; cyber-publicity muddle, 38–40; cyber-restraint hypocrisy, 36–38; cyber-sophistication vulnerability, 34–36; ideal dynamics, 32–34, 35*f*
cyberdeterrence planning, 172–89, 173*f*; coordination of cyberpolicy, 179–81; cyberattack containment, 182–86; cyberintelligence collection for, 172–76; cyberstrategy doctrine development, 177–79; harmonization of cybersecurity standards, 181–82; readiness for changing cyberattack methods, 176–77
cyberespionage, 18, 21, 37, 166–67, 218
cyber-hygiene, 201–2, 214, 232, 235
cyberintelligence collection, 172–76
cyber-liberty tension, 40–41, 242–43
cyber-publicity muddle, 38–40, 242
cyber-restraint hypocrisy, 36–38
cyber retaliation, 114–16, 120, 134, 160, 184, 222–23
cybersecurity standards, 181–82
cyber-sophistication vulnerability, 34–36, 242
cyberspace vs. real-world responses: cyberdeterrence best practices for, 222–24, 223*f*; cyber retaliation, 114–16, 120, 134, 160, 184, 222–23; execution of, 1, 195–96
cyberstrategy doctrine development, 177–79
cybertargets: attributes of, 154*f*, 157–61, 163–64, 213–14; cyberspace dependence/addiction of, 47–48; initiator-target cyber expertise imbalance, 45–46; patterns of case studies, 154*f*, 157–61, 163–64. *See also specific case studies*
cyberthreat contagion, 2, 185
Cyber Threat Intelligence Group, 119

Danchev, Dancho, 85
Darktrace (cybersecurity firm), 44
data corruption, 21, 22
data redundancy, 201
Decker, Benjamin, 92
decoy data techniques, 205
Defense Department (US), 237; Chinese cyberattacks against, 66, 68, 69, 70; cyberattack responses from, 23; cyberstrategy doctrine for, 190, 197, 199
Defense Intelligence Agency (US), 114
Defense Ministry (Israel), 91
Defense Science Board (US), 69
Deibert, Ronald, 88
democracy, 40
Denmark, Chinese cyberattacks against, 72
digital infrastructure, 25, 44–45, 80
Director of National Intelligence (US), 172
DirtJumper (network), 119
distributed denial-of-service (DDoS), 78–79, 82, 84, 86, 119

Doley, Boaz, 90
Dtex Systems, 101
dual-use technologies, 59, 61
Duqu (malware), 201

economic interdependence, 164–65, 247
economic sanctions. *See* sanctions
electromagnetic pulse (EMP) attack, 177
Energy Department (US), 12, 66
Enhanced Cybersecurity Services program (US), 52
Environmental Protection Agency (US), 12
espionage. *See* cyberespionage
Estonia targeted by Russian cyberattacks, 77–83; attribution, 79–80; description of attacks, 77–79; lessons learned, 82–83; response to, 81–82; security impact, 80–81
ethics dilemmas of cyberdeterrence, 2, 238–39, 240f, 241
European Command (US), 183
European Network and Information Security Agency, 81
Europe targeted by Syrian Electronic Army cyberattacks, 111–17; attribution, 113; description of attacks, 111–12; lessons learned, 116–17; response to, 114–16; security impact, 114
exfiltration and cleanup attacks, 21
exploit delivery attacks, 21
export controls, 59

Facebook, 112, 165
al-Falih, Khalid, 109
false flag attacks, 200
fearful prevention: cyberdeterrence best practices for, 224–26, 225f; cyberdeterrence execution, 1, 196–97
Federal Bureau of Investigation (FBI), 67, 124, 127, 134
Federal Reserve (US), 12
Federal Trade Commission (US), 105
Feinstein, Dianne, 75
Finland, technical assistance from, 81
FireEye, 112, 130
firewalls, 47, 54
Fitzgerald, Ben, 132
Five Eyes partnership, 180–81
Flashpoint Global Partners, 132

Food and Drug Administration (US), 13
Forbes targeted by cyberattacks, 112
foreign cyberthreats, 12–31; changing nature of, 14–23, 15f; defiance of cyberattackers, 25–28, 27f; goals of, 17–20, 19f; ineffective responses to, 23–25; motivations for, 17–20, 19f; perceived importance of, 12–13; styles, 20–23; targets for, 20. *See also* case studies; cyberattackers
Foreign Ministry (Israel), 91
France: cybersecurity strategy in, 82; ISIS cyberattacks against, 131; and Ukraine crisis, 118
France, Andrew, 44

GAO (Government Accountability Office, US), 12, 14, 180
Gaza Strip, 89, 91
Georgia targeted by Russian cyberattacks, 83–88; attribution, 84–85; description of attacks, 83–84; lessons learned, 87–88; response to, 86–87; security impact, 85–86
Germany: Chinese cyberattacks against, 72; cybersecurity strategy in, 82; Stuxent infected computers in, 98; technical assistance from, 81; and Ukraine crisis, 118
Gewirtz, David, 98
Ghosh, Anup, 75, 204
Al-Ghussian, Ihab, 91
Google targeted for cyberattacks, 10, 69, 134
Gourley, Bob, 114
Government Accountability Office (GAO, US), 12, 14, 180
Graham, Lindsey, 134
Graham, Robert, 125
Guardians of the Peace (hacker group), 124
The Guardian targeted by cyberattacks, 111

hacktivists, 16
Hagel, Chuck, 24
Hamas, 17, 65, 89–90, 93
Hathaway, Melissa, 99
Hawley, David, 103
Healey, Jason, 115, 129
Heartbleed (computer bug), 38
Hellman, Gretchen, 74–75
Hezbollah, 17, 65, 90, 92
Hidden Lynx (hacking group), 69

INDEX   283

Holden, Dan, 119
Home Depot targeted for cyberattacks, 10
Homeland Security Department (US):
  Chinese cyberattacks against, 66, 69;
  on cyberattack statistics, 12; and IMF
  cyberattacks, 105; National Cybersecurity
  and Communications Integration Center,
  95; National Infrastructure Protection
  Center, 45–46; on Sandworm hacking
  group, 21
Homeland Security Policy Institute, 129
honeypots and honeynets, 203–4, 207
Hong Kong, Chinese cyberattacks against, 72
hopeful persuasion: cyberdeterrence best
  practices for, 224–26, 225f; cyberdeterrence
  execution, 1, 196–97
Hosper, Nathan, 207
Huffington Post targeted by cyberattacks, 112
Hussain, Junaid, 131, 133
hybrid conflicts, 166

India: Chinese cyberattacks against, 72;
  Stuxent infected computers in, 98
indirect measures and effects, 164
Indonesia: Chinese cyberattacks against, 72;
  Stuxent infected computers in, 98
information sharing, 50–51
infrastructure design, 44–45
Institute for Science and International
  Security, 98
intellectual property theft, 69
Intelligence and National Security Alliance,
  173
intercorporate networks, 20
International Atomic Energy Agency, 94
International Cyber Security Protection
  Alliance, 101
International Monetary Fund targeted by
  cyberattacks, 101–6; attribution, 102–3;
  description of attacks, 101–2; lessons
  learned, 105–6; response to, 104–5;
  security impact, 103–4
International Olympic Committee, 72, 73
international organizations, 168–69. *See also
  specific organizations*
Internet Security Alliance, 51
The Interview (film), 123–24
Invincea, 204

Iranian cyberattacks on Aramco, 106–11;
  attribution, 107–8; description of attacks,
  106; lessons learned, 110–11; response to,
  17, 99, 109–10; security impact, 108–9
ISIS cyberattacks on US Central Command,
  130–36; attribution, 131–32; description of
  attacks, 130–31; lessons learned, 135–36;
  response to, 134–35; security impact,
  132–34
Israel and US cyberattack on Iran (Stuxnet),
  94–101; attribution, 96–97; case study
  patterns, 155; description of attacks, 94–95;
  lessons learned, 100–101; response to, 99;
  security impact, 97–98
Israel targeted by cyberattacks, 88–94;
  attribution, 90; description of attacks,
  88–90; lessons learned, 93–94; response to,
  92–93; security impact, 90–92
Italy, 118
Izzedine-Al-Qassam, 17, 92

Jalali, Gholam Reza, 97
Japan: Chinese cyberattacks against, 72; and
  Ukraine crisis, 118
Johnson, Rivers, 75
Juniper Networks, 69
Justice Department (US), 12, 70, 128

Kaspersky, Eugene, 59, 74
Kaspersky Lab, 69, 74, 76
Kassirer, Alex, 132
Kellerman, Tom, 101
Kim Jong-un, 123–24, 127, 129
kinetic warfare, 4–6, 59, 179, 198
Koo, Mohan, 101, 104

Labor Department (US), 12
Langner, Ralph, 95, 96, 97, 99
Latvia, 183
Lau, Hon, 74
Lavrov, Sergei, 78
legitimacy of cyberdeterrence, 2, 238–41, 240f
Levantine Group, 92
Lewis, James, 73
Lithuania, 183
Lockheed Martin, 66, 169
LookingGlass Cyber Solutions, 119
Lynn, William, 14, 77

Madory, Doug, 120, 128
Makhlouf, Rami, 113
Mandiant (cybersecurity firm), 69
McAfee, 70, 72, 76
McCaul, Michael, 134
McGurk, Seán, 95
Merchant Marine Academy (US), 183
MercyCorps International, 111
Mexico, cybersecurity strategy in, 181
Microsoft Windows, 94, 106
Military Academy (US), 183
Mills, Rich, 105
Moldova, 118
MonsterMind, 175
Morozov, Evgeny, 86–87
Moss, Jeff, 104
Mubarak, Hosni, 114
Murray, William, 102

Naida, Vitaly, 121
Napolitano, Janet, 75
Nashi (hacking group), 79–80
National Aeronautics and Space Administration (NASA, US), 12, 66
National Bank of Georgia, 86
National Counterintelligence and Security Center (US), 71
National Cyber Bureau (Israel), 92
National Cyber Directorate (Israel), 93
National Cybersecurity and Communications Integration Center (US), 95
National Infrastructure Protection Center (US), 45–46
National Public Radio, 112
National Security Agency (NSA), 7, 28, 37, 124, 174, 183
National Security Council (Ukraine), 118
National Weather Service (US), 13
NATO (North Atlantic Treaty Organization), 79, 80, 81, 165
Naval Academy (US), 183
Nazario, Jose, 57, 87, 88
NetBot Attacker, 46
Netherlands: cybersecurity strategy in, 82; and Ukraine crisis, 118
NetTraveler, 69
Newsweek targeted by cyberattacks, 130–31

New York Times: on Stuxnet, 96; targeted by cyberattacks, 112
New Zealand: Chinese cyberattacks against, 68; in Five Eyes partnership, 180–81
Night Dragon (Chinese cyberattacks on US), 69
nonstate cyberattackers: attributes of, 15–16; collusion with state entities, 16–17; orthodox vs. unorthodox restraints on, 194. *See also specific groups*
noobs, 217
North Atlantic Treaty Organization (NATO), 79, 80, 81, 165
North Korean cyberattacks on Sony Pictures Entertainment, 123–30; attribution, 124–26; description of attacks, 123–24; lessons learned, 128–30; response to, 127–28, 196, 215; security impact, 126–27
NSA (National Security Agency), 7, 28, 37, 124, 174, 183

Obama, Barack: on Chinese cyberattacks against US, 69; on cyberspace technology, 35; on digital infrastructure, 25; Enhanced Cybersecurity Services program, 52; on North Korean cyberattack on Sony Pictures Entertainment, 124, 125, 126, 127; and Stuxnet, 96
obstacles to progress, 43–64, 60–61*f*; attribution difficulties, 55–56; boomerang effects, 58–59; citizen attitudes, 52–53; cyberattack tools proliferation, 46; digital infrastructure design, 44–45; dual-use technologies, 59, 61; global tensions and power shifts, 2, 54–55; inappropriate deterrence models, 57–58; initiator-target cyber expertise imbalance, 45–46; plausible deniability issues, 16, 56–57; political regime constraints, 49–50; public-private sector friction, 50–52; scope of protection needs, 58; at societal levels, 49–55; static, rigid, predictable, and narrow cyberdeterrence, 47; systemic roots, 44–48; target cyberspace dependence/addiction, 47–48; time frames for, 55–61; value systems, 53
Olsen, Matthew, 133

Operation Armageddon (Russia), 119
Operation Cast Lead (Israel), 88–89
Operation Orchard (Israel), 97–98
Operation Pillar of Defense (Israel), 90–91
Operation Protective Edge (Israel), 91, 92
organized crime, 16, 54, 85–87
orthodox restraints: cyberdeterrence best practices for, 220–21, 221f; cyberdeterrence execution, 1, 194–95

Pakistan, Stuxent infected computers in, 98
Palestinian Islamic Jihad, 17, 90
Paller, Allan, 67, 71
Palmer, Jonathan, 101
Panetta, Leon, 23, 108
password protection, 47
patterns of case studies, 148–71, 149t; attribution challenges, 162; authoritarian states, 167; circumstances promoting cyberattack success, 150–61, 154f; cyberattacker attributes promoting cyberattack success, 154–57, 154f; cyberdeterrence case lessons, 161–69, 163f; cyberespionage penetration, 166–67; cybertarget attributes promoting cyberattack success, 154f, 157–61, 163–64; economic interdependence, 164–65; hybrid conflicts, 166; indirect measures and effects, 164; international organizations, 168–69; private sector, 169; social media, 165–66; terrorist groups, 167–68
payload injection attacks, 21
People's Liberation Army (China), 70, 71
Perfect Citizen project (US), 174
persuasion strategies: cyberdeterrence best practices for, 224–26, 225f; cyberdeterrence execution, 1, 196–97
plausible deniability, 16, 56–57, 68
Poland: and Combined Endeavor workshop, 183; technical assistance from, 87; and Ukraine crisis, 118
political regime constraints, 49–50
Poroshenko, Petro, 118
prevention strategies: cyberdeterrence best practices for, 224–26, 225f; cyberdeterrence execution, 1, 196–97
Prince, Matthew, 93
private sector: and cyberattack containment planning, 184; patterns of case studies, 169. *See also* public vs. private initiatives
protection equalization, 235–36
public-private cooperation, 33, 50, 52, 193, 233, 235–36
public vs. private initiatives: cyberdeterrence best practices for, 218–20, 219f; cyberdeterrence execution, 1, 192–93; as obstacles to progress, 50–52
Putin, Vladimir, 78, 118, 122

al-Qaddafi, Muammar, 111

real-world vs. cyberspace responses: cyberdeterrence best practices for, 222–24, 223f; execution of, 1, 195–96. *See also* kinetic warfare
reconnaissance attacks, 21
Red E-Digital, 126
Redstone Arsenal, 66
ResGas, 108
response thresholds, 178–79
reverse spoofing, 203, 207
RIA Novosti, 87
Rogers, Marc, 125
Rogers, Michael, 92, 130
Romania, cybersecurity strategy in, 181
Rouqa, Sami, 91
Royal United Services Institute, 70
RSA Security, 24
Rumsfeld, Donald, 70
Russian Business Network, 85
Russian cyberattacks on Estonia, 77–83; attribution, 79–80; description of attacks, 77–79; lessons learned, 82–83; response to, 81–82; security impact, 80–81
Russian cyberattacks on Georgia, 83–88; attribution, 84–85; description of attacks, 83–84; lessons learned, 87–88; response to, 86–87; security impact, 85–86
Russian cyberattacks on Ukraine, 117–23; attribution, 119–20; description of attacks, 117–18; lessons learned, 122–23; response to, 120–22, 196; security impact, 120

al-Saadan, Abdullah, 108
Saakashvili, Mikheil, 83, 84

Sample, Timothy, 178
sanctions, 57, 196, 198
Sandia National Laboratories, 66
Sandworm (hacking group), 21
SANS Institute, 71
Saudi Arabia. *See* Iranian cyberattacks on Aramco
Schmidt, Howard, 80
Schneier, Bruce, 124
script kiddies, 217
Segal, Adam, 115
Shady RAT (Chinese cyberattack on US), 72–77; attribution, 73–74; description of attacks, 72–73; lessons learned, 76–77; response to, 75–76; security impact, 74–75
Shamoon (virus), 106, 107, 108, 109
Shulman, Amichai, 74
Singapore, Chinese cyberattacks against, 72
Skype targeted by cyberattacks, 112
Slovenia, technical assistance from, 81
Snake (malware), 119
Snowden, Edward, 7, 28, 37, 175
social media: best practices for, 226; and cost maximization strategies, 206; cyberattack styles exploiting, 21; and ISIS cyberattacks on US Central Command, 130, 133, 135; patterns of case studies, 165–66; and Syrian Electronic Army cyberattacks, 112. *See also specific social networks*
Sony Pictures Entertainment targeted by North Korean cyberattacks, 123–30; attribution, 124–26; description of attacks, 123–24; lessons learned, 128–30; response to, 127–28, 196, 215; security impact, 126–27
South Korea: Chinese cyberattacks against, 72; and Ukraine crisis, 118
Stammberger, Kurt, 125
State Council Information Office (China), 67
State Department (US), 12, 66
Sterling, Bruce, 73
Stolfo, Salvatore, 205
Strauss-Kahn, Dominique, 103
Stuxnet (Israel and US cyberattack on Iran), 94–101; attribution, 96–97; case study patterns, 155; description of attacks, 94–95; lessons learned, 100–101; response to, 99; security impact, 97–98

Swedish Defence University, 85
Switzerland, Chinese cyberattacks against, 72
Symantec, 74, 76, 109
Syrian Electronic Army cyberattacks on US and Europe, 111–17; attribution, 113; description of attacks, 111–12; lessons learned, 116–17; response to, 114–16; security impact, 114
Syrian Observatory for Human Rights, 111
SyriaTel, 113

Taiwan, Chinese cyberattacks against, 72
Target targeted for cyberattacks, 10
technological diffusion, 2, 46, 55, 94, 186, 246
Teksoz, Bulent, 109
terrorist groups, 167–68, 176. *See also specific groups*
Titan Rain (Chinese cyberattack on US), 66–72; attribution, 67–68; case study patterns, 155; description of attacks, 66; lessons learned, 71–72; response to, 70–71; security impact, 68–70
Tkeshelashvili, Eka, 84–85
Torino Security, 184
trade secrets, 69
traffic tracing, 174
transparency, 28, 40, 129
Tubin, George, 116–17
Turkey, 118
Twitter, 112, 134, 165

Ukraine targeted by Russian cyberattacks, 117–23; attribution, 119–20; description of attacks, 117–18; lessons learned, 122–23; response to, 120–22, 196; security impact, 120
Ukrtelecom JSC, 121
Unintended breaches, 10
United Kingdom: Chinese cyberattacks against, 68, 72; cybersecurity strategy in, 82, 181; in Five Eyes partnership, 180–81; ISIS cyberattacks against, 131; and Ukraine crisis, 118
United Nations, 72, 74, 101, 118
United States: Chinese cyberattacks on, 66–77; and Cold War deterrence model, 2–3; and Combined Endeavor workshop, 183; cyberattack responses, 70–71,

75–76, 127–28, 196, 198, 215; and cyber-publicity muddle, 38–39; and cyber-restraint hypocrisy, 37–38; cybersecurity strategy in, 181; as cybertarget, 20; digital infrastructure in, 45; export control on dual-use technologies, 59; in Five Eyes partnership, 180–81; foreign cyberthreats in, 12–13; and global tensions and power shifts, 54–55; and IMF cyberattacks, 105; Iran targeted for Stuxnet cyberattack by, 94–101; Shady RAT cyberattack on, 72–77; Stuxnet infected computers in, 98; and Syrian Electronic Army cyberattacks, 115; Syrian Electronic Army cyberattacks on, 111–17; Titan Rain cyberattack on, 66–72; and Ukraine crisis, 118
United Telecom of Georgia, 86
University of Toronto, 88
unorthodox restraints: cyberdeterrence best practices for, 220–21, 221f; cyberdeterrence execution, 1, 194–95
US Army Information Systems Engineering Command, 66
US Central Command targeted by ISIS cyberattacks, 112, 130–35; attribution, 131–32; description of attacks, 130–31; lessons learned, 135–36; response to, 134–35; security impact, 132–34

US–China Economic and Security Review Commission, 68, 71
US Cyber Command, 20, 23–24, 115
US European Command, 183

Vietnam, Chinese cyberattacks against, 72
Vormetric, 75

Walla (email service), 91
Wall Street Journal on IMF as cybertarget, 102
Washington Post: on blowback, 201; on cyberthreats, 23; targeted by cyberattacks, 112
WBOC-TV targeted by cyberattacks, 130
Wilhoit, Kyle, 21
World Anti-Doping Agency, 72, 73
World Bank, 66, 101, 104–5

Yanukovych, Viktor, 117, 118, 119
Yisrael, Yitzhak Ben, 92
Yoran, Amit, 24
Youssef, Bassem, 114
YouTube, 114

"zero-day" vulnerabilities, 37
Zheng Zeguang, 67
Zuhri, Sami Abu, 90

About the Author

Robert Mandel is the Chair and Professor of International Affairs at Lewis & Clark College in Portland, Oregon. He has published over forty articles and book chapters as well as thirteen books. His most recent books include *Dark Logic: Transnational Criminal Tactics and Global Security* (2011), *Global Security Upheaval: Armed Nonstate Groups Usurping State Security Functions* (2013), and *Coercing Compliance: State-Initiated Brute Force in Today's World* (2015). He has worked for a number of US government intelligence agencies and testified before the US Congress.

www.ingramcontent.com/pod-product-compliance
Lightning Source LLC
Chambersburg PA
CBHW070754230426
43665CB00017B/2359